Renaissance Italy

Petty states ruled by princes and popes—a world of political ferment and social upheaval whose intellectual progress and artistic achievements have never been surpassed. . . .

This was Renaissance Italy, the world of Machiavelli, the Borgias, Dante, and Michelangelo. . . . This *is* Renaissance Italy, the multifaceted center of culture and conspiracy which comes vividly to life in Burckhardt's *The Civilization of the Renaissance in Italy*. Published in 1860, this classic work stands as the definitive history of the period. No other author, no other book has ever captured the mind and movement of the Renaissance, analyzed its achievements, or characterized its intellectual awakening with such perception and understanding.

This Mentor book offers the modern reader a definitive Burckhardt. It is based on the second German edition (the last edition on which Burckhardt worked) and is an up-to-date version of the S. G. C. Middlemore translation.

Other MENTOR Books
You Will Enjoy

The Civilization
Of The
Renaissance
In Italy

An Essay by Jacob Burckhardt

*The translation of S.G.C. Middlemore,
revised and edited by Irene Gordon*

A MENTOR BOOK from
NEW AMERICAN LIBRARY
TIMES MIRROR
New York and Toronto
The New English Library Limited, London

Library of Congress Catalog Card No. 61-8526

 MENTOR TRADEMARK REG. U.S. PAT. OFF. AND FOREIGN COUNTRIES
REGISTERED TRADEMARK—MARCA REGISTRADA
HECHO EN CHICAGO, U.S.A.

SIGNET, SIGNET CLASSICS, SIGNETTE, MENTOR AND PLUME BOOKS
are published *in the United States* by
The New American Library, Inc.,
1301 Avenue of the Americas, New York, New York 10019,
in Canada by The New American Library of Canada Limited,
295 King Street East, Toronto 2, Ontario,
in the United Kingdom by The New English Library Limited,
Barnard's Inn, Holborn, London, E.C. 1, England

PRINTED IN THE UNITED STATES OF AMERICA

INTRODUCTION

In a swift, malevolently nonchalant speech, Harry Lime, in the film version of Graham Greene's *The Third Man,* repels his antagonist's appeal to Goodness. "Remember what the fellow said," Lime tosses out, "—in Italy for 30 years, under the Borgias, they had warfare, terror, murder and bloodshed, but they produced Michelangelo, Leonardo da Vinci, and the Renaissance. In Switzerland they had brotherly love. They had 500 years of democracy and peace, and what did that produce? The cuckoo clock!" But Switzerland also produced Jacob Burckhardt, and it was Jacob Burckhardt who made the Renaissance.

The words Harry Lime utters have become the formula for those who believe they are "beyond good and evil." By taking unto themselves one of the most provocative periods in history, they seek to ennoble self-indulgence by identifying it with a group of men who have never ceased to excite the imagination and a body of art whose beauty, in the opinion of many, has never been surpassed. Those who mouth this formula generally overlook the circumstance that their facts are incorrect and that they are distorting the ideas of a gentle man who was born in Basel and died there, who rejected personal fame and academic glory, sought neither following nor disciples, never committed a violent action in his life and achieved, through one small and quiet book, an immortality almost equal to that of the gusty, troubled men who intrigued him and the works of art he loved. For if it can ever be said that one man alone established and characterized a historical period, then it may be said that it was Jacob Burckhardt who established the concept and characterized the essence of that time in Italy which remains, despite all dispute, the Renaissance.

Volumes of erudition have not earned such a unique position for dozens of scholars; that one man should have established an orthodoxy and revolutionized the writing of history with one book is, to say the least, startling. And Burckhardt himself would have been the most startled, and amused. A month before the book was published he described it as "a thoroughly wild plant dependent upon nothing already

v

existing." Two months after publication he wrote, "Reasonable people with some intelligence will perhaps acknowledge that the book *had* to be written from sheer inner necessity, even though the world ignores it," and two years later, "The melancholy fact is that we have not sold 200 copies. . . . I had warned the publisher . . . not to print more than 500; he printed 750 and now holds the surplus in bales in his store." And years later, the melancholy intact, ". . . thirty years ago one was completely alone with such thoughts, and the crowd of impressions of what was new to me was so great that it was impossible to preserve a sense of proportion among so many. And . . . how little I knew compared with the vast extent these studies have since attained."

The vast extent to which studies of the Renaissance had attained thirty years after the book was published was as nothing compared with the extent these studies have attained today, one hundred years later, in which Burckhardt persists as the dominant figure, as either target or rampart and occasionally both simultaneously. He has been exaggerated, misinterpreted, distorted, amplified, revised, disputed and refuted. Extended debates on whether the Renaissance is the beginning of modern times, as he proposes, or was actually the end of the Middle Ages led finally to a contention that there never was a Renaissance at all. To art historians it is thoroughly fitting that it was an art historian, one whose name is as magical as that of Burckhardt, Erwin Panofsky, who indicated with charm, wit, and graceful genius that there was a Renaissance. And to art historians it follows just as logically that it was, and perhaps even had to be, an art historian who wrote with compassion, humor, irony, and diffident genius, *The Civilization of the Renaissance in Italy*.

The question of whether there was a Renaissance would never occur to an art historian. It was, in fact, art history, trying to draw distinctions and recognize similarities among the works of art created through the ages, that developed the periodization Gothic, Renaissance, Baroque, as it was art history that transformed the descriptive phrase "renaissance of arts and letters" into the definite noun "the Renaissance." To reduce this activity to total simplicity: Anyone who has stood in the cathedral at Chartres and then in Santo Spirito in Florence has known instantly, unless he was devoid of his senses, that he had moved from one world into another. "Anyone" lets it go at something called an aesthetic experience, the art historian hangs on. He finds the nature of the objects before him more important than his own experience and devotes his time to the objective, historical analysis and interpretation of these objects. But because it has been difficult to arrive at universal agreement on the exact character of this analysis and interpretation, art history, although one of the youngest of the academic disciplines, has already developed a complex internal history. Is art history, or should it be, the analysis of the style of these objects as revealed by the changes of form, thus the history of form, or should it be the interpretation of the style of these objects as an expression of the intellectual, or spiritual character of a given time or people, thus one of the elements in the history of ideas? To those who have experienced first the writings of Heinrich Wölfflin, the greatest exponent of the formal school (and Burckhardt's most famous pupil), and Max Dvořák, one of the most brilliant expositors of the history-of-ideas school, and then come to Burckhardt, it is as if these two men are the separate streams into which the thoughts of this one man were divided.

Art history as it is known today had hardly been conceived when Burckhardt was young; by the end of his life he had done much to help it toward its birth. Burckhardt was not the first to see that art was not an isolated thing and was involved with the total life of a people, but he saw this involvement in a new way. In his student days in Berlin he had been part of a group that was imbued with the Romantic reverence of the Middle Ages and dreams of national destiny, and the Romantic emphasis of the national spirit did not leave him unaffected. But the Romantic interpretation of art as the expression of an age which often reduced art to illustrative material was to him unbearable, and the Romantic notion that feeling was all, that if emotion were strong enough form would automatically follow, left him cold. Mere melancholy never painted a landscape, he demurred. To Burckhardt the ideas that men had held through the ages were of supreme importance, but so was the actual work of art. Art was affected by extra-artistic circumstances, and art, in turn, affected these circumstances, but art also had an independent life with roots and a course of development all its own. This belief led Burckhardt to reject the history of art as a history of expression or a history of artists, and led him to a concept of *Kunstgeschichte nach Aufgaben*—art history according to genres—which was the first step toward a history of styles. He began a lecture on Gothic art, the final section of a course on the Middle Ages, by remarking, "If we are to have a complete picture of the culture of any past age, we must not omit the visual arts. A past age expresses its political character very clearly in reports and documents, its customs and morals in its literature and religious beliefs; but the deepest hopes and ideals are entrusted to future generations perhaps only in the guise of art, the greater the truth, the more unconsciously." But he prefaced the *Cicerone*, his book on the art of Italy, with the statement that he does not pretend to investigate and elucidate the deepest thoughts, the idea, of a work of art: "If these could be wholly expressed in words, art would be superfluous and the particular work could have remained unbuilt, unsculpted, unpainted."

Although he was probably more fit than most, Burckhardt, who occupied two professorial Chairs at Basel—history and art history—could not, ultimately, synthesize art and culture. *The Civilization of the Renaissance in Italy*, which reigns as Burckhardt's masterpiece as well as the masterwork on the Italian Renaissance, was to have done it. "The Renaissance was to have been portrayed," he wrote King Maximilian II of Bavaria, "in so far as she was the mother and source of modern man, in thought and sensibility as well as in the shaping of form. It seemed possible to deal with these two great movements in a worthwhile parallel, to fuse the history of art and the history of civilization." What we have now is the result of Burckhardt's personal failure, a failure conditioned by time, and perhaps by the task itself.

Jacob Burckhardt (1818-1897) was born into a family that had settled in Basel in the sixteenth century and had occupied prominent positions throughout the years. An interest in history and in art were counterpoised throughout his life. At his father's request, he enrolled for the theology degree, but before beginning his studies he spent nine months in Neuchâtel, from which he returned, at eighteen, with an essay on Swiss churches (which became his first published work) and a sketchbook in which he had entered architectural and decorative motifs. Shortly before he was to receive his degree he realized that his newly developed doubts about the divinity of Christ prohibited his entering the ministry. It was Heinrich Schreiber, a priest turned historian who also wrote on art, who stimulated him to the study of history. Burckhardt went to Berlin to study history under the famous Leopold Ranke but he was drawn to the Professor of Art History, Franz Kugler, who had perhaps the greatest single influence on him. The twenty-two-year-old student wrote to his older friend Schreiber, "I should attend Ranke on Modern History but his classes coincide three times a week with Kugler's [History of Architecture]. . . . art history will always cast her spell over me." Two months later to a friend his own age he expressed his affection for the Professor of Art History: "I have made friends with Kugler. . . . The good man has to go for a walk every day on account of superfluous fat, and allows me to fetch him whenever I like. I have done so frequently, and then we toddle along for a couple of hours. . . . I wisely let the fat gentleman go first over the frozen bogs; if they carry him, they'll carry me." Three years later he would proclaim with delight that the Professor had proposed *Du,* the familiar form of address, and twenty years later, a few months after the *Civilization of the Renaissance* was published, he would say, "What qualities I have, I got from Kugler, who had a feeling for essentials."

We owe to Kugler Burckhardt's first published comments on the art of the Renaissance and cultural history. In 1846 Kugler invited Burckhardt to help him prepare the new editions of his handbooks on the history of art and the history of painting. The kind of research Burckhardt himself loathed—those who practiced it he labeled beetles—has to some degree established how much and what in the revised editions is Burckhardt. The portions that can be attributed to him indicate that at twenty-eight he was aware of the artistic problems that would concern him for the rest of his life and was already pondering their solution. In the section on Late Gothic art he considers the differences between the art of the North and the art of the South during the fifteenth century, and remarks, "It may be reserved for future historical research to make use of these differences to interpret the spiritual life of that time and to establish more exactly the connecting links in the literature and history of the respective peoples; here we can only mention the phenomena as such." And further, "With regard to the development of the different characters of nations, much will eternally remain a mystery, and much, even if one believes he has grasped it, will be difficult to put into words." And when he comes to the sixteenth century and the problem of classic art, we see the earliest stage of what he will develop into an entire section in the *Civilization of the Renaissance*—the rejection of the idea that the character of Renaissance art or Renaissance culture can be attributed to the simple fact of a rebirth of antiquity: "The age of Raphael did not come about because it copied from the Antique; it was stirred by its spirit in a marvelous way and took from it not the accidental or national, but the enduring and eternal. And thus this age too was able to produce the enduring and eternal."

As soon as his work in Berlin was done, Burckhardt returned to Italy, and it is here, in the winter of 1847-48, that he first thought of a book on the Renaissance. In 1842 he had outlined his plan for future work to Schreiber: "In two years' time I should like to go to Paris for a few months and then, if possible, to Italy for a year to use libraries and museums all over the place, so that I shall be in a position to write: 1. a history of art from Constantine to the Ottos or the Hohenstaufen, and 2. a history of the Counter Reformation in Switzerland." The plan intrigues by its singular omission: the Renaissance. Years later Burckhardt said that one day in Rome in 1847 someone lent him Vespasiano's biographies and it was then that he first thought of writing a book on the Renaissance. But a few months later, while he was still in Italy, this idea had expanded into a great literary plan and he speaks of a series of small, readable, inexpensive books, some written by himself, some by others, on the Age of Pericles, the Late Roman Empire, the Eighth Century, the Age of the Hohenstaufen, Germany in the Fifteenth Century, the Age of Raphael.

The earlier plan had taken care of, as separate projects, his two major interests: art (Early Christian and medieval), and history (especially the history of his own country). This new plan, which now includes the Renaissance, is more extensive and primarily historical in outlook—in fact he called it a library of cultural history—but in the light of the book that finally emerged it is interesting to note that the *Civilization of the Renaissance,* when it was first conceived, was seen by him as the final entry in a comprehensive survey of the Middle Ages, and that the figure who characterized the age was not a political one, but an artist—Raphael.

This scheme gives substance to those of Burckhardt's critics who refuse to accept his view that the Renaissance is the first stage in the history of modern man, and who insist that many of the qualities Burckhardt considers unique to the Italians of the Renaissance were already present in the men of the Middle Ages and thus view the Renaissance as the conclusion of the medieval period. That the plan had not been some fleeting publishing scheme but represented his views at the time is indicated in his response, some fourteen years after the Renaissance book had been published, to a compliment on the earlier *Age of Constantine*: "If in 1852, soon after finishing the book, I had not lost my job here [Basel] (which thrust me into art history), I should have written a series of cultural-historical descriptions of the Middle Ages, of which the *Civilization of the Renaissance* would have been the concluding picture." The development had been natural enough. He had shared the Romantic enthusiasm for the

Middle Ages, the papers he had written for Ranke's seminars were on medieval subjects, his first publications were on medieval architecture. He was, in fact, a medievalist, and could write to a friend just before he went to Rome on the trip during which he first considered a book on the age of Raphael, "Do drop your hostility to the Middle Ages! What oppresses us are the apes of the Middle Ages, not the real and genuine age of Dante and his associates. . . . I have historical proof that people enjoyed themselves quite wonderfully in the Middle Ages, and that life was more colorful and rich than can possibly be imagined." Burckhardt had spent his life in the north of Europe where the greatest architecture is medieval; an extended stay in Italy was necessary before he could include Mediterranean culture—the Age of Pericles, the Late Roman Empire, the Age of Raphael—in his program. When, then, did he begin to see the age of Dante and his successors as the beginning of a new civilization and not the concluding chapters of an older one?

During the years 1848-53 Burckhardt lectured in Basel. Although these lectures were primarily on history, there were some devoted to art: a series on the history of ancient art, and another on what was listed as the archeology of Christian art. It was also during these years, in 1852, that his first book was published, *The Age of Constantine the Great*, the first volume of the great plan that would never be accomplished. The book was dedicated to Heinrich Schreiber, the man who had turned him to history. His public lectures were on the Middle Ages, and it is in these that the change in his thinking becomes evident. He first gave a course on the history of the Middle Ages, which, except for some marginal notes and added sheets, seems to have been very much like a course he had given some years before. The course that followed immediately upon this one, however, betrays the change. It was called the Golden Age of the Middle Ages, which he began by denying there were such things as golden ages, and stated that golden ages were only the nostalgic longings of a hampered spirit. His love for the Middle Ages has not diminished, but the attitude is different. From the Romantic love of the individual and the special, he has started to search for the general and the characteristic, and for the first time he has tried to present a major epoch of European civilization as a totality. This was followed by a course on the last centuries of the Middle Ages, which, with a series of three lectures on the Archbishop Andreas von Krain and the last attempt to have a Council in Basel, demonstrates the gradual process by which he came to see a certain civilization in

Italy as something distinct from the civilization of the North.
The late Middle Ages of Basel and the early Renaissance of
Italy appear together in the lectures on Andreas von Krain,
and the pages in which Burckhardt outlines the background
of the period can almost serve as a preparatory study for the
book he will publish ten years later. He sketches the North
first and the meaning of the Councils, then the Papacy of
Sixtus IV. Aeneas Sylvius is here and already receives the
affection Burckhardt will lavish on him in the later book.
There are also phrases that sound so familiar now: "to rise,
to rule, to hold one's ground is the single aim of these fine,
cultivated princes"; "driven by ambition, the Italian prince
becomes a political artist"; "most of the Popes are immoral,
they are surrounded by the most shocking depravity, but the
Rome of that day is one of the birthplaces of the so-called
Renaissance, of the new methods of observation and representation in art, literature, and life which had been fructified
by antiquity," etc. There is much here of the Romantic interpretation of the Renaissance, but in these lectures on Archbishop Andreas von Krain and on the late Middle Ages,
Burckhardt seems to have taken his first steps toward moving
from the subject matter of a period to the content of a civilization.

In 1852 Burckhardt lost his job as history teacher in the
secondary school. The reorganization of the education system
added to his duties and he asked to be excused from having
to correct papers, a condition the board refused to meet. His
request was reasonable enough, but something more than
logic seems to have been involved. The Italian journey of
1847-48 had been a time of resolution of personal crisis
brought about by political events in Europe and the political
views of his closest friends, his own immediate past and the
problem of his future. He had shared much with his Berlin
friends, but never their radical and revolutionary politics, and
years before they, he had seen the dangers of the events that
would finally occur in 1848. Already in 1846, when he
returned from Italy to Berlin to work on the revision of
Kugler's books, he had not resumed his old friendships. Some
months before he left for the extended stay in Italy he had
written one of his disillusioned friends, "If I were any use in
the affairs of this world, and if I were not in perpetual need
of beauty in nature and art, I should say to you: let's go to
America together! But I could not live there; I need a
historical . . . terrain, otherwise I should die, which might not
be the worst thing after all." He went to Italy, to his land of

"chestnut trees and frescoes," and there seems to have reached certain decisions about himself and his future.

In 1848, at the age of thirty, he returned to Basel with the quiet decision that it would be there that he would teach and write his books. But although he had gained the confidence to pursue his own point of view and to trust his own vision, he had not yet arrived, as he would in later years, at the ability to put up with the loneliness this involved. Shortly after his return to Basel he complained, "What do these phantoms that I live with daily want of me? You at least have taken part and tried things; I just spin away by myself. It is a very curious feeling to have done with the world and to ask for nothing more than a spot in the sun, in which to hatch things that no one bothers about in the end. And yet it is not just egoistic epicureanism that makes me behave this way; every nature, after all, has its needs." His particular needs—observation, contemplation, meditation, beauty, harmony—and an incredible loneliness seem to have had more to do with his abandonment of Basel than a refusal to mark papers. His old friend Schreiber did not agree with his plan to go to Italy, but Burckhardt was determined.

After fourteen months in Italy Burckhardt came back to Basel with three quarters of a book finished. Seven months later it was published as the *Cicerone: A Guide to the Works of Art of Italy*. The book was dedicated to Franz Kugler, the man who had turned him to art history. Although the *Civilization of the Renaissance* has overshadowed it, the *Cicerone* established Burckhardt's fame during his own lifetime and remains an important book. It is not so much a guide book to the works of art of Italy as it is a tour through the history of Italian art. For the first time definite terminal points are set for the Renaissance, a distinction is made between Early and High Renaissance, and the "premature" appearance of a return to ancient art, as in the case of Nicola Pisano, which had always confused previous classifications, was seen for the first time as a proto-Renaissance. Kugler, in fact, described it as having no equal in the entire literature of art.

Burckhardt's lectures in Basel had been leading him from the kind of history that concerns itself with the course of events toward *Kulturgeschichte*, the kind of history that concerns itself with the character of events. Within his own field, the Middle Ages, he had begun to distinguish differences between the various generations, and had already observed that northern Basel and southern Florence at the same chronological point were different societies. This second extended stay in Italy, and especially the concentration on

Italian art, seems to have made him see the differences more sharply. The *Cicerone* was the first truly systematic review of Renaissance art, but it is concerned primarily with questions of style. He was, as he remarks in his foreword, concerned here with the language of art rather than the ideas. For the nature of this book this concern was sufficient, but for Burckhardt there must have been a certain incompleteness, which led him to pick up the subject he had listed in his great literary plan eight years before: the Age of Raphael. The convergence of language and ideas seems to have taken place in Florence; among the notebooks he kept in that city, there are six that form a separate group. They are the first tangible traces of the book that was to become finally the *Civilization of the Renaissance in Italy*.

The *Cicerone* was published toward the end of 1854. At the same time he applied for a position at the newly founded Polytechnical Institute in Zurich, and a few months later he was appointed Professor of Art History. His father described it as "the greatest turning point in his life. He enters a new atmosphere; he achieves a kind of independence he has never had and, what is most important: time to work, in which he can develop and become what his destiny demands." Burckhardt himself saw it as a chance to work: "One of the principal reasons why I have decided to go to Zurich is because I can live there practically incognito. . . . I am not going to Zurich as the only newly appointed Professor, but as one of thirty . . . . Among this crowd one can hide away unnoticed." The Age of Raphael was plaguing him; within two weeks of his arrival in Zurich he writes: "I am possessed by a scholarly spirit that may well lay claim to all the powers at my disposal for years to come, the serious examination into the history of the beautiful. I brought this 'infirmity' back with me from Italy last year, and feel I could not die in peace unless I had fulfilled my destiny in this respect."

In Zurich Burckhardt had all the time he wanted. He had only to lecture; there were no seminars, no dissertations, no examinations, no meetings. And the library of Zurich was rich in the material he needed. Day after day he trudged home with the volumes of Muratori's *Rerum italicarum scriptores*, excerpting chronicles and diaries of all the Italian cities; he excerpted the sixteen volumes of the *Archivio storico italiano*, the writings of Alberti, Bandello, Dante, Serlio, Vasari. During the two and a half years he was in Zurich he developed three courses: a history of Greek and Roman art, which was an expansion of the course he had given five years before in Basel; a history of medieval art, which also goes back to previous lectures but this time rearranged according to a point of view that seems almost to lead to a Civilization of the Middle Ages; and a course on the architecture of the Renaissance. This last reads almost like an outline of the *Civilization of the Renaissance* in which the history of art was to have been fused with the history of civilization. The course begins with a short presentation of the civilization of the Renaissance as an introduction to its art. The ideas he had sketched in the *Cicerone* with regard to the development of Italian art he now set into the broader framework of a total civilization. In this early picture of the Renaissance there is much that will find its way into the final book—the rise of the cities, the increase in wordliness without, however, a total abandonment of religion, the attraction and influence of the ancient world. But the two aspects in which he will find the essential character of the Renaissance as a new civilization are still absent: individualism, and the discovery of the world and of man. Probably because at this point the consideration of the nature of Renaissance art was dominant and not the nature of Renaissance man.

In January 1858 Burckhardt received a letter so shrewdly worded as to appeal to the best and the worst in him. Basel wanted him back; they offered him the Chair of History, total freedom of choice regarding his program and activities, and begged him to return to his native city to develop and raise the spiritual life of her people. This was an appeal Burckhardt would find hard to resist, and there must have been an element of satisfaction in being pursued by those who had rejected him. Why else then, just when he was beginning a work that he knew from the outset would take years of attention, should he have exchanged the peaceful existence of Zurich which afforded him so much time for a life in Basel that would make so many demands. A year after his arrival in Zurich he was still speaking of that "precious quiet in which one can really set fire to one's embers, e.g., pursue Renaissance studies whose notes already fill a whole shelf. Oh, if only a whole series of years proceed this way, without disturbance and with good health."

The same need that pushed him back to Basel seems also to have forced him, once he was there, into justifying the call. The conflict between what he believed he owed Basel and his desire to write the Renaissance book emerges in what is perhaps the only hysterical letter in his entire correspondence. Kugler had died the same month that Burckhardt returned to Basel. Within weeks Burckhardt had been asked to complete the books Kugler had been working on, a revision of the books Burckhardt had helped him revise years before. Burckhardt had refused because of his new position and his own work. When he is asked again, a few days after his first refusal, the storm breaks: "All the wishing and vowing in the world will not make the impossible possible. I cannot work sixteen hours a day instead of eight, and am especially not disposed, for any reason whatsoever, to offer up my tolerable health to my desk, as poor Kugler has done. I cannot share the first semester of a position, upon which my entire future depends, with another major work. I was brought here with a substantial payment, in order to have *all* of me, and now, just when I am being torn apart with wondering how I will ever fulfill these intentions, you come along and demand a great work from me. . . . Have you even glanced at this History of Architecture? really look at the book and you will see the principles and dimensions that govern it. No one 'completes' such a thing once the author dies. I have already brought my sacrifice to my present position: my work on the Renaissance will either remain unwritten or will shrink to a few articles. The research took me two whole years and filled me with the most beautiful fancies, which have now flown. Not that the world will have lost much; but you must understand at least that I am making other sacrifices to my position and that I do not refuse your request out of convenience and selfishness."

His response a few months later to the inquiry from King Maximilian of Bavaria indicates that he had definitely decided that he could not carry out his original plan. He comments sadly that the beauty of the plan had deceived him about his powers. During the next months he prepared the section of late medieval sculpture and painting for the third edition of Kugler's handbook of art history. In July 1858, during the summer vacation, he cut apart his Renaissance notes, rearranged them according to the new, reduced plan, and roughed out his categories: politics, war, the papacy, fame and individualism, antiquity, discovery of the world, discovery of man, festivals, poetry, the Renaissance man. There is no mention of the book again until August 1860 when he writes Schreiber that he has spent his holidays reading proofs. In September he is sending copies to friends.

What is the *Civilization of the Renaissance in Italy* and why has this "thoroughly wild plant" remained alive while other flowers have faded? The answer lies in the nature of the book and of the man who wrote it. Burckhardt was not the first man who tried to discover the spirit of an age or a nation, and he himself says in a letter that accompanied one of the first copies of the book, that the phenomena he deals with have been discovered and discussed by others. Stendhal and Goethe had even taken the same path as Burckhardt, from a love of the art to an interest in the society that had produced it; Voltaire, Hegel, Michelet—from whom Burckhardt borrowed the phrase "the discovery of the world and of man," which has ever since been identified more with the adopter than its author—tried to delineate the spirit of this age. Each of these men, and many others, had seen and touched the separate ingredients Burckhardt used, yet none had synthesized them into such an integrated whole. That these men could not accomplish what Burckhardt did may lie in the fact that whereas they had extraordinary quantities of a singular gift, he seems to have had large quantities of a variety of gifts. "Burckhardt knows everything," a friend once wrote, "he knows where the sweetest grapes grow on Lake Como and can tell you off the top of his head the best sources for a life of Nostradamus. He writes a Latin treatise on Charles Martel . . . things of which no mortal ever knew, then sits down on the sofa, smokes a dozen fine Manilla cigars, and composes a poetic fantasy on the love of an Elector of Cologne for the daughter of an alchemist."

Superior gifts, an excellent education, supreme intuition were only part of his equipment. Perhaps of greatest significance was the circumstance that Burckhardt had beliefs but no theories, and thus was not crippled by a system. Since to him history was neither man's parade toward progress nor his rendezvous with some ideal destiny, there was no need to play one age against the other. His work in art history and especially his work on the *Cicerone* had given him a clearer view of the extent and limits of that particular period of history, so that he, as others had not, could grasp it as a whole. From art history and the abundance of masterpieces that make up its subject matter he had learned that each age has its unique way of expressing itself, and that a personal preference for one style does not require disparagement of another. Each historical age creates its own language which is at the same time its mode of thinking and feeling.

The Burckhardt who in his youth had dreamed of being the historian of his native city and had concentrated on the medieval art of Germany passed from national interests to universal ones. He had begun his series of lectures on the Middle Ages by outlining his presentation: "Not politics but culture. . . . Not according to nations or chronology but ac-

cording to the pervasive spiritual currents. . . . Not princes
and their dynasties but people and their development in a
common spirit."

This outline for a course on the Middle Ages can stand as
his program for the *Civilization of the Renaissance* in which
he painted the portrait of Italy as she was between 1300 and
1530. He does not report in chronological order the wars,
pacts, treaties, and alliances that followed upon each other,
but cuts across the centuries and through the events to reveal
her essential nature. The point has been made that this
method has created a static picture and has "tended to
minimize the sense of historical development within the period
while exaggerating the contrast with the preceding age or
with the contemporary civilization of other countries." But
it might be answered that although the motion picture can
show greater development than a still photograph, the painted
portrait—the result of infinite selection—can reveal more
than either. Whether Jan Six was taller or shorter than other
men, or fatter or thinner, whether he had a young wife or
an old one, whether he had children, pets, or a windmill is of
no consequence; Rembrandt put Jan Six alone on his canvas
and revealed more about this one man in his isolation than
about all the members of the *Night Watch*. Burckhardt had
used the word *Kulturgeschichte* in the titles of his courses;
indeed, while he was working on the Renaissance book he was
repeating the course he called *Die Kulturgeschichte der
letzten Jahrhunderte des Mittelalters* (The History of the
Civilization of the Last Centuries of the Middle Ages). But
he named this book *Die Kultur der Renaissance in Italien*,
the civilization of the Renaissance in Italy. He was not portraying the history of that civilization, but the civilization
itself.

In creating his portrait of the Renaissance, Burckhardt
worked like an artist, and created a structure that has the
balance and harmony of the art he loved. Unlike the modern
artist, Burckhardt kept his preparatory drawings at home and
exhibited only the finished piece. His observations, contemplation, and research had revealed to him one outstanding
feature. He does not explain the steps by which he came to
it, but once having grasped it, takes it as given and proceeds
to show how it operated. To Burckhardt the essential characteristic that made the Renaissance man different from all
other men and gave its particular flavor to everything he did
and created was individualism. Burckhardt does not bother
to elucidate why this should have developed especially in
the Italians of the fourteenth, fifteenth, and sixteenth cen-

turies. He sketches the political conditions of Europe in the fourteenth century, the struggle between Pope and Emperor that vitiated the strength of both, the wars between the Spaniards and the Moors, the wars between France and England, as the external conditions that left Italy internally free to develop as she would. Devoid of a common external purpose, disturbed little by foreign interference, the Italians could devote themselves to their own affairs, from which came their energy and their individualism. With this beginning, Burckhardt goes on to build a composition conditioned by his artistic sense and his knowledge.

The book is divided into six parts. The two longest parts are the first, concerned with politics and the state, and the last, devoted to morality and religion. Between these two major structural supports, Burckhardt sets the individual and his activities. After the first, long part of the book, out of the struggle for political power, comes the Development of the Individual, the shortest section in the book. From here the arch rises to the third longest section, the Revival of Antiquity, from where it descends to a shorter section, the Discovery of the World and of Man, to a still shorter section, Society and Festivals, to arrive at the longest, concluding section on morality. Within these major sections Burckhardt portrays the Renaissance man exercising his individualism in various areas of his life.

It is perhaps symptomatic of the nature of subsequent generations that they have paid most attention and restricted themselves to what Burckhardt has given the least space— the development of individualism. Just as Burckhardt was not overly concerned with investigating why individualism developed, he was not particularly interested in individualism per se. Burckhardt's concept of individualism does not endorse powerful passions and ruthless action. He saw Renaissance individualism as the awakening of man's awareness of himself, as a being apart from a group or a class, and saw that man's consciousness of self not only allowed possibilities but contained problems. The awareness of himself gave the Renaissance man freedom to develop and create, to Burckhardt the highest freedoms, but it also put him in a new relation to God and the world, which he then had the responsibility to resolve. That Burckhardt was as concerned with the problems as with the possibilities probably accounts for the fact that the section on morality and religion is the longest in the book.

Both Burckhardt's picture and his method of painting it have been criticized. It has been said that in pursuing his image he has exaggerated, stressed, and suppressed all those features which would have marred his portrait. Philosophers have complained that there is no system, economists have complained that there is no economics, sociologists that there is sociability but no society, and some have even complained that he ignores art. Also, his use of sources has been criticized. The charge of omitting art would cause some pain, but to the rest, Burckhardt would probably answer that he knows and doesn't see that it matters much, that he has chosen only those aspects of society that seem to him to reveal most about the spirit of an age. In our day of precise research and the scientific method Burckhardt's attitude toward his sources may seem cavalier. But even here he is supremely himself and follows his own method. He had the advantage of a magnificent memory and marvelous intuition which gave him that special "feel" of a thing which acres of documentation cannot supply. Burckhardt was not interested in events, only in the ideas these events expressed. Thus, whether Pandolfini or Alberti wrote the treatise on domestic life is of concern only to those deeply involved with either of the two gentlemen. To Burckhardt, concerned with the spirit of the age, the only things that matter are that such a treatise was written, what the treatise says, and what the total occurrence indicates. That years of research have not altered appreciably Burckhardt's portrait of Renaissance civilization is proof that his beliefs were not prejudices.

The attraction of the book lies as much in Burckhardt's style and presentation as it does in his ideas and material. Burckhardt wrote all his lectures but never, as a principle of teaching, did he bring even a note to class. The first encounter is supposed to have been disappointing. He seemed distant, looked out of the windows, and appeared to be talking to himself. To judge from Wölfflin's report to his parents of his first interview with his teacher, "He was friendly but withdrawn. I didn't know what to make of him," the distance seems to have been an element of personality. That same day, after the first lecture, Wölfflin noted in his diary, "Aroused no enthusiasm." But after the second lecture he noted, "Stirring," and fifty years later he claimed he could still hear that low, vibrant voice. The book, too, follows this course. It begins slowly, quietly, as if the author were murmuring to himself. A footnote seems to indicate that he has momentarily noticed his listener. Gradually he becomes stronger, his humor begins to play, his irony emerges and the reader is captured by a delightful human being speaking warmly about other human beings, taking seriously many of the things they took seriously, shaking his head in disbelief over others. He can wonder, in the middle of a learned paragraph on the revival of rhetoric and Latin orations of two and three hours, how it was possible to endure such infliction. A serious discussion of the new attitude toward landscape and Dante's ascent of a mountain sheerly for the view, he footnotes with the sober reflection that he cannot imagine what else Dante could have found to do up there.

These may, however, be mere external justification for the enduring life of the book. The ultimate reason may lie in a special quality that characterized Burckhardt's entire professional life. In 1874, when he began to barricade himself from Nietzsche behind the refrain that he had been born without the capacity for philosophical speculation, he wrote Nietzsche what could almost amount to his credo: "I have done everything I possibly could to lead them on to acquire personal possession of the past—in whatever form—and at least not to sicken them of it; I wanted them to be capable of plucking the fruits for themselves; I never dreamed of training scholars and disciples in the narrower sense, but only wanted to make every member of my audience feel and know that everyone may and must appropriate those aspects of the past which appeal to him personally, and that there might be happiness in doing so." The secret of Burckhardt's attraction, which grows with the years, may be that he cared deeply about what he produced for others and for what others had created for him. *The Civilization of the Renaissance in Italy,* which had been born as the Age of Raphael in the mind of a thirty-year-old, was written by a man who in his sixty-fifth year could say, "In *my* life nothing much matters any more since this morning; I saw the Raphaels in the Vatican again and now I can die."

New York
November, 1960

—IRENE   GORDON

EDITOR'S NOTE

The Civilization of the Renaissance in Italy was first published in German in 1860. The second German edition, prepared by the author, was published in 1868. In 1876 Burckhardt sent an annotated copy to his Italian translator. This represents Burckhardt's total activity with the book; thereafter his only contribution was to allow those who would to do as they liked with it. Under other hands the essay of some 400 pages grew into a reference book twice the original size. The present edition is based on the volume prepared by Professor Werner Kaegi for the German edition of Burckhardt's collected works, and follows the second German edition in form and in content. Dates are as Burckhardt gave them and have not been changed to agree with modern research, no material has been added to his text, and bits that had been deleted by previous editors have been restored. Material set between parallels (||) are the additions Burckhardt made for the Italian translation; material enclosed by brackets ([ ]) are notations by the present editor. A good part of Burckhardt's footnotes have been included; those which have been omitted were mainly citations to material in foreign languages, which can be obtained only in specialized libraries.

Burckhardt's lectures mentioned in the Introduction are discussed in detail in Professor Kaegi's biography of Burckhardt now in process of publication, which will surely bring about a new evaluation and understanding of Burckhardt and his work.

Contents

CONTENTS

CONTENTS

PART TWO

THE DEVELOPMENT OF THE INDIVIDUAL

CONTENTS

PART THREE

THE REVIVAL OF ANTIQUITY

CONTENTS

CONTENTS

CONTENTS

Contents

PART FIVE

SOCIETY AND FESTIVALS

CONTENTS

PART SIX

MORALITY AND RELIGION

CONTENTS

CONTENTS

Preface to the Second Edition [1868]

The changes that have been made in this new edition are limited to some sentences in the text and additions to the notes. The author would have preferred to revise the book completely, but he lacked the necessary leisure and the possibility of another lengthy stay in Italy. Therefore, instead of altering individual parts and adding new ones, he would rather risk having the work reappear in the same form in which it found its previous approval. Perhaps, too, many views and judgments that already seem somewhat immature to the author would have been even less acceptable in their revised form.

May this work recommend itself anew to friends of the study of the history of civilization, which is making such great strides at the present time.

PART ONE

THE STATE AS A WORK OF ART

This work is called an "essay" in the strictest sense of the word. The author is well aware of the limited means and powers with which he undertook so arduous a task; and even if he could view his research with greater confidence, he would not feel any more assured of the approval of the experts. To each eye the outlines of a given civilization probably present a different picture; and when we discuss a civilization that, as mother of our own, still influences us, the individual judgment and feeling of both writer and reader must come into play at every moment. On the vast ocean upon which we venture, the possible ways and directions are many; and the same studies that have served for this work might easily, in other hands, not only receive a wholly different treatment and interpretation, but might also lead to essentially different conclusions. In fact, the subject is so important that it still calls for fresh investigation, and may be studied with advantage from the most varied points of view. Meanwhile we hope that a patient hearing is granted us, and that this book is taken and judged as a whole. It is the most serious difficulty of the history of civilization that a great intellectual process must be broken up into single, and what often seem arbitrary, categories in order to be in any way intelligible.—It was formerly our intention to fill up the greatest gap in this book by a special work on the Art of the Renaissance—an intention, however, that we have been able to fulfill only in part.[1]

---

1. *Geschichte der Baukunst* by Franz Kugler (vol. IV, part 1: *Die Architektur und Dekoration der italienischen Renaissance*).

[These quiet words on an unfulfilled intention and this matter-of-fact footnote are typical of Burckhardt. They conceal a frustration that was to last until his death, and hide the hesitancy,

The struggle between the Popes and the Hohenstaufen left Italy in a political condition that was fundamentally different from that of other countries of the West. While in France, Spain, and England the feudal system was so organized that, at the close of its existence, it was naturally transformed into a unified monarchy, and while in Germany it helped to maintain, at least outwardly, the unity of the empire, Italy had shaken it off almost entirely. The Emperors of the fourteenth century, even in the most favorable circumstance, were no longer received and respected as feudal lords, but as possible leaders and supporters of powers already in existence; the Papacy, with its creatures and allies, though strong enough to hinder national unity in the future, was not strong enough itself to bring about that unity.[2] Between the two lay a multitude of political units—republics and despots—some of long standing, some of recent origin, whose existence had come to be taken for granted.[3] In them for the first time we detect the modern political spirit of Europe, surrendered freely to its own instincts, often displaying the worst features of an unbridled egotism, outraging every right

honesty, depression, humor, modesty, integrity, and pride that were part of Burckhardt's delightful but complex attitude toward himself, his work, and the world. "The Architecture and Decoration of the Italian Renaissance," which had been published in 1867, two years before this second edition of the *Civilization,* is a brilliant and important book; but it is, actually, "merely" a continuation of a history of architecture which Franz Kugler began in 1856 and worked on until his death in 1858. It is, also, the very child Burckhardt had disowned in 1864.

In the earliest stages of his work on the Italian Renaissance, Burckhardt had intended "to fuse art and the history of civilization." But he eventually succumbed to the realization that he would have to treat the art of the Renaissance and the history of that civilization separately. Thus, two books were planned. Immediately after Kugler's death, Burckhardt had been asked to complete the interrupted history of architecture, but he refused, pleading too much work and too little time. By 1863, three years after the *Civilization* was published, he had finished seven-eighths of his "Art of the Renaissance," but then experienced "the kind of sorrows that do not make men young." He found his work "inadequate in principle and execution," and put it back in his desk, "probably forever." The next year he gave the manuscript to Wilhelm Lübke ". . .to do with as he pleases, so that he may at least use some of this material for a ivth volume of Kugler's History of Architecture." He complained that he did not want to publish something that "instead of ending in periods, keeps ending in question marks," and recommended that the title page read, "Kugler's History of Architecture, vol. IV, by W. Lübke, and killing every germ of a healthier culture. But wherever this vicious tendency was overcome or in any way counterbalanced, a new being appeared in history: the State as a calculated conscious creation, as a work of art. This new life displayed itself in hundreds of ways, both in the republican and in the despotic States, and determined their internal form as well as their foreign policy. We shall limit ourselves to the consideration of the completer and more clearly defined type that is offered by the despotic States.

The internal condition of the despotically governed States had a memorable counterpart in the Norman Empire of Lower Italy and Sicily as it had been transformed by Emperor Frederick II. Bred amid treason and peril among Saracens, Frederick had early accustomed himself to a thoroughly objective treatment of affairs, the first modern man to sit upon a throne. His acquaintance with the internal condition and administration of the Saracenic States was close and intimate; and the mortal struggle in which he was engaged with the Papacy compelled him, no less than his adversaries,

---

with the use of material by J. Burckhardt (my name in small print)." He preferred, actually, that his name not appear at all. Despite this early disavowal, in later years Burckhardt participated in two more editions, which bear the anomalous title *Geschichte der Renaissance in Italien* (History of the Renaissance in Italy), and 1894, three years before his death, he was interested in bringing out a fourth edition.

The manuscript that had been seven-eighths finished had stopped somewhere in the middle of the section on painting. Toward the end of his life, Burckhardt used some of this material in his essays "Das Altarbild" (The Altarpiece), "Das Porträt in der italienischen Malerei" (The Portrait in Italian Painting), and "Die Sammler" (Collectors), which were published in 1898, the year after his death, as *Beiträge zur Kunstgeschichte von Italien* (Contributions to the Art History of Italy). In his last days he inscribed his sculpture notes with trembling hand: "Not to be published." But in 1934 these notes were included in the grand edition of Burckhardt's Collected Works as "Randglossen zur Skulptur der Renaissance" (Marginalia on the Sculpture of the Renaissance).

Small wonder Burckhardt wrote to friend, "I count on your tried and true good nature as I lay this infant at your breast," when he sent him one of the first copies of the *Civilization of the Renaissance* in September 1860. "It is, after all, a child of sorrow."]

2. Machiavelli, *The Discourses*, Book I, ch. 12.

3. The rulers and their dependents were called *lo stato;* this name later came to mean the collective existence of a territory.

to bring into the field all the resources at his command. Frederick's measures (especially after the year 1231) aimed at the complete destruction of the feudal State, at the transformation of the people into a multitude destitute of will and of means of resistance, but profitable in the utmost degree to the treasury. He centralized, in a manner hitherto unknown in the West, the whole judicial and political administration. No office was henceforth to be filled by popular election, under penalty of the devastation of the offending district and the enslavement of its inhabitants. Taxes, based on a comprehensive assessment and in accordance with Mohammedan practice, were collected by those cruel and vexatious methods without which, it is true, it is impossible to obtain any money from Orientals. Here, in short, we find, not a people, but simply a disciplined multitude of subjects, who were forbidden, for example, to marry out of the country without special permission, and under no circumstances were allowed to study abroad. The University of Naples was the first we know of to restrict the freedom of study, whereas the East, in these respects at least, left its youth unfettered. But it was after genuine Mohammedan fashion that Frederick traded on his own account in all parts of the Mediterranean, reserving to himself the monopoly of many commodities and restricting the commerce of his subjects. The Fatamid caliphs, with all their esoteric unbelief, were (at least in their earlier history) tolerant of the religious differences of their subjects; Frederick, on the other hand, crowned his system of government by a religious inquisition that appears even more reprehensible when we remember that in the persons of the heretics he was persecuting the representatives of a free municipal life. Lastly, the internal police and the core of the army for foreign service were composed of Saracens who had been brought over from Sicily to Nocera and Lucera— men who were deaf to the cry of misery and indifferent to the ban of the Church. At a later period the subjects, who had long forgotten the use of weapons, were passive witnesses of the fall of Manfred and of the seizure of the government by Charles of Anjou, who continued to use the existing system.

By the side of the centralizing Emperor appeared a usurper of the most individual kind: his vicar and son-in-law, Ezzelino da Romano. He does not represent any system of government or administration, for all his activity was spent in struggles for supremacy in the eastern part of Upper Italy; but as a political type he was a figure of no less importance for the future than his imperial protector. The conquests and usurpations which had hitherto taken place in the Middle Ages rested on real or pretended inheritance and other such claims, or else were effected against unbelievers and excommunicated persons. Here for the first time the attempt was openly made to found a throne by wholesale murder and endless barbarities, by the adoption, in short, of any means with a view to nothing but the end pursued. None of his successors, not even Cesare Borgia, rivaled the magnitude of Ezzelino's crimes; but the example once set was not forgotten, and his fall led to no return of justice and served as no warning to future transgressors.

It was in vain at such a time that St. Thomas Aquinas, a born subject of Frederick, developed the theory of a constitutional monarchy in which the prince would be assisted by an upper house named by himself and a representative body elected by the people. Such theories remained in the lecture room, and Frederick and Ezzelino were and remain for Italy the greatest political phenomena of the thirteenth century. Their personalities, already half legendary, form the most important subject of *Le cento novelle antiche* [*The Hundred Old Tales*] whose original composition certainly falls within this century. In them Ezzelino is spoken of with the awe that all mighty impressions leave behind them. His person became the center of a whole literature, from the chronicle of eyewitnesses to the half-mythical tragedy of later poets.

The despotisms, great and small, of the fourteenth century afford constant proof that such examples were not ignored. Their flagrant crimes have been reported in detail by historians; but as States depending for existence on themselves alone, and scientifically organized with a view to this object, they hold a higher interest.

The deliberate adaptation of means to ends, of which no prince of that time outside Italy had any idea, joined to almost absolute power within the limits of the State, produced men and modes of life of a peculiar character. For the more prudent tyrants the chief secret of government lay in leaving taxation as far as possible where they found it, or as they had first arranged it. The chief sources of income were: a land tax, based on a valuation; definite taxes on articles of consumption; duties on exported and imported goods; and, in addition, the revenues from the private holdings of the ruling house. The only possible increase was derived from the growth of business and of general prosperity. Loans, such as we find in the free cities, were unknown here; a well-planned confiscation was held a preferable means of raising money, provided only that it left public credit unshaken—an end attained, for example, by the truly Oriental practice of deposing and plundering the director of finance.

Out of this income the expenses of the little court, of the bodyguard, of the mercenary troops, and of the public buildings were met, as well as of the buffoons and men of talent who belonged to the personal entourage of the prince. The illegitimacy of his rule isolated the tyrant and surrounded him with constant danger; the most honorable alliance that he could form was with intellectual merit, without regard to its origin. The liberality of the Northern princes of the thirteenth century was confined to the knights, to the nobility that served and sang. It was otherwise with the Italian despot. With his thirst for fame and his passion for monumental works, it was talent not birth that he needed. In the company of the poet and the scholar he felt himself in a new position, almost, indeed, in possession of a new legitimacy.

Renowned in this respect is the ruler of Verona, Can Grande della Scala, who numbered among the illustrious exiles whom he entertained at his court representatives of all Italy. The men of letters were not ungrateful. Petrarch, whose visits at the courts of such men have been so severely censured, sketched an ideal picture of a prince of the fourteenth century.[4] He demands great things from his patron, the lord of Padua, but in a manner that shows that he holds him capable of them. "Thou must not be the master but the father of thy subjects, and must love them as thy children; yea, as members of thy body. Weapons, guards, and soldiers thou mayest employ against the enemy—with thy subjects good will is sufficient. By citizens, of course, I mean only those who love the existing order; for those who daily desire change are rebels and traitors, and against such, a stern justice may take its course." Then follows, worked out in detail, the purely modern fiction of the omnipotence of the State. The prince is to take everything into his charge, to maintain and restore churches and public buildings, to keep up the municipal police,[5] to drain the marshes, to look after the supply of wine and corn, to distribute the taxes justly, to support the sick and the helpless, and to give his protection and

4. Not till a hundred years later is the princess spoken of as the mother of the people.
5. With the parenthetical request that the keeping of pigs in the streets of Padua be forbidden, as the sight of them is unpleasant and they frighten the horses.

society to distinguished scholars, on whom his fame in after ages will depend.

But whatever might be the brighter sides of the system and the merits of individual rulers, the men of the fourteenth century were aware of the brief and uncertain tenure of most of these despotisms. Inasmuch as political institutions like these are naturally secure in proportion to the size of the territory in which they exist, the larger principalities were constantly tempted to swallow up the smaller. The hecatombs of petty rulers that were sacrificed at this time to the Visconti alone! But this external danger almost always corresponded to an internal ferment, and the effect of the situation on the character of the ruler was generally of the most sinister kind. Absolute power, with its temptations to luxury and unbridled selfishness, and the perils to which he was exposed from enemies and conspirators, turned him almost inevitably into a tyrant in the worst sense of the word. Fortunate man who could trust his nearest relations! But where all was illegitimate, there could be no regular law of inheritance, either with regard to the succession or to the division of the ruler's property; and consequently the heir, if incompetent or a minor, was liable in the interest of the family itself to be supplanted by an uncle or cousin of more resolute character. The acknowledgment or exclusion of the bastards was a constant source of strife; and consequently most of these families were plagued with a crowd of discontented and vindictive kinsmen. This circumstance gave rise to continual outbreaks of treason and to frightful scenes of domestic bloodshed. Sometimes the pretenders lived abroad in exile and, like the Visconti who practiced the fisherman's craft on the Lago di Garda, viewed the situation with patient indifference. When asked by his rival's messenger when and how he thought he would return to Milan, he replied, "Not until his crimes have outweighed mine."[6] Sometimes, too, the despot was sacrificed by his relations to the public conscience that he had too grossly outraged, in order to save the rest of the house.[7] In a few cases the government was in the hands of the whole family, or at least the ruler was bound to take their advice; and here, too, the distribution of property and influence often led to bitter disputes.

The Florentine writers of the time display a deep and

6. Matteo I Visconti and Guido della Torre, then ruling Milan, are the persons referred to.
7. The secret murder of Matteo II Visconti by his brother.

persistent hatred for this whole system. Even the pomp and
display, with which the despot was perhaps less anxious to
gratify his own vanity than to impress the popular imagination, awakened their keenest sarcasm. Woe to an adventurer
if he fell into their hands, like the upstart Doge Agnello of
Pisa (1364), who used to ride out with a golden scepter, and
show himself at the window of his house, "as relics are
shown," reclining on embroidered drapery and cushions; he
had to be served like a pope or emperor, by kneeling attendants.[8] More often, however, the old Florentines speak
on this subject in a tone of lofty seriousness. Dante [9] saw
and characterized well the vulgarity and commonplace which
marked the ambition of the new princes. "What else mean
their trumpets and their bells, their horns and their flutes,
but 'come, hangmen—come, vultures!' " The castle of the
tyrant is pictured as lofty and solitary, full of dungeons and
listening tubes, the home of cruelty and misery. Misfortune
is foretold to all who enter the service of the despot, who
finally himself becomes an object of pity: he must become
the enemy of all good and honest men; he can trust no one,
and can read in the faces of his subjects the expectation of
his fall. "As despotisms rise, grow, and are consolidated, so
grows in their midst the hidden element that must produce
their dissolution and ruin." But the deepest ground of dislike
has not been stated; Florence was then the scene of the richest
development of human individuality, whereas for the despots
no other individuality could be suffered to live and thrive
but their own and that of their nearest dependents. The
control of the individual was rigorously carried out, even
down to the establishment of a system of passports.[10]

The astrological superstitions and the religious unbelief of
many of the tyrants gave, in the minds of their contemporaries,
a peculiar color to this awful and God-forsaken existence.
When the last Carrara could no longer defend the walls and
gates of the plague-stricken Padua that was hemmed in on

8. Even Petrarch finds the despots gotten up "like altars at a
festival."
9. *De vulgari eloquentia*, Book I, ch. 12: ...*qui non heroico
more, sed plebeo sequuntur superbiam,* etc. [...who not in a
heroic way, but in a common way, follow pride].
10. The passport office of Padua at about the middle of the fourteenth century is described by Franco Sacchetti as *quelli delle
bullette* [the filing people]. In the last ten years of the reign of
Frederick II, when the strictest control was exercised over the
personal conduct of his subjects, this system of passports must
have been very highly developed.

all sides by the Venetians (1405), the soldiers of the guard heard him cry to the devil to come and kill him.

The most complete and most instructive type of despotism of the fourteenth century is to be found unquestionably among the Visconti of Milan, from the death of the Archbishop Giovanni onward (1354). There is an unmistakable family likeness between Bernabò and the worst of the Roman emperors; the most important public object was the prince's boar-hunting; whoever interfered with it was put to death by torture; the terrified people were forced to maintain 5,000 boar hounds, with strict responsibility for their health and safety. The taxes were extorted by every conceivable sort of compulsion; seven daughters of the prince received a dowry of 100,000 gold florins apiece; and an enormous treasure was collected. On the death of his wife (1384) an order was issued "to the subjects" to share his grief as once they had shared his joy, and to wear mourning for a year. – The *coup de main* (1385) by which his nephew Gian Galeazzo got him into his power—one of those brilliant plots which make the heart of even subsequent historians beat more quickly—was strikingly characteristic of the man. In Gian Galeazzo that passion for the colossal which was common to most of the despots exhibited itself on the grandest scale. At the cost of 300,000 gold florins, he undertook the construction of gigantic dikes to divert, in case of need, the Mincio from Mantua and the Brenta from Padua, and thus to render these cities defenseless. Indeed, it is not impossible that he thought of draining the lagoons of Venice. He founded "that most wonderful of all convents," the Certosa di Pavia, and the cathedral of Milan, "which exceeds in size and splendor all the churches of Christendom." The Palace in Pavia, which his father Galeazzo began and which he himself finished, was probably the most magnificent of the princely dwellings of Europe at that time. There he transferred his famous library, and the great collection of relics of the saints in which he placed a peculiar faith. It would have been strange had a prince of this character not also cherished the highest ambitions in political matters. King Wenceslaus made him Duke (1395); he was hoping for nothing less than the Kingdom of Italy or the Imperial crown, when (1402) he fell ill and died. His territories are said to have paid him in a single year, besides the regular taxes of 1,200,000 gold florins, no less than 800,000 more in extraordinary subsidies. After his death the dominions that he had brought together by every sort of violence fell to pieces; and for a

time even the original nucleus was barely maintained by his
successors. What might have become of his sons Giovanni
Maria (d. 1412) and Filippo Maria (d. 1447), had they
lived in a different country and among other traditions,
cannot be said. But, as heirs of their house, they inherited
that monstrous capital of cruelty and cowardice which had
been accumulated from generation to generation.

Giovanni Maria, too, is famed for his dogs, which were no
longer, however, used for hunting boars but for tearing
human bodies. Tradition has preserved their names, like
those of the bears of Emperor Valentinian I. In May 1409,
when war was taking place and the starving populace cried
Pace! Pace! in the streets, he loosed his mercenaries on them
and 200 lives were lost; under penalty of the gallows it was
forbidden to utter the words *pace* and *guerra,* and even the
priests were ordered to say *tranquillitatem,* instead of *dona
nobis pacem!* At last a band of conspirators took advantage
of the moment when Facino Cane, the chief *condottiere* of
the insane ruler, lay ill at Pavia, and cut down Giovanni
Maria in the church of San Gottardo at Milan; the dying
Facino on the same day made his officers swear to stand by
the heir Filippo Maria, whom he himself urged his wife to
take for a second husband. His wife, Beatrice di Tenda,
followed his advice. We shall have occasion to speak of
Filippo Maria later on.

And in times like these Cola di Rienzi dreamed of founding on the rickety enthusiasm of the corrupt population of
Rome a new dominion over Italy. By the side of rulers such
as these, he seems no better than a poor deluded fool.

The despotisms of the fifteenth century were of a different
character. Many of the lesser tyrants, and some of the greater,
such as the Scala and the Carrara, had disappeared, while the
more powerful ones, aggrandized by conquest, had developed
systems peculiar to themselves. Naples, for example, received
a fresh and stronger impulse from the new Aragonese dynasty.
A striking feature of this epoch was the attempt of the
condottieri to found independent dynasties of their own,
which further strengthened the tendency to accept the rule
of the stronger and put a high premium on shrewdness and
ruthlessness. To gain security, the petty despots began to
enter the service of the larger States, and themselves became
condottieri, receiving money in return for their services and
immunity for their misdeeds, perhaps even an increase of
territory. All, whether small or great, had to exert themselves
more, act with greater caution and calculation, learn to

refrain from too wholesale barbarities; only so much wrong was permitted as was demonstrably necessary for the end in view, and those not directly concerned could find no fault with this. There is no trace here of that half-religious loyalty by which the legitimate princes of the West were supported; personal popularity is the closest approximation we can find. Talent and calculation were the only means of advancement. A character like that of Charles the Bold, which wore itself out in the passionate pursuit of impracticable ends, was a riddle to the Italians. "The Swiss were only peasants, and if they were all killed it would be no satisfaction for the Burgundian nobles who might fall in the war. Were the Duke to get possession of all Switzerland without a struggle, his income would not be 5,000 ducats the greater." The medieval features in Charles's character, his chivalrous aspirations and ideals, had long become unintelligible to the Italians. When the diplomats of the South saw him strike his officers and yet keep them in his service, when he maltreated his troops to punish them for a defeat and then threw the blame on his counsellors in the presence of the same troops, they gave him up for lost. Louis XI, on the other hand, whose policy surpassed that of the Italian princes in their own style, and who was an avowed admirer of Francesco Sforza, must be placed far below these rulers in all that regards culture and refinement.

Good and evil lie strangely mixed together in the Italian States of the fifteenth century. The personality of the ruler was so highly developed, often of such deep significance, and so characteristic of the conditions and needs of the time,[11] that to form an adequate moral judgment on it is no easy task.

The foundation of the system was and remained illegitimate, and nothing could remove the curse that clung to it. Imperial approval or investiture could not change it, since the people attached little weight to the fact that the despot had bought a piece of parchment in some foreign country or from some stranger passing through his territory. If the Emperor had been good for anything—so ran the logic of uncritical common sense—he would never have let the tyrant rise at all. Since the Roman expedition of Charles IV, the emperors had done nothing more in Italy than *sanction* a tyranny which had arisen without their help; they could give

11. This compound of force and talent is what Machiavelli calls *virtù* [courage] and is also considered compatible with *scelleratezza* [monstrousness], see, e.g., *The Discourses*, Book I, ch. 10, on Septimus Severus.

it no other *guarantee* than what might flow from an imperial charter. The whole conduct of Charles in Italy was a scandalous political comedy. Matteo Villani relates how the Visconti escorted him round their territory, and at last out of it; how he went about like a hawker selling his wares (privileges) for money; what a mean appearance he made in Rome, and how at the end, without even drawing his sword, he returned across the Alps with full coffers. Sigismund came, on the first occasion at least (1414), with the good intention of persuading John XXIII to take part in his council; it was on that journey, when Pope and Emperor were gazing from the lofty tower of Cremona on the panorama of Lombardy, that their host, the tyrant Gabrino Fondolo, was seized with the desire to throw them both over. On his second visit Sigismund came as a mere adventurer; for more than half a year he remained shut up in Siena, like a debtor in jail, and only with difficulty, and at a later period, succeeded in being crowned in Rome. And what are we to think of Frederick III? His journeys to Italy have the air of holiday trips or pleasure tours made at the expense of those who wanted him to confirm their prerogatives, or whose vanity it flattered to entertain an emperor. The latter was the case with Alfonso of Naples, who paid 150,000 florins for the honor of an imperial visit. At Ferrara, on his second return from Rome (1469), Frederick spent a whole day without leaving his chamber, distributing no less than eighty titles; he created knights, counts, doctors, notaries—counts, indeed, of various degrees: counts palatine, counts with the right to create doctors up to the number of five, counts with the right to legitimatize bastards, to appoint notaries, to declare dishonorable notaries honorable, etc. His Chancellor, however, expected in return for the patents in question a gratuity which was thought excessive at Ferrara. What Duke Borso thought of his imperial patron distributing patents and furnishing the entire little court with titles is not mentioned. The humanists, then the chief spokesmen of the age, were divided in opinion according to their personal interests. Whereas the Emperor was greeted by some of them with the conventional acclamations of the poets of Imperial Rome, Poggio confessed that he no longer knew what the coronation meant; in the old times only the victorious Imperator had been crowned, and then he was crowned with laurel.

With Maximilian I begins not only the general intervention of foreign nations, but a new imperial policy with regard to Italy. The first step—the investiture of Lodovico Sforza (Il Moro) and the exclusion of his unfortunate nephew—was not

of a kind to bear good fruit. According to the modern theory of
intervention, when two parties are tearing a country to pieces,
a third may step in and take its share; and on this principle
the Empire could claim its portion. But right and justice
were no longer the issue. When Louis XII was expected in
Genoa (1502), and the imperial eagle was removed from
the hall of the ducal palace and replaced by painted lilies,
the historian Senarega asked what, after all, was the meaning
of the eagle which so many revolutions had spared, and what
claims did the Empire have on Genoa. No one knew more
than the old phrase, that Genoa was a *camera imperii*. In
fact, nobody in Italy could give a clear answer to any such
questions. Only when Charles V held Spain and the Empire
together was he able by means of Spanish forces to make
good imperial claims; but it is notorious that what he thereby
gained turned to the profit, not of the Empire, but of the
Spanish monarchy.

Closely connected with the political illegitimacy of the
dynasties of the fifteenth century was the public indifference
to legitimate birth, which to foreigners—for example, to
Comines—appeared so remarkable. The two things went naturally hand in hand. Whereas in Northern countries, as in
Burgundy, the illegitimate offspring were provided for by a
distinct class of appanages, such as bishoprics and the like,
and in Portugal an illegitimate line maintained itself on the
throne only by constant effort, in Italy there no longer existed
a princely house where, even in the direct line of descent,
bastards were not patiently tolerated. The Aragonese monarchs
of Naples belonged to the illegitimate line, Aragon itself
falling to the lot of the brother of Alfonso I. The great
Federigo of Urbino was, perhaps, no Montefeltro at all. When
Pius II was on his way to the Congress of Mantua (1459),
eight bastards of the House of Este rode to meet him at
Ferrara, among them the reigning Duke Borso himself and
two illegitimate sons of his illegitimate brother and predecessor
Lionello. The latter had also had a lawful wife, herself an
illegitimate daughter of Alfonso I of Naples by an African
woman. Bastards were often admitted to the succession where
the lawful children were minors and the dangers of the situation were pressing; and a rule of seniority became recognized,
which took no account of pure or impure birth. The fitness
of the individual, his worth and capacity, were of more
weight here than all the laws and usages that prevailed
elsewhere in the West. It was the age, indeed, in which the
sons of the Popes were founding dynasties. In the sixteenth
century, through the influence of foreign ideas and of the

Counter Reformation which was then beginning, the whole question was judged more strictly: Varchi discovers that the succession of the legitimate children "is ordered by reason, and is the will of heaven from eternity." Cardinal Ippolito de' Medici founded his claim to the lordship of Florence on the fact that he was perhaps the fruit of a lawful marriage, and at all events son of a gentlewoman and not (like Duke Alessandro) of a servant girl. At this time began those morganatic marriages of affection which in the fifteenth century, on grounds either of policy or morality, would have had no meaning at all.

But the highest and the most admired form of illegitimacy in the fifteenth century was presented by the *condottiere* who, whatever may have been his origin, raised himself to the position of an independent ruler. At bottom, the occupation of Lower Italy by the Normans in the eleventh century was of this character, but now attempts of this kind began to keep the peninsula in a constant ferment.

It was possible for a *condottiere* to obtain the lordship of a district even without usurpation, when his employer, through want of money or troops, provided for him in this way; under any circumstances the *condottiere*, even when he dismissed temporarily the greater part of his forces, needed a safe place where he could establish his winter quarters and lay up his stores and provisions. The first example of a captain thus portioned is John Hawkwood, who was invested by Pope Gregory XI with the lordship of Bagnacavallo and Cotignola. But when with Alberigo da Barbiano Italian armies and leaders appeared upon the scene, the chances of founding a principality, or of increasing one already acquired, became more frequent. The first great bacchanalian outbreak of military ambition took place in the duchy of Milan after the death of Gian Galeazzo (1402). The policy of his two sons was aimed chiefly at the destruction of the new despotisms founded by the *condottieri;* and from the greatest of them, Facino Cane, the house of Visconti inherited, together with his widow, a long list of cities, and 400,000 gold florins, let alone the soldiers of her first husband whom Beatrice di Tenda brought with her. From that time that thoroughly immoral relation between the governments and their *condottieri,* which is characteristic of the fifteenth century, became more and more common. An old story—one of those which are true and not true, everywhere and nowhere—describes it as follows: The citizens of a certain town—Siena seems to be meant—once had an officer in their service who had freed them from foreign aggression; daily they took counsel how to recompense him, and concluded that no reward in their power was great enough, not even if they made him lord of the city. At last one of them rose and said, "Let us kill him and then worship him as our patron saint." So they did, following the example set by the Roman senate with Romulus. In fact, the *condottieri* had reason to fear none so much as their employers; if they were successful, they became dangerous, and were put out of the way, like Roberto Malatesta just after the victory he had won for Sixtus IV (1482); if they failed, the vengeance of the Venetians on Carmagnola (1432) showed to what risks they were exposed. It is characteristic of the moral aspect of the situation that the *condottieri* had often to give their wives and children as hostages, and yet neither felt nor inspired confidence. They must have been heroes of abnegation, natures like Belisarius himself, not to be cankered by hatred and bitterness; only the most perfect goodness could save them from the most monstrous iniquity. No wonder then if we find them full of contempt for all sacred things, cruel and treacherous to their fellows—men who did not care if they died under the ban of the Church. At the same time, and through the force of the same conditions, the genius and capacity of many of them attained the highest conceivable development, and won for them the admiring devotion of their followers; their armies are the first in modern history in which the personal credit of the leader is the one moving power. A brilliant example is shown in the life of Francesco Sforza; no prejudice of birth could prevent him from winning and turning to account when he needed it a boundless devotion from each individual with whom he had to deal; his enemies laid down their arms at the sight of him, greeting him reverently with uncovered heads, each honoring in him "the common father of the men-at-arms." The family of the Sforza has this special interest, that from the very beginning of its history we seem able to trace its endeavors after the crown. The foundation of its fortune lay in the remarkable fruitfulness of the family; Francesco's father, Jacopo, himself a celebrated man, had twenty brothers and sisters, all brought up roughly at Cotignola, near Faenza, amid the perils of one of the endless Romagnole vendettas between their own House and that of the Pasolini. The family dwelling was a mere arsenal and fortress, the mother and daughters as warlike as their kinsmen. In his thirteenth year Jacopo ran away and fled to Panicale to the papal *condottiere* Boldrino—the man who even in death continued to lead his troops, the orders being given from the bannered tent in which the embalmed body lay, till at last a fit leader was

found to succeed him. As Jacopo gradually prospered under
the service of various *condottieri,* he summoned his relations,
and derived from them the same advantages that a prince
obtains from a numerous dynasty. It was these relations who
kept the army together when he lay a captive in the Castel
dell' Ovo at Naples; his sister took the royal envoys prisoners
with her own hands, and by this reprisal saved him from death.
It was an indication of the breadth and range of his plans
that in monetary affairs Jacopo was thoroughly trustworthy;
even after his defeats he found credit with the bankers. He
habitually protected the peasants against the license of his
troops, and disliked the destruction of a conquered city. He
gave his well-known mistress, Lucia, the mother of Francesco,
in marriage to another, in order to be free for a princely
alliance. Even the marriages of his relations were arranged on
a definite plan. He kept clear of the impious and profligate
life of his contemporaries, and brought up his son Francesco
to three rules: "Let other men's wives alone; strike none of
your followers, or, if you do, send the injured man far away;
don't ride a hard-mouthed horse, or one that drops his shoe."
But his chief source of influence lay in the qualities, if not of a
great general, at least of a great soldier. His frame was powerful; his peasant's face and frank manners won general popularity; his memory was marvelous, and after the lapse of years
he could recall the names of his followers, the number of
their horses, and the amount of their pay. His education was
purely Italian: he devoted his leisure to the study of history,
and had Greek and Latin authors translated for his use. Francesco, his still more famous son, set his mind from the first
on founding a powerful State, and through brilliant generalship and a faithlessness that hesitated at nothing, got possession of the great city of Milan (1447-1450).

His example was contagious. Aeneas Sylvius wrote about
this time: "In our change-loving Italy, where nothing stands
firm and where no ancient dynasty exists, a servant can
easily become a king." One man in particular, who styled
himself "the man of fortune," captured the imagination of the
whole country: Giacomo Piccinino, the son of Niccolò. It
was a burning question of the day if he, too, would succeed
in founding a princely house. The greater States had an
obvious interest in hindering it, and even Francesco Sforza
thought it would be better if the list of self-made sovereigns
were not enlarged. But the troops and captains sent against
him when, for instance, he was aiming at the lordship of
Siena, saw their own advantage in supporting him: "If it
were all over with him, we should have to go back and plough

our fields." Even while besieging him at Orbetello, they supplied him with provisions; and he got out of his difficulties with honor. But at last fate overtook him. All Italy was betting on the result, when (1465), after a visit to Sforza at Milan, he went to King Ferrante at Naples; in spite of the pledges given, and of his high connections, he was murdered in the Castel Nuovo. Even the *condottieri* who had obtained their dominions by inheritance, never felt themselves safe. When Roberto Malatesta and Federigo of Urbino died on the same day (1482), one at Rome, the other at Bologna, it was found that each had commended his State to the care of the other. In the presence of a class of men who permitted themselves everything, everything seemed permissible. Francesco Sforza, when quite young, had married a rich Calabrian heiress, Polissena Ruffo, Countess of Montalto, who bore him a daughter; an aunt poisoned both mother and child, and seized the inheritance.

From the death of Piccinino onward, the founding of new States by the *condottieri* became a scandal not to be tolerated. The four "great powers," Naples, Milan, the Papacy, and Venice, formed among themselves a political equilibrium that refused to allow any disturbance. In the States of the Church, which swarmed with petty tyrants who in part were or had been *condottieri*, the *nipoti* [nephews] of the Popes, since the time of Sixtus IV, monopolized the right to all such undertakings. But at the first sign of a political crisis, the soldiers of fortune appeared again upon the scene. Under the wretched administration of Innocent VIII a certain Boccalino, who had formerly served in the Burgundian army, almost surrendered himself and the town of Osimo, of which he was master, to the Turkish forces; fortunately, through the intervention of Lorenzo the Magnificent, he proved willing to be paid off, and took himself away. In the year 1495, when the wars of Charles VIII had shattered Italy, the *condottiere* Vidovero, of Brescia, tried his strength; he had already seized the town of Cesena and murdered many of the nobles and burghers; but the citadel held out, and he was forced to withdraw. Then, at the head of a band lent him by another scoundrel, Pandolfo Malatesta of Rimini, son of the Roberto already spoken of and Venetian *condottiere*, he wrested the town of Castelnuovo from the Archbishop of Ravenna. The Venetians, fearing that worse would follow and urged on by the Pope, ordered Pandolfo, "with the kindest intentions," to take the opportunity to arrest his good friend: the arrest was made, though "with great regret," whereupon the order came to bring the prisoner to the gallows. Pandolfo was considerate enough to strangle him in prison, and then show his corpse to the people. – The last notable example of such usurpers is the famous Castellan of Musso who, during the confusion in the Milanese territory which followed the battle of Pavia (1525), improvised a sovereignty on the Lake of Como.

In general it may be said of the despotisms of the fifteenth century, that the greatest crimes were most frequent in the smallest States. In these, where the family was numerous and all the members wished to live in a manner befitting their rank, disputes respecting the inheritance were unavoidable. Bernardo Varano of Camerino put two of his brothers to death (1434), wishing to divide their property among his sons. Where the ruler of a single town was distinguished by a wise, moderate, and humane government, and by zeal for intellectual culture, he was generally a member of some great family, or politically dependent on it. This was the case, for example, with Alessandro Sforza, Prince of Pesaro, brother of the great Francesco and stepfather of Federigo of Urbino (d. 1473). Prudent in administration, just and affable in his rule, he enjoyed, after years of warfare, a tranquil reign, collected a noble library, and passed his leisure in learned or religious conversation. A man of the same class was Giovanni II Bentivoglio of Bologna (1462-1506), whose policy was determined by that of the Este and the Sforza. What ferocity and bloodthirstiness is found, on the other hand, among the Varani of Camerino, the Malatesta of Rimini, the Manfreddi of Faenza, and above all among the Baglioni of Perugia. We have a striking picture of the events in the last-named family toward the close of the fifteenth century, in the admirable historical narratives of Graziani and Matarazzo.

The Baglioni were one of those families whose rule never took the shape of an avowed despotism. It was rather a leadership exercised by means of their vast wealth and of their practical influence in the choice of public officers. Within the family one man was recognized as head; but deep and secret jealousy prevailed among the members of the different branches. Opposed to the Baglioni stood another aristocratic party, led by the family of the Oddi. The city (about 1487) was turned into a camp, and the houses of the leading citizens swarmed with bravoes; scenes of violence were a daily occurrence. At the burial of a German student who had been assassinated, two colleges took arms against each other; sometimes the bravoes of the different Houses even battled in the public square. The complaints of the merchants and artisans were vain; the papal governors and *nipoti* held their tongues, or took themselves off at the first opportunity. At last the Oddi were forced to abandon Perugia, and the city became a beleaguered fortress under the absolute despotism of the Baglioni who used even the cathedral as barracks. Plots and surprises were met with cruel vengeance; after 130 conspirators, who had forced their way into the city, were killed and hung up at the Palazzo Communale (in the year 1491), thirty-five altars were erected in the square, and for three days mass was performed and processions held, to remove the curse from the city. A *nipote of* Innocent VIII was stabbed in broad daylight; a *nipote* of Alexander VI, who was sent to smooth matters over, was dismissed with public contempt. All the while the two leaders of the ruling House, Guido and Ridolfo, were holding frequent interviews with Suor Colomba of Rieti, a Dominican nun of saintly reputation and miraculous powers, who under penalty of some great disaster ordered them to make peace—naturally in vain. Nevertheless the chronicle takes this opportunity to point out the devotion and piety of the better men in Perugia during this reign of terror. When Charles VIII approached (1494), the Baglioni from Perugia and the exiles encamped in and near Assisi conducted the war with such ferocity that every house in the valley was leveled, the fields lay untilled, the peasants were turned into plundering and murdering savages, the fresh-grown bushes were filled with stags and wolves, and the beasts grew fat on the bodies of the slain, on so-called "Christian flesh." When Alexander VI withdrew into Umbria before Charles VIII who was returning from Naples (1495), it occurred to him, when at Perugia, that he might now rid himself of the Baglioni once and for all; he proposed to Guido a festival or tournament, or something of the kind, which would bring the whole family together. Guido, however, was of the opinion "that the most impressive spectacle of all would be to see the whole military force of Perugia collected in a body," whereupon the Pope abandoned his project. Soon after, the exiles made another attack in which only the personal heroism of the Baglioni won them the victory. It was then that the eighteen-year-old Simonetto Baglione fought in the square with a handful of followers against hundreds of the enemy: he fell at last with more than twenty wounds, but rose again when Astorre Baglione came to his help, and, mounting his horse, in gilded armor with a falcon on his helmet, "like Mars in bearing and in deeds, plunged into the struggle."

At that time Raphael, a boy of twelve, was in the workshop of Pietro Perugino. The impressions of these days are perhaps immortalized in the small, early pictures of St. Michael and St. George; something of them, it may be, lives eternally in the large painting of St. Michael; and if Astorre Baglione has anywhere found his apotheosis, it is in the figure of the heavenly horseman in the Heliodorus.[12]

The opponents of the Baglioni were partly destroyed, partly scattered in terror, and were henceforth incapable of another enterprise of the kind. After a time a partial reconciliation took place, and some of the exiles were allowed to return. But Perugia became neither safer nor more tranquil: the inner dissension of the ruling family broke out in frightful excesses. An opposition was formed against Guido and Ridolfo and their sons Gianpaolo, Simonetto, Astorre, Gismondo, Gentile, Marcantonio, and others by two great-nephews, Grifone and Carlo Barciglia; the latter was also a nephew of Varano, Prince of Camerino, and brother-in-law of one of the former exiles, Girolamo della Penna. In vain did Simonetto, warned by sinister presentiments, entreat his uncle on his knees to allow him to put this Penna to death: Guido refused. The plot ripened suddenly on the occasion of the marriage of Astorre to Lavinia Colonna, at Midsummer 1500. The festival began and lasted several days amid gloomy forebodings, whose deepening effect is admirably described by Matarazzo. Varano himself encouraged them; with devilish ingenuity he taunted Grifone with the prospect of undivided authority, and by an imaginary intrigue between his wife Zenobia and Gianpaolo. Finally each conspirator was provided with a victim. (The Baglioni lived in separate houses, mostly on the site of the present castle.) Each received fifteen of the bravoes at hand; the remainder were set on the watch. In the night of July 15 the doors were forced, and Guido, Astorre, Simonetto, and Gismondo were murdered; the others succeeded in escaping.

As the corpses of Astorre and Simonetto lay in the street, the spectators, "and especially the foreign students," compared Astorre to an ancient Roman, so great and imposing did he seem. In the features of Simonetto could still be traced the audacity and defiance that death itself had not tamed. The victors went round among the friends of the family, and did their best to recommend themselves; they found all in tears and preparing to leave for the country. Meantime the escaped Baglioni collected forces outside the city, and on the following

12. [Burckhardt refers here to three paintings now in the Louvre —*St. Michael* (about 1502), *St. George and the Dragon* (about 1502), *St. Michael* (1518)—and to the *Expulsion of Heliodorus* (1511-12) in the Vatican.]

day, with Gianpaolo at their head, forced their way in and speedily found adherents among others whom Barciglia had been threatening with death. When Grifone fell into their hands near Sant' Ercolano, Gianpaolo handed him over for execution to his followers. Barciglia and Penna fled to Camerino to Varano, the chief author of the tragedy; and in a moment, almost without loss, Gianpaolo became master of the city.

Atalanta, the still young and beautiful mother of Grifone, who the day before had withdrawn to a country house with the latter's wife Zenobia and two children of Gianpaolo, and who more than once had repulsed her son with a mother's curse, now returned with her daughter-in-law in search of the dying man. All stood aside as the two women approached, each man shrinking from being recognized as the slayer of Grifone, and dreading the malediction of the mother. But they were deceived: she herself besought her son to pardon him who had dealt the fatal blow, and he died with her blessing. The eyes of the crowd followed the two women reverently as they crossed the square with bloodstained garments. It was for Atalanta that Raphael later painted the famous *Deposition*[13] with which she laid her own sorrow at the feet of the highest and holiest of maternal sorrows.

The cathedral, in the immediate neighborhood of which the greater part of this tragedy had been enacted, was washed with wine and consecrated afresh. The triumphal arch erected for the wedding still remained standing, painted with the deeds of Astorre and with the laudatory verses of the narrator of these events, the worthy Matarazzo.

A legendary history arose for the Baglioni, which was simply a reflection of these atrocities. All the members of this family, from the beginning, were supposed to have died a violent death—on one occasion twenty-seven at the same time; their houses were said to have been leveled once before and the streets of Perugia paved with the bricks, and more of the same. Under Paul III the destruction of their palaces really took place.

For a time they seemed to have formed good resolutions, to have brought their own party into order, and to have protected the public officials against the arbitrary acts of the nobility. But the old curse broke out again like a smoldering fire. In 1520 Gianpaolo was enticed to Rome under Leo X, and there beheaded; one of his sons, Orazio, who ruled Perugia for a short time only and by the most violent means,

13. [Signed and dated 1507. Borghese Gallery, Rome.]

as the partisan of the Duke of Urbino (himself threatened by the Pope), repeated in his own family the atrocities of the past. His uncle and three cousins were murdered, whereupon the Duke sent word that enough had been done. His brother, Malatesta Baglione, the Florentine general, has made himself immortal by the treason of 1530; and Malatesta's son Ridolfo, the last of the House, attained, by the murder of the legate and the public officers in the year 1534, a brief but sanguinary authority.

Here and there we shall meet the tyrants of Rimini again. Unscrupulousness, impiety, military skill, and high culture have seldom been combined in one individual as in Sigismondo Malatesta (d. 1467). But the accumulated crimes of such a family must at last outweigh all talent, however great, and drag the tyrant into the abyss. Pandolfo, Sigismondo's nephew, who has already been mentioned, succeeded in holding his ground for the sole reason that the Venetians refused to abandon their *condottiere*, whatever his crimes; when his subjects, after ample provocation, bombarded him in his castle at Rimini (1497) and then allowed him to escape, a Venetian commissioner brought him back, stained as he was with fratricide and every other abomination. Thirty years later the Malatesta were penniless exiles. The time around 1527 was, as had been the time of Cesare Borgia, epidemic years for these minor dynasties; few of them outlived this date, and none to their own good. At Mirandola, which was governed by insignificant princes of the house of Pico, there lived in the year 1533 a poor scholar, Lilio Gregorio Giraldi, who had fled from the sack of Rome to the hospitable hearth of the aged Giovanni Francesco Pico, nephew of the famous Giovanni; their discussions about the sepulchral monument the prince was constructing for himself gave rise to a treatise, the dedication of which bears the date of April of that year. The postscript is a sad one: "In October of the same year the unhappy prince was attacked in the night and robbed of life and throne by his brother's son; and I myself, having barely escaped with my life, am in the deepest misery."

An unscrupulous half-tyranny such as Pandolfo Petrucci exercised from after 1490 in Siena, then torn by faction, is hardly worth close attention. Insignificant and malicious, he governed with the help of a professor of jurisprudence and an astrologer, and frightened his people by an occasional murder. His pastime in the summer months was to roll blocks of stone from the top of Monte Amiata, without caring what or whom they hit. After succeeding where the most prudent failed, in escaping from the devices of Cesare Borgia, he died forsaken and despised. His sons maintained a qualified supremacy for many years afterward.

In discussing the chief dynasties it is best to treat the Aragonese separately. The feudal system, which from the days of the Normans had survived in the form of a territorial supremacy of the barons, gave a distinctive color to the political constitution of Naples; while elsewhere in Italy, excepting only the southern part of the ecclesiastical dominion and a few other districts, a direct tenure of land prevailed and no hereditary powers were permitted. The great Alfonso, who reigned in Naples from 1435 (d. 1458), was not like his real or alleged descendants. Brilliant, fearless in mixing with his people, dignified and affable in intercourse, admired rather than blamed even for his old man's passion for Lucrezia d'Alagno, he had the one bad quality of extravagance, from which the natural consequence followed. Unscrupulous financiers were long omnipotent at the court, till the bankrupt king robbed them of their spoils; a crusade was preached as a pretext for taxing the clergy; after a great earthquake in the Abruzzi, the survivors were compelled to pay the taxes of the dead. By such means Alfonso was able to entertain distinguished guests with unrivaled splendor; he found pleasure in ceaseless expense, even for the benefit of his enemies; and in rewarding literary work he knew no bounds, so that Poggio received 500 pieces of gold for translating into Latin Xenophon's *Cyropaedia*.

Ferrante [Ferdinand I],[14] who succeeded him, passed as his illegitimate son by a Spanish lady, but was probably the son of a Valencian marrano. Whether it was his blood or the plots formed against his life by the barons that embittered and darkened his nature, it is certain that in ferocity he had no equal among the princes of his time. Restlessly active, recognized as one of the most powerful political minds of the day, and free from the vices of the profligate, he concentrated all his powers—among which must be reckoned profound dissimulation and an irreconcilable spirit of vengeance—on the destruction of his opponents. Insulted in every area in which a ruler is open to offense, for the leaders of the barons, though related to him by marriage, were the allies of his foreign enemies, extreme measures became part of his daily policy. The means for this struggle with his barons and for

14. Comines, *Charles VIII*, ch. 17, and the characteristics of the Aragonese in general.

his external wars were exacted in the same Mohammedan fashion that Frederick II had introduced: only the Government dealt in corn and oil; the entire commerce of the country was put by Ferrante into the hands of a wealthy merchant, Francesco Coppola, who had complete control of the anchorage on the coast, and shared the profits with the King; deficits were made up by forced loans, by executions and confiscations, by open simony, and by contributions levied on the ecclesiastical corporations. Besides hunting, which he practiced regardless of all rights of property, his pleasures were of two kinds: he liked to have his opponents near him, either alive in well-guarded prisons, or dead and embalmed, dressed in the clothing they wore in their lifetime. He would chuckle in talking of the captives with his friends, and make no secret whatever of the museum of mummies. His victims were mostly men whom he had got into his power by treachery; some were even seized while guests at the royal table. His conduct to his prime minister, Antonello Petrucci, who had grown sick and gray in his service, and from whose increasing fear of death he extorted present after present, was literally devilish. At length a suspicion of complicity with the last conspiracy of the barons gave the pretext for his arrest and execution. With him died Coppola. The way in which all this is narrated in Caracciolo and Porzio makes one's hair stand on end. – The elder of the King's sons, Alfonso, Duke of Calabria, enjoyed in later years a kind of co-regency with his father. He was a savage, brutal profligate, who in point of frankness had the advantage of Ferrante, and who openly avowed his contempt for religion and its usages. The better and nobler features of the Italian despotisms are not to be found among the princes of this line; all that they possessed of the art and culture of their time served the purpose of luxury or display. Even the genuine Spaniards seem to have almost always degenerated in Italy; but the end of this crossbred house (1494 and 1503) gives clear proof of a want of blood. Ferrante died of mental care and trouble; Alfonso accused his brother Federigo, the only honest member of the family, of treason, and insulted him in the vilest manner. At length, though he had hitherto passed for one of the ablest generals in Italy, he lost his head and fled to Sicily, leaving his son, the younger Ferrante, a prey to the French and to domestic treason. A dynasty that had ruled as this had done must at least have sold its life dear, if its children were ever to hope for a restoration. But, as Comines one-sidedly, and yet on the whole rightly observes on this occasion, *Jamais homme cruel ne fut hardi* (No cruel man was ever without fear).

The despotism of the Dukes of Milan, whose government from the time of Gian Galeazzo onward was a thoroughgoing absolute monarchy, shows the genuine Italian character of the fifteenth century. The last of the Visconti, Filippo Maria (r. 1412-1447), is a man of particular interest, of whom, fortunately, an admirable description has been left us. What fear can do to a man of uncommon gifts and high position is here shown with what may be called a mathematical completeness. All the resources of the State were devoted to the one end of securing his personal safety, though happily his cruel egotism did not degenerate into a purposeless thirst for blood. He lived in the citadel of Milan, surrounded by magnificent gardens, arbors, and lawns. For years he never set foot in the city, making his excursions only in the country, where he had several splendid castles; the flotilla, drawn by the swiftest horses, that carried him to them along canals constructed for the purpose, was arranged to allow the practice of the most rigorous etiquette. Whoever entered the citadel was watched by a hundred eyes; it was forbidden even to stand at the window, lest signals should be given to those outside. All who were admitted to the entourage of the Prince were subjected to ingenious tests; then, once accepted, they were charged with the highest diplomatic commissions, as well as with the humblest personal services—both being equally honorable in this court. And this was the man who conducted long and difficult wars, who dealt habitually with important political affairs, and every day sent his plenipotentiaries to all parts of Italy. His safety lay in the fact that not one of his servants trusted the others, that his *condottieri* were watched and misled by spies, and that the ambassadors and higher officials were baffled and kept apart by artificially nourished jealousies, in particular by the device of coupling an honest man with a knave. His inward faith, too, rested on opposed and contradictory systems; he believed in blind necessity and in the influence of the stars, and offered prayers simultaneously to all gods; he was a student of the ancient authors and of French tales of chivalry. And yet the same man, who would never suffer death to be mentioned in his presence and had his dying favorites removed from the castle so that no shadow might fall on this abode of happiness, deliberately hastened his own death by closing up a wound, and, refusing to be bled, died at last with dignity and grace.

His son-in-law and successor, the fortunate *condottiere*

Francesco Sforza (r. 1450-1466), was perhaps of all the Italians of the fifteenth century the man most after the heart of his age. Never was the triumph of genius and individual power more brilliantly displayed than in him; and those who would not recognize his merit had at least to honor him as Fortune's favorite. The Milanese avowed it an honor to be governed by so distinguished a master; when he entered the city the thronging populace bore him on horseback into the cathedral, without giving him the chance to dismount. Let us read the balance sheet of his life, drawn up by Pope Pius II, a judge in such matters:[15] "In the year 1459, when the Duke came to the Congress at Mantua, he was 60 (really 58) years old; on horseback he looked like a young man, of lofty and imposing figure, serious expression, calm and affable in conversation, princely in his whole bearing, a combination of bodily and intellectual gifts unrivaled in our time, unconquered on the field of battle—this was the man who raised himself from a humble position to rule an empire. His wife was beautiful and virtuous, his children like the angels of heaven; he was seldom ill; all his chief desires were fulfilled. And yet he was not without misfortune; his wife, out of jealousy, killed his mistress, his old comrades and friends, Troilo and Brunoro, deserted him and went over to King Alfonso; another, Ciarpollone, he was forced to hang for treason; he lived to see his brother Alessandro set the French against him; one of his sons formed intrigues against him, and was imprisoned; the March of Ancona, which he had won in war, he lost in war. No man enjoys so serene a fortune that he has not somewhere to struggle with adversity. He is happy who has few troubles." With this negative definition of happiness the learned Pope dismisses the reader. Had he been able to see into the future, or been willing to stop and discuss the consequences of an uncontrolled despotism, one pervading fact would not have escaped his notice —the absence of all guarantee for the future. Those children, beautiful as angels, carefully and thoroughly educated as they were, fell victims, when they grew up, to the corruption of a measureless egotism. Galeazzo Maria (r. 1466-1476), a master of appearances, took pride in the beauty of his hands, in the high salaries he paid, in the financial credit he enjoyed, in his treasure of two million pieces of gold, in the distinguished people who surrounded him, and in the army and birds of chase which he maintained. He was fond of the sound of his own voice and spoke well, most fluently, perhaps,

15. *The Commentaries of Pius II,* Book III. Cf. Book II.

when he had the chance of insulting a Venetian ambassador. He was subject to caprices, such as having a room painted with figures in a single night; and, what was worse, to fits of senseless debauchery and revolting cruelty to his nearest friends. To a few fanatics he seemed to possess all the characteristics of a tyrant; they murdered him, and thereby delivered the State into the power of his brothers, one of whom, Lodovico (Il Moro), threw his nephew into prison, and took the government into his own hands. From this usurpation followed the intervention of the French and the disasters that befell the whole of Italy. Il Moro is the most perfect type of despot of that age and, as a kind of natural phenomenon, almost disarms our moral judgment. He practiced a profound immorality with perfect ingenuousness and probably no one would have been more astonished than he to learn that man is morally responsible for the means he chooses, as well as the ends; indeed, he would have reckoned it as a singular virtue that so far as possible he had abstained from too free a use of punishment by death. He accepted as no more than his due the almost fabulous respect of the Italians for his political genius. In 1496 he boasted that Pope Alexander was his chaplain, Emperor Maximilian his *condottiere,* Venice his chamberlain, and the King of France his courier, who must come and go at his bidding. With marvelous presence of mind he weighed, even in his last extremity (1499), all possible means of escape, and at length decided, to his honor, to trust to the goodness of human nature; because of a former quarrel, he rejected the offer of his brother, Cardinal Ascanio, who wished to remain in the citadel of Milan: "Monsignore, take it not ill, but I trust you not, brother though you be"; and appointed to the command of the castle, as "pledge of his return," a man to whom he had always done good, but who betrayed him. – At home Il Moro was a good and useful ruler, and to the last he reckoned on his popularity both in Milan and in Como. In later years (after 1496) he overstrained the resources of his State, and at Cremona ordered, out of pure expediency, a respected citizen, who had spoke against the new taxes, to be quietly strangled; and from that time, when holding audiences, he kept his visitors away from his person by means of a bar, so that in conversing with him they were compelled to speak at the top of their voices. – At his court, the most brilliant in Europe since that of Burgundy had ceased to exist, immorality of the worst kind was prevalent; daughter was sold by father, wife by husband, sister by brother. The Prince himself was always active, and, as son of his own deeds, claimed relationship with all who, like himself, stood on their personal merits—scholars, poets, artists, and musicians. The academy he founded served rather for his own purposes than for the instruction of scholars; nor was it the fame of the distinguished men who surrounded him that he required, so much as their society and their services. It is certain that Bramante was scantily paid at first; Leonardo, on the other hand, was, up to 1496, suitably remunerated—and what kept him at the court, if not his own free will? The world lay open to him, as perhaps to no other mortal of that day; and if proof were wanting of the loftier element in the nature of Il Moro, it is found in the long stay of the enigmatic master at his court. That Leonardo later entered the service of Cesare Borgia and Francis I was probably due again to the interest he felt in the unusual and striking character of these men.

Of his sons, who after the fall of Il Moro were badly brought up among strangers, the elder, Massimiliano, resembled him not at all; the younger, Francesco, was at all events not without spirit. Milan, which in those years changed its rulers so often and suffered so unspeakably in the change, endeavored to secure itself against a reaction. In the year 1512 the French, retreating before the arms of Maximilian and the Spaniards, were induced to make a declaration that the Milanese had taken no part in their expulsion, and, without being guilty of rebellion, might yield themselves to a new conqueror. It is a fact of some political importance that in such moments of transition the unhappy city, like Naples at the flight of the Aragonese, was apt to fall prey to gangs of (often highly aristocratic) scoundrels.

The House of Gonzaga at Mantua and that of Montefeltro of Urbino were among the best ordered and richest in men of ability during the second half of the fifteenth century. The Gonzaga were a tolerably harmonious family; for a long period no murder had been known among them, and their dead could be shown to the world without fear. The Marquis Francesco Gonzaga [16] and his wife, Isabella d'Este, in spite of some few irregularities, were a united and respectable couple, and raised their sons to be successful and remarkable men at a time when their small but most important State was exposed to incessant danger. That Francesco, either as statesman or as soldier, should adopt a policy of exceptional

16. Born, 1466; betrothed to six-year-old Isabella, 1480; succeeded, 1484; married, 1490; died, 1519. Isabella died, 1539. Their sons: Federigo, ruled 1519-40, made Duke, 1530; and the famous Ferrante Gonzaga. What follows is taken from the correspondence of Isabella.

honesty, was what neither the Emperor, nor Venice, nor the King of France could have expected or desired; but certainly since the battle at the Taro (1495), so far as military honor was concerned, he felt and acted as an Italian patriot, and imparted the same spirit to his wife. Every deed of loyalty and heroism, such as the defense of Faenza against Cesare Borgia, she felt as a vindication of the honor of Italy. Our judgment of her need not rest on the praises of the artists and writers who made the fair princess a rich return for her patronage; her own letters show her to us as a woman of unshaken calm, witty and gracious in her observations. Bembo, Bandello, Ariosto, and Bernardo Tasso sent their works to this court even though it was small and powerless and its treasury was often empty. A more polished and charming circle had not been seen in Italy since the dissolution of the old court of Urbino (1508); and the Mantuan court even surpassed the Ferrarese in respect to freedom of movement. In artistic matters Isabella was especially gifted, and no lover of art can read without emotion the catalogue of her small but choice collection.

In the great Federigo (1444-1482), whether he were a genuine Montefeltro or not, Urbino possessed a brilliant representative of the princely order. As a *condottiere* he shared the political morality of *condottieri*, a morality for which they are only partially to blame; as ruler of his little territory he practiced the policy of spending at home the money he had earned abroad, and taxing his people as lightly as possible. Of him and his two successors, Guidobaldo and Francesco Maria, we read: "They erected buildings, furthered the cultivation of the land, lived at home, and gave employment to a large number of people: their subjects loved them." Not only the State, but the court too, was a work of art and organization, and in every way. Federigo had 500 persons in his service; the arrangements of his court were as complete as those of the greatest monarchs, but nothing was wasted—everything had its purpose and all was carefully controlled. Here was no vice and dissipation, for the court served also as a military academy for the sons of other great houses, whose education was a matter of honor for the Duke. The palace he built was not one of the most splendid, but it had a classical perfection; there he assembled his greatest treasure, the celebrated library. Feeling secure in a land where all gained profit or employment from his rule and none were beggars, he habitually went about unarmed and almost unaccompanied; he alone among the princes of his time walked in public gardens and took his frugal meals in an open chamber, while Livy (or in time of fasting, some devotional work) was read to him. In the same afternoon he would listen to a lecture on some classical subject, and then go to the Clarice monastery and through the grille talk of sacred things with the abbess. In the evenings he would supervise the exercises of the young people of his court on the magnificent meadow of San Francesco, and saw to it that all the feats were done in the most perfect manner. He strove always to be affable and accessible, visiting in their shops the artisans who worked for him, holding frequent audiences, and, if possible, attending to the requests of each individual on the same day they were presented. No wonder that the people, as he walked along the street, knelt down and cried: *Dio ti mantenga, Signore* [May God keep you, Sir]!" Intelligent people called him "the light of Italy." [17] – His gifted son Guidobaldo, plagued by sickness and every kind of misfortune, was finally able (1508) to place his State into the sure hands of his nephew Francesco Maria (*nipote* also of Pope Julius II), who succeeded at least in preserving the territory from any permanent foreign occupation. It is remarkable with what confidence these two yielded and fled— Guidobaldo before Cesare Borgia, Francesco before the troops of Leo X; they knew that their restoration would be that much easier and more popular the less the country suffered through a fruitless defense. When Lodovico counted on the same thing at Milan, he forgot the many grounds of hatred that existed against him. – The court of Guidobaldo has been made immortal as the school of polished manners by Baldassare Castiglione, who presented his eclogue *Tirsi* before and in honor of that society (1506), and who afterward (1518) laid the dialogue of his *Courtier* in the circle of the accomplished Duchess (Elisabetta Gonzaga).

The government of the Este at Ferrara, Modena, and Reggio displays a remarkable balance of violence and popularity. Within the palace frightful deeds were perpetrated; a princess was beheaded for alleged adultery with a stepson (1425); legitimate and illegitimate children fled from the court, and even abroad were threatened by assassins sent in pursuit of them (1471). Plots from without were incessant; the bastard of a bastard tried to wrest the crown from the lawful heir (Ercole I) who later (1493) is supposed to have poisoned his wife on discovering that she, at the instigation

17. Castiglione, *The Courtier*, Book I.

of her brother Ferrante of Naples, was going to poison him. This list of tragedies is closed by the plot of two bastards against their brothers, the ruling Duke Alfonso I and Cardinal Ippolito (1506), which was discovered in time and was punished with life imprisonment. – But the financial system in this State was perfectly developed, and had to be, since among the large and secondary powers of Italy, it was the most threatened and was in constant need of arms and fortifications. It was hoped that the increasing prosperity of the people would keep pace with the increasing taxation, and the Marquis Niccolò (d. 1441) openly expressed the wish that his subjects might be richer than other peoples. If rapid increase of population is a measure of prosperity actually attained, it is then important to note that in 1497 there were no houses for rent. Ferrara is the first really modern city in Europe; here, at the bidding of the ruler arose the first large, systematically laid-out quarters; here, by concentration of civil service and active promotion of trade, was formed a true capital; wealthy fugitives from all parts of Italy, Florentines especially, were invited to settle and build their palaces here. But the indirect taxation, at all events, must have reached a point at which it could only just be borne. The prince, it is true, took the kind of precautionary measures that were adopted by other Italian despots, such as Galeazzo Maria Sforza: in time of famine, he imported corn and, apparently, distributed it gratuitously; but in ordinary times he compensated himself by the monopoly, if not of corn, of many other necessaries of life—fish, salt, meat, fruit and vegetables, which last were carefully planted on and near the walls of the city. The most considerable source of income, however, was the annual sale of public offices, a practice that was common throughout Italy but about which we know most at Ferrara. It is reported, for example, that at the new year 1502 the majority of the officials bought their places at excessive prices (*salati*); public servants of the most various kinds, custom house officers, bailiffs (*massari*), notaries, *podestà* [magistrates], judges, and even *capitani*, i.e., governors of provincial towns, are cited by name. As one of the "devourers of the people" who paid dearly for their places, and who were hated "more than the devil," Tito Strozza—let us hope not the famous Latin poet—is mentioned. About the same time every year the incumbent duke would make a round of visits in Ferrara, the so-called *andar per ventura* [venturing forth], during which he took presents from, at any rate, the more wealthy citizens. The gifts, however, did not consist of money, but of natural products.

It was the pride of the Duke for all Italy to know that at Ferrara the soldiers received their pay and the professors at the University their salary not a day later than it was due; that the soldiers never dared lay arbitrary hands on citizen or peasant; that Ferrara was impregnable to assault; and that vast sums of coined money were stored up in the citadel. It was not necessary to keep two sets of accounts: the Minister of Finance was also manager of the ducal household. The buildings erected by Borso (1430 to 1471), by Ercole I (till 1505), and by Alfonso I (till 1534), were numerous, but mostly of small size; they are characteristic of a princely house that, with all its love of splendor—Borso never appeared but in embroidery and jewels—indulged in no ill-considered expense. Alfonso may perhaps have foreseen the fate that was in store for his charming little villas, the Belvedere with its shady gardens and Montana with its fountains and beautiful frescoes.

It is undeniable that the dangers to which these princes were constantly exposed developed in them remarkable capacities. In so artificial a world only a virtuoso could succeed, and each candidate for distinction had to justify his claims and prove himself worthy of the dominion he sought. Their characters are not without dark sides; but in each of them there was something of those qualities that Italy then pursued as its ideal. What European monarch of that time exerted so much energy on his own education as, for instance, Alfonso I? His travels in France, England, and the Netherlands were undertaken for the purpose of study, and gave him a greater knowledge of the industry and commerce of these countries.[18] It is ridiculous to reproach him with the turner's work that he practiced in his leisure hours, connected as it was with his skill in casting cannon, and with the unprejudiced freedom with which he surrounded himself by masters of every art. The Italian princes were not, like their contemporaries in the North, dependent on the society of an aristocracy which held itself to be the only class worth consideration, and which infected the monarch with the same conceit. In Italy the prince was permitted and compelled to know and to use men of every class; and the nobility, though by birth a caste, were forced in social intercourse to

18. The journey of Leo X, undertaken when he was a cardinal, may also be mentioned here. His object was less serious, and was directed rather to amusement and knowledge of the world. The spirit is wholly modern; no Northerner of that time traveled with such purposes.

stand upon their personal qualifications alone. But this is a point that we shall discuss more fully below.

The feeling of the Ferrarese toward the ruling house was a strange compound of silent dread, of the truly Italian sense of well-calculated interest, and of the loyalty of the modern subject: personal admiration was transferred into a new sentiment of duty. In 1451 the city of Ferrara set up in the piazza a bronze equestrian statue to their Prince Niccolò, who had died ten years earlier; Borso (1454) did not scruple to place his own seated bronze statue close by, in addition to which the city, at the very beginning of his reign, decreed to him a "marble triumphal column." A citizen, who, when abroad in Venice, had openly spoken ill of Borso, was informed against on his return home, and condemned to banishment and the confiscation of his goods, indeed a loyal subject almost struck him down before the tribunal itself; with a rope round his neck the offender went to the Duke and begged for a full pardon. The government was especially well provided with spies, and the Duke inspected personally the daily list of travelers that the innkeepers were strictly ordered to present. Under Borso, who was anxious to leave no distinguished stranger unhonored, this regulation served a hospitable purpose; but Ercole I used it purely as a security measure. In Bologna, too, it was then the rule, under Giovanni II Bentivoglio, that every passing traveler who entered at one gate had to obtain a ticket in order to go out at the other.[19] – A perfect way for the prince to gain popularity was his sudden dismissal of oppressive officials. When Borso personally arrested his chief and confidential counselors, when Ercole I removed and disgraced a tax collector who for years had been sucking the blood of the people, bonfires were lighted and the bells were pealed in their honor. With one of his officials, however, Ercole let things go too far, with the director of the police, or whatever we choose to call him (*capitaneo di giustizia*), Gregorio Zampante of Lucca (a native being unsuited for an office of this kind). Even the sons and brothers of the Duke trembled before this man; the fines he inflicted amounted to hundreds and thousands of ducats, and torture began before the trial. Bribes were accepted from wealthy criminals, and their pardon obtained from the Duke by false representations. What sums would the people cheerfully have paid the Duke had he cashiered this enemy of God and man! But Ercole had knighted him and made him godfather to his children; and year by year

19. Vasari, Life of Michelangelo.

Zampante laid by 2,000 ducats. He dared eat only pigeons bred in his own house, and did not venture on the streets without a band of archers and bravoes. It was time to get rid of him; in 1496 two students and a converted Jew whom he had mortally offended, killed him in his house while he was taking his siesta, and then rode through the town on horses held in waiting, crying, "Come out! come out! we have slain Zampante!" The pursuers were too late, for the slayers were already safely across the frontier. Now of course it rained satires—some in the form of sonnets, others in odes. – It was wholly in the spirit of this dominion that the sovereign imposed his own respect for useful servants on the court and on the people. When in 1469 Borso's privy councilor Ludovico Casella died, no court of law or place of business in the city, and no lecture room at the University, was allowed to be open on the day of the funeral; all had to follow the body to San Domenico, since the Duke intended to be present. And, in fact, "the first of the House of Este to attend the corpse of a subject" walked, clad in black, after the coffin, weeping, while behind him came the relatives of Casella, each conducted by a gentleman of the court: nobles carried the body of the commoner from the church into the cloister, where it was buried. Indeed this official sympathy with princely emotion arose first in the Italian States.[20] At bottom may be a beautiful, humane sentiment; the utterance of it, especially in the poets, is, as a rule, equivocal. One of the youthful poems of Ariosto, on the Death of Leonora of Aragon, wife of Ercole I,[21] contains besides the flowery compliments that are lavished on the dead of all ages, some thoroughly modern features: "This death has given Ferrara a blow from which it will not recover for years: its benefactress is now its advocate in heaven, since earth was not worthy of her; truly the angel of Death did not come to her, as to us common mortals, with bloodstained scythe, but fair to behold (*onesta*), and with so kind a face that every fear was allayed." But we meet, also, with sympathy of a different kind. Novelists, depending wholly on the favor of their patrons, tell us the love stories of the prince even before his death, in a way which, to later times, would seem the height of indiscretion, but which passed then simply as an innocent compliment. Lyrical poets even went so far as to sing the illicit love affairs of their lawfully married lords,

20. An early example, Bernabò Visconti, see above.
21. Without doubt, the cause of this death was unknown to the nineteen-year-old poet.

e.g. Angelo Politian those of Lorenzo the Magnificent, and Gioviano Pontano, with singular gusto, those of Alfonso of Calabria. The poem in question betrays unconsciously the odious disposition of the Aragonese ruler; in these things too, he must be the most fortunate, else woe to those who are more successful! – That the greatest artists, for example Leonardo, should paint the mistresses of their patrons was no more than a matter of course.

But the House of Este was not satisfied with the praises of others; it undertook to celebrate itself. In the Palazzo Schifanoia Borso had himself painted in a series of historical representations, and Ercole (beginning in 1472) celebrated the anniversary of his accession by a procession that was compared to the feast of Corpus Christi; shops were closed as on Sunday; in the center of the line walked all the members of the princely house, even the bastards, clad in embroidered robes. That the prince was the fountain of honor and authority, that all personal distinction flowed from him, had long been expressed at this court by the Order of the Golden Spur—an order which no longer had anything in common with medieval chivalry. Ercole I added to the spur a sword, a gold-laced mantle, and a grant of money, in return for which, there is no doubt, regular service was required.

The patronage of art and letters for which this court has obtained a world-wide reputation, was exercised through the University, which was one of the best in Italy, and by the gift of places in the personal or official service of the Prince; thus, no additional expense was incurred. Boiardo, as a wealthy country gentleman and high official, belonged to this class. When Ariosto began to distinguish himself, there existed no court, in the true sense of the word, either at Milan or Florence, soon there would be none at Urbino, and Naples is not even worth mentioning. He had to content himself with a place among the musicians and jugglers of Cardinal Ippolito till Alfonso took him into his service. It was otherwise at a later time with Torquato Tasso, whose presence at court was jealously sought.

In face of this centralized authority, all opposition within the State was futile. The elements needed for the restoration of a republic had been forever destroyed; everything was directed toward power and despotism. The nobles, deprived of political rights even where they held feudal possessions, might call themselves and their bravoes Guelphs or Ghibellines, and might dress up in padded hose or feathered caps or however they pleased—thoughtful men like Machiavelli[22] knew well enough that Milan and Naples were too "corrupt" for a republic. Curious things are revealed in the records of the trials involving these two so-called parties, whose power had for a long time served only to give official status to old family feuds. An Italian prince who was advised by Agrippa of Nettesheim to destroy them, replied that their quarrels brought him more than 12,000 ducats a year in fines. — And when, for example, in the year 1500, during the brief return of Il Moro to his States, the Guelphs of Tortona summoned a part of the neighboring French army into the city in order to make an end once for all of their opponents, the French began by plundering and ruining the Ghibellines, but finished by doing the same to the Guelphs, till Tortona was laid utterly waste. — Even in Romagna, the hotbed of every ferocious passion, these two names had long lost all political meaning. It was a sign of the political delusion of the people that they frequently believed that the Guelphs were the allies of the French and the Ghibellines of the Spaniards. I do not see that those who tried to profit by this error gained much by it. France, after all her interventions, had to abandon the peninsula at last, and what became of Spain, after she had destroyed Italy, is known to all of us.

But to return to the despots of the Renaissance. A pure and simple mind might perhaps even then have argued that, since all power is derived from God, these princes, if they were loyally and honestly supported by all their subjects, *must* in time improve and lose all traces of their violent origin. But from characters and imaginations inflamed by passion and ambition, reasoning of this kind cannot be expected. Like bad physicians, they thought to cure the disease by removing the symptoms, and fancied that if the tyrant were killed, freedom would naturally follow. Or else, without reflecting even to this extent, they sought only to give vent to the general hatred, or to take vengeance for some family misfortune or personal affront. Just as the governments were absolute and free from all legal restraints, so did the opposition use methods that were equally lawless. Boccaccio declares openly: "Shall I call the tyrant king or prince, and obey him loyally as my lord? No! for he is the enemy of the commonwealth. Against him I may use arms, conspiracies, spies, ambushes, and fraud; to do so is a sacred, necessary work. There is no more pleasing sacrifice than the blood of a tyrant." We need not occupy ourselves with individual cases; Machiavelli, in a famous chapter of his *Discourses*,

22. Machiavelli, *The Discourses*, Book I, ch. 17.

discusses the conspiracies of ancient and modern times from the days of the Greek tyrants and cold-bloodedly classifies them according to their various plans and results. We shall make only two observations: on the murders committed in church, and on the influence of classical antiquity.

It was almost impossible to lay hands on the well-guarded tyrant other than at solemn religious services; and on no other occasion was the entire royal family to be found assembled in one place. The Fabrianese murdered the members of their ruling house, the Chiavelli, during high mass (1435), indeed, using as the signal the words of the Creed, *Et incarnatus est* [and was made flesh]. At Milan, Duke Giovanni Maria Visconti was assassinated at the entrance of the church of San Gottardo (1412), Galeazzo Maria Sforza inside the church of Santo Stefano (1476), and Il Moro escaped the daggers of the adherents of the widowed Duchess Bona only by entering the church of Sant' Ambrogio by another door than that by which he was expected (1484). No impiety was intended; before the murder the assassins of Galeazzo prayed to the patron saint of the church, and even listened to the first mass. One cause of the partial failure of the Pazzi conspiracy against Lorenzo and Giuliano de' Medici (1478) was that the bandit Montesecco, who had bargained to commit the murder at a banquet, declined to undertake it in the Cathedral of Florence; in his stead were recruited certain of the clergy "who were familiar with the sacred place and thus had no fear."

As to the effect of antiquity—the influence of which on moral, and more especially on political, questions we shall often refer to—the example was set by the rulers themselves, who, both in their conception of the State and in their personal conduct, avowedly took the old Roman empire as their model. In like manner their opponents, when they acted on a conscious theory, patterned themselves on the ancient tyrannicides. It may be hard to prove that in the main point —in forming the resolve itself—they consciously followed a classical example; but the reference to antiquity was not merely a matter of rhetoric. Most remarkable information has come down to us with respect to Lampugnani, Olgiati, and Visconti, the murderers of Galeazzo Sforza. All three had personal motives, yet their enterprise may in part be ascribed to a more general reason. About this time Cola de' Montani, a humanist and professor of eloquence, had fired among many of the young Milanese nobility a vague passion for glory and patriotic achievements, and had mentioned to Lampugnani and Olgiati his hope of delivering Milan. Sus-

picion was soon aroused against him, he was banished from
the city, and his pupils were abandoned to the fanaticism
he had excited. Some ten days before the deed they took a
solemn oath in the monastery of Sant' Ambrogio. "Then,"
says Olgiati, "in a remote corner I raised my eyes to the
picture of St. Ambrose and implored his help for ourselves
and for *his* people." The heavenly protector of the city was
called on to bless the undertaking, as was afterward St.
Stephen, in whose church it was fulfilled. Now many more
were informed of the plot, nightly meetings were held in the
house of Lampugnani, and the conspirators practiced for
the murder with the sheaths of their daggers. The attempt
was successful, but Lampugnani was killed on the spot by
the attendants of the Duke and the others were captured.
Visconti was penitent, but Olgiati through all his tortures
maintained that the deed was a suitable offering to God,
and exclaimed while the executioner was breaking his ribs,
"Courage, Girolamo! thou wilt long be remembered; death
is bitter, but glory is eternal."

But however idealistic the object and purpose of such
conspiracies may appear, the manner in which they were
conducted betrays the influence of the most heinous of all
conspirators, a man in whose thoughts freedom had no place
whatever: Catiline. The annals of Siena tell us expressly
that the conspirators had studied their Sallust, and the fact
is indirectly confirmed by the confession of Olgiati. Elsewhere, too, we shall meet the awesome name of Catiline.
For conspiracy there was no pattern more attractive, if one
ignored his purpose.

Whenever the Florentines got rid of, or tried to get rid of,
the Medici, tyrannicide was accepted and approved. After
the flight of the Medici in 1494, Donatello's bronze group
of Judith with the dead Holofernes was taken from their
palace and placed before the Palazzo della Signoria, on the
spot where Michelangelo's *David* now stands,[23] with the
inscription, *Exemplum salutis publicae cives posuere 1495*
[The citizens have placed an example of public safety]. No
example was more popular than that of the younger Brutus,
who, in Dante,[24] lies with Cassius and Judas Iscariot in the
lowest pit of hell because of his treason to the empire. Pietro
Paolo Boscoli, whose plot against Giuliano, Giovanni, and

23. [In 1919 Donatello's *Judith and Holofernes* was returned to
its place before the Palazzo della Signoria (Palazzo Vecchio).
Michelangelo's *David* had already been moved to the Accademia,
and was replaced by a replica that still stands before the Palazzo.]
24. *Inferno,* xxxiv, 64.

Giulio de' Medici failed (1513), was an enthusiastic admirer of Brutus, and in order to follow in his steps only waited to find a Cassius. He found such a partner in Agostino Capponi. His last utterances in prison—one of the most striking pieces of evidence of the religious feeling of the time—show with what an effort he rid his mind of those Roman fantasies in order to die like a Christian. A friend and the confessor had to assure him that St. Thomas Aquinas condemned conspirators absolutely; but the confessor afterward admitted to the same friend that St. Thomas drew a distinction and permitted conspiracies against a tyrant who had forced himself on a people against their will. – After Lorenzino de' Medici murdered Duke Alessandro (1537), and then escaped, an apology for the deed appeared, which is probably his own work, or was at least written at his request, in which he praises tyrannicide as an act of the highest merit; on the grounds that Alessandro was a legitimate Medici and therefore related to him (if only distantly), he boldly compares himself with Timoleon, who slew his brother for his country's sake. Others used the comparison with Brutus, and that Michelangelo himself, even late in life, was not unfriendly to ideas of this kind, may be inferred from his bust of Brutus (in the Uffizi).[25] He left it unfinished, like nearly all his works, but certainly not because the murder of Caesar was repugnant to his feeling, as the couplet beneath declares.

One seeks in vain in the despotic States of the Renaissance for the kind of popular radicalism that opposed the monarchies of later times. Each individual protested inwardly against despotism but was more readily disposed to make tolerable or profitable terms with it rather than combine with others for its destruction. Things had to be as bad as they were at Camerino, Fabriano, or Rimini before the citizens united to destroy or expel the ruling house. In most cases they knew only too well that this would only mean a change of masters. The star of the Republics was certainly on the decline.

The Italian municipalities had, in earlier days, given signal proof of that force which transforms city into State. It remained only that these cities should combine in a great confederation; and this idea constantly recurred to Italian statesmen, whatever differences of form it might from time to time display. During the struggles of the twelfth and thirteenth centuries, great and formidable leagues actually were formed

25. [Now in the Museo Nazionale (Bargello), Florence.]

by the cities; and Sismondi believes that the time of the final armaments of the Lombard confederation against Barbarossa (from 1168 on) was the point at which a universal Italian league had been possible. But the more powerful States had already developed characteristic features which made any such scheme impracticable. In their commercial dealings they shrank from no measures, however extreme, that might damage their competitors and held their weaker neighbors in a condition of helpless dependence—in short, each fancied he could get on by himself without the assistance of the rest, and thus paved the way for future despotism. This came when long conflicts between the nobility and the people, and between the different factions of the nobility, had awakened the desire for a stable government, and when bands of mercenaries ready to sell their support to the highest bidder superseded the general levy of the citizens which party leaders had already discovered did not serve their purposes. The tyrants destroyed the freedom of most of the cities; here and there they were expelled, but only partially, or only for a short time; and they always returned, since the internal conditions were favorable to them and the opposing forces were exhausted.

Among the cities that maintained their independence, two hold the greatest significance for the history of mankind: Florence, the city of incessant movement, which has left us a record of the thoughts and aspirations of individuals and the people as a whole, who, for three centuries, took part in this movement; and Venice, the city of apparent stagnation and of political secrecy. No stronger contrast can be imagined than that which is offered us by these two, and neither can be compared to anything else that the world has hitherto produced.

The Venetians regarded Venice as a marvelous and mysterious creation in which, from the very beginning, something other than human ingenuity was involved. The solemn foundation of the city was the subject of a legend: on March 25, 413, at midday, emigrants from Padua laid the first stone at the Rialto, that they might have a sacred, inviolable asylum amid the devastations of the barbarians. Later writers attributed to the founders the presentiment of the future greatness of the city; M. Antonio Sabellico, who has celebrated the event in magnificent flowing hexameters, has the priest who completes the act of consecration cry to heaven, "When in days to come we attempt great things, grant us prosperity! Now we kneel before a poor altar; but if our vows are not made in vain, a hundred temples, O God, of gold and marble shall arise to Thee." – At the end of the fifteenth century the island city was the jewel box of the world. The same Sabellico describes it as such, with its ancient cupolas, its leaning towers, its inlaid marble façades, its compressed splendor, where the richest decoration did not hinder the practical employment of every corner of space. He takes us to the crowded piazza before San Giacomo di Rialto, where the business of the world is transacted, not amid shouting and confusion, but with the subdued hum of many voices; where in the porticoes [26] round the square and in those of the adjoining streets sit the money-changers and hundreds of goldsmiths, with endless rows of shops and warehouses above their heads. He describes the great Fondaco dei Tedeschi [warehouse of the Germans] beyond the bridge, where their goods and their dwellings lay, and before which their ships are drawn up side by side in the canal; higher up, a whole fleet laden with wine and oil, and parallel with it, on the shore swarming with porters, the vaults of the merchants; then from the Rialto to the Piazza di San Marco, the inns and the perfumers' stalls. So he conducts the reader from quarter to quarter, till he comes at last to the two hospitals, which were among those institutions of public utility that were nowhere so numerous as at Venice. Care for the people, in peace as well as in war, was characteristic of the Venetian government, and its attention to the wounded, even to those of the enemy, astounded the other States. Public institutions of every kind could find their model in Venice; the pensioning of retired servants was carried out systematically, and even included a provision for widows and orphans. Wealth, political security, and acquaintance with other countries had matured the understanding of such questions. These slender fair-haired men, with quiet cautious steps and deliberate speech, differed from one another only slightly in costume and bearing; ornaments, especially pearls, were reserved for the women and girls. At that time the general prosperity, notwithstanding the losses sustained from the Turks, was still dazzling; but years later the stores of energy that the city possessed and the prejudice in its favor diffused throughout Europe enabled Venice to survive the heaviest blows: the discovery of the sea route to the Indies, the fall of the Mamelukes in Egypt, and the war of the League of Cambrai.

Sabellico, who was born in the neighborhood of Tivoli and was accustomed to the frank loquacity of the scholars

26. This whole quarter was later altered by the rebuilding that took place at the beginning of the sixteenth century.

of his day, remarks elsewhere with some astonishment that the young nobles who came to hear his morning lectures could not be prevailed upon to enter into political discussions: "When I ask them what people think, say, and expect about this or that movement in Italy, they all answer with one voice that they know nothing about the matter." Still, in spite of the strict inquisition of the State, much was to be learned from the more corrupt members of the aristocracy by those who were willing to pay enough for it. In the last quarter of the fifteenth century there were traitors among the highest officials; the popes, the Italian princes, even second-rate *condottieri* in the service of the government had their informers, some on regular salary; things went so far that the Council of Ten found it prudent to conceal important political news from the Council of the Pregadi, and it was even supposed that Il Moro had control of a definite number of votes among the Pregadi. Whether the nightly hanging of single offenders and the high rewards for informing (e.g., a pension of sixty ducats for life) were of much avail is hard to decide; one of the chief causes of this evil, the poverty of many of the nobility, could not be removed in a day. In the year 1492 two nobles proposed that the State spend 70,000 ducats for the relief of those poor nobles who held no public office; the matter was close to coming before the Gran Consiglio, in which it might have had a majority, when the Council of Ten interfered in time and banished the two proposers for life to Nicosia in Cyprus. About this time a Soranzo was hanged, though not in Venice itself, for sacrilege, and a Contarini was put in chains for burglary; in 1499 another of the same family came before the Signoria and complained that for many years he had been without an office, that he had only sixteen ducats a year and nine children, that his debts amounted to sixty ducats, that he knew no trade and had lately been turned out on the street. We can understand why some of the wealthier nobles built houses which provided free lodging for their needy comrades. The construction of houses for the ~ake of God, whole rows of them, figure in wills as deeds of charity.

But if the enemies of Venice ever founded serious hopes upon abuses of this kind, they were greatly in error. It might be thought that the commercial activity of the city, which put within reach of the humblest a rich reward for his labor, and the colonies on the eastern shores of the Mediterranean would have diverted from political affairs the dangerous elements of society. But did not Genoa, notwithstanding similar advantages, have the stormiest political history? The cause of the stability of Venice lies rather in a set of circumstances that were found in combination nowhere else. As an unassailable city, Venice had been able from the beginning to conduct its foreign affairs with cool deliberation, to ignore nearly altogether the political intrigues of the rest of Italy, to avoid permanent alliances and to set the highest price on those it thought fit to make. The keynote of the Venetian character was, consequently, a spirit of proud and contemptuous isolation, which, joined to the hatred felt for the city by the other States of Italy, gave rise to a strong sense of solidarity within. The inhabitants were thus united by the most powerful ties of interest in dealing with both the colonies and the possessions on the mainland, forcing the population of the latter, that is, of all the towns up to Bergamo, to buy and sell only in Venice. The conviction that such an advantageous position could be maintained only by internal harmony and unity was so widely diffused among the citizens that conspirators found few elements to work upon. If there were any malcontents, they were held so far apart by the division between noble and burgher that a mutual understanding was not easy. And within the ranks of the nobility the ones who might have been dangerous, namely, the rich, were deprived of the major source of all conspiracies—idleness—by their extensive commercial enterprises and travel, and by the incessant wars with the Turks. In these wars they were spared, often to a criminal extent, by the commanding officers, and a Venetian Cato predicted the fall of the city if this fear of the nobles "to give one another pain" continued at the expense of justice. Nevertheless this free movement in the open air gave the Venetian aristocracy, as a whole, a healthy bias. And when envy and ambition called for satisfaction, an official victim was found and legal means and authorities were ready. The moral torture suffered for years by Doge Francesco Foscari (d. 1457) before the eyes of all Venice is perhaps the most frightful example of a vengeance that is possible only in an aristocracy. The Council of Ten, which had a hand in everything, which disposed without appeal life and death, financial affairs and military appointments, which included the Inquisitors, and which overthrew Foscari as it had overthrown so many powerful men before—this Council was yearly chosen afresh from the whole governing body, the Gran Consiglio, and was consequently the most direct expression of its will. It is not probable that serious intrigues occurred at these elections, as the short duration of the office and the accountability that followed rendered it an object of no great desire. But violent and mysterious as the proceedings of this and other authorities might be, the genuine Venetian courted rather than fled their sentence, not only because the Republic had long arms, and if it could not catch him might punish his family, but because in most cases it acted from rational motives and not from a thirst for blood. Indeed, no State has ever exercised a greater moral influence over those of its subjects who were abroad. If there were traitors among the Pregadi, there was ample compensation for this in the fact that every Venetian away from home was a born spy for his government. It was a matter of course that the Venetian cardinals at Rome sent home news of the transactions of the secret papal consistories. Cardinal Domenico Grimani had the dispatches which Ascanio Sforza was sending to his brother Il Moro intercepted near Rome (1500) and forwarded them to Venice; his father, then exposed to a serious accusation, claimed credit for this service of his son before the Gran Consiglio, in other words, before all the world.

The conduct of the Venetian government to its *condottieri* has already been spoken of. A further guarantee of their fidelity lay in their great number, by which treachery was made as difficult as its discovery was easy. In looking at the Venetian army list, one is only surprised that among forces of such miscellaneous composition any common action was possible. In the catalogue for the campaign of 1495 we find 15,526 horsemen, broken up into a number of small divisions. Only Gonzaga of Mantua had as many as 1,200, and Gioffredo Borgia 740; then follow six officers with a contingent of 700 to 600, ten with 400, twelve with 400 to 200, fourteen or thereabouts with 200 to 100, nine with 80, six with 60 to 50, and so forth. These forces were composed partly of old Venetian troops, some of whom were led by Venetian city or country nobles; the majority of the leaders, however, were princes and rulers of cities, or their relatives. To these forces must be added 24,000 infantry—we are not told how they were raised or commanded—with 3,300 additional troops, who probably belonged to the special services. In time of peace the cities of the mainland were wholly unprotected or occupied by insignificant garrisons. Venice relied, if not exactly on the loyalty, at least on the good sense of its subjects; in the war of the League of Cambrai (1509) it absolved them, as is well known, from their oath of allegiance, and let them compare the amenities of a foreign occupation with the mild government to which they had been accustomed. As there had been no treason in their desertion of

St. Mark, and consequently no punishment was to be feared, they returned to their old masters with the utmost eagerness. This war, we may remark parenthetically, was the result of a century's outcry against the Venetian desire for aggrandizement. The Venetians, in fact, were not free from the mistake of those over-clever people who refuse to credit even their opponents with irrational and unjust conduct. Misled by this optimism, which is, perhaps, a peculiar weakness of aristocracies, they had utterly ignored not only the preparations of Mohammed II for the capture of Constantinople, but even the armaments of Charles VIII, till the unexpected blow fell at last. The League of Cambrai was an event of the same character, in so far as it was clearly opposed to the interests of the two chief members, Louis XII and Julius II. The agelong hatred of all Italy for the victorious city was concentrated in the Pope, and blinded him to the consequences of foreign intervention; and Venice ought long before to have recognized the policy of Cardinal d'Amboise and his king as a piece of malicious imbecility, and to have been thoroughly on its guard. The other members of the League took part in it from that envy which may be a salutary corrective to great wealth and power, but which is in itself a beggarly sentiment. Venice came out of the conflict with honor, but not without lasting damage.

A power whose foundations were so complicated, whose activity and interests filled so wide a stage, cannot be imagined without a systematic supervision of the whole, without a regular estimate of means and burdens, of profits and losses. Venice can easily make good its claim to be the birthplace of modern statistics, together, perhaps, with Florence, and followed by the more enlightened despotisms. The feudal State of the Middle Ages knew of nothing more than catalogues of signorial rights and possessions (urbariae); it looked on production as a fixed quantity, which it approximately is, so long as we have to do with landed property only. The towns throughout the West, however, seem from very early times to have treated production, which with them depended on industry and commerce, as exceedingly variable; but even in the most flourishing times of the Hanseatic League, they never got beyond a simple commercial balance sheet. Fleets, armies, political power and influence fall under the debit and credit of a tradesman's ledger. It was in the Italian States that a clear political consciousness, the pattern of Mohammedan administration, and the long and active exercise of trade and commerce combined to produce for the first time a true science of statistics. The absolute monarchy of Frederick II in Lower Italy was organized with the sole object of securing a concentrated power for the life-and-death struggle in which he was engaged. In Venice, on the contrary, the supreme objects were the enjoyment of life and power, the increase of inherited advantages, the creation of the most lucrative forms of industry, and the opening of new channels for commerce.

The writers speak of these things with the greatest freedom. We learn that in the year 1422 the population of the city amounted to 190,000 souls; the Italians were, perhaps, the first to reckon, not according to hearths, or men able to bear arms, or people able to walk, and so forth, but according to *anime* [lives], and thus to get the most neutral basis for further calculation. About this time, when the Florentines wished to form an alliance with Venice against Filippo Maria Visconti, they were for the moment refused, in the belief, resting on accurate commercial estimates, that a war between Milan and Venice, that is, between buyer and seller, was foolish. Even if the Duke were merely to increase his army, the Milanese, through the heavier taxation that must ensue, would become worse customers. "Better let the Florentines be defeated, and then, accustomed as they are to the life of a free city, they will settle with us and bring their silk and woolen industry with them, as the Lucchese did in their distress." The speech of the dying Doge Mocenigo (1423) to a few of the senators whom he had summoned to his bedside is still more remarkable. It contains the chief elements of a statistical account of the entire resources of Venice. I cannot say whether or where a thorough elucidation of this perplexing document exists; but by way of illustration, the following may be mentioned. After repaying a war loan of four million ducats, the public debt *(il monte)* still amounted to six million ducats. The current trade (it seems) amounted to ten million, which yielded, (so the text informs us) a profit of four million. The 3,000 *navigli*, the 300 *navi*, and the 45 galleys were manned respectively by 17,000, 8,000 and 11,000 seamen (more than 200 for each galley). To these must be added 16,000 shipwrights. The houses in Venice were valued at seven million, and brought in a rent of half a million.[27] There were 1,000 nobles whose incomes ranged from 70 to 4,000 ducats. – In another passage the ordinary income of the State in that same year is put at 1,100,000

27. Here all the houses, not merely those owned by the State, are meant. The latter, however, sometimes yielded enormous rents. Cf. Vasari, Life of Jacopo Sansovino.

ducats; through the disturbance of trade caused by the wars it sank about the middle of the century to 800,000 ducats.

If Venice, by this kind of computation and by the practical turn that she gave it, was the first fully to represent one important side of modern political life, she was, on the other hand, somewhat retarded in the kind of culture that was prized most highly at that time in Italy. The literary impulse, in general, was absent here, and especially that enthusiasm for classical antiquity which prevailed elsewhere.[28] The aptitude of the Venetians for philosophy and eloquence, says Sabellico, was in itself as great as that for commerce and politics. In 1459 George of Trebizond laid the Latin translation of Plato's *Laws* at the feet of the Doge and was appointed professor of philology with a yearly salary of 150 ducats, and even dedicated his book on rhetoric to the Signoria. If, however, we look through the history of Venetian literature which Francesco Sansovino appended to his well-known book, we find in the fourteenth century almost nothing but history and special works on theology, jurisprudence, and medicine; and even in the fifteenth century, till we come to Ermolao Barbaro and Aldus Manutius, humanistic culture is, for a city of such importance, most scantily represented. The library that Cardinal Bessarion bequeathed to the State narrowly escaped dispersion and destruction. Learning could be had at Padua, where, however, physicians and jurists (for their interpretation of points of law) received by far the highest pay. The share of Venice in the poetical creations of the country was long insignificant, till, at the beginning of the sixteenth century, her deficiencies were made good. Even the art of the Renaissance was imported, and it was only toward the end of the fifteenth century that she began to move in this field with independence and strength. But we find more striking instances still of intellectual backwardness. This government, which had the clergy so thoroughly in its control, which reserved to itself the appointment to all important ecclesiastical offices, and which time and again dared to defy the Curia, displayed an official piety of a most singular kind. The bodies of saints and other relics imported from Greece after the Turkish conquest were bought at the greatest sacrifices and received by the Doge in solemn procession.[29]

28. This dislike seems to have amounted to positive hatred in Pope Paul II, who called the humanists, every one of them, heretics. Platina, *Lives of the Popes*.
29. When the body of St. Luke was brought from Bosnia, a dispute arose with the Benedictines of Santa Giustina at Padua, who claimed that they already possessed it, and the Pope had to decide between the two parties.

For the coat without a seam it was decided (1455) to offer 10,000 ducats, but it was not to be had. These actions were not the fruit of any popular enthusiasm, but of the calm resolutions of the heads of the government, and could have been omitted without attracting any comment, and at Florence, under similar circumstances, would certainly have been omitted. We are not concerned here with the piety of the masses and their firm belief in the indulgences of an Alexander VI. But the State itself, after absorbing the Church to a degree unknown elsewhere, had in truth a certain ecclesiastical element in its composition, and the Doge, the symbol of the State, appeared in twelve great processions *(andate)* in a semi-clerical character. They were almost all festivals commemorating political events, and vied with the great feasts of the Church; the most brilliant of all, the famous marriage with the sea, fell on Ascension Day.

The most elevated political thought and the most varied forms of human development are found united in the history of Florence, which in this sense deserves the name of the first modern State in the world. Here a whole community was involved with what in the despotic cities was the affair of a single family. That wondrous Florentine spirit, at once keenly critical and artistically creative, incessantly transformed the social and political condition of the State, and just as incessantly described and judged the change. Florence thus became the home of political doctrines and theories, of experiments and sudden changes, but also, like Venice, the home of statistics, and alone and above all other States in the world, the home of historical representation in the modern sense of the phrase. The spectacle of ancient Rome and a familiarity with its leading writers were not without influence, and Giovanni Villani confesses that he received the first impulse to his great work at the jubilee of the year 1300,[30] and began it immediately on his return home. Yet how many among the 200,000 who made the pilgrimage to Rome that year may have been like him in gifts and tendencies and still did not write the history of their native cities! For not all of them could encourage themselves with the thought: "Rome is sinking; my native city is rising and ready to achieve great things, and therefore I wish to relate its entire past history, and hope to continue the story to the present time, and as long as my life shall last." And besides the evidence of its past, Florence obtained through its historians something further—a greater fame than that of any other city of Italy.

30. The year 1300 is also a fixed date in Dante's *Divine Comedy*.

It is not our present task to write the history of this remarkable State, but merely to give a few indications of the intellectual freedom and independence that was produced in the Florentines by this history.

About the year 1300 Dino Compagni described the civic quarrels of his day. His description of the political situation of the city, the motivating forces within the parties, the personalities of the leaders, in short, the whole web of direct and indirect causes and effects shows clearly the superiority of Florentine judgment and observation.[31] And what a politician is the great victim of these crises, Dante Alighieri, matured alike by home and by exile! He poured forth his scorn of the incessant changes and experiments in the constitution of his native city in ringing verses which will remain proverbial wherever similar events occur;[32] he addressed his home in words of defiance and yearning which must have sent shivers through the hearts of the Florentines. But his thoughts ranged over Italy and the whole world; and if his passion for the Empire, as he conceived it, was no more than an illusion, it must still be admitted that the youthful dreams of a newborn political speculation are in his case not without a poetic grandeur. He is proud to be the first who trod this path,[33] certainly in the footsteps of Aristotle, but in his own way independently. His ideal emperor is a just and humane judge, dependent on God only, the heir of the Roman Empire, which had been sanctioned by nature, by right, and by the will of God. The conquest of the world had been, according to this view, rightful, resting on a divine judgment between Rome and the other nations, and God gave his approval to this Empire, since under it He became Man, submitting at His birth to the census of the Emperor Augustus, and at His death to the judgment of Pontius Pilate, etc. We may find it hard to appreciate these and other arguments, but Dante's passion never fails to move us. His letters[34] reveal him as one of the earliest publicists, and he is perhaps the first layman to issue independent political tracts in epistolary form. He began early. Soon after the death of Beatrice he addressed a

31. [These sentences have always been omitted from the English translation on the grounds that the chronicle of Dino Compagni is spurious.]
32. *Purgatorio,* vi, at the end.
33. *De monarchia,* Book I, ch. 1.
34. He wanted the Emperor, as well as the Pope, to be permanently in Italy. See his letter [Epistle VIII] written during the conclave of Carpentras, 1314.

pamphlet on the state of Florence "to the great ones of the earth," and even the public pronouncements of his later years, dating from the time of his banishment, are all directed to emperors, princes, and cardinals. In these letters and in his book *De vulgari eloquentia* [*On the Vernacular*] the feeling, paid for with such bitter pains, constantly recurs that the exile may find elsewhere than in his native city an intellectual home in language and culture, which cannot be taken from him. We shall have more to say on this point.

To the Villani, Giovanni as well as Matteo, we owe not so much deep political reflection as fresh, practical observations and the elements of Florentine statistics, as well as important notices of other States. Here, too, trade and commerce had given the impulse to economic as well as political science. Nowhere else in the world was such accurate information to be had on financial affairs. The wealth of the Papal court at Avignon, which at the death of John XXII amounted to twenty-five million gold florins, would be incredible on any less trustworthy authority. Only here do we meet with colossal loans, e.g., the loan contracted by the King of England from the Florentine Houses of Bardi and Peruzzi, who lost to His Majesty the sum of 1,365,00 gold florins (1338) —their own money and that of their partners—and nevertheless recovered. The most important facts, however, are those regarding the condition of Florence at this time: the public income (over 300,000 gold florins) and expenditure; the population of the city (here only roughly estimated, according to the consumption of bread, in *bocche*, i.e., mouths, put at 90,000) and the population of the whole territory; the excess of 300 to 500 male children among the 5,800 to 6,000 baptized annually;[35] the schoolchildren, of whom 8,000 to 10,000 learned reading, 1,000 to 1,200 in six schools learned arithmetic; and besides these, 600 students who were taught Latin grammar and logic in four schools. Then follow the statistics of the churches and monasteries; of the hospitals (with more than a thousand beds); of the wool trade, with most valuable details; of the mint, the provisioning of the city, the public officials, and so on.[36] Merely by chance we learn other things: for example, when the public funds (*monte*) were first established, in the year 1353, the Franciscans spoke from the pulpit in favor of the measure, the Dominicans and Augustinians against it. Finally, nowhere else

35. The priest put aside a black bean for every boy and a white one for every girl. This was the only means of registration.
36. There was already a permanent fire brigade in Florence.

in Europe were the economic consequences of the Black Death observed and described as they are here.[37] Only a Florentine could have left it on record how it was expected that the scanty population would make everything cheap, and how instead, labor and commodities doubled in price; how the common people at first would do no work at all, but simply gave themselves up to enjoyment; how in the city itself servants and maids were to be had only at extravagant wages; how the peasants would till only the best lands, and left the rest uncultivated; and how the enormous legacies bequeathed to the poor at the time of the plague seemed useless afterward, since the poor had either died or had ceased to be poor. Lastly, on the occasion of a great bequest, by which a childless philanthropist left six denarii to every beggar in the city, the attempt is made to give a comprehensive statistical account of Florentine mendicancy.

This statistical view of things subsequently became still more highly cultivated at Florence. The noteworthy point about it is that, as a rule, we can perceive its connection with the higher aspects of history, with art, and with culture in general. An inventory of the year 1422 mentions, within the compass of the same document, the seventy-two exchange offices around the Mercato Nuovo; the amount of coined money in circulation (two million gold florins); the then-new industry of gold spinning; the silk wares; Filippo Brunelleschi, who was excavating classical architecture, and Leonardo Aretino, secretary of the republic, who was reviving ancient literature and eloquence; and, finally, the general prosperity of the city, then free from political conflicts, and of the good fortune of Italy, which had rid itself of foreign mercenaries. The Venetian statistics quoted above, which date from about the same year, certainly give evidence of larger property and profit and of a more extensive scene of action; Venice had long been mistress of the seas when (1422) Florence sent out its first galleys (to Alexandria). But who can fail to recognize the higher spirit of the Florentine documents? These and similar lists recur at intervals of ten years, systematically arranged and tabulated, while elsewhere we find at best occasional notices. We can form an approximate estimate of the property and the business of the first Medici; from 1434 to 1471 they paid for charities, public buildings, and taxes no less than 663,755 gold florins, of which more than 400,000 fell on Cosimo alone, and Lorenzo

---

37. Of primary importance for the plague itself is the famous description by Boccaccio at the beginning of the *Decameron*.

the Magnificent was delighted that the money had been so
well spent. In 1478 we have again a most important and in
its way complete view of the commerce and trades of this
city, some of which may be wholly or partly reckoned among
the fine arts: gold and silver embroidery, damasks, woodcarving and marquetry (intarsia), sculpture of arabesques in
marble and sandstone, portraits in wax, jewelry and work in
gold. The inborn talent of the Florentines for the systemati-
zation of outward life is shown by their books on agriculture,
business, and domestic economy, which are markedly superior
to those of other European people of the fifteenth century. It
has rightly been decided to publish selections of these works,
although much study will be needed to extract clear and
definite results from them. At all events, we have no difficulty
recognizing the city where parents petitioned the government
in their wills to fine their sons 1,000 florins if they declined
to practice a regular profession.

For the first half of the sixteenth century probably no
State in the world possesses a document like the magnificent
description of Florence by Varchi. In descriptive statistics, as
in so many other things, here yet another model is left to
us, before the freedom and greatness of this city sank into the
grave.[38]

38. As regards prices and wealth in Italy, I am only able, in
default of further means of investigation, to bring together some
scattered facts, which I have picked up here and there. Obvious
exaggerations are ignored. The gold coins worth referring to are:
the ducat, the sequin, the *fiorino d'oro,* and the *scudo d'oro.*
Their value is approximately the same—11 to 12 francs of our
money [roughly, about $2.25].

In Venice, for example, Doge Andrea Vendramin passed, with
170,000 ducats, for an exceedingly rich man (1476).

In the 1460s the Patriarch of Aquileia, Lodovico Patavino, was
called, with 200,000 ducats, "perhaps the richest of all Italians."

Antonio Grimani paid 30,000 ducats for his son's election as
cardinal. His ready money was put at 100,000 ducats.

In 1522 it was no longer Venice, but Genoa, that ranked as
the richest city in Italy, after Rome.

For Florence the data are wholly exceptional and do not
justify our making generalizations. For example, the loans to
foreign princes, which refer to only one or two Houses but
which were actually the business of large companies. So, too, the
enormous fines levied on defeated parties, e.g., between 1430-35,
77 families paid 4,875,000 gold florins.

The fortune of Giovanni de' Medici amounted at his death
(1428) to 179,221 gold florins, but of his two sons Cosimo and
Lorenzo, the latter alone left at his death (1440) 235,137 gold
florins.

This statistical estimate of outward life is, however, accompanied by the narrative of political events to which we have already referred. Florence not only existed under political forms more varied than those of the free States of Italy and of Europe generally, but it reflected upon them far more deeply. It is the most faithful reflection of the relations of individuals and classes to a variable whole. The pictures of the great civic demagogies in France and in Flanders, as they are delineated in Froissart, and the narratives of the German chronicles of the fourteenth century are certainly of high importance; but in comprehensiveness of thought and in the rational development of the story, none bear comparison with the Florentines. The rule of the nobility, the tyrannies, the struggles of the middle class with the proletariat, limited and unlimited democracy, pseudo-democracy, the primacy of a single house, theocracy (Savonarola), and the mixed forms of government that prepared the way for the Medicean despotism—all are so described that the inmost motives of the actors are laid bare.[39] Machiavelli, finally, in his Florentine history (to 1492) represents his native city as a living organism and its development as a natural and individual process; he is the first of the moderns to rise to such a conception. It lies outside our province to determine whether and in what points Machiavelli may have done violence to history, as is notoriously the case in his life of Castruccio Castracani—a highly colored picture of the typical despot. We might find something to say against every line of the *Istorie fiorentine* [*History of Florence*], and yet the great and unique value of the whole would remain unaffected. And his contemporaries and successors, Jacopo Pitti, Guicciardini, Segni, Varchi, Vettori, what a crown of illustrious names! And what a story these masters tell! The great and memorable drama of the last decades of the Florentine republic

As proof of the general rise of trade, e.g., in the fourteenth century the 44 goldsmiths on the Ponte Vecchio paid the State 800 gold florins in rent. Vasari, Life of Taddeo Gaddi. – The diary of Buonaccorso Pitti is full of figures, which only prove, however, the high prices of commodities and the low value of money.

For Rome we can have no criterion, since the income of the Curia was derived from all Europe; nor can statements about Papal treasures and the fortunes of cardinals be trusted. The well-known banker Agostino Chigi left (1520) a total fortune of 800,000 ducats.

39. So far as Cosimo (r. 1433-65) and his grandson Lorenzo the Magnificent (d. 1492) are concerned, the author refrains from any judgment on their internal policies.

unfolds before us. This voluminous record of the collapse of
the highest and most original life that the world could then
show may appear to one as nothing more than a collection of
curiosities, may awaken in another a devilish delight at the
shipwreck of so much nobility and grandeur, to a third may
seem like a great historical assize; in any case, it will remain
an object of thought and study till the end of time. The evil
that was forever troubling the state of affairs was the rule
of Florence over once powerful and now conquered rivals
like Pisa—a rule of which the necessary consequence was
a chronic state of violence. The only remedy, certainly an
extreme one and one which none but Savanarola could
have accomplished, and that only with the help of favorable
circumstances, would have been the well-timed dissolution of
Tuscany into a federal union of free cities. At a later period
this scheme, then no more than the dream of a past age,
brought a patriotic citizen of Lucca to the scaffold (1548).[40]
From this evil and from the ill-starred Guelph sympathies of
Florence for a foreign prince, which accustomed it to foreign
intervention, came all the disasters which followed. But who
does not admire these people who were brought by their venerated preacher to a mood of such sustained loftiness that for
the first time in Italy they set the example of sparing a conquered foe, when the whole history of their past taught
nothing but vengeance and extermination? The glow that
fused patriotism and moral regeneration may seem, when
looked at from a distance, to have soon passed away; but
its best results shine forth again in the memorable siege of
1529-1530. They were, as Guicciardini then wrote, "fools"
who drew down this storm upon Florence, but himself confesses that they achieved things that seemed incredible; and
when he declares that sensible people would have got out
of the way of the danger, he means no more than that
Florence ought to have yielded herself silently and ingloriously
into the hands of her enemies. Her splendid suburbs and
gardens, and the lives and prosperity of countless citizens
would thus have been preserved, but she would have been the
poorer by one of her greatest and most ennobling memories.

40. Franc. Burlamacchi, father of the head of the Lucchese
Protestants, Michele B. – It is well known how Milan, by its
severe treatment of the neighboring cities from the eleventh to
the thirteenth centuries, prepared the way for the creation of a great
despotic State. Even at the time of the extinction of the Visconti
in 1447, Milan frustrated the deliverance of North Italy prin-
cipally because it would not accept a confederation of equal
cities.

In many of their chief merits the Florentines are the pattern and the earliest expression of Italians and modern Europeans generally; they are so also in many of their defects. When Dante compares the city that was always mending its constitution with the sick man who continually changes his position to ease his pain, he touches a permanent feature of the political life of Florence. The great modern fallacy that a constitution can be *made*, can be manufactured by a combination of existing forces and tendencies,[41] was constantly cropping up in stormy times; and even Machiavelli was not wholly free from this idea. There was no lack of political theorists who, by an ingenious distribution and division of political power, by indirect elections of the most complicated kind, by the establishment of nominal offices, etc., sought to establish a lasting order, and to satisfy or to deceive rich and poor alike. They naïvely modeled themselves after classical antiquity, and even borrowed the party names *ottimati* [optimates], *aristocrazia* [aristocracy].[42] It is only since then that the world has become used to these expressions and given them a conventional European meaning, whereas all former party names were purely national, and either characterized the cause at issue or sprang from the caprice of accident. But how a name colors or discolors the cause!

But of all who thought it possible to construct a State, the greatest beyond all comparison was Machiavelli. He treats existing forces as living and active, takes a large and accurate view of alternative possibilities, and seeks to mislead neither himself nor others. There is in him neither vanity nor ostentation; indeed, he does not write for the public, but either for princes and administrators or for friends. The danger for him does not lie in an affectation of genius or in a false order of ideas, but rather in a powerful imagination which he evidently controls with difficulty. The objectivity of his political judgment is sometimes appalling in its sincerity; but it was formed in a time of extraordinary need and peril, when it was no easy matter to believe in right, or to credit others with just dealing. Virtuous indignation at his expense is thrown away on us who have seen in what sense political

41. On the third Sunday in Advent 1494 Savonarola preached as follows on the method for bringing about a new constitution: The 16 companies of the city were each to work out a plan, the Gonfalonieri were to choose the four best, and from these, the Signoria would select the very best. — But things took a different turn, indeed, under the influence of the preacher himself.
42. The latter was first used in 1527, after the expulsion of the Medici.

morality is understood by the statesmen of our own century. Machiavelli, at all events, was able to forget himself in his cause. He was a patriot in the fullest sense of the word, notwithstanding that his writings, with the exception of very few words, are altogether destitute of enthusiasm, and that the Florentines themselves treated him in the end as a criminal. But free as he was, like most of his contemporaries, in speech and morals, the welfare of the State was his first and last thought. His most complete program for the construction of a new political system at Florence is set forth in the memorial to Leo X, composed after the death of the younger Lorenzo de' Medici, Duke of Urbino (d. 1519), to whom he had dedicated the *Prince.* The State was by that time in extremities and utterly corrupt, and the remedies proposed are not always morally justifiable; but it is most interesting to see how he hopes to set up the republic in the form of a moderate democracy, as heiress to the Medici. A more ingenious scheme of concessions to the Pope, to the Pope's various adherents, and to the different Florentine interests, cannot be imagined; we might fancy ourselves looking into the works of a clock. More principles, observations, comparisons, political forecasts, etc., abound in the *Discourses,* among them flashes of wonderful insight. He recognizes, for example, the law of a continuous though not uniform development in republican institutions, and requires the constitution to be flexible and capable of change, as the only means of dispensing with bloodshed and banishments. For a like reason, in order to guard against private violence and foreign intervention—"the death of all freedom"—he wishes to see introduced a judicial procedure (*accusa*) against hated citizens, in place of which Florence had hitherto had nothing but the court of scandal. With a masterly hand he characterizes the tardy and involuntary decisions which at critical moments play so important a part in republican States. Once, it is true, he is misled by his imagination and the pressure of events into unqualified praise of the people, who choose their officers, he says, better than any prince, and who can be cured of their errors by "good advice."[43] With regard to the government of Tuscany, he has no doubt that it belongs to his native city, and maintains (in a separate discourse) that the reconquest of Pisa is a question of life or death; he deplores that Arezzo, after the rebellion of 1502, was not razed to the ground; he admits in general that Italian republics must be allowed

43. This same view, without doubt borrowed from here, appears in Montesquieu.

to expand freely and add to their territory in order to prevent attack by others and to enjoy peace at home; but Florence had always begun at the wrong end, and from the first made deadly enemies of Pisa, Lucca, and Siena, whereas Pistoia, "treated like a brother," had submitted voluntarily.

It would be unreasonable to draw a parallel between the few other republics that still existed in the fifteenth century and this unique city—the most important workshop of the Italian, and indeed of the modern European, spirit. Siena suffered from the gravest organic maladies, and its relative prosperity in art and industry must not mislead us. Aeneas Sylvius[44] looks with longing from his native town to the "happy" German imperial cities, where life is not embittered by confiscations of land and goods, arbitrary officials, and political factions. Genoa scarcely comes within range of our task, as before the time of Andrea Doria it took almost no part in the Renaissance. Indeed, the inhabitant of the Riviera was proverbial among Italians for its contempt of all higher culture. Party conflicts here assumed so fierce a character and disturbed so violently the whole course of life, that we can hardly understand how, after so many revolutions and invasions, the Genoese ever contrived to return to an endurable condition. Perhaps it was because all who took part in public affairs were at the same time almost without exception active men of business. The example of Genoa shows in a striking manner with what insecurity wealth and vast commerce, and with what internal disorder the possession of distant colonies, are compatible.

Lucca was of little significance in the fifteenth century. || There has come down to us a report by the Lucchese historian Giovanni di Ser Cambio, which dates from the first decades of the century, when the city was under the half-despotism of the Guinigi, and which gives us a vivid glimpse into the position of all such ruling houses in Republics. The author discusses: the number and distribution of mercenary troops in the city and outlying districts; the bestowal of all offices on selected supporters; the number of weapons in private ownership and the disarmament of suspect persons; the control of exiles, who are restrained, by threat of total

44. [It might be well to remember at this point that Aeneas Sylvius is Enea Silvio de Piccolomini, who became Pope Pius II. He is Burckhardt's favorite and is the "hero" of this book, as Raphael would have been the hero of the "Art of the Renaissance" had it been written. Burckhardt mentions Aeneas Sylvius-Pope Pius II often, calling him by whichever name is appropriate to the particular time in question.]

confiscation, from leaving their appointed places of banishment; the removal of dangerous rebels by secret violence;
the compelling of emigrated merchants and craftsmen to
return; the prevention of further meetings of the general
council (*consiglio generale*) by replacing it with a commission consisting of only 12 or 18 supporters; the restriction of
all expenditures in favor of the indispensable mercenary soldiers without whom there would be constant danger and who
must be kept in good humor (*i soldati si faccino amici, con-
fidanti e savi* [the soldiers should be turned into friends and
confidants, and should be kept informed]); finally, he con-
cedes the prevailing economic distress, particularly the decline
of the silk industry but also that of all the other trades, including wine-growing, and as a temporary measure proposes
a higher duty on foreign wine and an absolute compulsion
of the country people (*contado*) to buy everything, with the
exception of food, in the city. This remarkable document
would require a detailed commentary; we mention it here
only as further evidence that in Italy systematic political
thought was developed much earlier than in the North. ||

The majority of the Italian States were in their internal
construction works of art, that is, the fruit of reflection and
careful adaptation; and their relation to one another and to
foreign countries was also a work of art. The fact that nearly
all of them were the result of recent usurpations exercised
as fatal an influence in their foreign as in their internal
policy. Not one of them recognized another without reserve;
the same game of chance that had helped to found and con-
solidate one dynasty might upset another. Nor was it always
a matter of choice with the despot whether to keep quiet or
not. The necessity of movement and aggrandizements is common to all illegitimate powers. Thus Italy became the home
of a "foreign policy" which gradually, in other countries also,
acquired the position of a recognized system of public law.
The purely objective treatment of international affairs, as free
from prejudice as from moral scruples, attained a perfection
which sometimes is not without a certain beauty and grandeur
of its own; but as a whole it gives the impression of a bot-
tomless abyss.

Intrigues, armaments, leagues, corruption, and treason make
up the external history of Italy at this period. Venice in particular was long accused by all sides of seeking to conquer
all Italy, or of gradually so reducing its strength that one
State after another must fall into her hands. But on closer
inspection it is evident that this complaint did not come from
the people, but rather from the courts and official classes,

which were commonly abhorred by their subjects, whereas
through its mild government, Venice enjoyed a general confidence.[45] Even Florence, with its restive subject cities, found
itself in a false position with regard to Venice, apart from
all commercial jealousy and from the progress of Venice in
Romagna. At last the League of Cambrai actually did strike
a serious blow at the State which all Italy ought to have
supported with united strength.

But even the other States trusted each other only so far
as their own evil intentions would suggest, and were always
ready to act on the worst. Il Moro, the Aragonese king of
Naples, and Sixtus IV—to say nothing of the smaller powers
—kept Italy in a state of perilous agitation. It would have
been well if the atrocious game had been confined to Italy;
but it lay in the nature of the case that intervention and
help should be sought from abroad—in particular from the
French and the Turks.

The sympathies of the people at large were throughout on
the side of France. Florence had never ceased to confess
with shocking naïveté its old Guelph preference for the
French. And when Charles VIII actually appeared on the
south of the Alps, all Italy accepted him with an enthusiasm
which to himself and his followers seemed unaccountable.[46]
In the imagination of the Italians, to take Savonarola for an
example, the ideal picture of a wise, just, and powerful savior
and ruler was still alive, with the difference that he was no
longer the emperor invoked by Dante, but the Capetian king of
France. With his departure the illusion was broken; but it
took a long time before it was understood how completely
Charles VIII, Louis XII, and Francis I had mistaken their
true relation to Italy, and by what inferior motives they had
been led. The princes, for their part, tried to make use of
France in a wholly different way. When the Franco-English
wars came to an end, when Louis XI began to cast his
diplomatic nets on all sides, when, finally, Charles of Burgundy embarked on his foolish adventures, the Italian cabinets
met them halfway on every point and the intervention of
France was only a question of time—even without the claims

45. Indeed, in 1467 Galeazzo Maria Sforza declared the contrary to the Venetian agent, but this was only braggadocio. On
every occasion, cities and villages surrendered voluntarily to Venice
—chiefly, it is true, those that escaped from the hands of some
despot—whereas Florence had to keep down neighboring republics,
which were accustomed to freedom.
46. Comines, *Charles VIII*. The French were considered *commes
saints* [as saints].

on Naples and Milan—as had already occurred in Genoa and Piedmont. The Venetians, in fact, expected it as early as 1462. The mortal terror of Duke Galeazzo Maria of Milan during the Burgundian war, in which he was apparently the ally of Charles as well as of Louis, and consequently had reason to dread an attack from both, is strikingly shown in his correspondence. The plan of a balance of power among the four chief Italian States, as understood by Lorenzo the Magnificent, was only the assumption of a cheerful optimistic spirit that had outgrown both the recklessness of an experimental policy and the superstitions of Florentine Guelphism, and persisted in hoping for the best. When Louis XI offered him aid in the war against Ferrante of Naples and Sixtus IV, he replied, "I cannot set my own advantage above the safety of all Italy; would to God it never enters the minds of the French kings to try their strength in this country! Should they ever do so, Italy is lost." For the other princes, the King of France was alternately a bugbear to themselves and their enemies, and they threatened to call him in whenever they saw no more convenient way out of their difficulties. The Popes, in their turn, fancied that they could make use of France without any danger to themselves, and even Innocent VIII imagined that he could withdraw to sulk in the North, and return to Italy as a conqueror at the head of a French army.

Thoughtful men foresaw the foreign conquest long before the expedition of Charles VIII. And when Charles was back again on the other side of the Alps, it was plain to everyone that an era of intervention had begun. Misfortune now followed on misfortune; it was understood too late that France and Spain, the two chief invaders, had become great European powers, that they would no longer be satisfied with superficial homage but would fight to the death for influence and territory in Italy. They had begun to resemble the centralized Italian States and indeed to copy them, but on a gigantic scale. Schemes of annexation or exchange of territory were for a time indefinitely multiplied. The end, as is well known, was the complete victory of Spain, which, as sword and shield of the Counter Reformation, for a long time counted even the Papacy among its subjects. The melancholy reflections of the philosophers were filled with only one theme at that time—the indication of how all who had called in the barbarians came to a bad end.

Alliances were at the same time formed with the Turks too, with as little scruple or disguise; they were reckoned no worse than any other political expedients. The belief in the unity of Western Christendom had at various times in the course of the Crusades been seriously shaken, and Frederick II had probably outgrown it. But the fresh advance of the Eastern nations, the need and the ruin of the Greek Empire, had revived the old feeling (though not in its former strength) throughout Western Europe. Italy, however, was a striking exception. Great as was the terror felt for the Turks, and the actual danger from them, there was scarcely a government of any consequence that did not conspire against other Italian States with Mohammed II and his successors. And when they did not do so, they still had the credit of it; it was no worse than the sending of emissaries to poison the cisterns of Venice, which was the charge brought against the heirs of Alfonso, King of Naples. From a scoundrel like Sigismondo Malatesta nothing better could be expected than that he should call the Turks into Italy. But even the Aragonese monarchs of Naples, from whom Mohammed—at the instigation, supposedly, of other Italian governments—had once wrested Otranto (1480), afterward incited Sultan Bajazet II against the Venetians. The same charge was brought against Il Moro: "The blood of the slain, and the misery of the prisoners in the hands of the Turks, cry to God for vengeance against him," says the State historian. In Venice, where the government was informed of everything, it was known that Giovanni Sforza, ruler of Pesaro, the cousin of Il Moro, had entertained the Turkish ambassadors on their way to Milan. The two most respectable among the Popes of the fifteenth century, Nicholas V and Pius II, died in the deepest grief at the progress of the Turks, the latter indeed amid the preparations for a crusade which he hoped to lead in person; their successors, however, embezzled the contributions sent for this purpose from all parts of Christendom, and degraded the indulgences granted in return for them into a private commercial speculation. Innocent VIII consented to be jailer to the fugitive Prince Djem, for a salary paid by the prisoner's brother Bajazet II, and Alexander VI supported the steps taken by Il Moro in Constantinople to further a Turkish assault on Venice (1498), whereupon the latter threatened him with a Council. It is clear that the notorious alliance between Francis I and Soliman II was nothing new or unheard of.

Indeed, we find instances of whole populations to whom it seemed no particular crime to go over bodily to the Turks. Even if it were only held out as a threat to oppresive governments, this is at least proof that the idea had become familiar. As early as 1480 Baptista Mantuanus makes it quite clear that most of the inhabitants of the Adriatic coast foresaw something of this kind, and that Ancona in particular desired it. When Romagna was suffering from the oppressive government of Leo X, a deputy from Ravenna said openly to the Legate, Cardinal Giulio de' Medici: "Monsignore, the honorable Republic of Venice will not have us, for fear of a dispute with the Holy See; but if the Turk comes to Ragusa, we will put ourselves into his hands."

It was a poor but not wholly groundless consolation for the Spanish enslavement of Italy that the country was at least secured from the relapse into barbarism which would have awaited it under the Turkish rule.[47] By itself, divided as it was, it could hardly have escaped this fate.

If, with all these drawbacks, the Italian statesmanship of this period deserves our praise, it is based only on its practical and unprejudiced treatment of those questions which were not affected by fear, passion, or malice. Here was no feudal system after the Northern fashion, with its artificial scheme of rights; but the power which each possessed he possessed (as a rule) in practice as in theory. Here was no attendant nobility to foster in the mind of the prince the medieval sense of honor with all its strange consequences; but princes and counselors were agreed in acting according to the exigencies of the particular case and to the end they had in view. Toward the men whose services were used and toward allies, come from what quarter they might, no pride of caste was felt which could possibly estrange a supporter; and the class of the *condottieri*, in which birth was a matter of indifference, shows clearly enough in what sort of hands the real power lay; and lastly, the governments, in the hands of enlightened despots, had an incomparably more accurate acquaintance with their own country and with that of their neighbors than was possessed by their Northern contemporaries, and estimated the economical and moral capacities of friend and foe down to the smallest particular. Notwithstanding grave errors, they were born masters of statistical science.

With such men negotiation was possible; one could hope that they would be convinced and their opinion modified when practical reasons were laid before them. When the great

47. Ranke, *History of the Latin and Teutonic Nations.* — Michelet's view, that the Turks would have become Occidentalized in Italy, does not satisfy me. — This designation of Spain is hinted at, perhaps for the first time, in the speech delivered by Fedra Inghirami in 1510 before Julius II at the celebration of the capture of Bugia by the fleet of Ferdinand the Catholic.

Alfonso of Naples was a prisoner of Filippo Maria Visconti
(1434), he was able to satisfy his jailer that the rule of the
House of Anjou instead of his own at Naples would make
the French the masters of Italy; Filippo Maria set him free
without ransom and made an alliance with him. A Northern
prince would scarcely have acted in the same way, certainly
not one whose morality in other respects was like that of
Visconti. The confidence felt in the power of practicality is
shown by the celebrated visit Lorenzo the Magnificent, to the
astonishment of the Florentines, paid the faithless Ferrante at
Naples—a man who would certainly be tempted to keep him
a prisoner, and who was by no means too scrupulous to do so.
For to arrest a powerful monarch, and then to let him go
alive, after extorting his signature and otherwise insulting
him, as Charles the Bold did to Louis XI at Péronne (1468),
seemed madness to the Italians.[48] Lorenzo was expected to
come back covered with glory, or not to come back at all.
The art of political persuasion was at this time raised to an
art—especially by the Venetian ambassadors—of which Northern nations first obtained a conception from the Italians,
and of which the official addresses give a most imperfect
idea, since these are mere pieces of humanistic rhetoric. Nor,
in spite of an otherwise ceremonious etiquette, was there in
case of need any lack of rough and frank speaking
in diplomatic intercourse. A man like Machiavelli appears in
his *Legazioni* in an almost pathetic light. Furnished with
scanty instructions, shabbily equipped, and treated as an
agent of inferior rank, he never loses his gift of free and
wide observation or his pleasure in picturesque description.
– ‖ Italy was and remained the land of political *istruzioni*
[instructions] and *relazioni* [reports]; certainly, excellent diplo-
macy, was practiced in other States, but only Italy has preserved so many records from so early a period. The long
dispatch (January 17, 1494) on the last painful weeks of
Ferrante of Naples, written by Pontano to the cabinet of
Alexander VI, gives us the best idea of this class of political
writing. And this has been mentioned only in passing and as
one of the numerous dispatches by Pontano. How many
other dispatches, just as important and as vigorously written,
of other cabinets of the end of the fifteenth and the beginning
of the sixteenth centuries remain unknown, not to mention
those of later times. ‖ – A special division of this work will

48. If Comines on this occasion, and many others, observes and
judges as objectively as any Italian, his intercourse with Italians,
particularly with Angelo Catto, must be taken into account.

be devoted to the study of man, as individual and as nation, which with these Italians goes hand in hand with the study of social conditions.

Here we will indicate only briefly the steps by which war assumed the character of a work of art. During the Middle Ages the education of the individual soldier of the Western countries was perfect within the limits of the then prevalent system of defense and attack. There were always ingenious inventors in the arts of besieging and of fortification, but the development of both strategy and tactics was hindered by the character and duration of military service, and by the ambition of the nobles, who, for example, disputed questions of precedence in the face of the enemy, and through simple want of discipline caused the loss of great battles like Crécy and Maupertuis. Italy, on the contrary, was the first country to adopt the system of mercenary troops, which demanded a wholly different organization; and the early introduction of firearms did its part in making war a democratic pursuit, not only because the strongest castles were unable to withstand a bombardment, but because the skill of the engineer, of the gunfounder, and of the artillerist—men belonging to another class than the nobility—was now of the first importance in a campaign. It became clear, not without regret, that the value of the individual, which had been the soul of the small and admirably organized bands of mercenaries, would suffer from these novel means of destruction, which did their work at a distance; and there were *condottieri* who opposed to the utmost the introduction at least of the musket, which had lately been invented in Germany; thus Paolo Vitelli, while recognizing and himself adopting the cannon, put out the eyes and cut off the hands of the captured *schioppettieri* [harquebusiers].[49] On the whole, however, the new discoveries were accepted and turned to useful account, till the Italians became the teachers of all Europe, both in the building of fortifications and in the means of attacking them. Princes like Federigo of Urbino and Alfonso of Ferrara acquired a mastery of the subject compared to which the knowledge even of Maximilian I appears superficial. In Italy there was, earlier than elsewhere, a comprehensive science and art of military affairs; we meet here, for the first time, that impartial delight in able generalship for its own sake, which might, indeed, be expected from the frequent change of party and from the wholly practical attitude of the *condottieri*.

49. One is reminded of Federigo of Urbino, who "would have been ashamed" to have a printed book in his library.

During the Milano-Venetian war of 1451 and 1452 between Francesco Sforza and Jacopo Piccinino, the latter's headquarters were attended by the scholar Gian Antonio Porcellio dei Pandoni, who had been commissioned by Alfonso of Naples to write a report of the campaign. It is written, not in the purest but in a fluent Latin, a little too much in the style of the humanistic bombast of the day, modeled on Caesar's *Commentaries*, and interspersed with speeches, prodigies, and the like; and since for the past hundred years it had been seriously disputed whether Scipio Africanus or Hannibal was the greater, Piccinino through the whole book must be called Scipio and Sforza Hannibal. But something positive had to be reported, too, respecting the Milanese army; the sophist presented himself to Sforza, was led along the ranks, praised highly all that he saw, and promised to hand it down to posterity. The Italian literature of the day is rich in descriptions of wars and military strategy written for specialists as well as educated laymen, whereas the contemporary narratives of Northerners, such as Diebold Schilling's description of the Burgundian War, still retain the shapelessness and matter-of-fact dryness of a mere chronicle. Machiavelli, the greatest dilettante who has, as such, ever treated military affairs, was then writting his *Arte della guerra* [*The Art of War*]. But the development of the individual soldier found its most complete expression in those public and solemn conflicts between one or more pairs of combatants which were practiced long before the famous Battle of Barletta (1503). The victor was assured an honor denied to the Northern warrior—the praises of poets and scholars. The result of these combats was no longer regarded as Divine judgment, but as a triumph of personal merit, and—to the spectators—the decision of an exciting competition and a satisfaction for the honor of the army or the nation.

It goes without saying that this purely rational treatment of military affairs allowed, under certain circumstances, the worst atrocities, even in the absence of a strong political hatred, as, for instance, the plunder of a city that had been promised to the troops. After the forty-day devastation of Piacenza (1447), which Sforza was compelled to permit to his soldiers, the town stood empty for a long time, and had to be repopulated by force. Yet outrages like these were nothing compared with the misery which was afterward brought upon Italy by foreign troops, most of all by the Spaniards, in whom perhaps a touch of non-Western blood, perhaps familiarity with the spectacles of the Inquisition, had unleashed the diabolical side of human nature. Who, once aware of their atrocities at Prato, Rome, etc., can take any interest in Ferdinand the Catholic and Charles V, who knew what these hordes were, and yet unchained them. The mass of documents that gradually come to light from the cabinets of these rulers will always remain an important source of historical information—but no one will ever again seek a fruitful political conception in the deeds of such princes.

The Papacy and the dominions of the Church[50] are such exceptional creations that we have hitherto, in determining the general characteristics of Italian States, referred to them only in passing. That deliberate choice and adaptation of political expedients, which makes the other States so interesting, is what we find least of all at Rome, since here the spiritual power could constantly conceal or supply the defects of the temporal. And what fiery trials did this State undergo in the fourteenth century and the beginning of the fifteenth! When the Papacy was led captive to the South of France, all was, at first, thrown into confusion; but Avignon had money, troops, and a great statesman and general, the Spaniard Albornoz, who again brought the ecclesiastical State into complete subjection. The danger of a final dissolution was still greater at the time of the schism, when neither the Roman nor the French Pope was rich enough to reconquer the newly lost State; but this was done under Martin V, after the unity of the Church was restored, and done again under Eugenius IV, when the same danger was renewed. But the ecclesiastical State was and remained a thorough anomaly among the powers of Italy; in and near Rome itself, the Papacy was defied by the great families of the Colonna, Orsini, Savelli, Anguillara, etc.; in Umbria, in the Marches, and in Romagna, those civic republics, for whose devotion the Papacy had shown so little gratitude, had almost ceased to exist and their place had been taken by a crowd of princely dynasties, great or small, whose loyalty and obedience signified little. As self-dependent powers, standing on their own merits, they have a special interest, and from this point of view the most important of them have already been discussed.

Nevertheless, we can hardly dispense with a few general remarks on the Papacy. New and strange perils and trials came upon it in the course of the fifteenth century, as the political spirit of the nation began to take hold of it from

50. Here, once for all, we refer the reader to Ranke's *History of the Popes,* vol. I.

various sides, and to draw it within the sphere of its action. The least of these dangers came from the populace or from abroad; the greatest lay in the characters of the Popes themselves.

Let us, for the moment, ignore the countries beyond the Alps. When the Papacy was exposed to mortal danger in Italy, it neither received nor could receive the slightest assistance from France, then under Louis XI, nor from England, distracted by the Wars of the Roses, nor from the then disorganized Spanish monarchy, nor even from the Germany that had been betrayed at the Council of Basel. In Italy itself there were a number of educated and even uneducated people whose national vanity was flattered by the Italian character of the Papacy; the personal interests of very many depended on its having and retaining this character; and vast masses of the people still believed in the efficacy of the Papal blessing and consecration,[51] even notorious transgressors like Vitelozzo Vitelli, who still prayed to be absolved by Alexander VI, when the Pope's son had him strangled. But even all this sympathy would not have saved the Papacy had its enemies been really in earnest, and had they known how to take advantage of the envy and hatred with which the institution was regarded.

And just when the prospect of help from without was so small, the most dangerous symptoms appeared within the Papacy itself. Living, as it now did, and acting in the spirit of the secular Italian principalities, it was compelled to go through the same dark experiences as they; but its own exceptional nature gave a peculiar color to the shadows.

As far as the city of Rome itself was concerned, small account was taken of its internal agitations, so many were the Popes who had returned after they had been expelled by popular tumult, and so greatly did the presence of the Curia suit the interests of the Roman people. Rome displayed at times a specific anti-Papal radicalism, and the most serious plots which were then contrived gave proof of the working of unseen hands from without. It was so in the case of the conspiracy of Stefano Porcari against Nicholas V (1453),

---

51. Even professional murderers would not venture an attack on the Pope. – The great offices of the Church were treated with much importance by the pomp-loving Paul II (Platina, *Lives of the Popes*) and by Sixtus IV, who, despite the gout, conducted Easter mass while seated. Curiously, the people distinguished between the magical power of the blessing and the unworthiness of the blesser; when, in 1481, Sixtus IV was unable to give the benediction on Ascension Day, they muttered and cursed him.

the very Pope who had done most for the prosperity of the city. Porcari aimed at the complete overthrow of the Papal authority, and had distinguished accomplices, who, though their names are not handed down to us, are certainly to be found among the Italian governments of the time. Under the same Pontificate, Lorenzo Valla concluded his famous declamation against the gift of Constantine with the wish for the speedy secularization of the States of the Church.

The Catilinarian gang with which Pius II had to contend (1460) avowed with equal frankness their resolution to overthrow the government of the priests, and its leader, Tiburzio, blamed the soothsayers, who had fixed the accomplishment of his wishes for this very year. Several of the chief men of Rome, the Prince of Taranto, and the *condottiere* Jacopo Piccinino, were accomplices and supporters of Tiburzio. Indeed, when we think of the booty that was accumulated in the palaces of wealthy prelates—the conspirators had their eyes on the Cardinal of Aquileia especially—we are surprised that, in an almost unguarded city, such attempts were not more frequent and more successful. It was not without reason that Pius II preferred to reside anywhere rather than in Rome, and even Paul II suffered no small anxiety (1468) with regard to a plot, real or imaginary, of a similar kind. The Papacy had either to succumb to such enterprises, or to stamp out the aristocratic factions under whose protection these bands of robbers grew.

This task was undertaken by the terrible Sixtus IV. He was the first Pope who had Rome and its environs thoroughly under his control, especially after his successful attack on the House of Colonna, and consequently, both in his Italian policy and in the internal affairs of the Church, could venture to act with a defiant audacity, and to scorn the complaints and threats to summon a Council which arose from all parts of Europe. He supplied himself with the necessary funds by a simony that suddenly grew to unheard-of proportions and extended from the appointment of cardinals down to the granting of the smallest favors. Sixtus himself had not obtained the Papal dignity without recourse to the same means.

A corruption so universal might sooner or later bring disastrous consequences on the Holy See, but they lay in the uncertain future. It was otherwise with nepotism, which at one time threatened to destroy the Papacy altogether. Of all the *nipoti*, Cardinal Pietro Riario enjoyed at first the chief and almost exclusive favor of Sixtus. He soon drew upon himself the eyes of all Italy, partly by the fabulous luxury

of his life, partly through the reports of his irreligion and
his political plans. He arranged with Duke Galeazzo Maria
of Milan (1473), that the latter should become King of
Lombardy, and then aid him with money and troops to return
to Rome and ascend the Papal throne; Sixtus, it appears,
would have yielded to him voluntarily. This plan, which, by
making the Papacy hereditary, would have ended in the
secularization of the Papal State, was frustrated by Pietro's
sudden death.[52] The second *nipote,* Girolamo Riario, remained a layman, and did not seek the Pontificate. But from
this time the *nipoti,* by their endeavors to found principalities
for themselves, became a new source of confusion to Italy.
The Popes had already tried to make good their feudal
claims on Naples in favor of their relatives, but since the
failure of Calixtus III, such a scheme was no longer practicable, and Girolamo Riario, after the attempt to conquer
Florence (and who knows how many other places) had
failed, was forced to content himself with founding a State
within the limits of the Papal dominions themselves. This
was justifiable in so far as Romagna, with its princes and
civic despots, threatened to shake off the Papal supremacy
altogether, and may have fallen prey to Sforza or the
Venetians, had Rome not interfered to prevent it. But who,
in those times and circumstances, could guarantee the continued obedience of *nipoti* and their descendants, now turned
into sovereign rulers, to Popes with whom they had no
further concern? Even during his lifetime the Pope was not
always sure of his own son or nephew; thus the temptation
was strong to expel the *nipote* of a predecessor and replace
him by one of his own. The effect of the whole system on
the Papacy itself was most serious; all means of compulsion,
even spiritual, were used without scruple for the most questionable ends, and to these ends the other aims of the Throne
of St. Peter were made subordinate. And when ends were
attained, at whatever cost of revolutions and proscriptions,
a dynasty had been founded whose greatest interest was the
destruction of the Papacy.

At the death of Sixtus, Girolamo was able to maintain
himself in his usurped principality (Forlì and Imola) only
by the utmost exertions of his own, and by the aid of the
House of Sforza (to which his wife belonged). In the conclave
(1484) that followed the death of Sixtus—in which Innocent
VIII was elected—an incident occurred which seemed to

---

52. According to Machiavelli, the Venetians poisoned him. They
were not without motives.

furnish the Papacy with a new external guarantee. Two cardinals, who were princes of ruling houses—Giovanni d'Aragona, son of King Ferrante, and Ascanio Sforza, brother of Il Moro—sold their votes with shameless effrontery. Thus the ruling houses of at least Naples and Milan became interested, by their participation in the booty, in the continuance of the Papal system. Again, in the following conclave, when all but five cardinals sold themselves, Ascanio accepted enormous bribes, not without cherishing the hope that at the next election he himself would be the favored candidate.

Lorenzo the Magnificent, on his part, was anxious that the House of Medici should not be sent away with empty hands. He married his daughter Maddalena to Franceschetto Cibo, the son of the new Pope, and expected not only favors of all kinds for his own son, Cardinal Giovanni (afterward Leo X), but also the rapid promotion of his son-in-law. But with respect to the latter, he demanded impossibilities. Under Innocent VIII there was no opportunity for the audacious nepotism by which States had been founded, since Franceschetto himself was a poor creature who, like his father the Pope, sought power only for the lowest purpose of all—the acquisition and accumulation of money. The manner, however, in which father and son practiced this occupation would have had to lead sooner or later to a final catastrophe—the dissolution of the State.

If Sixtus had filled his treasury by the sale of spiritual dignities and favors, Innocent and his son, for their part, established an office for the sale of secular favors, in which pardons for murder and manslaughter could be bought for large sums of money. Out of every fine, 150 ducats were paid into the Papal treasury, and whatever remained to Franceschetto. During the latter part of this Pontificate, Rome swarmed with licensed and unlicensed assassins; the factions, which Sixtus had begun to put down, became as active as ever; the Pope, well guarded in the Vatican, was satisfied with laying an occasional trap, in which a wealthy offender might be caught. But for Franceschetto there was only one problem: how, when the Pope died, to escape with well-filled coffers. He betrayed himself at last, on the occasion of a false report (1490) of his father's death; he tried to carry off all the money on hand—the Papal treasury—and when this proved impossible, insisted that, at all events, the Turkish prince, Djem, go with him and serve as living capital, to be advantageously disposed of, perhaps to Ferrante of Naples. It is difficult to estimate the political possibilities of past times, but we cannot help wondering whether Rome could have survived two or three Pontificates of this kind. Even in relation to the believing countries of Europe, it was imprudent to let matters go so far that not only travelers and pilgrims, but a whole embassy of Emperor Maximilian were stripped to their shirts in the neighborhood of Rome, and that many envoys turned back without setting foot inside the city.

Such a condition of things was incompatible with *the* conception of power and its pleasures that inspired the gifted Alexander VI (1492-1503), and the first event that occurred was the restoration, at least temporarily, of public order and the punctual payment of every salary.

Strictly speaking, this Pontificate might be passed over, since we are discussing aspects of Italian civilization and the Borgias are no more Italian than the House of Naples. Alexander spoke Spanish in public with Cesare; Lucrezia, at her entrance to Ferrara, where she wore a Spanish costume, was sung to by Spanish buffoons; their confidential servants consisted of Spaniards, as did also the most ill-famed company of the troops of Cesare in the war of 1500; and even his hangman, Don Michelotto, and his poisoner, Sebastiano Pinzòn, seem to have been Spanish. Among his other achievements, Cesare, in true Spanish fashion, killed, according to the rules of the craft, six wild bulls in an enclosed court. But the corruption, which seemed to culminate in this family, was already far advanced when they came to Rome.

What they were and what they did has been often and fully described. Their immediate purpose, which, in fact, they attained, was the complete subjugation of the Pontifical State. All the petty despots,[53] who were mostly more or less refractory vassals of the Church, were expelled or destroyed; and in Rome itself the two great factions—the so-called Guelph Orsini as well as the so-called Ghibelline Colonna— were annihilated. But the means employed were of so frightful a character that they must certainly have ended in the ruin of the Papacy, had not the contemporaneous poisoning of both father and son suddenly intervened to alter the whole situation. − The moral indignation of Christendom was certainly no great source of danger to Alexander; at home he extorted terror and obedience; foreign rulers were won over to his side, and Louis XII even aided him to the utmost of his power. The mass of the people throughout Europe had

---

53. Except the Bentivoglio at Bologna and the House of Este at Ferrara. The latter were compelled to form a family relationship, Lucrezia marrying Prince Alfonso.

hardly a conception of what was passing in Central Italy. The only moment that was really fraught with danger—when Charles VIII was in Italy—went by with unexpected fortune, and even then it was not the Papacy as such that was in peril, but Alexander, who risked being supplanted by a more respectable Pope. The great, permanent, and increasing danger for the Papacy lay in Alexander himself, and, above all, in his son Cesare Borgia.

In the nature of the father, ambition, avarice, and sensuality were combined with strong and brilliant qualities. From the first day of his Pontificate he granted himself in the fullest measure all the pleasures of power and luxury. In the choice of means to this end he was wholly without scruple; it was known at once that he would more than compensate himself for the sacrifices his election had involved, and that the simony of the seller would far exceed the simony of the buyer. It must be remembered that the vice-chancellorship and other offices that Alexander had formerly held had taught him to know better and turn to more practical account the various sources of revenue than any other member of the Curia. As early as 1494, a Carmelite, Adam of Genoa, who had preached at Rome against simony, was found murdered in his bed with twenty wounds. Hardly a single cardinal was appointed without the payment of enormous sums of money.

But when in course of time the Pope fell under the influence of his son, his violent measures assumed that satanic character which necessarily reacts upon the ends pursued. What was done in the struggle with the Roman nobles and with the tyrants of Romagna exceeded in faithlessness and barbarity even that measure to which, for example, the Aragonese rulers of Naples had already accustomed the world; and the genius for deception was also greater. The manner in which Cesare isolated his father, murdering brother, brother-in-law, and other relations or courtiers, whenever their favor with the Pope or their position in any other respect became inconvenient to him, is literally appalling. Alexander was forced to acquiesce in the murder of his best-loved son, the Duke of Gandia, since he himself lived in hourly dread of Cesare.

What were the ultimate aims of the latter? Even in the last months of his tyranny, when he had murdered the *condottieri* at Sinigaglia, and was to all intents and purposes master of the ecclesiastical State (1503), those who were close to him gave the modest reply that the Duke merely wished to put down the factions and the despots, and all only for the good of the Church; that for himself he desired nothing more than the lordship of Romagna, and that he had earned the gratitude of all the following Popes by ridding them of the Orsini and Colonna. But no one will accept this as his ultimate design. Pope Alexander himself, in his discussions with the Venetian ambassador, went further than this, when committing his son to the protection of Venice: "I will see to it," he said, "that one day the Papacy shall belong either to him or to you." Cesare indeed added that no one could become Pope without the consent of Venice, and for this end the Venetian cardinals needed merely to keep together. Whether he referred to himself we are unable to say; at all events, the declaration of his father is sufficient to prove his designs on the Pontifical throne. We further obtain from Lucrezia Borgia a certain amount of indirect evidence, in so far as certain passages in the poems of Ercole Strozza may be the echo of expressions which she as Duchess of Ferrara may easily have permitted herself. Cesare's hopes of the Papacy are chiefly spoken of; now and then a supremacy over all Italy is hinted at; and finally we are given to understand that as temporal ruler Cesare's projects were of the greatest, and that for their sake he had surrendered his cardinalate. In fact, there can be no doubt whatever that Cesare, whether chosen Pope or not after the death of Alexander, meant to keep possession of the Pontifical State at any price, and that this, after all the enormities he had committed, he could not as Pope have succeeded in doing permanently. He, if anybody, could have secularized the States of the Church,[54] and he would have been forced to do so in order to keep them. Unless we are much deceived, this is the real reason for the secret sympathy with which Machiavelli treats the great criminal; from Cesare, or from nobody, could it be hoped that he "would draw the steel from the wound," in other words, annihilate the Papacy— the source of all foreign intervention and of all the divisions of Italy. – The intriguers who thought they divined Cesare's aims, when they held out to him hopes of the Kingdom of Tuscany, seem to have been dismissed with contempt.

But all logical conclusions from his premises are idle, not because of the unaccountable genius which, in fact, character-

---

54. He was married to a French princess of the House of Albret and had a daughter with her; in some way or other he would have tried to found a dynasty. It is not known whether he took steps to regain the cardinal's hat, although (according to Machiavelli) he must have counted on the early death of his father.

ized him as little as it did the Duke of Friedland [Wallenstein], but because the means he employed were not compatible with any large and consistent course of action. Perhaps in the very excess of his wickedness some prospect of salvation for the Papacy may have existed, even without the accident that put an end to his rule.

Even if we assume that the destruction of the petty despots in the Pontifical State had gained nothing but sympathy for Cesare, even if we take as proof of his great prospects the army that followed his fortunes in 1503—the best soldiers and officers of Italy with Leonardo da Vinci as chief engineer —there is so much else that is irrational, our opinion becomes as confused as that of his contemporaries. To this irrationality belongs the devastation and maltreatment of the newly won State that Cesare still intended to keep and to rule. Also, the condition of Rome and of the Curia in the last decades of the Pontificate. Whether father and son had drawn up a formal list of proscribed persons, or whether murders were resolved upon one by one, in either case the Borgias were bent on the secret destruction of all who stood in their way or whose inheritance they coveted. Money and movable goods formed the smallest part; it was a much greater source of profit for the Pope that the incomes of the clerical dignitaries in question were suspended by their death, and that he received the revenues of their offices while vacant and the price of these offices when they were filled by the successors of the murdered men. The Venetian ambassador Paolo Capello reported in the year 1500: "Every night four or five murdered men are discovered—bishops, prelates, and others —so that all Rome trembles for fear of being murdered by the Duke (Cesare)." He himself used to wander about the frightened city in the nighttime with his guards, and there is every reason to believe that he did so not only because, like Tiberius, he shrank from showing his now repulsive features by daylight, but also to gratify his insane thirst for blood, perhaps even on persons unknown to him. As early as the year 1499 the despair was so great and so general that many of the Papal guards were waylaid and put to death. But those whom the Borgias could not assail with open violence fell victims to their poison. For those cases in which a certain amount of discretion seemed requisite, that white powder of an agreeable taste was used, which did not work on the spot, but which took effect slowly and gradually, and which could be mixed without notice in any dish or goblet. Prince Djem had taken some of it in a sweet draught, before Alexander surrendered him to Charles VIII (1495), and at the end of their career father and son poisoned themselves with the same powder by accidentally tasting wine intended for a wealthy cardinal. The official epitomizer of the history of the Popes, Onofrio Panvinio, mentions three cardinals (Orsini, Ferrerio, and Michiel) whom Alexander had poisoned, and hints at a fourth (Giovanni Borgia) who should be charged to Cesare's account. Although at that time in Rome wealthy prelates seldom died without giving rise to suspicions of this sort. Even tranquil scholars who had withdrawn to some provincial town were not out of reach of the merciless poison. It began to be distinctly uncomfortable to be near the Pope; in earlier days he had been terrified by storms and thunderbolts crumbling walls and buildings; in the year 1500, when these phenomena recurred, they were held to be *cosa diabolica* [the work of the devil]. The report of these events seems at last, through the well-attended jubilee of 1500, to have been carried far and wide throughout the countries of Europe, and the infamous traffic in indulgences did what else was needed to draw all eyes on Rome. Besides the returning pilgrims, strange white-robed penitents came from Italy to the North, among them disguised fugitives from the Papal State, who are not likely to have been silent. Yet who can calculate how far the scandal and indignation of Christendom might have gone, before they became a source of pressing danger to Alexander. "He would," says Panvinio elsewhere, "have put all the remaining rich cardinals and prelates out of the way, to get their property, had he not, in the midst of his great plans for his son, been struck down by death." And what might not Cesare have achieved if, at the moment his father died, he himself had not been deathly ill! What a conclave that would have been, in which, armed with all his weapons, he extorted his election from a college whose numbers he had judiciously reduced by poison—and when there was no French army at hand! In pursuing such a hypothesis the imagination loses itself in an abyss.

Instead of this there followed the conclave in which Pius III was elected, and, after his speedy death, that which chose Julius II—both elections the results of a general reaction.

Whatever may have been the private morals of Julius II, in all essential respects he was the savior of the Papacy. His familiarity with the course of events since the Pontificate of his uncle Sixtus had given him a profound insight into the grounds and conditions of the Papal authority. On these he founded his own policy, and devoted to it the whole force and passion of his unshakable soul. He ascended the steps of the Throne of St. Peter without simony and amid general

applause, and with him ceased, at all events, the undisguised
traffic in the highest offices of the Church. Julius had favorites, and among them were some who were not worthy, but
a special fortune put him above the temptation to nepotism.
His brother, Giovanni della Rovere, was the husband of the
heiress of Urbino, sister of Guidobaldo, the last Montefeltro,
and from this marriage was born, in 1491, a son, Francesco
Maria della Rovere, who was at the same time Papal *nipote*
and lawful heir to the duchy of Urbino. Whatever Julius
acquired, either on the field of battle or by diplomatic means,
he proudly bestowed on the Church, not on his family; the
ecclesiastical territory, which he found in a state of dissolution, he bequeathed to his successor completely subdued and
increased by Parma and Piacenza. It was not his fault that
Ferrara, too, was not added to the dominions of the Church.
The 700,000 ducats which were stored up in the Castel Sant'
Angelo were to be delivered by the governor to none but
the future Pope. He made himself heir of the cardinals,
indeed, of all the clergy who died in Rome, and this by the
most despotic means; [55] but he murdered or poisoned none
of them. That he himself should lead his forces to battle was
for him an unavoidable necessity, and certainly did him nothing but good in Italy at a time when a man had to be either
hammer or anvil, and when personality was a greater power
than the most indisputable right. If despite all his high-
sounding "Away with the barbarians!" he nevertheless contributed more than any man to the firm settlement of the
Spaniards in Italy, he may have thought it a matter of
indifference to the Papacy, or even, as things stood, a relative
advantage. And to whom, sooner than to Spain, could the
Church look for a sincere and lasting respect, in an age when
the princes of Italy cherished none but sacrilegious projects
against her? — Be this as it may, the powerful, original nature,
which could swallow no anger and conceal no genuine good
will, made on the whole the impression most desirable in his
situation—that of the *Pontefice terribile* [passionate Pope].
With comparatively clear conscience, he could even venture
to summon a Council to Rome, and so bid defiance to that
outcry for a Council which was raised by the opposition all
over Europe. A ruler of this stamp needed some great outward symbol of his conceptions; Julius found it in the
reconstruction of St. Peter's. The plan of St. Peter's, as

55. Hence the splendor of the tombs the prelates erected during
their lifetime; in this way a part of the booty was kept from
the Papacy.

Bramante wanted it, is perhaps the grandest expression of unified power that can be imagined. In other arts besides architecture the face and the memory of the Pope live on in their most ideal form, and it is not without significance that even the Latin poetry of those days gives proof of an enthusiasm for Julius which was wholly different from that shown for his predecessors. The entry into Bologna, at the end of the *Iter Julii Secundi* by Cardinal Adriano da Corneto, has a splendor of its own, and Giovanni Antonio Flaminio, in one of the finest elegies,[56] appealed to the patriot in the Pope to grant his protection to Italy.

In a thunderous constitution of his Lateran Council, Julius had forbidden the simony of the Papal elections. After his death (1513) the money-loving cardinals tried to evade the prohibition by proposing that the endowments and offices hitherto held by the chosen candidate be equally divided among themselves, in which case they would have elected the best-endowed cardinal (the incompetent Raphael Riario). But a reaction, arising chiefly from the younger members of the Sacred College, who, above all, desired a liberal Pope, rendered the miserable combination futile; Giovanni de' Medici was elected—the famous Leo X.

We shall meet with him often, whenever there is mention of the noonday of the Renaissance; here we wish only to point out that under him the Papacy was again exposed to great internal and external dangers. Among these we do not reckon the conspiracy of Cardinals Petrucci, Sauli, Riario, and Corneto, which at most could have occasioned a change of persons, and to which Leo found the true antidote in the unheard-of creation of thirty-one new cardinals, a measure that had the additional advantage of rewarding, in some cases at least, real merit.[57]

But some of the paths Leo allowed himself to tread during the first two years of his office were extremely dangerous. He endeavored to secure, by serious negotiation, the kingdom of Naples for his brother Giuliano, and for his nephew Lorenzo a powerful North Italian State, to comprise Milan, Tuscany, Urbino, and Ferrara. It is clear that the Pontifical

56. Although when Julius once lay unconscious for hours and was thought to be dead (August 1511), the more restless members of the noblest families—Pompeo Colonna and Antimo Savelli—dared to call the "people" to the Capitol and to urge them to throw off the Papal yoke.

57. And is supposed to have brought in 500,000 gold florins; the Order of the Franciscans alone, whose general was made a cardinal, paid 30,000.

State, thus hemmed in on all sides, would have become a mere Medicean appanage, in fact, there would have been no further need to secularize it.

The plan found an insuperable obstacle in the political conditions of the time. Giuliano died early. To provide for Lorenzo, Leo undertook to expel Duke Francesco Maria della Rovere from Urbino, but reaped from the war nothing but hatred and poverty, and was forced, when in 1519 Lorenzo died, to hand over the hard-won conquests to the Church. He did on compulsion and without credit what, if it had been done voluntarily, would have been to his eternal honor. What he then attempted against Alfonso of Ferrara, and actually achieved against a few petty despots and *condottieri*, was assuredly not of a kind to raise his reputation. And all this when the monarchs of the West year by year grew more and more accustomed to a colossal political card game in which the stakes were this or that province of Italy. Who could guarantee that, since the last decades had seen so great an increase of their power at home, their ambition would stop short of the States of the Church? Leo himself witnessed the prelude of what was fulfilled in 1527; a few bands of Spanish infantry appeared—of their own accord, it seems—at the end of the year 1520, on the borders of the Pontifical territory, with a view to laying the Pope under contribution, but were driven back by the Papal forces. The public feeling, too, against the corruptions of the hierarchy had of late years been drawing rapidly to a head, and men with an eye for the future, like the younger Pico della Mirandola, called urgently for reform. Meantime Luther had already appeared on the scene.

Under Adrian VI (1521-1523), the few and timid improvements carried out in the face of the great German Reformation came too late. He could do little more than proclaim his horror of the course that things had taken hitherto, of simony, nepotism, prodigality, brigandage, and profligacy. The danger from the side of the Lutherans was by no means the greatest; an acute observer from Venice, Girolamo Negro, uttered his fears that a speedy and terrible disaster would befall the city of Rome.[58]

Under Clement VII the whole horizon of Rome was filled with vapors, like that leaden veil the sirocco draws over

---

58. Rome, March 17, 1523: For many reasons this city stands on a needle's point, and God grant that we do not have to flee to Avignon or to the end of the ocean. I see before me the impending fall of this spiritual monarchy. . . . Unless God helps us, we are lost.

the Campagna which can make the last months of summer so deadly. The Pope was as hated at home as he was abroad. Thoughtful people were filled with anxiety; hermits appeared on the streets and squares of Rome, foretelling the fall of Italy and of the world, and calling the Pope the Antichrist; the Colonna faction raised its head defiantly; the indomitable Cardinal Pompeo Colonna, whose mere existence was a permanent menace to the Papacy, ventured to surprise the city (1526), hoping, with the help of Charles V, to become Pope then and there, as soon as Clement was killed or captured. It was no piece of good fortune for Rome that the latter was able to escape to the Castel Sant' Angelo, and the fate for which he himself was reserved may well be called worse than death.

By a series of those falsehoods on which only the powerful can venture but which bring ruin upon the weak, Clement brought about the advance of the Germano-Spanish army under Bourbon and Frundsberg (1527). It is certain that the Cabinet of Charles V intended to inflict on him a severe castigation, and that it could not calculate beforehand how far the zeal of the unpaid hordes would carry them. It would have been vain to attempt to enlist men in Germany without paying any bounty, had it not been well known that Rome was the object of the expedition. It may be that the written orders to Bourbon will be found some day, and it is not improbable that they will prove to be worded mildly. But historical criticism will not allow itself to be led astray. The Catholic King and Emperor owed it to luck and nothing else that Pope and cardinals were not murdered by his troops. Had this happened, no sophistry in the world could clear him of his share in the guilt. The massacre of countless people of less consequence, the plunder of the rest with the help of torture and traffic in human life, show clearly enough what was possible in the *sacco di Roma* [sack of Rome].

Charles seems to have wished to bring the Pope, who had fled a second time to the Castel Sant' Angelo, to Naples, after extorting from him vast sums of money, and Clement's flight to Orvieto must have happened without any connivance on the part of Spain. Whether the Emperor ever thought seriously of the secularization of the States of the Church (for which the world was quite prepared) and whether he was really dissuaded from it by the representations of Henry VIII of England, will probably never be made clear.

But if such projects really existed, they cannot have lasted long: from the devastated city a new spirit of reform arose in both Church and State. It made itself felt immediately;

Cardinal Sadoleto, for example, writes: "If through our suffering, atonement is made to the wrath and justice of God, if these fearful punishments again open to us the way to better laws and morals, then our misfortune is perhaps not of the greatest. . . . What belongs to God He will take care of; before us, however, lies a life of reformation, which no violence can take from us. Let us so direct our deeds and thoughts as to seek in God only the true glory of the priesthood and our own true greatness and power."

In point of fact, this critical year of 1527 bore such fruit that the voices of serious men could again make themselves heard. Rome had suffered too much to return, even under a Paul III, to the gay corruption of Leo X.

The Papacy, too, when its sufferings became so great, began to excite a sympathy half religious and half political. The kings could not tolerate that one of their number should arrogate to himself the position of Papal jailer, and concluded (August 18, 1527) the Treaty of Amiens, one of the objects of which was the deliverance of Clement. Thus, they at least turned to their own account the unpopularity that the deeds of the imperial troops had excited. At the same time, however, the Emperor became seriously embarrassed, even in Spain, where the prelates and grandees never saw him without making the most urgent remonstrances. When a general deputation of the clergy and laity, all clothed in mourning, was projected, Charles, fearing that troubles might arise out of it, like those of the insurrection quelled a few years before, forbade the scheme. Not only did he not dare to prolong the maltreatment of the Pope, but he was absolutely compelled, even apart from all considerations of foreign politics, to be reconciled with the Papacy, which he had so grievously wounded. For the temper of the German people, which had pointed to a different course, seemed to him, like German affairs generally, to afford little foundation for support. It is possible, too, as a Venetian maintains, that the memory of the sack of Rome lay heavy on his conscience, and thus hastened that expiation which was sealed by the permanent subjection of the Florentines to the Medicean family of which the Pope was a member. The *nipote* and new Duke, Alessandro de' Medici, was married to the natural daughter of the Emperor.

In the following years the idea of a Council enabled Charles to keep the Papacy in all essential points under his control, and at the same time both protect and oppress it. The greatest danger of all—secularization—the danger that came from within, from the Popes themselves and their *nipoti,* was set aside for centuries by the German Reformation. Just as this alone had made the expedition against Rome (1527) possible and successful, so did it compel the Papacy to become once more the expression of a world-wide spiritual power, to raise itself from the soulless debasement in which it lay, and to place itself at the head of all the enemies of this reformation. Thus, the institution that developed during the latter years of Clement VII, and under Paul III, Paul IV, and their successors, in face of the defection of half Europe, was a new, regenerated hierarchy that avoided all the great and dangerous scandals of former times, particularly nepotism and its attendant territorial aggrandizement, and which, in alliance with the Catholic princes impelled by a newborn spiritual force, made its chief work the recovery of what had been lost. It only existed and is only intelligible in opposition to the seceders. In this sense it can be said with perfect truth that the moral salvation of the Papacy was due to its mortal enemies. And now its political position, too, though certainly under the permanent tutelage of Spain, became impregnable; almost without effort it inherited, on the extinction of its vassals (the legitimate line of Este and the House of Della Rovere), the duchies of Ferrara and Urbino. Without the Reformation—if, indeed, it is possible to think it away—the whole ecclesiastical State would have passed into secular hands long ago.

In conclusion, let us briefly consider the effect of these political circumstances on the spirit of the nation as a whole.

It is evident that the general political uncertainty in Italy during the fourteenth and fifteenth centuries had to evoke in nobler spirits a patriotic disgust and opposition. Dante and Petrarch had proclaimed loudly a common Italy as the object of the highest efforts of all her children. It may be objected that this was only the enthusiasm of a few highly instructed men, in which the mass of the people had no share; but it can hardly have been otherwise even in Germany, although in name at least that country was united, and recognized in the Emperor one supreme head. The first patriotic utterances of German literature (if we except some verses of the *Minnesänger*) belong to the humanists of the time of Maximilian I and after, and read like an echo of Italian declamations. And yet, Germany was, in a wholly different degree it is true, a nation before Italy ever was since the time of ancient Rome. France owes the consciousness of its national unity mainly to its conflicts with the English, and Spain has never permanently succeeded in absorbing Portugal, closely related as the two countries are. For Italy, the existence of the ecclesiastical State, and the conditions under which it could continue, were a permanent obstacle to national unity, an obstacle whose removal seemed hopeless. When, therefore, in the political intercourse of the fifteenth century, the common fatherland is sometimes emphatically named, it is done in most cases to annoy some other Italian State. Those deeply serious and sorrowful appeals to national sentiment were not heard again till the sixteenth century, when it was too late, when the country was inundated with Frenchmen and Spaniards. It may be said that local patriotism in some measure took the place of this feeling, but it was a poor substitute.

PART TWO

THE DEVELOPMENT OF THE INDIVIDUAL

IN the character of these States, whether republics or despotisms, lies, not the only, but the chief reason for the early development of the Italian into modern man. It is this that made it inevitable that he should be the first-born among the sons of modern Europe.

In the Middle Ages both sides of human consciousness— that which was turned within and that which was turned without—lay as though dreaming or half awake beneath a common veil. The veil was woven of faith, illusion, and childish prepossession, through which the world and history were seen clad in strange hues. Man was conscious of himself only as a member of a race, people, party, family, or corporation—only through some general category. It is in Italy that this veil dissolved first; there arose an *objective* treatment and consideration of the State and of all the things of this world, and at the same time the *subjective* side asserted itself with corresponding emphasis. Man became a spiritual *individual*,[59] and recognized himself as such. In the same way the Greek had once distinguished himself from the barbarian, and the Arab had felt himself an individual at a time when other Asiatics knew themselves only as members of a race. It will not be difficult to show that this result was due above all to the political circumstances of Italy.

In far earlier times we can occasionally detect a development of free personality which in Northern Europe either did not occur at all, or could not reveal itself in the same manner. The band of audacious wrongdoers of the tenth century described to us by Liudprand, some of the con-

59. Observe the expressions *uomo singolare* [singular man] and *uomo unico* [unique man] for the higher and highest stages of individual development.

temporaries of Gregory VII (for example, Benzo of Alba), and a few of the opponents of the first Hohenstaufen, exhibit traits of this kind. But at the close of the thirteenth century Italy began to swarm with personalities; here the spell cast on individuality was completely broken, and a thousand different figures appear, each with its own special face. Dante's great poem would have been impossible in any other country of Europe, if only for the reason that they all still lay under the spell of race. For Italy the august poet, through the wealth of individuality, became the most national herald of his time. But this unfolding of the treasures of human nature in literature and art—this many-sided representation and criticism—will be discussed in separate chapters; here we have to deal only with the psychological fact itself. This fact appears in the most decisive and unmistakable form. The Italians of the fourteenth century knew little of false modesty or hypocrisy; not one of them was afraid of singularity, of being and seeming [60] unlike his neighbors.

Despotism, as we have already seen, fostered the utmost individuality not only in the tyrant or *condottiere*,[61] but also in the men he protected or used as his tools—the secretary, minister, poet, and companion. These people were forced to know all the inward resources of their own nature, the momentary as well as the permanent; and their enjoyment of life was enhanced and concentrated by the desire to obtain the greatest satisfaction from a period of power and influence that might be very brief.

But even the subjects were not free from the same impulse. We will ignore completely those who wasted their lives in secret opposition and conspiracies, and consider only those who were content with a strictly private station, like most of the urban population of the Byzantine Empire and the Mohammedan States. No doubt it was often hard for the subjects of a Visconti to maintain the dignity of their persons and families, and multitudes must have suffered in moral character through the servitude they lived under. But this was not the case with regard to individuality; for political impotence does not hinder the different tendencies and manifestations of private life from thriving in the fullest vigor and

60. By the year 1390 there was no longer any prevailing fashion of dress for men in Florence, each preferring to clothe himself in his own way.
61. And also of their wives, as is seen in the House of Sforza and among other North Italian ruling families. There was more than one genuine virago among them, and in several cases natural gifts were supplemented by great humanistic culture.

variety. Wealth and culture, so far as display and rivalry
were not forbidden to them, combined with an always considerable municipal freedom and a Church that, unlike that
of the Byzantine or of the Mohammedan world, was not
identical with the State—all these conditions undoubtedly
favored the growth of individual thought, for which the necessary leisure was furnished by the cessation of party conflicts.
The politically indifferent private man busied partly with
serious pursuits, partly with the interests of a dilettante,
seems to have been first fully formed in these despotisms
of the fourteenth century. Documentary evidence cannot, of
course, be expected on such a point. The novelists, from
whom we might expect information, describe to us oddities
in plenty, but only from one point of view and only in so
far as the needs of the story demand. Their scene, too, lies
chiefly in the republican cities.

In the latter, circumstances were also, but in another way,
favorable to the growth of individual character. The more
frequently the governing party was changed, the more the individual was led to make the utmost of the exercise and
enjoyment of power. The statesmen and popular leaders,
especially in Florentine history,[62] acquired so marked a personal character that we can scarcely find, even exceptionally,
a parallel to them in contemporary history, hardly even in
Jacob van Arteveldt.

The members of the defeated parties, on the other hand,
often came into a position like that of the subjects of the
despotic States; but the freedom or power already enjoyed,
perhaps even the hope of recovering them, gave a higher
energy to their individuality. Among these men of involuntary
leisure we find, for instance, an Agnolo Pandolfini (d. 1446),
whose work on domestic economy [63] is the first program
of a completely developed private life. His estimate of the
duties of the individual as against the dangers and thanklessness of public life is in its way a true monument of the age.

But it is banishment, above all, that either wears the exile

---

62. About 1390 Franco Sacchetti enumerates the names of more
than 100 distinguished people in the ruling parties who had
died within his memory. However many mediocrities there may be
among them, the list is still remarkable as evidence of the
awakening of individuality.
63. *Trattato del governo della famiglia* [Treatise on the Administration of the Family]. A recent study proposes that this work was
written by L.B. Alberti. [It is now generally accepted that the
document in question is actually part of a larger treatise by Alberti. Cf. footnote 68.]

out or develops whatever is greatest in him. "In all our
more populous cities," says Gioviano Pontano, "we see a
crowd of people who have left their homes of their own
free will; but a man takes his virtues with him wherever he
goes." And in fact, they were by no means only men who
had been formally exiled, but thousands who had left their
native cities voluntarily, because they had found the political
or economic condition intolerable. The Florentine emigrants
at Ferrara, the Lucchese in Venice, etc., formed whole
colonies by themselves.

The cosmopolitanism that grew up in the most gifted
exiles is one of the highest stages of individualism. Dante,
as we have already said, finds a new home in the language
and culture of Italy, but goes beyond even this in the words,
"My country is the whole world." [64] – And when return to
Florence was offered him on unworthy conditions, he wrote
back: "Can I not behold the light of the sun and the
stars everywhere; everywhere meditate on the noblest
truths, without appearing ingloriously and shamefully before
the city and the people? Even my bread will not fail me."
The artists exult no less defiantly in their freedom from the
constraints of fixed residence. "Only he who has learned
everything," says Ghiberti, "is nowhere a stranger; robbed
of his fortune and without friends, he is yet the citizen
of every country, and can fearlessly despise the changes of
fortune." In the same strain an exiled humanist writes:
"Wherever a learned man fixes his seat, there is home." [65]

An acute and practiced eye might be able to trace, step by
step, the increase in the number of complete men during the
fifteenth century. Whether they strove consciously toward
the harmonious development of their spiritual and material
existence, is hard to say; but several of them attained it, so

64. *De vulgari eloquentia,* Book I, ch. 6. – On the ideal Italian
language, ch. 17. – The spiritual unity of cultured men, ch. 18. –
But on homesickness, cf. the famous passages in *Purgatorio,*
viii, 1ff and *Paradiso,* xxv, 1.
65. This certainly borders on the saying: *Ubi bene, ibi patria*
[where it is well, there is my country]. – The abundance of
neutral intellectual pleasure, which is independent of local circumstances and of which the educated Italian became more and
more capable, rendered exile more tolerable to them. Cosmopolitanism is a sign of an epoch in which new worlds are discovered,
and men no longer feel at home in the old. We see it among the
Greeks after the Peloponnesian War; Plato, as Niebuhr says, was
not a good citizen, and Xenophon was a bad one; Diogenes went
so far as to proclaim homelessness a pleasure and calls himself,
Laërtius tells us, $\alpha\pi o\lambda\iota s$ [stateless].

far as is possible given the imperfection of all that is earthly. If we forego the attempt to estimate the share that fortune, character, and talent had in the life of Lorenzo the Magnificent, then let us look at a personality such as that of Ariosto, especially as shown in his satires. How harmoniously are expressed the pride of the man and the poet, the irony with which he treats his own enjoyments, the most delicate satire, and the deepest good will!

When this impulse to the highest individual development was combined with a powerful and varied nature that had mastered all the elements of the culture of the age, then there arose the "all-sided man"—*l'uomo universale*—who belonged exclusively to Italy. There were men of encyclopedic knowledge in many countries during the Middle Ages, for this knowledge was confined within narrow limits; and even in the twelfth century there were universal artists, but the problems of architecture were comparatively simple and uniform, and in sculpture and painting, subject matter was more important than form. But in Italy at the time of the Renaissance, we find artists who created new and perfect works in all branches of the arts, and who also made the greatest impression as men. Others, outside the arts they practiced, were masters of a vast range of spiritual interests.

Dante, who, even in his lifetime, was called by some a poet, by others a philosopher, by others a theologian,[66] pours forth in all his writings a stream of personal force by which the reader, even apart from the interest of the subject, feels himself carried away. What power of will must the steady, unbroken elaboration of the *Divine Comedy* have required! And if we look at the contents of the poem, we find that in the whole spiritual or physical world there is hardly an important subject which the poet has not fathomed, and on which his utterances—often only a few words—are not the most weighty of his time. For the visual arts he is of the first importance, and this for better reasons than the few references to contemporary artists—he himself soon became a source of inspiration.[67]

The fifteenth century is, above all, that of the many-sided men. There is no biography which does not, besides the chief work of its hero, speak of other pursuits, all of which pass

---

66. Boccaccio, *Life of Dante.*
67. The angels he drew on tablets on the anniversary of the death of Beatrice (*La vita nuova*) may have been more than the work of a dilettante. Leonardo Aretino says he drew *egregiamente* [perfectly] and was a great lover of music.

beyond mere dilettantism. The Florentine merchant and statesman was often learned in both classical languages; the most famous humanists read the *Ethics* and *Politics* of Aristotle to him and his sons; even the daughters of the house were highly educated. It is in these circles that private education was first treated seriously. The humanist, for his part, was compelled to the most varied attainments, since his philological learning was not limited, as it is now, to the theoretical knowledge of classical antiquity, but had to serve the practical needs of daily life. While studying Pliny, for example, he assembled a museum of natural history; the geography of the ancients was his guide to modern cosmography; their history was his pattern in writing contemporary history; he not only translated the comedies of Plautus, but acted as manager when they were put on the stage; he did his best to imitate every effective form of ancient literature down to the dialogues of Lucian; and besides all this, he acted as secretary and diplomat—not always to his own advantage.

But above these many-sided men, tower some who may truly be called all-sided. Before we discuss in detail the characteristics of life and culture at that time, let us consider here, on the threshold of the fifteenth century, the figure of one of these giants—Leon Battista Alberti. His biography, which is only a fragment, speaks of him only little as an artist, and makes no mention at all of his great significance in the history of architecture. We shall now see what he was, even without these special claims to distinction.

In everything that wins praise, Leon Battista was, from his childhood, first. Of his various gymnastic feats and exercises we read with astonishment how, with his feet together, he could jump over a man's head; how, in the cathedral, he threw a coin in the air till it was heard to ring against the distant roof; how the wildest horses trembled under him. In three things he desired to appear faultless to others: in walking, in riding, and in speaking. He learned music without a master, and yet his compositions were admired by professional musicians. Under the pressure of poverty, he studied both civil and canonical law for many years, till exhaustion brought on a severe illness; and when, in his twenty-fourth year, he found his memory for words weakened but his sense of facts unimpaired, he set to work at physics and mathematics. And all the while he acquired every sort of accomplishment by cross-examining artists, scholars, and artisans of all descriptions, even shoemakers, about the secrets and peculiarities of their craft. He practiced both painting and sculpture, and excelled in making admirable likenesses, even when only from memory. Great admiration was excited by his mysterious camera obscura, in which he showed the stars and the moon rising over rocky hills, wide landscapes with mountains and gulfs receding into misty distance, and fleets advancing on the waters in shade or sunshine. And that which others created he welcomed joyfully, and held as almost divine every human achievement that followed the laws of beauty. To all this must be added his literary works, first of all those on art, which are landmarks and authorities of the first order for the renaissance of form, especially in architecture; then his Latin prose writings—novels and other works—of which some have been taken for productions of antiquity; his elegies, eclogues, and humorous dinner speeches. He also wrote an Italian treatise on domestic life in four books,[68] and even a funeral oration on his dog. His serious and witty sayings were thought worth collecting, and specimens of them, many columns long, are quoted in his biography. And all that he had and knew he imparted, as rich natures always do, without the least reserve, giving away his chief discoveries for nothing. But the deepest spring of his nature has yet to be spoken of—the sympathetic intensity with which he entered into everything around him. At the sight of noble trees and waving cornfields he shed tears; handsome and dignified old men he honored as "a delight of nature," and could never look at them enough. Perfectly formed animals won his good will as being specially favored by nature; and more than once, when he was ill, the sight of a beautiful landscape cured him.[69] Small wonder that those who saw him in this close and mysterious communion with the world ascribed to him the gift of prophecy. He was said to have predicted accurately, many years in advance, a bloody catastrophe in the family of Este, the fate of Florence and that of the Popes, and to have been able to read from their countenances the hearts of men. It goes without saying that an iron will pervaded and sustained

68. This is the work that has, until recently, been considered to be a treatise by Pandolfini (cf. footnote 63).
69. In his *De re aedificatoria* [*The Architecture of Leone Battist Alberti*], Book VIII, ch. 1, there is a definition of what might be considered a beautiful road: *si modo mare, modo montes, modo lacum fluentem fonesve, modo aridam rupem aut planitiem, modo nemus vallemque exhibebit* [if only it will have now a sea, now hills, now a following lake, or a spring, now a bare rock, now a plain, wood, or valley].

his whole personality; like all the great men of the Renaissance, he said, "Men can do all things if they will."

And Leonardo da Vinci was to Alberti as the finisher is to the beginner, as the master to the dilettante. If only Vasari's work were supplemented here by a description like that of Alberti! The colossal outlines of Leonardo's nature can never be more than dimly and distantly conceived.

To this inward development of the individual corresponds a new sort of outward distinction—the modern idea of fame.

In the other countries of Europe the different classes of society lived apart, each with its own medieval sense of caste honor. The poetic fame of the Troubadours and *Minnesänger* was peculiar to the knightly order. But in Italy social equality had appeared before the time of the tyrannies or the democracies; there are, also, early traces of a general society having, as will be shown more fully, a common ground in Latin and Italian literature; and such a ground was necessary to nourish this new element in life. To this must be added that the Roman authors, who were now zealously studied, are filled and saturated with the conception of fame, and that their very subject matter—the universal empire of Rome —stood as a permanent ideal before the minds of Italians. From this time all the aspirations and achievements of the people were governed by a moral postulate that was still unknown elsewhere in Europe.

Here, as in all essential points, Dante must be heard first. He strove for the poet's garland with all the power of his soul.[70] Even as publicist and man of letters, he laid stress on the fact that what he did was new, and that he not only was, but wanted to be known as, the first to walk these paths.[71] But in his prose writings he touches also on the inconveniences of fame; he knows how often personal acquaintance with famous men is disappointing, and explains

---

70. *Paradiso*, xxv, at the beginning: *Se mai continga* etc. [Should it e'er come to pass]. – Cf. Boccaccio, *Life of Dante*, *Vaghissimo fu e d'onore a di pompa, a per avventura più che alle sua inclinata virtù non si sarebbe richiesto* [He longed most ardently for honor and glory; perchance more than befitted his illustrious virtue].

71. *De vulgari eloquentia*, Book I, ch. 1, and especially *De monarchia*, Book I, ch. 1, where he wishes to set forth the idea of monarchy not only for the good of the world, but also *ut palmam tanti bravii primus in meam gloriam adipiscar* [that I may be the first to win for my glory the palm of so great a prize].

how this is due partly to the childish fancy of men, partly to
envy, and partly to the imperfections of the hero himself.[72]
And in his great poem he firmly maintains the emptiness of
fame, although in a manner that betrays that his heart was
not yet free from longing for it. In the *Paradiso* the sphere
of Mercury is the seat of such blessed ones [73] who on earth
strove after glory and thereby dimmed "the rays of true
love." It is characteristic, however, that the lost souls in hell
beg Dante to keep alive for them their memory and fame
on earth,[74] while those in the *Purgatorio* only entreat his
prayers and those of others for their deliverance.[75] And in a
famous passage,[76] the passion for fame—*lo gran disio dell'
eccellenza* [the great desire of excelling]—is reproved for the
reason that intellectual glory is not absolute, but is relative
to the times and may be surpassed and eclipsed by greater
successors.

The new race of poet-scholars that arose soon after Dante
quickly made themselves masters of this fresh tendency. They
did so in a double sense, being themselves the most acknowl-
edged celebrities of Italy, and at the same time, as poets and
historians, consciously disposing of the reputation of others.
An outward symbol of this sort of fame was the coronation
of the poets, of which we shall speak later on.

A contemporary of Dante, Albertinus Musattus or Mus-
satus, crowned poet at Padua by the bishop and rector,
enjoyed a fame that approached deification. Every Christmas
Day the doctors and students of both colleges of the University came in solemn procession before his house with
trumpets and, it seems, burning tapers, to salute him and
bring him presents. His glory lasted until he fell into disgrace
with the ruling tyrant of the House of Carrara (1318).

This new incense, which once was offered only to saints
and heroes, was given in clouds to Petrarch, who persuaded
himself in his later years that it was a foolish and trouble-
some thing. His *Letter to Posterity* is the confession of an
old and famous man, who is forced to gratify public curiosity.
He admits that he wishes for fame in the times to come, but
would rather be without it in his own day. In his dialogue

---

72. *Convivio*, Book I, ch. 4.
73. *Paradiso*, vi, 112ff.
74. E.g., *Inferno*, vi, 89; xiii, 53; xvi, 85; xxxi, 127.
75. *Purgatorio*, v, 70, 87, 133; vi, 26; viii, 71; xi, 31; xiii, 147.
76. *Purgatorio*, xi, 79-117. Besides *gloria* [glory], we find here
close together: *grido* [the cry], *fama* [fame], *rumore* [noise],
nominanza [repute], *onore* [honor]—all different names for the
same thing.

on fortune and misfortune, the interlocutor, who maintains the futility of fame, has the best of the contest. Then should we take him at his word when he is so pleased that by his writings the autocrat of Byzantium knows him as well as Emperor Charles IV knows him? And in fact, even in his lifetime, his fame extended far beyond Italy. And the emotion he felt was natural when his friends, on the occasion of a visit to his native Arezzo, took him to the house where he was born, and told him that the city had provided that no change should be made in it. In former times the dwellings of certain great saints were preserved and revered in this way, as, for example, the cell of St. Thomas Aquinas in the Dominican convent at Naples, and the Portiuncula of St. Francis near Assisi; and one or two great jurists enjoyed the half-mythical reputation which led to this honor. Thus, toward the close of the fourteenth century the people at Bagnolo, near Florence, called an old building the "studio" of Accorso (b. about 1150), but, nevertheless, allowed it to be destroyed. It is probable that the great incomes and the political influence that some jurists obtained (as consulting lawyers) made a lasting impression on the popular imagination.

To the cult of the birthplaces of famous men must be added that of their graves, and, in the case of Petrarch, of the spot where he died. In memory of him Arquà became a favorite resort of the Paduans, and was dotted with graceful little villas—at a time when in the North there were no "classic spots" and pilgrimages were made only to pictures and relics. It was a point of honor for the different cities to possess the bones of their own and foreign celebrities; and it is most remarkable how seriously the Florentines, even in the fourteenth century—long before the building of Santa Croce—labored to make their cathedral a Pantheon. Accorso, Dante, Petrarch, Boccaccio, and the jurist Zanobi della Strada were to have had magnificent tombs there. Late in the fifteenth century, Lorenzo the Magnificent applied in person to the Spoletans, asking them to give up the corpse of the painter Fra Filippo Lippi for the cathedral, and received the answer that they had none too many ornaments to the city, especially in the shape of distinguished people, for which reason they begged him to spare them; and, in fact, he had to content himself with erecting a cenotaph. And even Dante, in spite of all the applications to which Boccaccio urged the Florentines with bitter emphasis, remained sleeping tranquilly in San Francesco at Ravenna, "among ancient tombs of emperors and vaults of saints, in more honorable company than thou, O Florence, couldst offer him." Even at that time a remarkable man remained unpunished when he took the candles from the altar on which the crucifix stood, and set them by the grave, with the words, "Take them; thou art more worthy of them than He—the Crucified One!"

And now the Italian cities began to remember their ancient citizens and inhabitants. Naples, perhaps, had never forgotten its tomb of Vergil, since a kind of mythical halo had become attached to the name. The Paduans, even in the sixteenth century, firmly believed that they possessed not only the genuine bones of their Trojan founder, Antenor, but also those of the historian Livy. "Sulmona," says Boccaccio, "bewails that Ovid lies buried far away in exile, Parma rejoices that Cassius sleeps within its walls." In the fourteenth century the Mantuans coined a medal with the bust of Vergil, and raised a statue that was supposed to represent him. In a fit of aristocratic insolence, the guardian of the young Gonzaga, Carlo Malatesta, had it pulled down in 1392, and was then forced, when he found the fame of the old poet too strong for him, to set it up again. Even then, perhaps, the grotto two miles from the town, where Vergil was said to have meditated, was shown to strangers, as the Scuola di Virgilio at Naples was. Como claimed both the Plinys for its own, and at the end of the fifteenth century erected in their honor seated statues under graceful baldachins on the façade of the cathedral.

History and the new topography were now careful to leave no local celebrity unnoticed, while the Northern chronicles only here and there, among the list of popes, emperors, earthquakes, and comets, remark, that at such a time this or that famous man "flourished." We shall discuss elsewhere how, mainly under the influence of the idea of fame, an admirable biographical literature was developed. Here we limit ourselves to the local patriotism of the topographers who recorded the claims to distinction of their native cities.

In the Middle Ages, the cities were proud of their saints and of the bones and relics in their churches. With these even the panegyrist of Padua of about 1450, Michele Savonarola, begins his list; but then he passes to "the famous men who were no saints, but who, by their great intellect and force *(virtus)*, deserve to be added *(adnecti)* to the saints" —just as in classical antiquity the distinguished man followed close upon the hero. The further enumeration is most characteristic of the time. First comes Antenor, the brother of Priam, who founded Padua with a band of Trojan fugitives;

King Dardanus, who defeated Attila in the Euganean hills, pursued him and struck him dead at Rimini with a chessboard; Emperor Henry IV, who built the cathedral; a King Marcus, whose head was preserved in Monselice; then a couple of cardinals and prelates as founders of colleges, churches, and so forth; the famous Augustinian theologian, Fra Alberto; a string of philosophers beginning with Paolo Veneto and the celebrated Pietro of Abano; the jurist Paolo Padovano; then Livy and the poets Petrarch, Mussato, Lovato. If there is any want of military celebrities in the list, the poet consoles himself by the abundance of learned men and by the more durable character of intellectual glory, whereas the fame of the soldier is buried with his body, and, if it lasts, owes its permanence only to the scholar. It is nevertheless honorable to the city that foreign warriors lie buried there by their own wish, like Pietro de' Rossi of Parma, Filippo Arcelli of Piacenza, and especially Gattemelata of Narni (d. 1442), whose bronze equestrian statue,[77] "like a triumphant Caesar," already stood by the church of the Santo. The author then names a crowd of jurists and physicians, nobles who had not only, like so many others, "received, but deserved, the honor of knighthood." Then follows a list of famous artisans, painters, and musicians, and closes with the name of a fencing master, Michele Rosso, who, as the most distinguished man in his profession, was to be seen painted in many places.

By the side of these local temples of fame, which myth, legend, popular admiration, and literary tradition combined to create, the poet-scholars built up a pantheon of world-wide celebrity. They made collections of famous men and famous women, often in direct imitation of Cornelius Nepos, Pseudo-Suetonius, Valerius Maximus, Plutarch (Mulierum virtutes), St. Jerome (De viris illustribus), and others. Or they wrote of imaginary triumphal processions and Olympian assemblies, as was done by Petrarch in his Trionfo della fama, and Boccaccio in the Amorosa visione, with hundreds of names, of which three fourths at least belong to antiquity and the rest to the Middle Ages. Step by step this new and comparatively modern element was treated with greater emphasis; the historians began to insert descriptions of character, and collections arose of the biographies of distinguished contemporaries, such as those by Filippo Villani, Vespasiano Fiorentino, Bartolommeo Fazio, and lastly by Paolo Giovio.

The North, until Italian influence began to tell on its

77. [By Donatello.]

writers (e.g., Trithemius), had only legends of the saints, or descriptions of princes and churchmen partaking largely of the character of legends and showing no traces of the idea of fame, that is, of distinction won by a man's personal efforts. Poetic glory was still confined to certain classes of society, and the names of Northern artists are known to us at this period only in so far as they were members of certain guilds or corporations.

The poet-scholar in Italy had, as we have already said, the fullest consciousness that he was the dispenser of fame and immortality, or, if he chose, of oblivion. Boccaccio complains of a fair one to whom he had done homage and who remained hardhearted so that he might go on praising her and thus make her famous, and he hints that he will try the effect of a little faultfinding. Sannazaro, in two magnificent sonnets, threatens Alfonso of Naples with eternal obscurity because of his cowardly flight before Charles VIII. Angelo Politian seriously exhorts (1491) King John of Portugal to consider his immortality with regard to the new discoveries in Africa, and to send the material to him in Florence "to be put into shape" *(operosius excolenda)*, otherwise it might befall him as it had befallen all the others whose deeds, unsupported by the help of the learned, "lie hidden in the vast heap of human frailty." The king (probably his humanistic chancellor) agreed and promised that at least the Portuguese chronicles of African affairs would be translated into Italian, and sent to Florence to be done into Latin. Whether the promise was kept is not known. These pretensions are by no means as groundless as they may at first appear; for the form in which events, even the greatest, are told to the living and to posterity is anything but a matter of indifference. The Italian humanists, with their mode of exposition and their Latin style, long had complete control of the reading world of Europe, and up to the last century even Italian poets were more widely known and studied than those of any other nation. The baptismal name of the Florentine Amerigo Vespucci was given, on account of his book of travels, to a new quarter of the globe, and if Paolo Giovio, with all his superficiality and graceful caprice, promised himself immortality, his expectation has not been altogether disappointed.

Amid all these preparations to win fame, a curtain is drawn aside here and there, and we see frightful evidence of a boundless ambition and thirst after greatness, regardless of all means and consequences. Thus, in the preface to Machiavelli's Florentine history, in which he blames his predecessors (Leonardo Aretino, Poggio) for their too considerate reticence with regard to the political parties in the city: "They erred greatly and showed that they understood little the ambition of men and the desire to perpetuate a name. How many who could distinguish themselves by nothing praiseworthy, strove to do so by infamous deeds! Those writers did not consider that actions that are great in themselves, as is the case with the actions of rulers and of States, always seem to bring more glory than blame, of whatever kind they are and whatever the result may be."[78] In more than one remarkable and dreadful undertaking the motive assigned by serious writers is the burning desire to achieve something great and memorable. Here is revealed not merely an extreme case of ordinary vanity, but something demonic, i.e., a surrender of the will, involving the use of any means, however atrocious, and even an indifference to success itself. It is in this sense, for example, that Machiavelli conceives the character of Stefano Porcari;[79] of the murderers of Galeazzo Maria Sforza, the documents tell us about the same; and the assassination of Duke Alessandro of Florence (1537) is ascribed by Varchi himself to the thirst for fame which tormented the murderer Lorenzino de' Medici. Still more stress is laid on this motive by Paolo Giovio. Lorenzino, according to him, pilloried by a pamphlet of Molza because of the mutilation of some ancient statues at Rome, broods over a deed whose "novelty" would make his disgrace forgotten, and ends by murdering his kinsman and prince. – These are characteristic features of this age of highly excited but already despairing passions and forces, and remind us of the burning of the temple at Ephesus in the time of Philip of Macedon.

The corrective, not only of fame and the modern desire for fame but of all highly developed individuality, is ridicule and scorn, especially when expressed in the victorious form of wit. In the Middle Ages hostile armies, princes, and nobles provoked one another with symbolic insult, or the defeated party was loaded with symbolic outrage. Here and there, under the influence of classical literature, wit began to be used as a weapon in theological disputes, and the

78. Cf. *The Discourses,* Book I, ch. 27. *Tristizia* [crime], can have *grandezza* [magnanimity] and be *in alcuna generosa* [to an extent generous]; *grandezza* can remove *infamia* [infamy] from a deed; man can be *onorevolmente* [honorably criminal] in contrast to *perfattamente buono* [perfectly good].
79. *History of Florence,* Book VI.

poetry of Provence produced a whole class of satirical compositions. Even the *Minnesänger,* as their political poems show, could adopt this tone when necessary.[80] But wit could become an independent element in life only when its appropriate victim, the developed individual with personal pretensions, appeared. Then it was by no means limited to the tongue and the pen, but included tricks and practical jokes—the so-called *burle* [humorous tricks] and *beffe* [nasty tricks]—which form a chief subject of many collections of novels.

The Hundred Old Tales, which must have been composed about the end of the thirteenth century, have as yet neither wit, the fruit of contrast, nor the *burla,* for their subject; their aim is merely to give simple and elegant expression to wise sayings and pretty stories or fables. But if anything proves the old age of the collection, it is precisely this absence of satire. For with the fourteenth century comes Dante who, in the utterance of scorn, leaves all other poets far behind, and who, if only for his great picture of the deceivers,[81] must be called the chief master of colossal comedy. With Petrarch begin the collections of witty sayings after the pattern of Plutarch (*Apophthegmata,* etc.). What stores of wit were concentrated in Florence during this century is most characteristically shown in the novels of Franco Sacchetti. These are, for the most part, not stories but answers given under certain circumstances—shocking pieces of naïveté, with which fools, court jesters, rogues, and profligate women make their retort. The comedy lies in the startling contrast of this real or assumed naïveté to conventional morality and the ordinary relations of the world —everything is topsy-turvy. All means of picturesque representation are used, including the introduction of certain North Italian dialects. Often wit is replaced by mere insolence, clumsy trickery, blasphemy, and obscenity; one or two jokes told of *condottieri* are among the most brutal and malicious that are recorded. Many of the *burle* are thoroughly comic, but many are only real or supposed evidence of personal superiority, of triumph over another. How much people were willing to put up with, how often the victim used a retaliatory trick to bring the laughter back to his side, we

80. The Middle Ages are rich in so-called satirical poems, but the satire is not personal and is aimed at classes, professions, and whole populations, and it easily assumes the didactic tone. The spirit of this literature is best represented by *Reynard the Fox,* in all its forms among the different nations of the West.

81. *Inferno,* xxi, xxii. The only parallel possible is Aristophanes.

do not know; there was much heartless and pointless malice mixed up with it all, and undoubtedly often made life in Florence downright unpleasant. The inventors and retailers of jokes soon became inevitable figures, and among them there must have been some who were classical—far superior to all the mere court jesters, who lacked competition, a changing public, and the quick apprehension of the audience (all advantages of life in Florence). Some Florentine wits toured the despotic courts of Lombardy and Romagna as performers, and found themselves much better rewarded than at home, where their talent was cheap and plentiful. The better type of these people is the amusing man (l'uomo piacevole), the worse is the buffoon and the vulgar parasite who presents himself at weddings and banquets with the argument, "If I haven't been invited, the fault is not mine." Now and then the latter combine to pluck a young spendthrift, but in general they are treated and despised as parasites, whereas wits of higher position bear themselves like princes, and consider their talent as something sovereign. Dolcibene, whom Charles IV had pronounced to be the "king of Italian jesters," said to him at Ferrara: "You will conquer the world, since you are my friend and the Pope's; you fight with the sword, the Pope with his bulls, and I with my tongue." This is no mere jest, but the foreshadowing of Pietro Aretino.

The two most famous jesters about the middle of the fifteenth century were Arlotto, a priest near Florence, for more refined wit (facezie), and Gonnella, the court fool of Ferrara, for buffoonery. We can hardly compare their stories with those of the Parson of Kalenberg and Till Eulenspiegel, since the latter arose in a different and half-mythical manner, as fruits of the imagination of a whole people, and touch rather on what is general and intelligible to all, whereas Arlotto and Gonnella were historical beings, colored and formed by local influences. But if we make the comparison and extend it to the jests of the non-Italian nations, we shall find in general that the joke in the French fabliaux,[82] as among the Germans, is directed chiefly to the attainment of some advantage or enjoyment; whereas the wit of Arlotto and the practical jokes of Gonnella are an end in themselves, and exist simply for the sake of triumph. (Till Eulenspiegel again forms a class by himself, as the personified quiz, mostly pointless enough, of particular classes and professions.) The court fool of the Este retaliated more than once by his keen satire and refined modes of vengeance.

82. And, consequently, in those Italian novels whose subjects are derived from them.

The type of the *uomo piacevole* and the *buffone* long survived the freedom of Florence. Under Duke Cosimo, Barlacchia flourished, and at the beginning of the seventeenth century, Francesco Ruspoli and Curzio Marignolli. In Pope Leo X, the genuine Florentine love of jesters showed itself strikingly. This prince, whose taste for the most refined intellectual pleasures was insatiable, endured and desired at his table a number of witty buffoons and merry-andrews, among them two monks and a cripple; at public feasts he treated them with deliberate scorn as parasites, setting before them monkeys and crows in the place of savory meats. Indeed, Leo showed a peculiar fondness for the *burla;* it was characteristic of his nature sometimes to treat his own favorite pursuits—music and poetry—ironically, parodying them with his factotum, Cardinal Bibbiena. Neither of them found it beneath his dignity to fool an honest old secretary till he thought himself a master of the art of music. The Improvisatore, Baraballo of Gaeta, was brought so far by Leo's flattery that he applied in all seriousness for the poet's coronation on the Capitol. On the feast day of SS. Cosmas and Damian, the patrons of the House of Medici, he was first compelled, adorned with laurel and purple, to amuse the Papal guests with his recitations, and at last, when all were ready to split with laughter, to mount a gold-harnessed elephant in the court of the Vatican, sent as a present to Rome by Emmanuel the Great of Portugal, while the Pope looked down from above through his eyeglass.[83] But the animal, was so terrified by the noise of the trumpets and kettledrums and the cheers of the crowd, there was no getting him over the bridge of Sant' Angelo.

The parody of what is solemn or sublime, which we meet here in the form of a procession, had already taken an important place in poetry.[84] It was, naturally, compelled to

83. The eyeglass I infer not only from the portrait by Raphael [Uffizi Gallery, Florence], where it can be explained as a magnifer for looking at the miniatures in the prayer book, but from a statement of Pellicanus according to which Leo views an advancing procession of monks through a *specillum* [roughly, telescope], and from the *cristallus concava* [concave crystal] which, according to Paolo Giovio, he used when hunting.
84. We find it also in the visual arts, e.g., in the famous print [by Boldrini, after Titian] portraying the *Laocoön* as three monkeys. But here parody seldom went beyond sketches and the like, though much, it is true, may have been destroyed. Caricature is something different; in his grotesque faces, Leonardo represents the hideous when and because it is comical, and in doing so heightens the ludicrous element at will.

choose victims of another kind than those of Aristophanes, who introduced the great tragedians into his plays. But the same maturity of culture that at a certain period produced parody among the Greeks, did the same in Italy. By the close of the fourteenth century, the lovelorn wailings of Petrarch's sonnets and others of the same kind were parodied and the solemn air of this form of verse was ridiculed in lines of mystic twaddle. A constant invitation to parody was offered by the *Divine Comedy*, and Lorenzo the Magnificent wrote the most admirable travesty in the style of the *Inferno* (*Simposio*, or *I Beoni*). Luigi Pulci obviously imitates the *improvisatori* in his *Morgante*, and both his poetry and Boiardo's are in part, at least, a half-conscious parody of the chivalrous poetry of the Middle Ages. Such a caricature was deliberately undertaken by the great parodist Teofilo Folengo (about 1520). Under the name of Limerno Pitocco, he composed the *Orlandino*, in which chivalry appears only as a ludicrous setting for a crowd of modern figures and ideas. Under the name of Merlinus Coccaius he described the journeys and exploits of his fantastic vagabonds (also in the same spirit of parody) in half-Latin hexameters, with all the affected pomp of the learned epos of the day. (*Opus macaronicorum.*) Since then caricature has been constantly, and often brilliantly, represented on the Italian Parnassus.

About the middle period of the Renaissance a theoretical analysis of wit was undertaken, and its practical application in good society was regulated more precisely. The theorist was Gioviano Pontano.[85] In his work on speaking, especially in the fourth book, he tries, by comparing numerous jokes or *facetiae*, to arrive at a general principle. How wit should be used among people of position is taught by Baldassare Castiglione in his *Courtier*.[86] Its chief function is, naturally, to amuse others by relating comic or graceful stories and sayings; personal jokes, on the contrary, are discouraged on the ground that they wound unhappy people, show too much honor to wrongdoers, and make enemies of the powerful and the spoiled children of fortune; and even in relating these stories, a prudent reserve in the use of dramatic gestures is recommended to the gentleman. Then follows, not only for purposes of quotation, but as patterns for future jesters, a large collection of puns and witty sayings, methodically

85. He attributes a special gift of wit, in addition to the Florentines, to the Sienese and Peruginese, and adds the Spanish court out of politeness.
86. Book II.

arranged according to their species, among them many that are first-rate. Some twenty years later Giovanni della Casa, in his guide to good manners, is much stricter and more cautious; with a view to the consequences, he wishes to see the desire of triumph banished altogether from jokes and *burle*. He is the herald of a reaction that had to appear.

In fact, Italy had become a school for scandal, the like of which the world has never seen since, not even in the France of Voltaire. Certainly, he and his confreres did not lack a negative spirit, but where, in the eighteenth century, was to be found the crowd of suitable victims, that countless assembly of highly developed individualists, celebrities of every kind, statesmen, churchmen, inventors and discoverers, men of letters, poets and artists, all of whom gave the fullest and freest play to their individuality? This host existed in the fifteenth and sixteenth centuries, and along with it the general culture of the time had educated a poisonous brood of impotent wits, of born critics and railers, whose envy called for hecatombs of victims; and to all this was added the envy of the famous men toward each other. In this the philologists notoriously led the way—Filelfo, Poggio, Lorenzo Valla, and others—whereas the artists of the fifteenth century lived in peaceful and friendly competition with one another. The history of art may take note of the fact.

Florence, the great market of fame, was in this point, as we have said, in advance of other cities. "Sharp eyes and pointed tongues" is the description given of the inhabitants.[87] An easygoing contempt of everything and everybody was probably the prevailing tone of society. Machiavelli, in the remarkable prologue to his *Mandragola*, charges, rightly or wrongly, the visible decline of moral force to the general habit of evil-speaking, and threatens his detractors that he, too, can say some pretty sharp things. Next comes the Papal court, which had long been a rendezvous of the bitterest and wittiest tongues. Poggio's *facetiae* are dated from the Chamber of Lies (*bugiale*) of the apostolic notaries; and when we remember the number of disappointed office seekers, of

87. Machiavelli, *History of Florence,* Book VII, says of the young gentlemen of Florence shortly after the middle of the fifteenth century: *gli studi loro erano apparire col splendidi, e col parlare sagaci ed astuti, e quello che più destramente mordeva gli altri, era più savio e da più stimato* [their desire was to appear splendid in their apparel and to speak shrewdly and wittily, and whoever could make the most pointed remark was considered the wisest and was the most esteemed].

hopeless competitors and enemies of the favorites, of idle, profligate prelates assembled there, it is no wonder that Rome became the home of the savage pasquinade as well as of more philosophical satire. If we add to this the widespread hatred borne the priests, and the well-known instinct of the mob to charge the most awful horrors to the great, there results an untold mass of infamy. Those who could, protected themselves best by contempt of both the false and the true accusations, and by brilliant and joyous display.[88] More sensitive natures sank into utter despair when they found themselves deeply involved in guilt, and still more deeply in slander. In course of time calumny became universal, and the strictest virtue was the surest way to arouse attacks of malice. Of the great pulpit orator, Fra Egidio of Viterbo, whom Leo elevated to cardinal because of his merit and who showed himself a man of the people and a brave monk in the calamity of 1527, Giovio gives us to understand that he preserved his ascetic pallor by the smoke of wet straw and other means of the same kind. Giovio is a genuine curial in these matters. He generally begins by telling his tale, then adds that he does not believe it, and finally hints that perhaps there may be something in it after all. But the true scapegoat of Roman scorn was the pious and moral Adrian VI. There seems to have been a general agreement to treat him only as a comic figure. He was ruined from the start by the formidable pen of Francesco Berni for threatening to throw into the Tiber not, as has been said, the statue of Pasquino, but the writers of the satires themselves. The vengeance for this was the famous *capitolo* "Against Pope Adrian," inspired not exactly by hatred but by contempt for the comical Dutch barbarian; the savage attacks were reserved for the cardinals who had elected him. Berni and others sketch the environment of the Pope with the same sparkling untruthfulness with which the modern *feuilletoniste* turns black into white, and everything into anything. The biography which Paolo Giovio was commissioned to write by the Cardinal of Tortosa, and which was to have been a eulogy, is, for anyone who can read between the lines, a paragon of satire. It is very funny (at least it was for the Italians of that time) to read how Adrian applied to the Chapter of Saragossa for the jawbone of St. Lambert; how the devout Spaniards decked him out till he looked "like a

88. This was the practice of Leo X, and he calculated correctly. Fearfully as his reputation was mangled after his death by the satirists, they were unable to modify the general estimate of him.

right well-dressed Pope"; how he came in a confused and tasteless procession from Ostia to Rome, took counsel about burning or drowning Pasquino, would suddenly break off the most important business when dinner was announced, and finally, how at the end of an unhappy reign, he died of drinking too much beer—whereupon the house of his physician was hung with garlands by midnight revelers, and decorated with the inscription, *Liberatori Patriae S.P.Q.R.* It is true that Giovio had lost his money in the general confiscation of public funds, and had received a benefice by way of compensation only because he was "no poet," i.e., no pagan. But it was decreed that Adrian should be the last great victim. After the disaster that befell Rome in 1527, slander visibly declined along with the unrestrained wickedness of private life.

But while it was still flourishing there developed, chiefly in Rome, the greatest scandalmonger of modern times, Pietro Aretino. A glance at his life and character spares us the trouble of noticing many inferior members of his breed.

We know him chiefly in the last thirty years of his life (1527-1556), which he passed in Venice, the only asylum possible for him. From here he kept all who were famous in Italy in a kind of state of siege, and here were delivered to him the presents of the foreign princes who needed or dreaded his pen. Charles V and Francis I both pensioned him at the same time, each hoping that Aretino would harm the other. Aretino flattered both, but naturally attached himself more closely to Charles, because he remained master in Italy. After the Emperor's victory at Tunis in 1535, this adulation passed into the most ludicrous worship, in observing which it must not be forgotten that Aretino constantly cherished the hope that Charles would help him to a cardinal's hat. It is probable that he enjoyed special protection as a Spanish agent, since his speech or silence could have an effect on the smaller Italian courts and on public opinion in Italy. He affected utterly to despise the Papal court because he knew it so well; the true reason was that Rome neither could nor would pay him any longer. Venice, which sheltered him, he was wise enough to leave unassailed. The rest of his relations with the great is mere beggary and vulgar extortion.

Aretino affords the first great instance of the abuse of publicity to such ends. The polemical writings which a hundred years earlier Poggio and his opponents exchanged, are just as infamous in their tone and purpose, but they were not composed for the press, but for a sort of private circulation. Aretino made all his profit out of a complete publicity, and in a certain sense he may be considered the father of modern journalism. He had collections of his letters and miscellaneous articles printed periodically, after they had already been circulated among a fairly extensive public.[89]

Compared with the sharp pens of the eighteenth century, Aretino had the advantage that he was not burdened with principles, neither with liberalism nor philanthropy nor any other virtue, nor even with science; his whole baggage consisted of the well-known motto, *Veritas odium parit* [Truth produces hatred]. Consequently, he never found himself in the false position of Voltaire, for example, who was forced to disown his *Pucelle* and conceal all his life the authorship of other works. Aretino put his name to all he wrote, and all his life openly gloried in his notorious *Ragionamenti*. His literary talent, his clear sparkling style, his varied observation of men and things, would have made him worthy of notice under any circumstances, even though he was devoid of the power of conceiving a genuine work of art, such as a true dramatic comedy; and to the coarsest as well as the most refined malice he added a grotesque wit so brilliant that in some cases it does not fall short of that of Rabelais.

In such circumstances, with such aims and means, did he attack or circumvent his prey. The tone in which he appealed to Clement VII not to complain but to forgive, just when the wailings of the devastated city were ascending to the Castel Sant' Angelo, where the Pope himself was a prisoner, is the mockery of a devil or a monkey. Sometimes, when he is forced to give up all hope of presents, his fury breaks out into a savage howl, as in the *capitolo* to the Prince of Salerno who, after paying him for some time, refused to do so any longer. On the other hand, it seems that the terrible Pierluigi Farnese, Duke of Parma, never took any notice of him at all. As this gentleman had probably renounced all claim to a good reputation, it was not easy to harm him; Aretino tried, by comparing his personal appearance to that of a constable, a miller, and a baker. Aretino is most comical in the expression of whining mendicancy, e.g., in the *capitolo* to Francis I; but the letters and poems made up of menaces and flattery cannot, notwithstanding all that is ludicrous in them, be read without the deepest disgust. A letter such as the one

---

89. The fear he created among artists in particular by this means will be described elsewhere. – The propaganda weapon of the German Reformation was essentially the pamphlet that dealt with specific events; Aretino, however, was a journalist in the sense that with him the occasion for publicity was self-created.

written to Michelangelo in November 1545, is unique; along with all the admiration he expresses (for the *Last Judgement*) he charges Michangelo with irreligion, indecency, and theft (from the heirs of Julius II), and adds in a conciliating postscript, "I only want to show you that if you are *divino* (*di-vino*), I am not *d'acqua*." Aretino laid great stress upon it—whether from the insanity of conceit or by way of caricaturing famous men—that he, too, should be called divine, and he certainly attained so much personal celebrity that his house at Arezzo passed for one of the sights of the city. Indeed, there were whole months during which he never ventured to cross his threshold at Venice, lest he should fall into the hands of some incensed Florentine, e.g., the younger Strozzi. Nor did he escape the cudgels and the daggers of his enemies, although they failed to have the effect that Berni prophesied in a famous sonnet. Aretino died in his house, of apoplexy.

The variations in his modes of flattery are remarkable: with non-Italians he was grossly fulsome; people like Duke Cosimo of Florence he treated very differently. He praised the beauty of the then youthful prince, who in fact did share this quality with Augustus to an extraordinary degree; he praised his moral conduct, with an oblique reference to the financial pursuits of Cosimo's mother, Maria Salviati, and concluded with a mendicant whine about the bad times, etc. When Cosimo pensioned him, which he did liberally, considering his habitual parsimony—to the extent, toward the end, of 160 ducats a year—he doubtless had an eye to Aretino's dangerous character as a Spanish agent. Aretino could ridicule and revile Cosimo, and in the same breath threaten the Florentine agent that he would obtain from the Duke his immediate recall; and if the Medicean prince felt that Charles V had at last seen through him, he would naturally not be anxious that Aretino's jokes and rhymes against him should circulate at the Imperial court. A curiously qualified piece of flattery is that addressed to the notorious Marquis of Marignano who, as Castellan of Musso, had attempted to found an independent State. Thanking him for the gift of a hundred scudi, Aretino writes: "All the qualities that a prince should have are present in you, and all men would think so, were it not that the acts of violence inevitable at the beginning of all undertakings cause you to appear a trifle rough (*aspro*)."

It has often been noticed as something singular that Aretino only reviled the world, and not God. The religious belief of a man who lived as he did is a matter of perfect indifference, as are also the edifying writings which he composed for the sake of appearances.[90] It is in fact hard to say why he should have been a blasphemer. He was neither professor nor theoretical thinker nor writer; he could extort no money from God by threats or flattery, and was consequently never goaded into blasphemy by a refusal. A man like Aretino does not take trouble for nothing.

It is a good sign for the present spirit of Italy that such a character and such a career have become impossible. But for historical criticism Aretino will always occupy an important place.

90. He may have done so either with the hope of obtaining the red hat, or from fear of the new activity of the Inquisition, which he had dared to attack bitterly in 1535, but which, after the reorganization of that institution in 1542, suddenly rose again and silenced every opposing voice.

———◆———

PART THREE

THE REVIVAL OF ANTIQUITY

Now that this point in our historical view of Italian civilization has been reached, it is time to speak of the influence of antiquity, the "rebirth" of which has been unilaterally chosen as the name to sum up the whole period. The conditions that have been described up till now would have sufficed, apart from antiquity, to shake and mature the national mind; and most of the intellectual tendencies that still remain to be noted would be conceivable without it. But as what has gone before, so that which we have still to discuss is colored in many ways by the influence of the ancient world; and though the essence of the phenomena might still have been the same without the classical revival, it is only with and through this revival that it is actually manifested to us. The Renaissance would not have been the process of world-wide significance that it is, were its elements to be so easily separated from one another. We must insist, as one of the chief propositions of this book, that it was not the revival of antiquity alone, but its union with the genius of the Italian people, that achieved the conquest of the Western world. The amount of independence that the national spirit maintained in this union varies; in the modern Latin literature of the period, it is very small, whereas in the visual arts, as well as in other spheres, it is remarkably great; and hence, the alliance between two distant epochs in the civilization of the same people, because it was concluded with the greatest independence, proved justifiable and fruitful. The rest of Europe was free either to repel or to accept partly or wholly the mighty impulse that came from Italy. Where the latter was the case we may as well be spared the complaints over the early decay of medieval faith and civilization. Had these been strong enough to hold their ground, they would be alive to this day. If those elegiac natures which long to see them return had to spend but one hour in their midst, they would gasp to be back in modern air. That in a great historical process of this kind, flowers of exquisite beauty may perish without being made immortal in poetry or tradition, is undoubtedly true; nevertheless, we cannot wish the process undone. The process consists in this—that by the side of the Church, which had until then held the countries of the West together (though it was unable to do so much longer), there arose a new spiritual influence which, spreading out from Italy, became the breath of life for all the more instructed minds in Europe. The worst that can be said of the movement is that it was antipopular, that through it Europe became for the first time sharply divided into educated and noneducated classes. This reproach becomes groundless, however, as soon as we realize that even now the fact, though clearly recognized, cannot be altered. And this separation is by no means so cruel and absolute in Italy as elsewhere. The most artistic of her poets, Tasso, is in the hands of even the poorest.

The civilization of Greece and Rome, which, from the fourteenth century, obtained so powerful a hold on Italian life as the source and basis of culture, as the object and ideal of existence, partly also as an avowed reaction against preceding tendencies—this civilization had long been exerting an occasional influence on medieval Europe, even beyond the boundaries of Italy. The culture that Charlemagne advocated was, in face of the barbarism of the seventh and eighth centuries, essentially a renaissance, and could not be anything else. Just as in the Romanesque architecture of the North, beside the general outlines inherited from antiquity, remarkable direct imitations of the antique also occur, so, too, monastic scholarship had not only gradually absorbed an immense mass of subject matter from Roman writers, but the style, from the time of Einhard, is not without imitation.

But in Italy the revival of antiquity took a different form from that which it assumed in the North. The wave of barbarism had scarcely subsided before the people, in whom the antique heritage was not completely effaced, showed a consciousness of their past and a wish to reproduce it. Outside Italy there was a deliberate and conscious borrowing of this or that element of classical civilization; in Italy the sympathies both of the learned and of the people were directed toward antiquity as a whole, which stood to them as a symbol of past greatness. The Latin language was easy to an Italian, and the numerous monuments and documents in which the country abounded facilitated a return to the past. With this tendency other elements—the popular character which time had now greatly modified, the Germanic political institutions of the Lombards, chivalry and other Northern forms of civilization, and the influence of religion and the Church—combined to produce the modern Italian spirit, which was destined to serve as the model and ideal for the whole Western world.

How antiquity made itself felt in the visual arts, as soon as the flood of barbarism had abated, is clearly shown in the Tuscan buildings of the twelfth century and in the sculptures of the thirteenth. In poetry, too, there is no want of similar analogies to those who hold that the greatest Latin poet of the twelfth century, the writer who struck the keynote of a whole class of Latin poems, was an Italian. We mean the author of the best pieces in the so-called *Carmina Burana*. A frank enjoyment of life and its pleasures, as whose patrons the gods of heathendom are invoked, flows in full current through the rhymed verses. Reading them through at a stretch, we can scarcely help coming to the conclusion that an Italian, probably a Lombard, is speaking; in fact, there are positive grounds for thinking so.[91] To a certain degree these Latin poems of the *clerici vagantes* [wandering scholars] of the twelfth century, with all their remarkable frivolity, are doubtless a product in which the whole of Europe had a share; but the writer of the song *De Phyllide et Flora* and the *Aestuans interius*, etc. [Boiling in my spirit's veins] can have been a Northerner as little as the polished Epicurean observer to whom we owe *Dum Dianae vitrea sero lampas oritur* [When Diana lighteth late her crystal lamp]. Here, in truth, is a renaissance of the ancient view of life, which is all the more striking in the medieval form of verse in which it is set. There are many works of this and the following centuries in which a careful imitation of the antique appears both in the hexameter and pentameter of the meter and in the classical, often mythological, character of the subject, and which still do not have anything like the same spirit of antiquity about

91. The stay in Pavia, the local references to Italy generally, the scene with the *pastorella* [shepherdess] under the olive tree, the mention of the *pinus* [pine] as a shady tree in the open country, the frequent use of the word *bravium*, but especially the form *madii* for *maji* all seem to justify our view. – That the poet calls himself Walther gives us no clue to his origin. He has generally been identified as Walter Map, a canon of Salisbury and chaplain to the English kings toward the end of the twelfth century. Recently he has been thought to be identical with Walter of Lille or Walter of Châtillon.

them. In the hexametric chronicles and other works of William of Apulia and his successors we find frequent traces of a diligent study of Vergil, Ovid, Lucan, Statius, and Claudian; but this classical form is merely a matter of erudition as is the classical matter in compilers like Vincent of Beauvais, or in the mythological and allegorical writer, Alanus ab Insulis. The Renaissance, however, is not a fragmentary imitation or compilation, but a new birth; and the signs of this are visible in the poems of the unknown *clericus* of the twelfth century.

But the great and general enthusiasm of the Italians for classical antiquity really begins in the fourteenth century. For this a development of civic life was required, which took place only in Italy, and there not till then: that noble and burgher live together on equal terms, that a society arise which felt the need for culture, and had the leisure and the means to obtain it. But culture, as soon as it freed itself from the reverie of the Middle Ages, could not at once and without help find its way to understanding the physical and intellectual world. It needed a guide, and found one in the ancient civilization, with its wealth of truth and knowledge in every spiritual interest. Both the form and the substance of this civilization were adopted with admiring gratitude; it became the chief part of the culture of the age. The general condition of the country was favorable to this transformation. The medieval empire, since the fall of the Hohenstaufen, had either renounced or was unable to make good its claims on Italy. The Popes had migrated to Avignon. Most of the political powers actually in existence owed their origin to violent and illegitimate means. The spirit of the people, now awakened to self-consciousness, sought for some new and stable ideal, and thus the vision of the world-wide empire of Italy and Rome so possessed the popular mind that Cola di Rienzi could actually attempt to put it into practice. The conception he formed of his task, particularly when tribune for the first time, could only end in some extravagant comedy; nevertheless, the memory of ancient Rome was no slight support to the national sentiment. Armed afresh with its culture, the Italian soon felt himself in truth citizen of the most advanced nation in the world.

It is now our task to sketch this spiritual movement, not in all its fullness but only in its most salient features, and especially in its first beginnings.[92]

---

92. For particulars we recommend Roscoe: *The Life of Lorenzo*

Rome itself, the city of ruins,[93] now became the object of a wholly different sort of piety from that of the time when the *Mirabilia urbis Romae* [*The Marvels of Rome*] and the collection of William of Malmesbury were composed. The imagination of the devout pilgrim, or of the seeker after marvels and treasures,[94] is supplanted in contemporary records by the interests of the patriot and the historian. It is in this sense that Dante's words must be understood: that the stones of the walls of Rome deserve reverence, and that the ground on which the city is built is more worthy than men say.[95] The jubilees, incessant as they were, have scarcely left a single devout record in what we would call literature. The best thing that Giovanni Villani brought back from the jubilee of the year 1300 was the resolution to write his history, which had been awakened in him by the sight of the ruins of Rome. Petrarch gives evidence of a taste divided between classical and Christian antiquity. He tells us how he and Giovanni Colonna often ascended the gigantic vaults of the Baths of Diocletian, and there in the transparent air, in the deep silence, with the broad panorama stretching far around them, they spoke not of business or political affairs but of the history that the ruins beneath their feet suggested, Petrarch appearing in these dialogues as the partisan of classical, Giovanni of Christian, antiquity; they would discourse, too,

---

de' Medici and *The Life and Pontificate of Leo the Tenth*. – To form a conception of the extent that studies at the beginning of the sixteenth century had reached, we cannot do better than to turn to the *Commentarii urbani* of Raphael Volaterranus. Here we see how antiquity formed the introduction to and the chief matter of study in every branch of knowledge, from geography and local history, the lives of great and famous men, popular philosophy, morals, and the special sciences, to the analysis of the whole of Aristotle, with which the work closes. To understand its significance as an authority for the history of culture, we must compare it with all the earlier encyclopedias.

93. ‖This subject, which is mentioned here only in passing, has since been treated at length in Gregorovius' *History of the City of Rome in the Middle Ages*, to which we refer the reader.‖

94. ‖In William of Malmesbury, *The History of the Kings of England*, Book II, chs. 10, 13, we find various fantasies of treasure hunters, then Venus as ghostly love, and, finally, the discovery of the gigantic body of Pallas, the son of Evander, about the middle of the eleventh century. – Besides his tales of treasure hunters, William also quotes the elegy of Hildebert of Mans, Bishop of Tours, which is one of the most singular examples of humanistic enthusiasm for the first half of the twelfth century.‖

95. *Convivio*, Book IV, ch. 5.

of philosophy and of the inventors of the arts. How often since that time, down to the days of Gibbon and Niebuhr, have the same ruins stirred men's minds to historical reflection!

This double current of feeling can also be recognized in the *Dittamondo* of Fazio degli Uberti, composed about the year 1360—a description of visionary travels, in which the author is accompanied by the old geographer Solinus, as Dante was by Vergil. Just as they visit Bari in memory of St. Nicholas and Monte Gargano in devotion to the archangel Michael, in Rome the legends of Aracoeli and of Santa Maria in Trastevere are mentioned. Still, the pagan splendor of ancient Rome unmistakably exercises the greatest charm upon them. A venerable matron in torn garments—Rome herself—tells them of the glorious past, and gives them a minute description of the old triumphs; she then leads the strangers through the city, and points out to them the seven hills and many of the ruins—*che comprender potrai, quanto fui bella* [so you may understand how beautiful I used to be]!

Unfortunately this Rome of the schismatic and Avignonese popes was no longer, in respect to classical remains, what it had been some generations earlier. The destruction of 140 fortified houses of Roman nobles by the senator Brancaleone about 1258 must have wholly altered the character of the most important buildings then standing: for the nobles had no doubt ensconced themselves in the loftiest and best-preserved ruins.[96] Nevertheless, far more was left than we find now, and probably many of the remains still had their marble facings, their columns, and other ornaments where we now see nothing but the brickwork skeleton. In this state of things was begun a serious topography of the old city. In Poggio's walks through Rome the study of the remains themselves was for the first time more intimately combined with the study of ancient authors and inscriptions (which he sought out from among the vegetation in which they were imbedded)—his imagination severely restrained and memories of Christian Rome carefully excluded. If only Poggio's work were fuller, and illustrated! Far more was left in his time than was found by Raphael eighty years later. Poggio saw the tomb of Caecilia Metella and the columns in front of one of the

---

96. Parenthetically we may mention foreign evidence that in the Middle Ages Rome was looked upon as a quarry: the famous Suger who (about 1140) was seeking lofty pillars for the rebuilding of Saint-Denis thought of nothing less than the granite monoliths of the Baths of Diocletian, but later changed his mind. – Charlemagne undoubtedly proceeded with greater diffidence.

temples on the slope of the Capitol, first in full preservation, and then partially destroyed, owing to that unfortunate quality which marble possesses of being easily burned into lime. A vast colonnade near the Minerva gradually fell victim to the same fate. A witness in the year 1443 tells us that this manufacture of lime still went on, "which is a shame, for the new buildings are pitiful, and the beauty of Rome is in its ruins." The inhabitants of that day, in their peasants' cloaks and boots, looked to foreigners like cowherds; and in fact the cattle were pastured in the city up to the Banchi. The only social gatherings were the services at church, on which occasions it was possible to get a look at the beautiful women.

In the last years of Eugenius IV (d. 1447) Flavio Biondo wrote his *Roma instaurata*, making use of Frontinus and of the old regional chronicles, as well as, it seems, of Anastasius. Far from confining himself to what still existed, he seeks to discover what had been lost. In accordance with the dedication to the Pope, he consoles himself for the general ruin by the thought of the precious relics of the saints in which Rome was so rich.

With Nicholas V (1447-1455) that new monumental spirit which was distinctive of the age of the Renaissance appeared on the Papal throne. The new passion for and embellishment of the city brought with it on the one hand a danger for the ruins, on the other a respect for them, as forming one of Rome's claims to distinction. Pius II was wholly possessed by antiquarian enthusiasm, and if he speaks little of the antiquities of Rome, he studied closely those of all other parts of Italy and was the first to know and describe accurately the remains in the districts for miles around the capital. It is true that as priest and cosmographer he was interested alike in classical and Christian monuments and in the marvels of nature. Or was he constraining himself when he wrote that Nola was more highly honored by the memory of St. Paulinus than by all its classical reminiscences and the heroic struggle of Marcellus? Not, indeed, that his faith in relics was assumed; but his mind was evidently more disposed to an inquiring interest in nature and antiquity, to a zeal for monumental works, to a keen and delicate observation of human life. In the last years of his Papacy, afflicted with the gout but in the most cheerful mood, he was borne in his litter over hill and dale to Tusculum, Alba, Tivoli, Ostia, Falerii, and Ocriculum, and whatever he saw he noted down. He followed the Roman roads and aqueducts, and tried to fix the boundaries of the old tribes that had dwelt round the city. On an excursion to Tivoli with the great Federigo of Urbino the time was spent happily in talk of the ancients and their military system, and particularly of the Trojan war. Even on his journey to the Congress of Mantua (1459) he searched, though unsuccessfully, for the labyrinth of Clusium mentioned by Pliny, and visited the so-called villa of Vergil on the Mincio. That such a Pope should demand a classical Latin style from his abbreviators, is no more than might be expected. It was he who, in the war with Naples, granted an amnesty to the men of Arpinum, as countrymen of Cicero and Marius, after whom many of them were named. It was only to him, as both judge and patron, that Biondo could dedicate his *Roma triumphans*, the first great attempt at a complete exposition of Roman antiquity.

Nor was the enthusiasm for the classical past of Italy confined at this period to the capital. Boccaccio had already called the vast ruins of Baiae "old walls, yet new for modern spirits," and from that time they were held to be the most interesting sight near Naples. Collections of antiquities of all sorts now became common. Cyriacus of Ancona traveled not only through Italy, but through other countries of the old *orbis terrarum*, and brought back countless inscriptions and sketches. When asked why he took all this trouble, he replied, "To wake the dead."[97] The histories of the various cities of Italy had from the earliest times laid claim to some true or imagined connection with Rome, had alleged some settlement or colonization which started from the capital; and obliging manufacturers of pedigrees seem constantly to have derived various families from the most famous blood of Rome. So highly was this distinction valued, that men clung to it even in the light of the dawning criticism of the fifteenth century. When Pius II was at Viterbo[98] he said frankly to the Roman deputies who begged his speedy return, "Rome is as much my home as Siena, for my House, the Piccolomini, came in early times from the capital to Siena, as is proved by the constant use of the names Aeneas and Sylvius in my family." He would probably have had no objection to being held a descendant of the Julii. Even Paul II, a Barbo of Venice, found his vanity flattered by deducing his House, notwithstanding an adverse pedigree according to which it came from Germany, from the Roman Ahenobarbus, who had led a

97. ||According to Leonardo Aretino, Cyriacus traveled through Aetolia, Acarnania, Boeotia, and the Peloponnesos, and knew Sparta, Argos, and Athens.||
98. *The Commentaries of Pius II*, Book IV.

colony to Parma and whose successors had been forced by party conflicts to migrate to Venice. That the Massimi claimed descent from Q. Fabius Maximus, and the Cornaro from the Cornelii, cannot surprise us. On the other hand, it is a strikingly exceptional fact for the sixteenth century that the novelist Bandello tried to connect his blood with a noble family of Ostrogoths.

To return to Rome. The inhabitants, "who then called themselves Romans," accepted greedily the homage that was offered them by the rest of Italy. Under Paul II, Sixtus IV, and Alexander VI magnificent processions formed part of the Carnival, representing the scene most attractive to the imagination of the time—the triumph of the Roman Imperator. The sentiment of the people expressed itself naturally in this form. In this mood of public feeling, a report arose on April 18, 1485, that the corpse of a young Roman lady of the classical period—wonderfully beautiful and in perfect preservation—had been discovered. Some Lombard masons digging out an ancient tomb on an estate of the convent of Santa Maria Nuova, on the Appian Way, beyond the tomb of Caecilia Metella, found a marble sarcophagus with the inscription, "Julia, daughter of Claudius." On this basis the following story was built. The Lombards disappeared immediately with the jewels and treasure that were found with the corpse in the sarcophagus. The body had been coated with an antiseptic essence, and was as fresh and flexible as that of a girl of fifteen the hour after death. It was said that she still retained the colors of life, with eyes and mouth half open. She was taken to the Palazzo dei Conservatori on the Capitol; and then began a veritable pilgrimage to see her. Many came to paint her, "for she was more beautiful than can be said or written, and, were it said or written, it would not be believed by those who had not seen her." But by order of Innocent VIII she was secretly buried one night outside the Pincian Gate, and only the empty sarcophagus remained in the court of the Conservatori. Probably a colored mask of wax or some other material had been modeled in the classical style on the head and face of the corpse, with which the gilded hair of which we read would harmonize admirably. The touching point in the story is not the fact itself, but the firm belief that an ancient body, which was now thought to be at last really before men's eyes, must be far more beautiful than anything of their own time.

Meanwhile the material knowledge of old Rome was increased by excavations. Under Alexander VI the so-called "grotesques," that is, the mural decorations of the ancients,

were discovered, and the *Apollo Belvedere* was found at
Porto d'Anzio. Under Julius II followed the memorable
discoveries of the *Laocoön,* of the *Vatican Venus,* of the
Belvedere Torso, of the *Cleopatra* [*Sleeping Ariadne*];[99] even
the palaces of the nobles and the cardinals began to be filled
with ancient statues and fragments. Raphael undertook for
Leo X that ideal restoration of the whole ancient city which
his (or Castiglione's) celebrated letter discusses. After a
bitter complaint over the devastations which had not even
then ceased, and which had been particularly frequent under
Julius II, he beseeches the Pope to protect the few relics
that were left to testify to the power and greatness of that
divine soul of antiquity whose memory was inspiration to all
who were capable of higher things. He then goes on to set
down with penetrating judgment the foundations of a comparative history of art, and concludes with the definition of
an architectural survey, which has been accepted since his
time: he requires a separate ground plan, section, and elevation of every building that remained. How archaeology devoted
itself from that time to the study of the venerated city and
grew into a special science, and how the Vitruvian Academy
at least proposed to itself great aims, cannot be related here.
Let us rather pause at the days of Leo X, under whom the
enjoyment of antiquity combined with all other pleasures to
give to Roman life a unique stamp and consecration. The
Vatican resounded with song and music, and their echoes
were heard through the city as a call to joy and gladness,
though Leo did not succeed thereby in banishing care and
pain from his own life, and his deliberate calculation to
prolong his days by cheerfulness was frustrated by an early
death. The Rome of Leo, as described by Paolo Giovio, forms
a picture too splendid to turn away from, unmistakable as
are also its darker aspects—the slavery of those who were
struggling to rise; the secret misery of the prelates, who,
notwithstanding heavy debts, were forced to live in a style
befitting their rank; Leo's system of literary patronage,
which drove men to be parasites or adventurers; and, lastly,
his scandalous maladministration of the finances. Yet the
same Ariosto who knew and ridiculed all this so well, gives
in the sixth satire a longing picture of his expected intercourse with the accomplished poets who would conduct him
through the city of ruins, of the learned counsel he would
find there for his own literary efforts, and of the treasures

99. As early as Julius II excavations were made with the purpose
of finding statues. Cf. Vasari, Life of Giovanni da Udine.

of the Vatican library. These, he says, and not the long-abandoned hope of Medicean protection, were the baits that really attracted him, if he were again asked to go as Ferrarese ambassador to Rome.

The ruins in and outside Rome awakened not only archaeological zeal and patriotic enthusiasm, but an elegiac, sentimental melancholy. In Petrarch and Boccaccio we find touches of this feeling. Poggio often visited the temple of Venus and Roma, in the belief that it was that of Castor and Pollux, where once the senate had met so often, and would lose himself in memories of the great orators Crassus, Hortensius, Cicero. The language of Pius II, especially in describing Tivoli,[100] has a thoroughly sentimental ring, and soon afterward appeared the first pictures of ruins, with a commentary by Polifilo:[101] ruins of mighty arches and colonnades, half hidden in plane trees, laurels, cypresses, and brushwood figure in his pages. In the sacred legends it became the custom, we can hardly say how, to lay the scene of the birth of Christ in the ruins of a magnificent palace.[102] That artificial ruins later became a necessity of landscape gardening is only a practical consequence of this feeling.

But the literary bequests of antiquity, Greek as well as Latin, were far more important than the architectural, indeed, more important than all the artistic remains it had left. They were held in the most absolute sense to be the wellsprings of all knowledge. The literary conditions of that age of great discoveries have often been set forth; no more can be attempted here than to point out a few less-known features.

Great as the influence of the ancient writers was on the Italian mind of the fourteenth century and before, that influence was due more to the wide diffusion of what had long been known than to the discovery of that which was new. The most popular Latin poets, historians, orators, and letter writers, together with a number of Latin translations of single works of Aristotle, Plutarch, and a few other Greek authors, constituted the treasure from which the generation of Petrarch and Boccaccio drew their inspiration. Petrarch, as is well known, owned and kept with religious care a Greek Homer, which he was unable to read; the first Latin translation of the *Iliad* and *Odyssey*, though a very bad one, was made by Boccaccio with what help he could get from a Calabrian

100. *The Commentaries of Pius II*, Book V.
101. [Francesco Colonna, *Hypnerotomachia Poliphili*, printed in 1499 at Venice by Aldus Manutius.]
102. Whereas all the Fathers of the Church and all the pilgrims speak only of a cave. The poets, too, do without the palace.

Greek. It is in the fifteenth century that there begins the long list of new discoveries, the systematic creation of libraries by means of copies, and the rapid multiplication of translations from the Greek.[103]

Had it not been for the enthusiasm of a few collectors of that age, who shrank from no effort or privation, we should certainly possess only a small part of the literature, especially that of the Greeks, which has come down to us. Pope Nicholas V, when only a simple monk, ran into debt through buying manuscripts or having them copied. Even then he made no secret of his passion for the two great interests of the Renaissance, books and buildings. As Pope he kept his word. Copyists wrote and spies searched for him through half the world. Perotto received 500 ducats for the Latin translation of Polybius; Guarino was paid 1,000 gold florins for his translation of Strabo, and would have received 500 more but for the death of the Pope. Nicholas left a collection of 5,000 or, according to another way of calculating, 9,000 volumes, for the use of the members of the Curia, which became the foundation of the Vatican Library. It was to be preserved in the palace itself, as its noblest ornament, like the library of Ptolemy Philadelphus at Alexandria. When the plague drove him and his court to Fabriano, he took his translators and compilers with him to protect them from death.

The Florentine Niccolò Niccoli, a member of the accomplished circle of friends that surrounded the elder Cosimo de' Medici, spent his whole fortune in buying books. At last, when his money was all gone, the Medici put their purse at his disposal for any sum this purpose might require. We owe to him the completion of Ammianus Marcellinus, the *De oratore* of Cicero, and other works; he persuaded Cosimo to buy the best manuscript of Pliny from a monastery at Lübeck. With noble confidence he lent his books, allowed all comers to study them in his own house, and was ready to converse with them on what they had read. His collection of 800 volumes, valued at 6,000 gold florins, passed after his death, through Cosimo's intervention, to the monastery of San Marco, on the condition that it should be accessible to the public.

Of the two great book-finders, Guarino and Poggio, the latter, on the occasion of the Council of Constance and acting partly as Niccoli's agent, searched industriously among the abbeys of South Germany. There he discovered six orations of Cicero, and the first complete Quintilian, the St. Gall

103. Forgeries, by which the passion for antiquity was turned to profit or amusement, were not, as we know, uncommon.

manuscript that is now at Zurich; he is said to have copied the whole of it in thirty-two days in a beautiful handwriting. He was able to make important additions to Silius Italicus, Manilius, Lucretius, Valerius Flaccus, Asconius Pedianus, Columella, Celsus, Aulus Gellius, Statius, and others; and with the help of Leonardo Aretino he unearthed the last twelve comedies of Plautus, as well as Cicero's Verrine orations.

The famous Greek, Cardinal Bessarion, spurred on by a patriotic zeal for the antique, collected, at a great sacrifice, 600 manuscripts of pagan and Christian authors. He then looked round for some place where they could lie safely until his unhappy country, if she ever regained her freedom, could reclaim her lost literature. The Venetian government declared itself ready to erect a suitable building, and to this day the Library of San Marco retains a part of these treasures.

The formation of the celebrated Medicean library has a history of its own, into which we cannot enter here. The chief collector for Lorenzo the Magnificent was Johannes Lascaris. It is well known that the collection, after the plundering in the year 1494, had to be recovered piecemeal by Cardinal Giovanni de' Medici (Leo X).

The library of Urbino (now in the Vatican) was entirely the work of the great Federigo da Montefeltro. As a boy he had begun to collect; later he kept thirty or forty *scrittori* employed in various places, and in the course of time spent more than 30,000 ducats on the collection. It was systematically extended and completed, chiefly with the help of Vespasiano and his account of it forms an ideal picture of a library of the Renaissance. At Urbino there were catalogues of the libraries of the Vatican, of San Marco at Florence, of the Visconti at Pavia, and even of the library at Oxford. It was noted with pride that none could rival Urbino in the completeness of works of individual authors. Theology and the Middle Ages were perhaps most fully represented. There was a complete Thomas Aquinas, a complete Albertus Magnus, a complete Bonaventura, etc. The collection, however, was a many-sided one, and included, for example, every work on medicine which was then to be had. Among the "moderns," the great writers of the fourteenth century—Dante and Boccaccio, with their complete works—occupied first place. Then followed twenty-five select humanists, invariably with both their Latin and Italian writings and with all their translations. Among the Greek manuscripts the Fathers of the Church far outnumbered the rest; yet in the list of the classics we find all the works of Sophocles, all of Pindar, and all of

Menander. This last codex must have disappeared early[104] from Urbino, otherwise, the philologists would soon have edited it.

We have, further, certain accounts from which we know the way in which manuscripts and libraries were multiplied. The purchase of an ancient manuscript that contained a rare, or the only complete, or the only existing text of an old writer was naturally a lucky accident that could not be counted on. Among the professional copyists those who understood Greek took the highest place, and it was they who bore the honorable name of *scrittori* [writers]. Their number was always limited, and the pay they received very large.[105] The rest, simply called *copisti*, were partly clerks who made their living by such work, partly scholars who needed an addition to their income. Strangely, the copyists at Rome in the time of Nicholas V were mostly Germans or Frenchmen, probably men who were seeking favors at the Papal court, who kept themselves alive by this means. When, for example, Cosimo de' Medici was in a hurry to form a library for his favorite foundation, the Badia below Fiesole, he sent for Vespasiano, and received from him the advice to give up all thoughts of purchasing books, since those that were worth getting could not be had easily, but to use copyists, whereupon Cosimo bargained to pay him so much a day, and Vespasiano, with forty-five writers under him, delivered 200 volumes in twenty-two months. The catalogue of the works to be copied was sent to Cosimo by Nicholas V, who wrote it with his own hand. (Naturally ecclesiastical literature and the books needed for the choral services outnumbered all the rest.)

The handwriting was that beautiful modern Italian which was already in use in the preceding century, and which makes

104. Perhaps at the capture of Urbino by the troops of Cesare Borgia? – The existence of the manuscript has been doubted, but I cannot believe that Vespasiano would have spoken of the gnomic extracts from Menander, which do not amount to more than a couple of hundred verses, as *tutte le opere* [all the works], nor have mentioned them in the list of comprehensive manuscripts (even if he had before him only our present Pindar and Sophocles). It is not inconceivable that this Menander may some day appear again.

105. When Piero de' Medici, at the death of Matthias Corvinus, the bibliophile King of Hungary, declared that the *scrittori* would now have to lower their prices or they would not be hired any more (*scil.*, except by us), he could only have meant the Greek copyists, since the calligraphers, to whom one might be tempted to refer his words, continued to be numerous throughout Italy.

the sight of one of the books of that time a pleasure. Pope Nicholas V, Poggio, Gianozzo Manetti, Niccolò Niccoli, and other distinguished scholars wrote a beautiful hand, and desired and tolerated no other. The decorative portions, even when miniatures formed no part of them, were full of taste, as may be seen especially in the Laurentian manuscripts with the light and graceful scrolls that begin and end the lines. When the work was ordered by the great, the material was always parchment; the binding, both in the Vatican and at Urbino, was crimson velvet with silver clasps. Where there was so much care to honor the contents of a book by the beauty of its form, it is understandable that the sudden appearance of printed books was resisted at first. Federigo of Urbino "would have been ashamed" to own a printed book.

But the weary copyists—not those who lived by the trade but the many who were forced to copy a book in order to have it—rejoiced at the German invention. It was soon used in Italy, and for a long time only in Italy, to reproduce first the Latin and then even the Greek authors, but it did not spread with the rapidity that might have been expected from the general enthusiasm for these works. After a while the modern relation between author and publisher began to develop, and under Alexander VI censorship appeared, since it was no longer easy to destroy a book, as Cosimo could still demand from Filelfo.

The growth of textual criticism, which accompanied the advancing study of languages and antiquity, belongs as little to the subject of this book as the history of scholarship in general. We are occupied here not with the learning of the Italians as such, but with the reproduction of antiquity in literature and life. Yet one word more on the studies themselves may still be permissible.

Greek scholarship was confined chiefly to Florence and to the fifteenth and the beginning of the sixteenth centuries. The impulse that had proceeded from Petrarch and Boccaccio seems not to have extended beyond the interests of a few enthusiastic dilettanti; on the other hand, the study of Greek literature died out about the year 1520 with the last of the colony of learned Greek exiles, and it was a singular piece of fortune that Northerners (Erasmus, the Stephani, Budaeus) had meanwhile made themselves masters of the language. That colony had begun with Manuel Chrysoloras and his relation John, and with George of Trebizond. Then followed, about the time of the conquest of Constantinople and after, John Argyropulos, Theodore Gaza, Demetrios Chalcondylas who brought up his sons Theophilos and Basilios to be excellent Hellenists, Andronikos Kallistos, Marcos Musuros, and the family of Lascaris, not to mention others. But after the subjugation of Greece by the Turks was completed, the succession of scholars was maintained only by the sons of the refugees and perhaps here and there by some Candian or Cyprian refugee. That the decay of Hellenistic studies began about the time of the death of Leo X was due in part to a general change of intellectual attitude, and to a certain satiety of classical influences which was making itself felt; but its coincidence with the death of the Greek scholars was not entirely a matter of accident. The study of Greek among the Italians appears, if we take the year 1500 as our standard, to have been pursued with extraordinary zeal. Those who learned the language at that time could still speak it half a century later, in their old age, as, e.g., Popes Paul III and Paul IV. But this sort of mastery presupposes intercourse with native Greeks.

Besides Florence, Rome and Padua nearly always maintained paid teachers of Greek, and Verona, Ferrara, Venice, Perugia, Pavia, and other cities employed occasional teachers. Greek studies owed a priceless debt to the press of Aldus Manutius at Venice, where the most important and most voluminous writers were for the first time printed in Greek. Aldus ventured his all in the enterprise; he was an editor and publisher whose like the world has rarely seen.

That along with this classical revival, Oriental studies now assumed considerable proportions must be at least briefly mentioned. The controversial writings of the great Florentine statesman and scholar, Giannozzo Manetti (d. 1459), against the Jews afford an early instance of a complete mastery of Hebrew and Jewish knowledge. His son Agnolo was from his childhood instructed in Latin, Greek, and Hebrew. Indeed, Pope Nicholas V commissioned Giannozzo to make a new translation of the Bible, since the philologists of the time insisted on giving up the Vulgate.[106] Many humanists began to study Hebrew long before Reuchlin, and Pico della Mirandola's knowledge of the Talmud equaled that of the most learned Rabbi. The study of Arabic was stimulated first by the medical profession, which was no longer satisfied with the older Latin translations of the great Arab physicians; easy access to the originals was offered by the Venetian consulates

---

106. Sixtus IV, who built the Vatican Library and enriched it with many purchases of his own, paid salaries to Latin, Greek, and Hebrew scribes (*librarios*). Platina, *Life of Sixtus IV.*

in the East, where Italian doctors were regularly in attendance. Girolamo Ramusio, a Venetian physician, translated from the Arabic and died at Damascus. Andrea Mongaio of Belluno lived long at Damascus for the purpose of studying Avicenna, learned Arabic, and emended his author's text. The Venetian government afterward appointed him professor of this subject at Padua.

We must linger for a moment over Pico della Mirandola before passing on to the general effects of humanism. He was the only man who loudly and vigorously defended the truth and science of all ages against the one-sided worship of classical antiquity. He knew how to value not only Averroës and the Jewish investigators, but also the scholastic writers of the Middle Ages, according to the matter of their writings. He seems to hear them say, "We shall live forever, not in the schools of word-catchers but in the circle of the wise, where they talk not of the mother of Andromache or of the sons of Niobe, but of the deeper causes of things human and divine; he who looks closely will see that even the barbarians had intelligence (*mercurium*), not on the tongue but in the breast." Writing a vigorous and not inelegant Latin and a master of clear exposition, he despised the purism of pedants and the overestimation of borrowed forms, especially when joined, as they often are, with one-sidedness and involving indifference to the wider truth of the things themselves. Looking at Pico, we can guess at the noble direction Italian philosophy would have taken had not the Counter Reformation annihilated the higher spiritual life of the people.

Who now were those who acted as mediators between their own age and a venerated antiquity, and made the latter a chief element in the culture of the former?

They were a crowd of the most miscellaneous sort, wearing one face today and another tomorrow; but they themselves clearly felt, and it was fully recognized by their time, that they formed a wholly new element in society. The *clerici vagantes* of the twelfth century, whose poetry we have already referred to, may perhaps be taken as their forerunners—the same unstable existence, the same free and more than free views of life, and the germs, at all events, of the same pagan tendencies in their poetry. But now, as competition to the whole culture of the Middle Ages, which was essentially clerical and fostered by the Church, there appeared a new civilization, which based itself on that which lay on the other side of the Middle Ages. Its active representatives became influential [107] because they knew what the ancients knew, because they tried to write as the ancients wrote, because they began to think, and soon to feel, as the ancients thought and felt. The tradition to which they devoted themselves was copied in thousands of ways.

Some modern writers deplore the fact that the germs of a far more independent and essentially national culture, such as appeared in Florence about the year 1300, were afterward so completely swamped by the humanists. There was then, we are told, nobody in Florence who could not read; even the donkey men sang the verses of Dante, and the best Italian manuscripts that we possess originally belonged to Florentine artisans; the publication of a popular encyclopedia such as the *Tesoro* [*Li livres dou trésor*] of Brunetto Latini, was possible then; and all this was founded on a strength and soundness of character due to the universal participation in public affairs, to commerce and travel, and to the systematic reprobation of idleness. The Florentines were at time respected and influential throughout the whole world, and not without reason did Pope Boniface VIII in that very year call them the "the fifth element." The rapid progress of humanism after the year 1400 paralyzed native impulses. Henceforth men looked only to antiquity for the solution of every problem, and consequently allowed literature to turn into mere quotation. The very fall of civil freedom is partly ascribed to all this, since the new learning rested on obedience to authority, sacrificed municipal rights to Roman law, and thereby both sought and found the favor of the despots.

These charges will occupy us now and then, when we shall attempt to reduce them to their true value and to weigh the losses against the gains. For the present we must confine ourselves to showing that the civilization of the vigorous fourteenth century necessarily prepared the way for the complete victory of humanism, and that the greatest representatives of the national Italian spirit were the very men who opened wide the gate for the measureless devotion to antiquity in the fifteenth century.

First, Dante. If a succession of men of equal genius had presided over Italian culture, whatever elements their natures might have absorbed from the antique, they still could not fail to retain a characteristic and strongly marked national stamp. But neither Italy nor Western Europe produced an-

---

107. Their own estimate of themselves is indicated by, e.g., Poggio, according to whom only those people could say that they had lived, *se vixisse,* who had written learned and eloquent books in Latin, or translated Greek into Latin.

other Dante, and he was and remained the man who first thrust antiquity into the foreground of national culture. In the *Divine Comedy* he treats the ancient and the Christian worlds, not indeed as of equal authority, but as parallel to one another. Just as, at an earlier period of the Middle Ages, types and antitypes were sought in the history of the Old and New Testaments, so does Dante constantly bring together a Christian and a pagan illustration of the same fact.[108] It must be remembered that the Christian cycle of history and legend was familiar, whereas the ancient was relatively unknown, was full of promise and of interest, and must necessarily have gained the upper hand in the competition for public sympathy when there was no longer a Dante to maintain the balance between the two.

Petrarch lives in the memory of most people nowadays as a great Italian poet, but among his contemporaries his fame was due more to the fact that he was a kind of living representative of antiquity, that he imitated all styles of Latin poetry, and wrote letters that, as treatises on matters of antiquarian interest, obtained a reputation which to us is unintelligible, but which is understandable in an age without handbooks.

It was the same with Boccaccio. For two centuries, when little was known of the *Decameron* north of the Alps, he was famous all over Europe simply because of his Latin compilations of mythology, geography, and biography. One of these, *De genealogia deorum*, contains in the fourteenth and fifteenth books a remarkable appendix, in which he discusses the position of the then youthful humanism with regard to his time. We must not be misled by his exclusive references to *poesia*, as closer observation shows that he means thereby the whole mental activity of the poet-scholars.[109] It is this activity whose enemies he combats so vigorously: the frivolous ignoramuses who have no soul for anything but debauchery; the sophistical theologian, to whom Helicon, the Castalian fountain, and the grove of Apollo are foolishness; the greedy lawyers, to whom poetry is a superfluity, since no money can be made by it; finally (described periphrastically but recognizable enough), the mendicant friars who made

108. *Purgatorio*, xvii, e.g., contains striking examples: Mary hastens over the mountains, Caesar to Spain; [xx] Mary is poor, Fabricius is unselfish.
109. *Poeta* [poet] even in Dante (*La vita nuova*) means only the writer of Latin verses, while for those writing in Italian, *rimatore* [rhymemaker], *dicitore per rima* [he who declaims in rhyme] are used. It is true that the names and ideas became mixed in the course of time.

free with their charges of paganism and immorality. Then
follows the positive defense of poetry, the praise of poetry,
and especially of the deeper and allegorical meanings that
we must always attribute to it, and of that calculated obscurity
which is intended to repel the dull minds of the ignorant.
And finally, with a clear reference to his own scholarly
work,[110] the writer justifies the new relation in which his age
stood to paganism. The case was wholly different, he pleads,
when the Early Church had to fight its way among the
heathen. Now—praised be Jesus Christ!—true religion is
strengthened, paganism destroyed, and the victorious Church
in possession of the hostile camp. It is now possible to touch
and study paganism almost (fere) without danger. This is
the same argument used in later times to defend the Renaissance.

There was, thus, a new cause in the world and a new class
of men to maintain it. It is idle to ask if this cause ought
not to have stopped short in its victorious advance, to have
restrained itself deliberately and conceded first place to purely
national elements of culture. No conviction was more firmly
rooted in the popular mind than that antiquity was the
greatest glory Italy possessed.

There was a symbolical ceremony peculiar to this first
generation of poet-scholars that lasted on into the fifteenth
and sixteenth centuries, though it lost the higher sentiment
that inspired it—the coronation of the poets with the laurel
wreath. The origin of this custom in the Middle Ages is
obscure, and the ritual of the ceremony never became fixed.
It was a public demonstration, an outward and visible expression of literary enthusiasm, [111] and thus somewhat variable form. Dante, for instance, seems to have understood it
in the sense of a half-religious consecration; he wanted to
receive the wreath in the baptistery of San Giovanni, where
he, like thousands of other Florentine children, had received
baptism.[112] In virtue of his fame he could, says his biographer, have received the crown anywhere, but he desired it

110. Boccaccio, in a (later) letter to Jacobus Pizinga, confines
himself more strictly to poetry proper. And yet he recognizes as
poetry only that which treats of antiquity, and ignores the
Troubadors.
111. Boccaccio, Life of Dante: la quale (laurea) non scienza
accresce, ma è dell' acquistata certissimo testimonio a ornamento
[which (the laurel) does not increase one's knowledge, but is
the most certain testament and adornment of its acquisition].
112. Paradiso, xxv, 1ff. – Boccaccio, Life of Dante. Cf. Paradiso,
i, 25.

nowhere but in his native city, and therefore died uncrowned. From the same source we learn that the custom was till then uncommon, and was held to be inherited by the ancient Romans from the Greeks. The most recent source to which the practice could be referred is to be found in the Capitoline contests of musicians, poets, and other artists founded by Domitian in imitation of the Greeks and celebrated every five years, which may possibly have survived for a time the fall of the Roman Empire. But as few other men would venture to crown themselves, as Dante desired to do, the question arises, to whom did this office belong? Albertino Mussato was crowned at Padua in 1310 by the bishop and the rector of the University. The University of Paris, the rector of which was then a Florentine, and the municipal authorities of Rome, competed for the honor of crowning Petrarch (1341). His self-elected examiner, King Robert of Anjou, would have liked to have the ceremony at Naples, but Petrarch preferred to be crowned on the Capitol by the senator of Rome. This honor was long the highest object of ambition, and so it seemed to Jacobus Pizinga, an illustrious Sicilian magistrate. Then came the Italian journey of Charles IV, who found it amusing to flatter the vanity of ambitious men and impress the ignorant multitude by means of gorgeous ceremonies. Starting from the fiction that the coronation of poets was a prerogative of the old Roman emperors, and consequently was now his, he crowned the Florentine scholar, Zanobi della Strada, at Pisa, to the great disgust of Boccaccio, who declined to recognize this *laurea pisana* as legitimate. Indeed, it might be asked with what right this stranger, half Slavonic by birth, came to sit in judgment on the merits of Italian poets. But from that time the emperors crowned poets wherever they went on their travels; and in the fifteenth century the Popes and other princes assumed the same right, till at last no regard whatever was paid to place or circumstances. In Rome, under Sixtus IV, the academy of Pomponius Laetus gave the wreath on its own authority. The Florentines had the good taste not to crown their famous humanists till after death. Carlo Aretino and Leonardo Aretino were thus crowned; the eulogy of the first was pronounced by Matteo Palmieri, of the latter by Giannozzo Manetti, before the members of the council and the people, the orator standing at the head of the bier on which the corpse lay clad in a silken robe. Carlo Aretino was further honored by a tomb (in Santa Croce) which is among the most beautiful of the entire Renaissance.

The influence of antiquity on culture, of which we have now to speak, presupposes that the new learning had gained possession of the universities. This was so, but by no means to the extent and with the results that might have been expected.

Few of the Italian universities [113] show themselves in their full vigor till the thirteenth and fourteenth centuries, when the increase of wealth rendered a more systematic care for education possible. At first there were generally three sorts of professorships—civil law, canonical law, and medicine; in course of time professorships of rhetoric, of philosophy, and of astronomy were added, the last commonly though not always identical with astrology. The salaries varied greatly in different cases. Sometimes a capital sum was granted. With the spread of culture, competition became so active that the different universities tried to entice distinguished teachers away from one another; under such circumstances Bologna is said to have sometimes devoted half of its public income (20,000 ducats) to the university. Appointments were as a rule made only for a certain time, sometimes for only half a year, so that the teachers were forced to lead a wandering life, like actors. But appointments for life were not unknown. Occasionally these teachers promised never to repeat their teaching elsewhere. There were also voluntary, unpaid professors.

Of the chairs that have been mentioned, that of rhetoric was especially sought by the humanist; yet it depended only on his familiarity with the matter of ancient learning whether he could aspire to the chairs of law, medicine, philosophy, or astronomy. The internal conditions of the science of the day were as variable as the external conditions of the teacher. Certain jurists and physicians received by far the largest salaries of all, the former chiefly as consulting lawyers for the suits and claims of the State that employed them. In Padua a lawyer of the fifteenth century received a salary of 1,000

---

113. Bologna, as is well known, was older, whereas Pisa was a late foundation by Lorenzo the Magnificent *ad solatium veteris amissae libertatis* [to console us for our ancient lost liberty], as Giovio says. The university of Florence had existed as early as 1321, with compulsory attendance for the natives of the city; it was founded afresh in 1348 after the Black Death, and endowed with an annual income of 2,500 gold florins; again fell into decay and was refounded in 1357. The chair for the exposition of Dante, established in 1373 at the request of many citizens, was afterward generally combined with the professorship of philology and rhetoric, as when Filelfo held it.

ducats, and it was proposed to appoint a celebrated physician with a yearly payment of 2,000 ducats, and the right of private practice, the same man having previously received 700 gold florins at Pisa. When the jurist Bartolommeo Socini, professor at Pisa, accepted a Venetian appointment at Padua, and was starting on his journey, he was arrested by the Florentine government which would release him only on payment of bail of 18,000 gold florins. The high estimation in which these branches of science were held makes it clear why distinguished philologists turned their attention to law and medicine; on the other hand, specialists in other fields were more and more compelled to acquire something of a wide literary culture. We shall presently have occasion to speak of the work of the humanists in other departments of practical life.

Nevertheless, the position of the philologists, as such, even where the salary was large and other sources of income were possible, was on the whole uncertain and temporary, so that the same teacher could be connected with a great variety of institutions. It is evident that change was desired for its own sake, and something new was expected from everyone, which was only natural at a time when science was in the making and thus depended greatly on the personal influence of the teacher. A lecturer on classical authors did not always belong to the university of the town where he taught. Transportation was so easy and the supply of suitable accommodation (in monasteries and elsewhere) so abundant, that a private appointment was often practicable. In the first decades of the fifteenth century, when the University of Florence was at its greatest brilliance, when the courtiers of Eugenius IV, and perhaps even those of Martin V crowded the lecture rooms, when Carlo Aretino and Filelfo were competing for the largest audience, there existed, not only an almost complete university among the Augustinians of Santo Spirito, not only an association of scholars among the Camaldolesi of the Angeli, but distinguished individuals arranged, either singly or jointly, to provide philosophical and philological teaching for themselves and others. Linguistic and antiquarian studies in Rome had for a long time had almost no connection with the university (Sapienza), and depended almost exclusively either on the favor of individual Popes and prelates, or on the appointments made in the Papal chancery. It was not till Leo X that the great reorganization of the Sapienza took place, with eighty-eight lecturers, among whom were the most able men of Italy, even for instruction in the classics. But this new brilliancy was of short duration. –

We have already spoken briefly of the Greek professorships in Italy.

To form an accurate picture of the method of scientific instruction pursued at that time, we must turn our eyes as far as possible from our present academic system. Personal intercourse between teacher and pupils, public disputations, the constant use of Latin and often of Greek, the frequent changes of lecturers and the scarcity of books, gave the studies of that time a color that we cannot visualize without effort.

There were Latin schools in every town of any importance, by no means merely as preparatory to higher education, but because knowledge of Latin was as necessary as reading, writing, and arithmetic; and after Latin came logic. It should be noted particularly that these schools did not depend on the Church, but on the municipality; some of them, too, were merely private enterprises.

This school system, directed by a few distinguished humanists, not only attained a remarkable perfection of organization, but became an instrument of higher education. The education of the children of two princely houses in North Italy was administered by institutions that may be called unique.

At the court of Giovanni Francesco Gonzaga at Mantua (r. 1407-1444) there appeared the illustrious Vittorino da Feltre, one of those men whose whole lives are dedicated to the one goal for which nature endowed them. He was first the educator of the sons and daughters of the princely house, and under his care one of the daughters became a woman of learning. But when his reputation extended over all Italy, and members of great and wealthy families came from near and far, even from Germany, in search of his instruction, Gonzaga was not only willing that they should be received, but seems to have held it an honor for Mantua to be the chosen school of the aristocratic world. Here for the first time gymnastics and all noble physical exercise were considered, along with scientific instruction, as indispensable to a liberal education. Besides these pupils came others, whose instruction Vittorino probably held to be his highest earthly aim, the gifted poor, whom he supported in his house and educated, *per l'amore di Dio* [for the love of God], along with the highborn youths who learned here to live under the same roof with untitled genius. Gonzaga paid him a yearly salary of 300 gold florins, and covered the entire deficit, which often amounted to an equal sum. He knew that Vittorino never saved a penny for himself, and doubtless realized that the education of the poor was the unspoken condition of the great man's service. The establishment was conducted on strictly religious lines, stricter than that of many monasteries.

More stress was laid on pure scholarship by Guarino of Verona who was called to Ferrara by Niccolò d'Este in 1429 to educate his son Lionello, and in 1436, when his pupil was nearly grown up, began to teach at the university as professor of eloquence and of the ancient languages. While still acting as tutor to Lionello, he had many other pupils from various parts of the country, and in his own house had a select number of poor scholars, whom he partly or wholly supported. His evening hours were devoted till far into the night to hearing lessons. His house, too, was the home of a strict religion and morality. It signified as little to him as to Vittorino that most of the humanists of their day deserved small praise in the matter of morals or religion. It is inconceivable how Guarino, with all the daily work that fell upon him, still found time to do translations from the Greek and to write voluminous original works.

Moreover, in most of the courts of Italy, the education of the princely families was at least in part and for a certain number of years in the hands of the humanists, who thereby mounted a step higher in the aristocratic world. The writing of treatises on the education of princes, which had formerly been the business of theologians, now fell within their province, and Aeneas Sylvius, for example, addressed detailed exhortations to two young German princes of the House of Hapsburg on the subject of their further education, in which they are both urged, as might be expected, to cultivate and nurture humanism. Perhaps he was aware that in addressing these youths he was wasting his breath, and therefore took measures to put his treatise into public circulation. But the relations of the humanists to the rulers will be discussed separately.

First claim to our attention belongs to those citizens, mainly Florentines, who made antiquarian interests one of the chief objects of their lives, and who were either distinguished scholars, or distinguished dilettanti who maintained the scholars. They were of particular significance during the period of transition at the beginning of the fifteenth century, since it was in them that humanism first showed itself as a practical, indispensable element in daily life. It was only after them that the Popes and princes began to take it seriously.

Niccolò Niccoli and Giannozzo Manetti have already been mentioned more than once. Niccoli is described to us by Vespasiano as a man who would tolerate nothing around him out of harmony with the classical spirit. His handsome long-robed figure, his kindly speech, his house adorned with the noblest remains of antiquity made a singular impression. He was scrupulously clean in everything, most of all at table, where ancient vases and crystal goblets stood before him on whitest linen. The way in which he won over a pleasure-loving young Florentine to intellectual interests is too charming not to be described.

Piero de' Pazzi, son of a distinguished merchant and destined to the same calling, fair to behold, and much given to the pleasures of the world, thought about nothing as little as he thought about literature. One day, as Piero was passing the Palazzo del Podestà, Niccolò called the young man to him, and although they had never exchanged a word, the youth obeyed the call of one so respected. Niccolò asked him who his father was. He answered, "Messer Andrea de' Pazzi." He was questioned further: what business was he in? Piero replied, as young people are wont to do, "I enjoy myself" (*attendo a darmi buon tempo*). Niccolò said to him, "As son of such a father, and so fair to look upon, it is a shame that thou knowest nothing of the Latin language, which would be so great an ornament to thee. If thou learnest it not, thou wilt be good for nothing, and as soon as the flower of youth is over, thou wilt be a man of no consequence (*virtù*)." When Piero heard this, he straightway perceived that it was true, and said that he would gladly take pains to learn, if only he had a teacher. Whereupon Niccolò answered that he would see to that. And he found him a learned man for Latin and Greek, named Pontano, whom Piero treated as one of his own house, and to whom he paid 100 gold florins a year. Quitting all the pleasures in which he had hitherto lived, he studied day and night, and became a friend of all learned men and a noble-minded statesman. He learned by heart the whole *Aeneid* and many speeches of Livy, chiefly on the way between Florence and his country house at Trebbio.

Antiquity was represented in another and higher sense by Giannozzo Manetti. Precocious from his first years, he was hardly more than a child when he had finished his apprenticeship in commerce and became bookkeeper in a bank. But soon the life he led seemed to him empty and frail, and he began to yearn after science, through which alone man can secure immortality. He was the first among the Florentine aristocracy to bury himself in books, and became, as has been said, one of the most profound scholars of his time. When appointed by the government as its representative magistrate and tax collector (at Pescia and Pistoia), he fulfilled his duties in accordance with the lofty ideal with which his religious feeling and humanistic studies combined to inspire him. He succeeded in collecting the most unpopular taxes that the Florentine State imposed, and declined payment for his services. As provincial governor he refused all presents, kept the country well supplied with corn, was indefatigable in settling lawsuits amicably, and did wonders in calming inflamed passions by his goodness. The Pistoiese were never able to discover to which of the two political parties he leaned. As if to symbolize the common rights and interests of all, he spent his leisure hours in writing the history of the city, which, bound in a purple cover, was then preserved as a sacred relic in the town hall. At his departure, the city presented him with a banner bearing the municipal arms and a splendid silver helmet.

For the other learned citizens of Florence at this period we must refer to Vespasiano (who knew them all personally), because the tone and atmosphere in which he writes, and the terms and conditions on which he mixed in their society, are of even more importance than the facts he records. In translation, and still more in the brief indications to which we are compelled to limit ourselves, this chief merit of his book is lost. He is not a great writer, but he was thoroughly familiar with the subject he wrote on, and had a deep sense of its intellectual significance.

If we try to analyze the charm the Medici of the fifteenth century, especially Cosimo the Elder (d. 1464) and Lorenzo the Magnificent (d. 1492), exercised over Florence and over all their contemporaries, we shall find that it lay less in their political capacity than in their leadership in the culture of the age. A man in Cosimo's position—a great merchant and party leader, who, in addition, had on his side all the thinkers, writers and investigators, who by birth was the first of the Florentines and by culture became the first of the Italians—such a man is indeed a prince. To Cosimo belongs the special glory of recognizing in the Platonic philosophy [114] the fairest flower of the ancient world of thought, of inspiring his friends with the same belief, and, thus, of fostering within humanistic circles another and a higher rebirth of antiquity. The story has come down to us in detail. It all hangs on

114. What was known of Plato before can only have been fragmentary. A strange discussion on the antagonism of Plato and Aristotle took place at Ferrara in 1438 between Ugo of Siena and the Greeks who came to the Council.

the calling of the learned Johannes Argyropulos, and on the personal enthusiasm of Cosimo himself in his last years, so that, so far as Platonism was concerned, the great Marsilio Ficino could call himself the spiritual son of Cosimo. Under Pietro de' Medici, Ficino was already at the head of a school; Pietro's son and Cosimo's grandson, the illustrious Lorenzo, came over to him from the Peripatetics. Among his most distinguished fellow scholars were Bartolommeo Valori, Donato Acciaiuoli, and Pierfilippo Pandolfini. The enthusiastic teacher has declared in several passages of his writings that Lorenzo sounded all the depths of the Platonic philosophy and uttered his conviction that without Plato it would be hard to be a good Christian or a good citizen. The famous group of scholars that surrounded Lorenzo was bound together, and distinguished from all other circles of the kind, by this passion for a higher and idealistic philosophy. Only in such a world could a man like Pico della Mirandola feel happy. But perhaps the best thing that can be said about it is, that, with all this worship of antiquity, Italian poetry found here a sacred refuge, and that of all the rays of light that streamed from the circle of which Lorenzo was the center, none was more brilliant than his. As a statesman, let each man judge him as he pleases; a foreigner will hesitate to pronounce what was due to human guilt and what to circumstances in the fate of Florence, but no more unjust charge was ever made than that in the field of culture Lorenzo was the protector of mediocrity, that through his fault Leonardo da Vinci and the mathematician Fra Luca Pacioli lived abroad, and that Toscanella, Vespucci, and others remained, at the least, unsupported. He was not, indeed, a man of universal mind; but of all the great men who have striven to favor and promote spiritual interests, few have been so many-sided, and in none probably was the inner need so deep.

The age in which we live is loud enough in proclaiming the worth of culture, and especially of the culture of antiquity. But the enthusiastic devotion to it, the recognition that this need is the first and greatest of all needs, is nowhere to be found to such an extent as among the Florentines of the fifteenth and the early part of the sixteenth centuries. On this point we have indirect proof which precludes all doubt. It would not have been so common to give the daughters of the house a share in the same studies, had these studies not been held to be the noblest of earthly pursuits; exile would not have been turned into a happy retreat, as was done by Palla Strozzi; nor would men who indulged in every conceivable excess have retained the strength and the spirit to write critical treatises on the *Natural History* of Pliny as Filippo Strozzi. Our business here is neither to praise nor to blame, but to understand the spirit of the age in all its vigorous individuality.

Besides Florence, there were many cities of Italy where individuals and social circles devoted all their energies to the support of humanism and the protection of the scholars who lived among them. The correspondence of that period is full of references to personal relations of this kind. The official view of the instructed classes was set firmly and almost exclusively in this direction.

But it is now time to speak of humanism at the Italian courts. The natural alliance between the despot and the scholar, each relying solely on his personal talent, has already been touched upon; that the scholar should prefer the princely courts to the free cities, was only to be expected from the higher pay that he received there. At a time when the great Alfonso of Aragon seemed likely to become master of all Italy, Aeneas Sylvius wrote to another citizen of Siena: "I had rather that Italy attained peace under his rule than under that of the free cities, for kingly generosity rewards excellence of every kind." [115] Too much stress has recently been laid on the unworthy side of this relation, and the mercenary flattery to which it gave rise, just as formerly the eulogies of the humanists led to too favorable a judgment of their patrons. Taking all things together, it is greatly to the honor of these patrons that they felt bound to place themselves at the head of the culture of their age and country, one-sided though this culture might be. In some of the Popes, the fearlessness of the consequences to which the new learning might lead strikes us as something truly, but unconsciously, imposing. Nicholas V was confident of the future of the Church, since thousands of learned men supported her. Pius II was far from making such splendid sacrifices for humanism as were made by Nicholas, and the poets who frequented his court were few in number; but he himself was much more the personal head of the republic of letters than his predecessor, and enjoyed his position without the least misgiving. Paul II was the first to dread and mistrust the culture of his secretaries, and his three successors, Sixtus, Innocent, and

115. We must not be misled by the fact that along with this, complaints were frequently heard of the inadequacy of princely patronage and of the indifference of many princes to their fame. – It was impossible to satisfy all.

Alexander, accepted dedications and allowed themselves to be poetized to the hearts' content of the poets—there was even a "Borgiad," probably in hexameters—but they were too busy elsewhere, and too occupied in seeking other footholds for their power, to trouble themselves much about the poet-scholars. Julius II found poets to eulogize him, because he himself was no mean subject for poetry, but he does not seem to have troubled himself much about them. He was followed by Leo X, "as Romulus by Numa"—in other words, after the warlike turmoil of the previous Pontificate, a new one was hoped for which would be completely dedicated to the Muses. The enjoyment of elegant Latin prose and melodious verse was part of the program of Leo's life, and his patronage certainly had the result that his Latin poets have left us in countless elegies, odes, epigrams, and orations a living picture of that joyous and brilliant spirit of the Leonine days, with which the biography by Giovio is filled. Probably in all European history there is no prince who, in proportion to the few striking events of his life, has received such manifold homage. The poets had access to him chiefly about noon, when the musicians had ceased playing; but one of the best among them tells how they also pursued him when he walked in his garden or withdrew to the privacy of his chamber, and if they failed to catch him there, would try to win him with a petition in the form of an elegy filled with the whole population of Olympus. For Leo, prodigal of his money and disliking to be surrounded by any but cheerful faces, displayed a generosity in his gifts that was fabulously exaggerated in the hard times that followed. His reorganization of the Sapienza has already been spoken of. In order not to underrate Leo's influence on humanism we must guard against being misled by the frivolity that was mixed up with it, and we must not allow ourselves to be deceived by the apparent irony with which he himself sometimes treated these matters. Our judgment must proceed from the countless spiritual possibilities included in the word "stimulus," which, though they cannot be computed, can, on closer study, be practically demonstrated in particular cases. Whatever influence the Italian humanists have had in Europe since 1520 depends in some way on the impulse that was given by Leo. He was the Pope who, in granting permission to print the newly found Tacitus, could say that the great writers were a rule of life and a consolation in misfortune; that helping learned men and obtaining excellent books had always been one of his highest aims; and that now he thanked heaven that he could benefit the human race by furthering the publication of this book.

The sack of Rome in the year 1527 scattered the scholars no less than the artists in every direction, and spread the fame of the great departed Maecenas to the farthest boundaries of Italy.

Among the secular princes of the fifteenth century, none displayed such enthusiasm for antiquity as Alfonso the Great of Aragon, King of Naples. It seems that his zeal was thoroughly unaffected, and that the monuments and writings of the ancient world made upon him, from the time of his arrival in Italy, an impression deep and powerful enough to reshape his life. With strange readiness he surrendered the stubborn Aragon to his brother, in order to devote himself completely to his new possession. He had in his service, either successively or at the same time, George of Trebizond, the younger Chrysoloras, Lorenzo Valla, and Bartolommeo Fazio and Antonio Panormita, who were his historians; Panormita daily instructed the King and his court in Livy, even during military expeditions. These men cost him 20,000 gold florins annually. For his history of Alfonso, Fazio received, besides a yearly income of 500 ducats, a present of 1,500 more when it was finished, with the words, "It is not given to pay you, for your work would not be paid for if I gave you the fairest of my cities; but in time I hope to satisfy you." When he took Giannozzo Manetti as his secretary on the most brilliant conditions, he said to him, "My last crust I will share with you." When Giannozzo first came to bring the congratulations of the Florentine government on the marriage of Prince Ferrante, the impression he made was so great, that the King sat motionless on the throne, "like a bronze statue," and did not even brush away the flies. His favorite haunt seems to have been the library of the castle at Naples, where he would sit at a window overlooking the bay, and listen to learned debates on, for example, the Trinity. For he was profoundly religious, and in addition to Livy and Seneca, had the Bible read to him, which he knew almost by heart. Who can fully understand the feeling with which he regarded the suppositious remains of Livy at Padua? When, by dint of great entreaties, he obtained an armbone of the skeleton from the Venetians, and received it with solemn pomp at Naples, how strangely Christian and pagan sentiment must have been blended in his heart! During a campaign in the Abruzzi, when the distant Sulmona, the birthplace of Ovid, was pointed out to him, he saluted the spot and returned thanks to its

tutelary genius. It gladdened him to make good the prophecy
of the great poet as to his future fame. Once indeed, at his
famous entry into the conquered city of Naples (1443), he
himself chose to appear before the world in ancient style. Not
far from the market a breach forty ells wide was made in
the wall, and through this he drove in a gilded chariot like
a Roman Triumphator. Even the memory of the scene is
preserved by a magnificent marble triumphal arch in the
Castel Nuovo. – His Neapolitan successors inherited as little
of this passion for antiquity as of his other good qualities.

Alfonso was far surpassed in learning by Federigo of
Urbino, who had few courtiers around him, squandered nothing, and in his appropriation of antiquity, as in all other
things, proceeded systematically. It was for him and for
Nicholas V that most of the translations from the Greek,
and a number of the best commentaries and other such
works, were written. He spent much on the scholars whose
services he used, but spent it to good purpose. There were
no traces of a poets' court at Urbino, where the Duke himself was the most learned in the whole court. Classical
antiquity was actually only a part of his culture. An accomplished ruler, captain, and gentleman, he had mastered
the greater part of the science of the day, and this with a
view to its practical application. As a theologian, for example,
he was able to compare Scotus with Aquinas, and was familiar
with the writings of the Fathers of the Eastern and Western
Churches, the former in Latin translations. In philosophy, he
seems to have left Plato to his contemporary Cosimo, but he
knew thoroughly not only the *Ethics* and *Politics* of Aristotle
but the *Physics* and some other works. The rest of his
reading lay chiefly among the ancient historians, all of whom
he possessed; these, and not the poets, "he was always reading
and having read to him."

The Sforza,[116] too, were men of learning, some more, some
less, and patrons of literature, as we have already mentioned
in passing. Duke Francesco probably viewed humanistic
culture as a matter of course in the education of his children,
if only for political reasons. It was felt universally to be an
advantage if a prince could mix with the most instructed men
of his time on an equal footing. Il Moro, who was an

116. The last Visconti was still torn between Livy and the French
chivalrous romances, and Dante and Petrarch. The humanists
who presented themselves and promised to "make him famous"
were generally sent away after a few days.

excellent Latin scholar, showed an interest in intellectual matters that extended far beyond classical antiquity.

Even the petty despots strove after similar distinctions, and we do them injustice by thinking that they supported the scholars at their courts only as a means of diffusing their own fame. A ruler such as Borso of Ferrara, with all his vanity, does not seem to have looked for immortality from the poets, eager as they were to propitiate him with a "Borseid" and the like. He had far too proud a sense of his own position as a ruler. But intercourse with learned men, interest in antiquarian matters, and a passion for elegant Latin correspondence were necessities for the princes of that age. Competent as he was in practical matters, how bitterly Duke Alfonso complained that his weakliness in youth had forced him to seek recreation in manual pursuits only! or was this merely an excuse to keep the humanists at a distance? A nature like his was not intelligible even to contemporaries.

Even the most insignificant despots of Romagna found it hard to do without one or two men of letters. The tutor and secretary were often the same person, who sometimes even became the court factotum. We are apt to dismiss these small courts with too ready a contempt, forgetting that the highest spiritual things are not matters of measurement.

Life and manners at the court of Rimini must have been a singular spectacle under the bold pagan *condottiere* Sigismondo Malatesta. He had a number of scholars around him, some of whom he provided for liberally, even giving them landed estates, and others earned at least a livelihood as officers in his army. In his citadel—*arx Sismundea*—they used to hold discussions, often of a very venomous kind, in the presence of the *rex*, as they termed him. In their Latin poems they sing his praises and celebrate his amour with the fair Isotta, in whose honor and as whose tomb, *Divae Isottae Sacrum* [sacred to the divine Isotta], the famous rebuilding of San Francesco at Rimini [Tempio Malatestiano] was undertaken. When the humanists themselves died, they were laid in (or under) the sarcophagi with which the niches of both side walls of the church are adorned, with an inscription testifying that they were laid here at the time when Sigismundus, the son of Pandulfus, ruled. It is hard for us nowadays to believe that a monster like this prince felt learning and the friendship of cultivated people to be a necessity of life; and yet the man who excommunicated him, made war upon him, and burned him in effigy, Pope Pius II, says: "Sigismondo knew history and had a great store of philosophy; he seemed born to all that he undertook." [117]

There were two purposes, however, for which the humanist was as indispensable to the republics as to princes or Popes: namely, the official correspondence of the State, and the making of speeches on public and solemn occasions.

Not only was the secretary required to be a competent Latinist, but conversely, only a humanist was credited with the knowledge and ability necessary for the post of secretary. And thus during the fifteenth century most of the greatest, most learned men devoted a considerable part of their lives to serving the State in this capacity. No importance was attached to a man's home or origin. Of the four great Florentine secretaries who filled the office between 1429 and 1465, three belonged to the subject city of Arezzo: Leonardo (Bruni), Carlo (Marzuppini), and Benedetto Accolti; Poggio was from Terra Nuova, also in Florentine territory. For a long period, indeed, many of the highest offices of State were on principle given to foreigners. Leonardo, Poggio, and Giannozzo Manetti were at one time or another private secretaries to the Popes, and Carlo Aretino was to become one. Flavio Biondo, and, in spite of everything, at last even Lorenzo Valla, filled the same office. From the time of Nicholas V and Pius II onward, the Papal chancery continued more and more to attract the ablest men, even under the last Popes of the fifteenth century, little as they cared for letters. In Platina's *Lives of the Popes,* the life of Paul II is a charming piece of vengeance taken by a humanist on the one Pope who did not know how to behave to his chancery—to that circle "of poets and orators who bestowed on the Papal court as much glory as they received from it." It is delightful to see the indignation of these haughty gentlemen, when there was some squabble about precedence, when, for instance, the *advocati consistoriales* [lawyers of the Curia] claimed equal or superior rank to theirs. The Apostle John, to whom the *secreta coelestia* [celestial mysteries] were revealed; the secretary of Porsenna, whom Mucius Scaevola mistook for the king; Maecenas, who was private secretary to Augustus; the archbishops, who in Germany were called chancellors—all are appealed to in turn. "The apostolic secretaries have the most weighty business of the world in their hands, for who but they decide on matters of the Catholic faith, combat heresy, re-establish peace, mediate

---

117. *The Commentaries of Pius II,* Book II. By "history" he means everything that has to do with antiquity.

between great monarchs? Who but they write the statistical accounts of Christendom? It is they who astonish kings, princes, and nations by what comes forth from the Pope. They write commands and instructions for the legates, and take their orders only from the Pope, on whom they wait every hour of the day and night." But the highest summit of glory was attained only by the two famous secretaries and stylists of Leo X: Pietro Bembo and Jacopo Sadoleto.

All the chanceries did not turn out equally elegant documents. A leathern official style, in the impurest Latin, was very common. In the Milanese documents preserved by Corio there is a remarkable contrast between this sort of composition and the few letters written by members of the princely house, which must have been written, too, in moments of critical importance. They are models of pure Latinity. To maintain a faultless style under all circumstances was a rule of good breeding, and a result of habit.

The letters of Cicero, Pliny, and others, were at this time diligently studied as models. As early as the fifteenth century there appeared a whole series of manuals and models for Latin correspondence (as off-shoots of the great grammatical and lexicographic works), the mass of which is astounding to us even now when we look at them in the libraries. But just as the existence of these aids tempted many to undertake a task for which they had no vocation, so were the really capable men stimulated to a more faultless excellence, and the letters of Politian and those of Pietro Bembo at the beginning of the sixteenth century took their place as unrivaled masterpieces, not only of Latin style, but of the more special art of letter writing.

Along with these there appeared in the sixteenth century the classical style of Italian correspondence, at the head of which stands Bembo again. Its form is wholly modern, and deliberately kept free from Latin influence, and yet its spirit is thoroughly permeated and determined by antiquity.

But at a time and among a people where "listening" was among the chief pleasures of life, and where every imagination was filled with the memory of the Roman senate and its great speakers, the orator occupied a far more brilliant place than the letter writer. Eloquence had shaken off the influence of the Church, in which it had found a refuge during the Middle Ages, and now became an indispensable element and ornament of all elevated lives. Many of the social hours which are now filled with music were at that time given over to Latin or Italian oratory, regarding which each reader may form his own opinion.

The social position of the speaker was a matter of perfect indifference; what was desired was simply the most cultivated humanistic talent. At the court of Borso of Ferrara, the Duke's physician, Girolamo da Castello, was chosen to deliver the congratulatory address on the visits of Frederick III and of Pius II. Married laymen ascended the pulpits of the churches at any scene of festivity or mourning, and even on the feast days of the saints. It struck the non-Italian members of the Council of Basel strange that the Archbishop of Milan should summon Aeneas Sylvius, who was not yet ordained, to deliver a public discourse at the feast of St. Ambrose; but they suffered it in spite of the murmurs of the theologians, and listened to the speaker with the greatest curiosity.[118]

Let us glance for a moment at the more frequent and important occasions of public speaking.

It was not for nothing that, above all, the ambassadors from one State to another received the title of orators. Whatever else might be done in the way of secret negotiation, the envoy never failed to make a public appearance and deliver a public speech, under circumstances of the greatest possible pomp.[119] As a rule, however numerous the embassy might be, one individual spoke for all; but Pius II, a critic before whom all were glad to be heard, had to sit and listen to a whole deputation, one after another. Learned princes who had the gift of speech were fond of discoursing in Latin or Italian. The children of the House of Sforza were trained to this exercise. In 1455 the boy Galeazzo Maria delivered a fluent speech before the Great Council at Venice, and in 1459 his sister Ippolita saluted Pope Pius II with a graceful address at the Congress of Mantua. Pius himself through all his life did much by his oratory to prepare the way for his final elevation to the Papal chair. Great as he was both as scholar and diplomat, he would probably never have become Pope without the fame and charm of his eloquence. "For nothing was more lofty than the dignity of his oratory." Without doubt this was why multitudes held him to be the fittest man for the office even before his election.

Princes were also received on public occasions with speeches, which sometimes lasted for hours. This happened of course only when the prince was known as a lover of

---

118. *The Commentaries of Pius II,* Book I.
119. The success of the fortunate orator was as great as the humiliation of the speaker who broke down before distinguished audiences.

eloquence, or wished to pass for such,[120] and when a competent speaker was present, whether university professor, official, ecclesiastic, physician, or court scholar.

Every other political opportunity was seized with the same eagerness, and speakers who enjoyed a reputation drew large crowds from among those who revered learning. At the yearly change of public officers, and even at the consecration of new bishops, a humanist was sure to come forward, and sometimes addressed his audience in hexameters or Sapphic verses. Often a newly appointed official was forced to deliver a speech more or less relevant to his department, as, for instance, on justice; and lucky for him if he were well up in his part! At Florence even the *condottieri*—whatever their origin or education—were compelled to accommodate themselves to the popular sentiment, and on receiving the insignia of their office, were harangued before the assembled people by the most learned secretary of state. It seems that beneath or close to the Loggia dei Lanzi—the porch where the government was wont to appear solemnly before the people—a tribune or platform *(rostra, ringhiera)* was erected for such purposes.

Anniversaries, especially those of the death of princes, were commonly celebrated by memorial speeches. Even the funeral oration proper was generally entrusted to a humanist, who delivered it in church, clothed in secular dress; nor was it only princes to whom this honor was paid, but also officials, or persons otherwise distinguished. This was also the case with the speeches delivered at betrothals and weddings, except that these (so it seems) were made in the palace, instead of in church, as, e.g., that of Filelfo at the betrothal of Anna Sforza to Alfonso d'Este in the castle of Milan. (But it may have taken place in the chapel of the castle.) Private families of distinction also employed such wedding orators as one of the luxuries of life. At Ferrara, Guarino was requested on these occasions to send one of his pupils. The clergy conducted only the purely religious ceremonies at weddings and funerals.

The academic speeches, both those made at the installation of a new teacher and at the opening of a new course of lectures, were delivered by the professor himself, and treated

120. Charles V, when unable on one occasion to follow the flourishes of a Latin orator at Genoa, sighed into the ear of Giovio: "Ah, my tutor Adrian was right when he told me I should be punished for my childish idleness in learning Latin."

as occasions of great rhetorical display. The ordinary university lectures also usually had an oratorical character.

With regard to forensic eloquence, the quality of the audience determined the form of speech. When necessary, it was enriched with all sorts of philosophical and antiquarian learning.

As a special class of speeches we may mention the address made in Italian on the battlefield, either before or after the combat. Federigo of Urbino was esteemed a classic in this style; he would pass among his squadrons as they stood drawn up in order of battle, inspiring them in turn with pride and enthusiasm. Many of the speeches in the military histories of the fifteenth century, as for instance in Porcellius, may be, in part, imaginary, but may also be in part faithful recordings of words actually spoken. The addresses which were delivered to the Florentine Militia, organized in 1506 chiefly through the influence of Machiavelli, and which were spoken first at reviews, and afterward at special annual festivals, were of another kind. They were simply general appeals to patriotism, and were addressed to the assembled troops in the church of each quarter of the city by a citizen in armor, sword in hand.

Finally, it occasionally becomes diffcult in the fifteenth century to distinguish between preaching and oratory, since many of the clergy had entered the circle of classical culture, and wanted to succeed in it. The street preacher Bernardino da Siena, who in his own lifetime passed for a saint and who was worshipped by the populace, was not above taking lessons in rhetoric from the famous Guarino, although he had only to preach in Italian. Never was more expected from preachers than at that time—especially from the Lenten preachers; and there were not a few audiences which could not only tolerate, but which demanded a strong dose of philosophy from the pulpit. But here we have to speak of the distinguished occasional preachers in Latin. Many of their opportunities had been taken away from them, as has been observed, by learned laymen. Speeches on particular saints' days, at weddings and funerals, at the installation of a bishop, and even the introductory speech at the first mass of a clerical friend, or the address at the festival of some religious order, were all left to laymen. But at least at the Papal court in the fifteenth century, whatever the occasion might be, the preachers were generally monks. Under Sixtus IV, Giacomo da Volterra regularly listed these preachers, and criticized them according to the rules of the art. Fedra Inghirami, famous as an orator under Julius II, had at least received holy orders and was canon at St. John Lateran; and besides him, elegant Latinists were now common enough among the prelates. In this matter, as in others, the exaggerated privileges of the profane humanists appear lessened in the sixteenth century—on which point we shall speak more fully.

What was the subject and general character of these speeches? The national gift of eloquence was not lacking in the Italians of the Middle Ages, and from the first, a so-called "rhetoric" belonged to the seven liberal arts; but so far as the revival of the ancient methods is concerned, this merit must be ascribed, according to Filippo Villani, to the Florentine Bruno Casini, who died, while still a young man, in the plague in 1348. With the wholly practical purpose of fitting the Florentines to speak with ease and effect in public, he treated, after the pattern of the ancients, invention, declamation, bearing, and gesticulation, each in its proper connection. Elsewhere, too, we find early reports of oratorical training directed solely to practical application. No accomplishment was more highly esteemed than the power of elegant improvisation in Latin. The growing study of Cicero's speeches and theoretical writings, of Quintilian and of the imperial panegyrists, the appearance of new and original handbooks, the general progress of antiquarian learning, and the stores of ancient matter and thought which now could and must be drawn from—all combined to shape the character of the new eloquence.

But this character differed widely according to the individual. Many speeches breathe a spirit of true eloquence, especially those that keep to the subject; of this kind is the mass of what is left to us of Pius II. The miraculous effects produced by Giannozzo Manetti point to an orator whose like has not often been seen. His great audiences as envoy before Nicholas V and before the Doge and Council of Venice were events not soon to be forgotten. Many orators, on the contrary, would seize the opportunity, not only to flatter the vanity of distinguished hearers, but to load their speeches with an enormous mass of antiquarian rubbish. How it was possible to endure this infliction for two and even three hours, can only be understood when we take into account the intense interest at that time in everything connected with antiquity, and the rarity and defectiveness of treatises on the subject before the time of universal printing. Such orations had at least the value that we have claimed for many of Petrarch's letters. But some speakers went too far. Most of Filelfo's speeches are an atrocious patchwork of classical

and biblical quotations tacked on to a string of common-
places, among which the great people he wishes to flatter
are arranged under the head of the cardinal virtues, or some
such category, and it is only with the greatest effort in his
case and in that of many others, that we can extricate the
few historical notices of any value that they really contain.
The speech, for instance, of a scholar and professor of
Piacenza at the reception of Duke Galeazzo Maria, in 1467,
begins with Julius Caesar, then proceeds to mix up a mass of
classical quotations with a number from an allegorical work
by the speaker himself, and concludes with some exceedingly
indiscreet advice to the ruler. Fortunately it was late at night,
and the orator had to be satisfied with presenting his
panegyric in its written form. Filelfo begins a speech at a
betrothal with the words, "Aristotle, the peripatetic." Others
start with P. Cornelius Scipio, and the like, as though neither
they nor their hearers could wait a moment for a quotation.
At the end of the fifteenth century public taste suddenly
improved, chiefly through Florentine influence; and the practice of quotation was restricted within due limits, since many
works of reference were now in existence, in which the
first comer could find as much as he wanted of what had
hitherto been the admiration of princes and people.

As most of the speeches were written out beforehand in
the study, the manuscripts served as a means of further publicity. The great extemporaneous speakers, on the other hand,
had to be attended by shorthand writers.[121] – We must
further remember that not all the orations that have come
down to us were intended to be actually delivered. The
panegyric, for example, of the elder Beroaldus on Il Moro
was presented to him in manuscript. In fact, just as letters
addressed to all conceivable persons and parts of the world
were composed as exercises, as formularies, or even to serve
a controversial end, so there were speeches for imaginary
occasions to be used as models for the reception of princes,
bishops, and other dignitaries.

For oratory, as for the other arts, the death of Leo X
(1521) and the sack of Rome (1527) mark the epoch of
decadence. Giovio, but just escaped from the desolation of
the eternal city, describes, not impartially but on the whole
correctly, the causes of this decline:

"The plays of Plautus and Terence, once a school of Latin
style for the educated Romans, are supplanted by Italian

---

121. So, Savonarola. But the stenographers could not always
follow him or, e.g., any inspired improvisor.

comedies. Graceful speakers no longer find the recognition and reward that they once did. The consistorial advocates no longer prepare anything but the introductions to their speeches, and deliver the rest—a confused muddle—on the inspiration of the moment. Sermons and occasional speeches have sunk to the same level. If a funeral oration is wanted for a cardinal or other great personage, the executors do not apply to the best orators in the city, to whom they would have to pay a hundred pieces of gold, but they hire for a trifle the first impudent pedant whom they come across, who only wants to be talked of, whether for good or ill. The dead, they say, are none the wiser if an ape stands in a black dress in the pulpit, and beginning with a hoarse, whimpering mumble, passes step by step into a loud howling. Even the sermons preached at great Papal ceremonies are no longer as profitable as they used to be. Monks of all orders have again got them into their hands, and preach as if they were speaking to the mob. Only a few years ago a sermon at mass before the Pope might easily lead to a bishopric."

In connection with the oratory and the epistolary writings of the humanists, we shall discuss here their other creations, which were all, to a greater or less extent, reproductions of antiquity.

Among these must be placed the treatise, which often took the form of a dialogue borrowed directly from Cicero. In order to do some justice to this class of literature—in order not to throw it aside at first sight as a bore—two things must be taken into consideration. The century that escaped from the influence of the Middle Ages felt the need of some special mediation between itself and antiquity in many questions of morals and philosophy; and this need was met by the writer of treatises and dialogues. Much that appears to us mere commonplace in their writings was for them and their contemporaries a new and hard-won view of things upon which mankind had been silent since the days of antiquity. The language, too, in this form of writing, whether Italian or Latin, moved more freely and flexibly than in historical narrative, in letters, or in oratory, and thus became in itself the source of a special pleasure. Several Italian compositions of this kind still hold their place as patterns of style. Many of these works have been, or will be mentioned because of their contents; here we refer to them as a class. From the time of Petrarch's letters and treatises down to almost the end of the fifteenth century, the main business of most of these writers was the heaping up of learned quotations, as in the case of the orators. Later the whole style, especially in Italian, was purified, until, in the *Asolani* of Bembo, and the *Vita sobria* [*The Sober Life*] of Luigi Cornaro, a classical perfection was reached. Here too the decisive fact was that antiquarian matter of every kind had begun to be deposited in encyclopedic works, now printed, and no longer stood in the way of the essayist.

It was inevitable that the humanistic spirit should also control the writing of history. A superficial comparison of the histories of this period with the earlier chronicles, especially with works so full of life, color, and brilliancy as those of the Villani, will lead us loudly to deplore the change. How insipid and conventional the best of the humanists appear next to them and, particularly, their immediate and most famous successors among the historians of Florence, Leonardo Aretino and Poggio! The enjoyment of the reader is incessantly marred by the sense that, in the classical phrases of Fazio, Sabellico, Foglietta, Senarega, Platina (in the chronicles of Mantua), Bembo (in the annals of Venice), and even of Giovio (in his histories), the best local and individual color and the full sincerity of interest in the truth of events have been lost. Our mistrust is increased when we realize that Livy was taken as a pattern just where he is least worthy of imitation—namely, because he "turned a dry and naked tradition into grace and richness." We find the suspicious declaration that it is the function of the historian to excite, charm, or overwhelm the reader—as if he were a poet. We ask ourselves, finally, whether the contempt for modern things, which these same humanists sometimes avowed openly,[122] must not *necessarily* have had an unfortunate influence on their treatment of them. Automatically the reader finds himself looking with more interest and confidence on the modest Latin and Italian annalists, as, e.g., those of Bologna and Ferrara, who remained true to the old style, and one feels even more grateful to the best of the genuine chroniclers who wrote in Italian—Marino Sanudo, Corio, Infessura—who were followed at the beginning of the sixteenth century by that new and illustrious group of great national historians who wrote in their mother tongue.

In point of fact, contemporary history was written far better in the language of the day than when forced into Latin. Whether Italian was also more suitable for the narrative of events long past, for historical research, is a ques-

122. In this the humanists resemble the writers of late antiquity, who also severed themselves from their own age. – Cf. Burkhardt, *The Age of Constantine the Great,* ch. 7.

tion which for that period admits more than one answer. Latin was at that time the lingua franca of instructed people, not only in an international sense, as a means of intercourse between Englishmen, Frenchmen, and Italians, but also in an interprovincial sense. The Lombard, the Venetian, and the Neapolitan modes of writing, though long modeled on the Tuscan and bearing only slight traces of the dialect, were still not recognized by the Florentines. This was of less consequence for local contemporary histories, which were sure of readers at the place where they were written, than for the histories of the past, for which a larger public was desired. In these the local interests of the people had to be sacrificed to the general interests of the learned. How far would the influence of a man such as, e.g., Flavio Biondo have reached had he written his great monuments of learning in the dialect of the Romagna? They would have sunk into certain neglect, if only through the contempt of the Florentines, whereas written in Latin they exercised the profoundest influence on the whole European world of learning. And even the Florentines of the fifteenth century wrote Latin, not only because their minds were imbued with humanism, but in order to be more widely read.

Finally, there exist certain Latin essays in contemporary history which stand on a level with the best Italian works of the kind. When the continuous narrative after the manner of Livy—that Procrustean bed of so many writers—is abandoned, the change is marvelous. The same Platina and Giovio, whose great histories we read only because and so far as we must, suddenly come forward as masters in the biographical style. We have already mentioned Tristano Caracciolo, the biographical works of Fazio, the Venetian topography of Sabellico, and we shall speak of others.

The Latin treatises on past history were, naturally, concerned, for the most part, with classical antiquity. What we are most surprised to find among these humanists are some considerable works on the history of the Middle Ages. The first of this kind was the chronicle of Matteo Palmieri, beginning where Prosper Aquitanus leaves off. On opening the Decades of Flavio Biondo we are surprised to find a universal history, *ab inclinatione Romanorum imperii* [from the decline of the Roman Empire], as in Gibbon, full of original sources of each century, in which the first 300 folio pages deal with early medieval history down to the death of Frederick II. And this when in Northern countries chronicles of the Popes and emperors, and local annals were still the rule. It is not our task to show what writings Biondo used and where he found his material, though this justice will some day be done to him by the modern historians. This book alone would entitle us to say that it was the study of antiquity that made the study of the Middle Ages possible, by first training the mind to habits of impartial historical criticism. To this must be added, that the Middle Ages were now over for Italy, and the Italian mind could appreciate them better because it stood outside them. It cannot be said that it judged them fairly, nor even with piety. In the arts a strong prejudice established itself against all that those centuries had created, and the humanists date the new era from the time of their own appearance. "I begin," says Boccaccio, "to hope and believe that God has had mercy on the Italian name, since I see that His infinite goodness puts souls into the breasts of the Italians like those of the ancients—souls that seek fame by other means than robbery and violence, but rather on the path of poetry, which makes men immortal." But this narrow and unjust temper did not preclude investigation by the more gifted men, at a time when elsewhere in Europe such investigation would have been out of the question. A historical criticism of the Middle Ages was practicable just because the rational treatment of all subjects by the humanists had trained the historical spirit. In the fifteenth century this spirit had so far penetrated the history even of individual cities of Italy that the fabulous tales about the origin of Florence, Venice, Milan, etc., vanished, whereas for a long time the chronicles of the North were stuffed with that fantastic rubbish, destitute for the most part of all poetic value, that had been fashioned since the thirteenth century.

The close connection between local history and fame has already been touched on in reference to Florence. Venice would not be left behind. Just as a great rhetorical triumph of the Florentines would cause a Venetian embassy to write home posthaste for an orator, so, too, did the Venetians feel the need for a history that would bear comparison with those of Leonardo Aretino and Poggio. And it was to satisfy this feeling that, in the fifteenth century, the Decades of Sabellico appeared, and in the sixteenth the *Historia rerum Venetarum* of Pietro Bembo, both written at the express charge of the Republic, the latter a continuation of the former.

The great Florentine historians at the beginning of the sixteenth century were from birth completely different from the Latinists Bembo and Giovio. They wrote Italian not only because they could no longer vie with the Ciceronian elegance of the philologists, but because, like Machiavelli, they could only record in a living tongue the living results of their own immediate observations,[123] and because, as in the case of Guicciardini, Varchi, and many others, what they most desired was that their view of the course of events should have as wide and deep a practical effect as possible. Even when they write only for a few friends, as Francesco Vettori, they feel an inner need to utter their testimony on men and events, and to explain and justify their share in the latter.

And yet, with all that is characteristic in their language and style, they were powerfully affected by antiquity, and without its influence, would be inconceivable. They were no longer humanists, but they had passed through the school of humanism and they have in them more of the spirit of the ancient historians than most of the imitators of Livy. Like the ancients, they were citizens who wrote for citizens.

We cannot attempt to trace the influence of humanism in the special sciences. Each has its own history, in which the Italian investigators of the period, chiefly through their rediscovery of the results attained by antiquity,[124] mark a new epoch, more or less distinctly, with which the modern period of the science in question begins. With regard to philosophy, too, we must refer the reader to the special historical works on the subject. The influence of the old philosophers on Italian culture appears at times immense, at times inconsiderable: the former, when we consider how the doctrines of Aristotle, chiefly drawn from the *Ethics* [125] and *Politics*— both widely diffused at an early period—became the common property of educated Italians, and how the whole method of abstract thought was governed by him; the latter, when we remember how slight was the dogmatic influence of the old philosophies, and even of the enthusiastic Florentine Platonists, on the spirit of the people at large. What looks like such an influence is generally no more than a consequence of the new culture in general, and of the special growth and development of the Italian mind. When we come to speak of religion, we shall have more to say on this. But in by far the greater number of cases, we have to do, not with the general culture of the people, but with the utterances of individuals or of learned circles; and here, too, a distinction must be drawn between the true assimilation of ancient doctrines and fashion-

123. In the case of Machiavelli, we may add, also his observation of the past.
124. In fact, it was already said that Homer alone contained the whole of the arts and sciences—that he was an encyclopedia.
125. A cardinal under Paul II had his cooks instructed in Aristotle's *Ethics*.

able affectation. For with many, antiquity was only a fashion, even among very learned people.

Nevertheless, all that looks like affectation to our age, need not actually have been so then. The giving of Greek and Latin names to children, for example, is certainly better and more estimable than the present practice of taking them (especially female names) from novels. When the enthusiasm for the ancient world was greater than for the saints, it was simple and natural enough that noble families called their sons Agamemnon, Tydeus, and Achilles, and that a painter named his son Apelles and his daughter Minerva.[126] Nor will it appear unreasonable that, instead of a family name, which people were often glad to get rid of, a well-sounding ancient name was chosen. A local name, shared by all residents in the place and not yet transformed into a family name, was willingly given up, especially when its religious associations made it inconvenient. Filippo da San Gimignano called himself Callimachus. The man, misunderstood and insulted by his family, who made his fortune as a scholar in foreign cities, was proud, even if he were a Sanseverino, to change his name to Julius Pomponius Laetus. Even the simple translation of a name into Latin or Greek (as was almost uniformly the custom in Germany) may be excused to a generation that spoke and wrote Latin and needed names that could not only be declined, but used with facility in verse and prose. What was blameworthy and often ridiculous was the change of *half* a name, baptismal or family, to give it a classical sound and a new sense. Thus Giovanni was turned into Jovianus or Janus, Pietro to Petreius or Pierius, Antonio to Aonius, Sannazaro to Syncerus, Luca Grasso to Lucius Crassus. Ariosto, who speaks with such derision of all this, lived to see children called after his own heroes and heroines.

Nor must we judge too severely the Latinization of many social relations, titles of officials, ceremonies, and the like, in the writers of the period. As long as people were satisfied with a simple, fluent Latin style, as was the case with most writers from Petrarch to Aeneas Sylvius, this practice was not so frequent and striking; it became inevitable when a faultless, above all, Ciceronian, Latin was demanded. Modern names and things no longer harmonized with the style, unless

---

126. Vasari, Life of Sodoma and Life of Garofalo. — It is not surprising that the profligate women of Rome took the most sonorous ancient names—Julia, Lucretia, Cassandra, Portia, Virginia, Penthesilea, under which they appear in Aretino.

they were first artificially changed. Pedants found pleasure in addressing municipal councilors as *patres conscripti*, nuns as *virgines vestales*, and titling every saint *Divus* or *Deus*; but men of better taste, such as Paolo Giovio, only did so when they could not help it. But as Giovio lays no special stress on it, we are not offended if, in his melodious language, the cardinals appear as *senatores*, their dean as *princeps senatus*, excommunication as *dirae*, and the carnival as *lupercalia*. The example of this author alone is enough to warn us against drawing a hasty inference from these peculiarities of style as to the writer's whole mode of thinking.

The history of Latin composition cannot be traced in detail here. For fully two centuries the humanists acted as though Latin were, and must remain, the only language worth writing. Poggio deplores that Dante wrote his great poem in Italian; and Dante, as is well known, actually made the attempt in Latin, and first wrote the beginning of the *Inferno* in hexameters. The whole future of Italian poetry hung on his not continuing in this way, but even Petrarch relied more on his Latin poetry than on the sonnets and *canzoni*, and even Ariosto was expected to write his poem in Latin. A stronger coercion never existed in literature; but poetry shook it off for the most part, and it may be said, without the risk of too great optimism, that it was good for Italian poetry to have had both means of expressing itself. In both something great and characteristic was achieved, and in each we can see the reason why Latin or Italian was chosen. Perhaps the same may be said of prose. The position and influence of Italian culture throughout the world depended on the fact that certain subjects were treated in Latin—*urbi et orbi* [for the city and the world]—whereas Italian prose was written best by those to whom it cost an inward struggle not to write in Latin.

From the fourteenth century Cicero was uncontested as the purest model of prose. This was by no means due solely to a dispassionate opinion in favor of his choice of language, the structure of his sentences, and his style of composition, but to the fact that the Italian spirit responded fully and instinctively to the amiability of the letter writer, to the brilliancy of the orator, and to the lucid exposition of the philosophical thinker. Even Petrarch recognized clearly Cicero's weaknesses as a man and as a statesman, but he respected him too much to rejoice over them. After Petrarch's time, the epistolary style was modeled entirely on Cicero; and the other forms, with the exception of the narrative, followed suit. Yet the true Ciceronianism, which rejected every phrase that could not be justified by the source, did not appear till the end of the fifteenth century, when the grammatical writings of Lorenzo Valla began to be felt throughout Italy, and when the opinions of the Roman historians of literature had been sifted and compared. Only then was every shade of difference in the style of the ancients studied with closer and closer attention, till the consoling conclusion was at last reached that the one perfect model was Cicero, or, if all forms of literature were to be included, "that immortal and almost heavenly age of Cicero." Men such as Pietro Bembo and Piero Valeriano now turned all their energies to this one object. Even those who had long resisted and had formed for themselves an archaic style based on earlier authors, finally yielded and bowed before Cicero. At Bembo's advice, Longolius determined to read nothing but Cicero for five years, and even took an oath to use no word which did not occur in this author. It was this temper that erupted at last in the great war among the scholars, in which Erasmus and the elder Scaliger led the battle.

But not all the admirers of Cicero were so one-sided as to consider him the only source of language. In the fifteenth century, Politian and Ermolao Barbaro made a conscious and deliberate effort to form a style of their own, on the basis, naturally, of an "overflowing" learning, and our informant, Paolo Giovio, pursued the same end. He first attempted, not always successfully but often with remarkable power and elegance and with great effort, to reproduce in Latin a number of modern, particularly aesthetic, ideas. His Latin characteristics of the great painters and sculptors of his time[127] contain a mixture of the most intelligent and most blundering interpretation. Even Leo X, who placed his glory in the fact, *ut lingua latina nostro pontificatu dicatur facta auctior* [that it is said that the Latin language was increased during our Pontificate], was inclined to a liberal and not too exclusive Latinity, which, indeed, was in harmony with his pleasure-loving nature. He was satisfied if the Latin he had to read and hear was lively, elegant, and idiomatic. Then, too, Cicero offered no model for Latin conversation, so that here other gods had to be worshiped beside him. The want was supplied by presentations of the comedies of Plautus and Terence, frequent both in and out of Rome, which for the actors were an incomparable exercise in Latin as the language of daily life. During the Pontificate of Paul II, the learned Cardinal

127. It is well known that Giovio had long wanted to undertake the great work that Vasari ultimately accomplished.

of Teano (probably Niccolò Forteguerra of Pistoia) became famous because he dared to work on even the most defective plays of Plautus, those that had lost the cast of the characters, and went carefully through all that was left by this author, chiefly with an eye to the language. It may well be that it was he who stimulated the public presentations of these plays. Later Pomponius Laetus took up the same subject, and acted as producer when Plautus was put on the stage in the houses of great churchmen. The fact that these presentations became less common after 1520, is reckoned by Giovio, as we have seen, among the causes of the decline of eloquence.

We may, in conclusion, mention a parallel to Ciceronianism in the sphere of art: the revival of Vitruvius by the architects. And here, too, the law that prevails elsewhere in the history of the Renaissance holds good, that each artistic movement is preceded by a corresponding movement in the general culture of the age. In this case, the interval is not more than about twenty years, if we reckon from Cardinal Adriano da Corneto (1505?) to the first avowed Vitruvians.

But the chief pride of the humanists was their modern Latin poetry. We must discuss this, too, to the extent that it serves to characterize the humanist movement.

How favorable public opinion was to this form of poetry, and how close it came to supplanting all others, has already been shown. We may be very sure that the most gifted and highly developed nation extant at that time did not renounce the use of a language such as Italian out of mere folly and without significant purpose. A powerful reason must have led them to do so.

This was the devotion to antiquity. Like all ardent and genuine devotion, it prompted men to imitation. At other times and among other nations we find many isolated attempts of the same kind. But only in Italy were the two chief conditions present that were necessary for the continuance and development of neo-Latin poetry: a general interest in the subject among the instructed classes, and a partial reawakening of the old Italian genius among the poets themselves—the wondrous echo of a far-off strain. The best of what is produced under such conditions is not imitation, but individual, free creation. If we refuse to tolerate any borrowed forms in art, if we either set no value on antiquity at all, or attribute to it some magical and unapproachable virtue, or if we will pardon no slips in poets who were forced, for instance, to guess or to discover a multitude of syllabic quantities, then we had better let this class of literature alone. Its best works were not created to defy criticism, but to give pleasure to the poet and to thousands of his contemporaries.

Least successful were the epics derived from ancient history or legends. The essential conditions for a living epic poetry were not, as we know, given to the Romans who now served as models, not even, apart from Homer, to the Greeks. How could they emerge among the Latins of the Renaissance? And yet Petrarch's *Africa* probably found as many and as enthusiastic readers and hearers as any epic of modern times. Purpose and origin of the poem are not without interest. The fourteenth century recognized with sound historical sense that the time of the second Punic war had been the noonday of Roman greatness; and Petrarch could not resist writing of this time. Had Silius Italicus already been discovered, Petrarch would probably have chosen another subject; but as it was, the glorification of Scipio Africanus the Elder was so much in accord with the spirit of the fourteenth century, that another poet, Zanobi di Strada, also undertook the same task, and only out of respect for Petrarch stopped writing the poem on which he had already made great progress. If any justification were needed for the *Africa*, it lies in the fact that in Petrarch's time and afterward, Scipio was as much an object of public interest as if he were alive, and that he was regarded as greater than Alexander, Pompey, and Caesar. How many modern epics have a subject so popular, so historical in its basis, and so striking to the imagination? As poetry, it is true, the poem is unreadable. For other historical subjects we refer the reader to the histories of literature.

A richer and more fruitful vein was the poetic amplification of antique mythology, filling in the lacunae. Even Italian poetry began to take part in this early, beginning with the *Teseide* of Boccaccio, which ranks as his best poetic work. Under Martin V, Maffeo Vegio wrote a thirteenth book to the *Aeneid* in Latin; and we find a number of less ambitious attempts especially in the style of Claudian, a *Meleagris*, a *Hesperis*, etc. But most remarkable are the newly invented myths that peopled the fairest regions of Italy with a primeval race of gods, nymphs, genii, and even shepherds, to the point where the epic and bucolic can no longer be separated. The fact that in the narrative or conversational eclogue after the time of Petrarch, pastoral life was treated in a purely conventional manner, as a vehicle of all possible feelings and fancies will be discussed below.[128] Here we are interested only in the new myths. In these we see more clearly than

128. The brilliant exceptions, where rural life is treated realistically, will also be mentioned below.

anywhere else the double significance the old gods had for the men of the Renaissance. On the one hand, they replace abstract terms in poetry and render allegorical figures superfluous; and, on the other, they serve as free and independent elements in art, as forms of beauty that can be turned to some account in any and every poem. The example was boldly set by Boccaccio with his fanciful world of gods and shepherds who people the country round Florence in his *Ninfale d'Ameto and Ninfale Fiesolano*, both written in Italian. But the masterpiece in this style was the *Sarca* of Pietro Bembo, which tells how the river god of that name wooed the nymph Garda; of the brilliant marriage feast in a cave of Monte Baldo; of the prophecies of Manto, daughter of Tiresias; of the birth of the child Mincius; of the founding of Mantua, and of the future glory of Vergil, son of Mincius and Magia, nymph of Andes. This humanistic rococo is set forth by Bembo in verses of great beauty, concluding with an address to Vergil that any poet might envy. Such works are often slighted as mere declamation. This is a matter of taste on which we are all free to form our own opinion.

Further, we find long epic poems in hexameters on biblical or ecclesiastical subjects. The authors were by no means always in search of preferment or Papal favor. In the best of them, and even in less gifted writers, as Baptista Mantuanus, the author of the *Parthenice*, there was probably an honest desire to serve religion by their Latin verses—a desire with which their half-pagan conception of Catholicism harmonized only too well. Gyraldus lists a number of these poets, among whom Vida, with his *Christiad*, and Sannazaro, with his three books, *De partu Virginis*, hold first place. Sannazaro is impressive by the steady and powerful flow of his verse, in which Christian and pagan elements are mingled without scruple, by the plastic vigor of his description, and by the perfection of his workmanship. He could introduce Vergil's fourth Eclogue into his song of the shepherds at the manger without fear of comparison. In treating the other world, he sometimes exhibits a boldness worthy of Dante, as when King David in the Limbo of the Patriarchs rises to sing and prophesy, or when the Eternal One, seated on the throne clad in a mantle shining with pictures of all the elements, addresses the heavenly host. At other times he does not hesitate to weave the old classical mythology into his subject, yet without spoiling the harmony of the whole, since the pagan deities are only accessory figures and play no important part in the story. To appreciate the artistic genius of that age in its full range we must not refuse to notice such works as these. The merit of Sannazaro will appear the greater, when we consider that the mixture of Christian and pagan elements is apt to disturb us much more in poetry than in the visual arts. The latter can still satisfy the eye by beauty of form and color, and in general are much more independent of the significance of the subject than poetry. In the visual arts, the imagination is interested chiefly in the form, in poetry, in the matter. Honest Baptista Mantuanus, in his calendar of the festivals, tried another expedient. Instead of making the gods and demigods serve the purposes of sacred history, he put them, as the Fathers of the Church did, in active opposition to it. When the angel Gabriel salutes the Virgin at Nazareth, Mercury flies after him from Carmel and listens at the door. Then he announces the result of his eavesdropping to the assembled gods, and stimulates them thereby to desperate resolutions. Indeed, elsewhere in his writings, Thetis, Ceres, Aeolus, and other pagan deities pay willing homage to the glory of the Madonna.

The fame of Sannazaro, the number of his imitators, the enthusiastic homage that was paid him by the greatest men, all show how dear and necessary he was to his age. On the threshold of the Reformation he solved the problem for the Church: that it was possible for a poet to be completely classical and still be a Christian, and Leo as well as Clement thanked him loudly for this.

And, finally, contemporary history was also treated in hexameters or distichs, sometimes in a narrative and sometimes in a panegyrical style, but most commonly in honor of some prince or princely family. Thus there was a Sforziad, a Borseid, a Borgiad, a Trivulziad, and the like, which failed completely in their purpose. Those who became famous and immortal did not owe it to this sort of poem, for which the world has always had an ineradicable dislike, even when it happens to be written by a good poet. A wholly different effect is produced by smaller, simpler, and more unpretentious scenes from the lives of distinguished men, such as the beautiful poem on Leo X's Hunt at Palo, or the Journey of Julius II [*Iter Julii Secundi*] by Adriano da Corneto. Brilliant descriptions of hunting parties are found in Ercole Strozzi, in the above-mentioned Adriano, and in others; and it is a pity that the modern reader should allow himself to be irritated or repelled by the adulation with which they are filled. The masterly treatment and the considerable historical value of many of these most graceful poems guarantee to them a longer existence than many popular works of our own day are likely to attain.

In general, these poems are better the less they indulge in the sentimental and the general. Some of the smaller epic poems, even of recognized masters, unintentionally produce, by the ill-timed introduction of mythological elements, an impression that is indescribably ludicrous. Such, for instance, is the lament of Ercole Strozzi on Cesare Borgia. We hear the complaint of Roma, who had set all her hopes on the Spanish Popes, Calixtus III and Alexander VI, and who saw her promised deliverer in Cesare, whose history is related down to the catastrophe of 1503. The poet then asks the Muse what the counsels of the gods were at that moment, and Erato tells how, on Olympus, Pallas took the part of the Spaniards, Venus of the Italians, how both embrace the knees of Jupiter, how he kisses them, soothes them, and explains to them that he is helpless against the fate woven by the Parcae, but that the divine promises will be fulfilled by the child of the House of Este-Borgia.[129] After relating the fabulous origin of both families, he declares that he can confer immortality on Cesare as little as he could once—despite earnest entreaties—on a Memmon or Achilles; he finally concludes with the consoling assurance that Cesare, before his own death, will destroy many people in war. Mars then hastens to Naples to stir up war and confusion, while Pallas goes to Nepi, and there appears to the dying Cesare in the form of Alexander VI. After giving him the good advice to submit to his fate and be satisfied with the glory of his name, the Papal goddess vanishes "like a bird."

Yet we should deprive ourselves needlessly of an enjoyment that is sometimes very great, were we to throw aside everything in which classical mythology plays a part, whether well or badly. Painting and sculpture have ennobled this purely conventional form to a degree unknown in any other art. And even the lover of parody has nothing to lose, for here are the beginnings of that class of literature, e.g., the Macaroniana, to which Giovanni Bellini's comic *Feast of the Gods*[130] already stands as a parallel.

Many of the narrative poems in hexameters are also merely exercises, or adaptations of histories in prose (which the reader will prefer, where he can find them). Finally everything—every quarrel and every ceremony—was put into verse, even by the German humanists of the Reformation.

129. Ercole II of Ferrara, born April 4, 1508, probably shortly before or shortly after the composition of this poem.
130. [National Gallery of Art, Washington, D.C. (Widener Collection).]

And yet it would be unfair to attribute this to mere laziness or to an excessive facility in stringing verses together. In Italy, at all events, it was due rather to an abundant sense of style, as is further proved by the mass of contemporary reports, histories, and even pamphlets, in *terza rima*. Just as Niccolò da Uzzano cast his scheme for a new constitution, Machiavelli his view of the history of his own time, a third, the life of Savonarola, and a fourth the siege of Piombino by Alfonso the Great in this difficult meter in order to produce a stronger effect, so did many others feel the need of hexameters in order to win *their* public. What was tolerated and demanded in this form is best shown by the didactic poetry of the time. Its popularity in the sixteenth century is astounding; the making of gold, the game of chess, the management of silkworms, astrology, venereal disease are celebrated in Latin hexameters, to say nothing of many long Italian poems of the same kind. Nowadays these didactic poems are condemned unread, and how much, as a matter of fact, they are really worth reading, we are unable to say. One thing is certain: epochs far above our own in the feeling for beauty—the Renaissance and the Greco-Roman world—could not dispense with this form of poetry. It may be urged in reply, that it is not the lack of a feeling for beauty, but the greater seriousness and the universal treatment of all knowledge that renders the poetic form inappropriate, on which point we shall not enter.

One of these didactic works is occasionally republished: the *Zodiac of Life*, by Marcellus Palingenius, a Ferrarese secret adherent of Protestantism. To the loftiest speculations on God, virtue, and immortality, the writer connects the discussion of many questions of practical life, because of which he is an important authority in the history of morals. On the whole, however, his work lies outside the boundaries of the Renaissance, since his serious didactic purpose allows allegory to outstrip mythology.

But it was in lyric, and especially in elegiac poetry, that the poet-scholar came closest to antiquity; and after these, in epigram.

In the lighter style, Catullus exercised a perfect fascination over the Italians. Many elegant Latin madrigals, many little satires and malicious epistles are mere adaptations from him; and the death of parrots and lap dogs is bewailed, even where there is no verbal imitation, in precisely the tone and style of the verses on Lesbia's sparrow. There are short poems of this sort, the date of which even critics would be unable to fix, were it not for positive evidence that places them firmly in the fifteenth and sixteenth centuries.

On the other hand, there is scarcely an ode in the Sapphic or Alcaic meter that does not clearly betray its modern origin. This shows itself mostly by a rhetorical verbosity, rare in antiquity before the time of Statius, and by a singular lack of the lyrical concentration that is indispensable to this style of poetry. Single passages in an ode, sometimes two or three consecutive strophes, may look like an ancient fragment; but a longer extract will seldom maintain this character. And where it does, as, for instance, in the fine Ode to Venus, by Andrea Navagero, it is easy to detect a simple paraphrase of ancient masterpieces. Some of the ode writers take the saints for their subject and invoke them in verses tastefully modeled after analogous odes of Horace and Catullus. This is the manner of Navagero in the Ode to the Archangel Gabriel, and particularly of Sannazaro who goes very far in his appropriation of pagan sentiment. He celebrates magnificently his patron saint, whose chapel was attached to his lovely villa on the shores of Posilippo, "there where the waves of the sea drink up the stream from the rocks, and surge against the walls of the little sanctuary." His delight is in the annual feast of St. Nazarius, and the branches and garlands with which the chapel is hung on this day seem to him like sacrificial gifts. Full of sorrow, and far off in exile, at St.-Nazaire, on the banks of the Loire, with the banished Federigo of Aragon, he brings wreaths of box and oak leaves to his patron saint on the same anniversary, thinking of former years, when all the youth of Posilippo would come forth to greet him on flower-hung boats, praying for his return.

The most deceptive likeness to classical style was achieved by a class of poems in elegiacs or hexameters, whose subject ranges from true elegy to epigram. The humanists dealt most freely with the text of the Roman elegiac poets, and thus felt most at home in imitating them. The elegy of Navagero addressed to Night, like other poems of the same age and kind, is full of points that remind us of his models; but it has the finest antique ring about it. Indeed, Navagero always begins by choosing a truly poetical subject, which he then treats, not with servile imitation but with masterly freedom, in the style of the Anthology, of Ovid, of Catullus, or of the Vergilian eclogues. He uses mythology sparingly, only, for instance, in a prayer to Ceres and other rural divinities to introduce a sketch of country life. An address to his country, on his return from an embassy to Spain, though left unfinished, might have been worthy of a place beside the *Bella Italia, amate sponde* of Vincenzo Monti, if the rest had been equal to this beginning:

> *Salve cura Deûm, mundi felicior ora,*
> *Formosae Veneris dulces salvete recessus;*
> *Ut vos post tantos animi mentisque labores*
> *Aspicio lustroque libens, ut munere vestro*
> *Sollicitas toto depello e pectore curas!* [131]

The elegiac or hexametric form became the carrier of all higher sentiment, of the noblest patriotic enthusiasm (the elegy to Julius II) and the most elaborate deification of the ruling houses, but also of the tender melancholy of a Tibullus. Francesco Maria Molza, who rivals Statius and Martial in his flattery of Clement VII and the Farnesi, gives us in his elegy to his "comrades," written from a sickbed, thoughts on death as beautiful and genuinely antique as can be found in any of the ancient poets, and without borrowing anything worth speaking of from them. The spirit and range of Roman elegy were best understood and reproduced by Sannazaro, and no other writer of his time offers us so varied a choice of good poems in this style. — Now and then we shall mention some of these elegies because of their subject matter.

The Latin epigram finally became an affair of serious importance in that time, since a few clever lines engraved on a monument or quoted with laughter in society could establish a scholar's celebrity. This tendency exhibited itself early. When it was known that Guido da Polenta wished to erect a monument at Dante's grave, epitaphs poured in from all directions, "written by such who wished to *show themselves*, or to honor the dead poet, or to win the favor of Polenta." On the tomb of Archbishop Giovanni Visconti (d. 1354) in the Cathedral at Milan, we read at the end of thirty-six hexameters: "Master Gabrius de Zamoreis of Parma, Doctor of Laws, wrote these verses." In course of time, chiefly under the influence of Martial, and also Catullus, an extensive literature of this sort grew up. The greatest of all triumphs

---

131. [Hail, darling of the gods, thou happiest spot of earth! /hail chosen haunt of beauty's queen!/What joy I feel to see you thus again, and tread your shores/after so many toils endured in mind and soul!/How from my heart by your free gift I cast all anxious cares! — J.A. Symonds tr.]

was to have an epigram mistaken for antique, as though it had been copied from some old marble, or to make one so good that all Italy learned it by heart, as, for example, happened to some of Bembo's. When the Venetian government paid Sannazaro 600 ducats for his eulogy in three distichs, no one thought it an act of generous prodigality. The epigram was prized for what it was to all the educated classes of that age—the concentrated essence of fame. Nor, on the other hand, was any man so powerful that he was above the reach of a satirical epigram, and even the most powerful needed, for every inscription they set before the public eye, the aid of careful and learned scholars, for a blunder could qualify it for a place in the collections of ludicrous epitaphs. Epigraphy and literary epigrams became helpmates; the former was based on the most diligent study of ancient monuments.

The capital city of epigrams and inscriptions was, and remained, Rome. In this State without hereditary honors each man had to look after his own immortality; at the same time the epigram was an effective weapon against competitors. Pius II enumerates with satisfaction the distichs his chief poet Campanus wrote on every suitable occurrence of his reign. Under the succeeding Popes, satirical epigrams came into fashion and reached, in the opposition to Alexander VI and his family, the highest pitch of defiant invective. Sannazaro, it is true, wrote his verses in a place of comparative safety, but others in the immediate neighborhood of the court dared the most reckless attacks. When eight threatening distichs were found fastened to the doors of the library, Alexander strengthened his guard by 800 men; we can imagine what he would have done to the poet had he caught him. – Under Leo X, Latin epigrams were daily bread. For complimenting or reviling the Pope, for punishing enemies and victims named or unnamed, for real or imaginary subjects of wit, malice, grief, or contemplation, no form was more suitable. On the famous group of the *Virgin and Child with St. Anne,* which Andrea Sansovino carved for Sant' Agostino, no fewer than 120 persons wrote Latin verses, not so much, it is true, from piety, as from regard for the man who had commissioned the work. This man, Johann Goritz of Luxemburg, Papal referendary of petitions, not only held a religious service on the feast of St. Anne, but gave a great literary dinner in his garden on the slopes of the Capitol. It was then worth mustering, in a long poem *De poetis urbanis,* the whole crowd of poets who sought their fortune at the court of Leo, which was done by Franciscus Arsillus—a man who needed the patronage neither of Pope nor prince, and who dared to speak his mind, even against his colleagues. – The epigram survived the Pontificate of Paul III only in a few rare echoes, while epigraphy continued to flourish till the seventeenth century, when it finally perished of bombast.

Even in Venice this form of poetry had its own history, which we are able to trace with the help of Francesco Sansovino's *Venezia*. A standing task was offered by the mottoes (*brievi*) on the pictures of the Doges in the great hall of the ducal palace—two or four hexameters, setting forth the most noteworthy facts in the government of each. In the fourteenth century the tombs of the Doges bore short inscriptions in prose, which only recorded facts, and beside them turgid hexameters or leonine verses. In the fifteenth century more care was taken with the style; in the sixteenth century it is seen at its best; soon after came pointless antithesis, prosopopoeia, false pathos, praise of abstract qualities—in a word, bombast. A good many traces of satire can be detected, and veiled criticism of the living is implied in open praise of the dead. At a much later period we find a few instances of deliberate recurrence to the old, simple style.

Architectural and decorative works were constructed with a view to receiving inscriptions, often in multitudinous repetition; whereas the Gothic art of the North provided space for them only with difficulty, and in sepulchral monuments, for example, left only the most exposed parts free—namely, the edges.

By what we have said so far, we have, perhaps, failed to convince the reader of the characteristic value of this Latin poetry of the Italians. Our task was only to indicate its position and necessity in the history of civilization. Even in its own day, a caricature of it appeared—the so-called macaronic poetry. The masterpiece of this style, the *opus macaronicorum*, was written by Merlinus Coccaius (Teofilo Folengo of Mantua). We shall now and then have occasion to refer to the subject matter of this poem. The comic effect of the form—hexameter and other verses made up of Latin words and Italian words with Latin endings—lies chiefly in the fact that these combinations sound like so many slips of the tongue, or like the effusions of an overhasty Latin *improvisatore*. Imitations in German and Latin do not give the slightest idea of this effect.

After a brilliant succession of poet-scholars had, since the beginning of the fourteenth century, filled Italy and the world with the worship of antiquity, had determined the forms of education and culture, had often taken the lead in political affairs, and had, to the best of their ability, reproduced ancient literature, in the sixteenth century, when there was no desire yet to dispense completely with their doctrines and scholarship, the whole class fell into deep and general disgrace. They still served as models to the poets, historians, and orators, but no one wanted to be reckoned of their number. To the two chief accusations against them—malicious self-conceit and abominable profligacy—a third charge was now loudly added by the rising powers of the Counter Reformation: irreligion.

Why, it may be asked, were these reproaches, whether true or false, not heard sooner? As a matter of fact, they were heard at a very early period, but the effect they produced was insignificant, for the simple reason that men were far too dependent on the scholars for their knowledge of antiquity —the scholars were in the most personal sense the possessors, carriers, and diffusers of ancient culture. But the spread of printed editions of the classics, and of large and well-arranged handbooks and encyclopedias, went far to free the people from the necessity of personal intercourse with the humanists, and, as soon as they could be even partly dispensed with, the change in popular feeling became manifest. It was a change under which good and bad suffered indiscriminately.

The first to make these charges were the humanists themselves. Of all men who ever formed a class, they had the least sense of their common interests, and least respected what there was of this sense. As soon as they began to vie for position, no holds were barred. From literary discussion they passed with astonishing suddenness to the fiercest and the most groundless vituperation. They were not satisfied with refuting an opponent, but sought to annihilate him. Some of this must have been caused by their position and circumstances; we have seen how fiercely the age, whose loudest spokesmen they were, was tossed to and fro by the passion for fame and the passion for satire. Their position, too, in practical life was one that they had continually to fight for. In such a temper they wrote and spoke and described one another. Poggio's works alone contain enough dirt to create a prejudice against the whole class—and these *opera Poggii* were just those most often printed, on the north as well as on the south side of the Alps. We must be careful not to rejoice too soon if, in the fifteenth century, we meet among these men a figure who seems immaculate; on further inquiry there is always a danger of meeting some foul charge that even if it is incredible, still discolors the picture. The

mass of indecent Latin poems in circulation, and such things
as ribaldry on the subject of one's own family, as in Pontano's
dialogue *Antonius,* did the rest to discredit the class. The
sixteenth century was not only familiar with all these ugly
symptoms, but had also grown tired of the humanist. They
had to pay both for their misdeeds and for the excess of
honor that had previously been accorded them. Their evil
fate willed it that the greatest poet of the nation [Ariosto]
wrote of them in a tone of calm and sovereign contempt.

Of the reproaches that now combined to excite so much
hatred, many were only too well founded. A clear and
unmistakable tendency to strictness in matters of religion and
morality was alive in many of the philologists, and it is proof
of little knowledge of the period if the whole class is condemned. Yet many, and among them the loudest, were guilty.

Three things explain and perhaps lessen their guilt: the
overflowing excess of favor and fortune when luck was on
their side; the uncertainty of their existence, in which luxury
or misery depended on the caprice of a patron or the malice
of an enemy; and, finally, the misleading influence of antiquity. This undermined their morality, without giving them its
own; and in religious matters, since they could never accept
the positive belief in the old gods, it affected them only on
the negative and skeptical side. Just because they conceived of antiquity dogmatically—as the model for all
thought and action—its influence had to be pernicious. But
that an age existed which idolized the ancient world and
its products with an exclusive devotion was no longer the
fault of individuals; it was the result of historical providence.
All the culture of the ages that have followed, and of the
ages to come, rests upon the fact that it was so, and that all
the ends of life but this one were then deliberately put aside.

The career of the humanist was, as a rule, of such a kind
that only the strongest characters could pass through it un-
scathed. The first danger came, in some cases, from the
parents, who sought to turn a precocious child into a miracle
of learning, with an eye to his future position in that class
which then was supreme. Youthful prodigies, however, seldom
rise above a certain level; or, if they do, are forced to achieve
their further progress and development at the cost of the
bitterest trials. For an ambitious youth, the fame and brilliant
position of the humanists were a perilous temptation; it
seemed to him that he, too, "through inborn pride, could no
longer regard the low and common things of life." And so
he plunged into a life of excitement and vicissitude, in which
exhausting studies, tutorships, secretaryships, professorships,

offices in princely households, mortal enmities and perils, luxury and beggary, boundless admiration and boundless contempt, followed confusedly one upon the other, and in which the most solid worth and learning were often pushed aside by superficial impudence. But the greatest evil was that the position of the humanist was almost incompatible with a fixed home, since it either made frequent changes of dwelling necessary for a livelihood, or so affected the mind of the individual that he could never be happy for long in one place. While he grew tired of the people and had no peace among the enmities he excited, the people in their turn demanded something new. Much as this life reminds us of the Greek sophists of the Empire, as described to us by Philostratus, the position of the sophists was more favorable. They often had money, or could do without it more easily, and as professional teachers of rhetoric rather than men of learning, their life was freer and simpler. But the scholar of the Renaissance was forced to combine great learning with the power of resisting the influence of ever-changing pursuits and situations. Add to this the deadening effect of licentious excess, and—since do what he might, the worst was believed of him—a total indifference to the moral laws that were recognized by others. Such men cannot exist without an inordinate pride. They needed it, if only to keep their heads above water, and were confirmed in it by the deification mixed with hatred that was their lot. They are the most striking examples and victims of an unbridled subjectivity.

The attacks and satirical pictures began, as we have said, at an early period. For all strongly marked individuality, for every kind of distinction, a corrective was at hand in the national taste for ridicule. And in this case the men themselves offered the most terrible materials, which satire had only to put to use. In the fifteenth century, Baptista Mantuanus, in discoursing of the seven monsters, includes the humanists and many others under the entry *superbia* [pride]. He describes how, fancying themselves children of Apollo, they walk with affected solemnity and with sullen, malicious looks, now gazing at their own shadow, now brooding over the popular praise they seek, like cranes in search of food. But in the sixteenth century the indictment was presented in full. Besides Ariosto, there is the testimony of their own historian Gyraldus, whose treatise, written under Leo X, was probably revised about the year 1540. Warning examples from ancient and modern times of the moral disorder and wretched existence of the scholars meet us in astonishing abundance, and along with these, accusations of the most serious nature are formally lodged against them. Among these are anger, vanity, obstinacy, self-adoration, a dissolute private life, immorality of all descriptions, heresy, atheism; further, the habit of speaking without conviction, a sinister influence on government, pedantry of speech, thanklessness toward teachers, and abject flattery of the great, who first give the scholar a taste of their favors and then leave him to starve. The description is closed by a reference to the golden age, when no such thing as science existed on the earth. Of these charges, that of heresy soon became the most dangerous, and Gyraldus himself, when he later republished a perfectly harmless youthful work, had to take refuge under the mantle of Duke Ercole II of Ferrara,[132] since the men who now had the upper hand held that people had better spend their time on Christian themes than on mythological research. He justifies himself on the ground that the latter, on the contrary, were at such a time almost the only harmless branches of study, since they deal with subjects of a perfectly neutral character.

But if it is the duty of the historian to seek evidence in which moral judgment is tempered by human sympathy, he will find no greater authority than the work by Pierio Valeriano, On the Infelicity of the Scholar, which has been mentioned so often. It was written under the gloomy impressions left by the sack of Rome, which seems to the writer not only the direct cause of untold misery to the men of learning, but, as it were, the fulfillment of an evil destiny that had long pursued them. Pierio is led here by a simple and, on the whole, just feeling. He does not introduce a special power that plagued the men of genius *because* of their genius; he substantiates events, in which an unlucky chance often wears the aspect of fate. He does not want to write a tragedy or to refer everything to the conflict of higher powers; he is content to lay before us the scenes of everyday life. We meet men who, in times of trouble, lose first their incomes and then their places; men who, in trying to get two appointments, miss both; misers who carry their money sewn into their clothes, and die mad when they are robbed; to others, who accept well-paid offices, and then sicken with a melancholy longing for their lost freedom. We read how some died young of a plague or fever, and how the writings that had cost them so much toil were burned with their bed and clothes; how others lived in terror of the murderous

132. The dedication is a striking evidence of the first threatening movements of the Inquisition.

threats of their colleagues; how one was slain by a covetous servant, and another caught by highwaymen on a journey and left to languish in a dungeon because he was unable to pay ransom. Many died of secret grief over insults and neglect; a Venetian died because of the death of his prodigy son, and mother and brothers followed, as if the lost child drew them all after him. Many, especially Florentines, ended their lives by suicide; others through the secret justice of a tyrant. Who, after all, is happy?—and how is that happiness achieved? by blunting all feeling for such misery? One of the speakers in the dialogue in which Pierio clothed his argument can answer these questions—the illustrious Gasparo Contarini, at the mention of whose name we should expect to hear at least something of the truest and deepest thoughts on such matters. As a type of the happy scholar, he mentions Fra Urbano Valeriano of Belluno, who for years taught Greek at Venice, who visited Greece and the East, and toward the end of his life traveled through many countries without once mounting a horse; who never had a penny of his own, rejected all honors and distinctions, and after a gay old age, died in his eighty-fourth year, without, if we except a fall from a ladder, ever having known an hour of sickness. And what was the difference between such a man and the humanists? The latter had more free will, more subjectivity than they could convert into happiness. But the mendicant friar, who had lived from boyhood in the monastery, and had never eaten or slept except by rule, no longer felt the restraint as restraint. The power of this habit allowed him to lead, amid all outward hardships, a life of inward peace, and made a greater impression on his audience by this than by his Greek. To them he was proof that it depends on ourselves whether we bear up against misfortune or surrender to it. "Amid want and toil he was happy, because he willed to be so, because he had contracted no evil habits, was not capricious, inconstant, immoderate, but was always content with little or nothing." – If we heard Contarini himself, religious motives would probably play a part in the argument—but the practical philosopher in sandals speaks plainly enough. An allied character, but in other surroundings, is revealed by Fabio Calvi of Ravenna, the commentator of Hippocrates. He lived to a great age in Rome, eating only pulse "like the Pythagoreans," and dwelt in a hovel little better than the barrel of Diogenes. Of the pension that Pope Leo gave him, he took enough to keep body and soul together, and gave the rest away. He was a healthy man, like Fra Urbano, nor is it likely that, like him, he died with a smile on his lips, for in the sack of Rome, the ninety-year-old man was dragged away by the Spaniards, who hoped for a ransom, and died of hunger in a hospital. But his name has passed into the kingdom of the immortals, for Raphael loved the old man like a father, and honored him as a teacher, and came to him for advice in all things. Perhaps they discoursed chiefly of the projected restoration of ancient Rome, perhaps of still higher matters. Who can tell what share Fabio may have had in the conception of the *School of Athens,* and in other great works by Raphael?

We would close this part of our essay with greater pleasure, with the picture of a pleasing and winning character, with that of Pomponius Laetus, if only we had more at our disposal than the letter of his pupil Sabellicus, in which an antique flavor is deliberately given to his character. Yet certain features emerge. He was a bastard of the House of the Neapolitan Sanseverini, princes of Salerno, whom he nevertheless refused to recognize, writing, in reply to an invitation to live with them, the famous letter: *Pomponius Laetus cognatis et propinquis suis salutem. Quod petitis fieri non potest. Valete* [Pomponius Laetus greets his friends and neighbors. What you request cannot be done. Farewell.]. An insignificant little figure, with small, quick eyes and quaint dress, he lived during the last decades of the fifteenth century, as professor in the University of Rome, either in his cottage in a garden on the Esquiline, or in his vineyard on the Quirinal. In one he bred his ducks and fowls; the other he cultivated according to the strictest precepts of Cato, Varro, and Columella. He spent his holidays fishing or bird catching in the Campagna, or feasting by some shady spring or on the banks of the Tiber. Wealth and luxury he despised. Free from envy and uncharitable speech, he would not suffer them in others. It was only against the hierarchy that he gave his tongue free play, and, till his latter years, was considered a scorner of religion. He was involved in the persecution of the humanists begun by Pope Paul II, and was surrendered to this Pontiff by the Venetians; but no unworthy confessions could be wrung from him. He was afterward befriended and supported by Popes and prelates, and when his house was plundered in the disturbances under Sixtus IV, more was collected for him than he had lost. No teacher was more conscientious. Before daybreak he was seen descending the Esquiline with his lantern, and on reaching his lecture room always found it filled to overflowing. A stutter compelled him to speak with care, but his delivery was even and effective. His few works give evidence of careful writing. No scholar treated the text of ancient authors more soberly and accurately. The remains of antiquity that surrounded him in Rome touched him so deeply that he would stand before them as if entranced, or would suddenly burst into tears. Since he was ready to lay aside his own studies in order to help others, he was much loved and had many friends; and at his death, even Alexander VI sent his courtiers to follow the corpse, which was carried by the most distinguished of his pupils. The funeral service in the Aracoeli was attended by forty bishops and by all the foreign ambassadors.

It was Laetus who introduced and conducted the presentations of ancient, chiefly Plautine, plays in Rome. Every year, he celebrated the anniversary of the foundation of the city by a festival at which his friends and pupils recited speeches and poems. Such meetings were the origin of what acquired, and long retained, the name of the Roman Academy. It was simply a free union of individuals, and was not connected to any fixed institution. Besides the occasions mentioned, it met at the invitation of a patron, or to celebrate the memory of a deceased member, as of Platina. At such times, a prelate belonging to the academy would first say mass; Pomponio would then ascend the pulpit and deliver a speech; someone else would then mount the pulpit and recite an elegy. The customary banquet, with declamations and recitations, concluded the festival, whether joyous or serious, and the academicians, notably Platina himself, early acquired the reputation of epicures. At other times, the guests performed farces in the old Atellan style. As a free association of very varied elements, the academy lasted in its original form down to the sack of Rome, and enjoyed the hospitality of Angelus Coloccius, Johannes Corycius, and others. Its precise value as an element in the intellectual life of the people is as hard to estimate as that of any other social union of this kind; yet even Sadoleto reckoned it among the most precious memories of his youth. – A quantity of other academies appeared and passed away in various cities, according to the number and significance of the resident humanists or to the patronage bestowed by the great and wealthy. Of these we may mention the Academy of Naples, of which Gioviano Pontano was the center, and which sent out a colony to Lecce, and that of Pordenone, which formed the court of the *condottiere* Alviano. The circle of Il Moro, and its peculiar importance for that prince, has already been spoken of.

About the middle of the sixteenth century, these associations seem to have undergone a complete change. The humanists, driven from their commanding position and viewed askance by the men of the Counter Reformation, lost the control of the academies: and here, as elsewhere, Latin poetry was replaced by Italian. Before long every town of the least importance had its academy, with some bizarre name, and its own endowment and subscriptions. Besides the recitation of verses, the new institutions inherited from their predecessors the regular banquets and the presentation of plays, sometimes acted by the members themselves, sometimes under their direction by young amateurs, and sometimes by paid players. The fate of the Italian stage, and later even of the opera, was for a long time in the hands of these associations.

---◆---

PART FOUR

THE DISCOVERY OF THE WORLD AND OF MAN

FREE from the countless bonds that checked progress in other parts of the world, having reached a high degree of individual development, and schooled by the teachings of antiquity, the Italian mind now turned to the discovery of the outward world, and to the representation of that world in speech and form. How art accomplished this will be discussed elsewhere.

We can make only a few general observations here on the journeys of the Italians to distant parts of the world. The Crusades had opened unknown distances to all Europeans, and had awakened in all the passion for travel and adventure. It may be hard to indicate the point at which this passion allied itself with, or became the servant of, the thirst for knowledge; but it was in the Italians that this occurred first and most completely. Even in the Crusades their participation was different from that of other nations, since they already were a naval power and had commercial relations with the East. The Mediterranean Sea had raised a people who differed from those who lived inland; and never, from the very structure of their character, could the Italians be adventurers in the sense the word bore among the Northerners. Once they were at home in all the eastern harbors of the Mediterranean, it was natural that the most enterprising among them should join that vast Mohammedan nomadism that was discharged there, which there found its outlet. A whole world lay, as it were, freshly discovered before them. Or, as Polo of Venice, they were caught in the current of the Mongolian peoples and were carried to the steps of the throne of the Great Khan. At an early period, we find Italians sharing in the discoveries made in the Atlantic Ocean, as, for example, the Genoese, who found the Canary Islands in the thirteenth century. In the same year, 1291, that Ptolemais, the last remnant of the Christian East, was lost, it was again the Genoese who made the first known attempt to find a sea passage to the East Indies. Columbus is but the greatest of a long list of Italians who, in the service of the Western nations, sailed into distant seas. The true discoverer, however, is not the man who is the first accidentally to stumble upon something, but the man who finds what he has sought. Only such a man is linked with the thoughts and interests of his predecessors, and this relationship will also determine the account he gives of his search. This is why the Italians, although their claim to be the first comers to this or that shore may be disputed, will always remain the nation of discoverers for the whole later part of the Middle Ages.

The fuller proof of this assertion belongs to the special history of discoveries. Yet again and again we turn with admiration to the august figure of the great Genoese, by whom a new continent beyond the ocean was demanded, sought, and found; and who was the first to be able to say: *il mondo è poco*—the world is not so large as men have thought. Whereas Spain gave Alexander VI to the Italians, Italy gave Columbus to the Spaniards. Only a few weeks before the death of that Pope, Columbus wrote (July 7, 1503) from Jamaica his noble letter to the thankless Catholic kings, which succeeding generations have never been able to read without profound emotion. In a codicil to his will, dated Valladolid, May 4, 1506, he bequeathed to "his beloved home, the Republic of Genoa, the prayer book which Pope Alexander had given him, and which in prison, in conflict, and in every kind of adversity, had been to him the greatest comfort." These words seem to cast upon the abhorred name of Borgia one last gleam of grace and mercy.

The development of geographical and allied sciences among the Italians will, like the history of their voyages, be touched upon only briefly. A superficial comparison of their achievements with those of other nations shows an early and striking superiority on their part. Where, in the middle of the fifteenth century, was there, anywhere but in Italy, such a union of geographical, statistical, and historical knowledge as there was in Aeneas Sylvius? Where such a harmonious exposition? Not only in his great geographical work, but in his letters and commentaries, he describes with equal mastery landscapes, cities, manners, industries and products, political conditions and constitutions, wherever he draws from his own observation or the evidence of eyewitnesses. What he takes from books is, naturally, of less moment. Even the short sketch [133] of that valley in the Tirolese Alps where he had received a benefice through Frederick III leaves none of the relations of human life untouched, and displays a power and method of objective observation and comparison impossible in any but a countryman of Columbus trained in the school of the ancients. Thousands saw and, in part, knew what he knew, but they felt no impulse to draw a picture of it, and were not aware that the world desired such pictures.

In geography [134] as in other matters, it is vain to attempt to distinguish how much is to be attributed to the study of the ancients, and how much to the special genius of the Italians. They saw and treated the things of this world from an objective point of view, even before they were familiar with ancient literature, partly because they were themselves a half-antique people, and partly because their political circumstances predisposed them to it; but they would not have attained such perfection so rapidly had not the old geographers shown them the way. Finally, the influence of the existing Italian geographies on the spirit and tendencies of the travelers and discoverers was incalculable. Even the simple dilettante of a science—if, in the present case, we should assign to Aeneas Sylvius so low a rank—can diffuse just that sort of general interest in the subject which prepares for new pioneers the indispensable groundwork of a favorable predisposition in the public mind. True discoverers in any science know very well what they owe to such mediation.

For the position of the Italians in the sphere of the natural sciences, we must refer the reader to the special treatises on the subject; the only one with which we are familiar is the superficial and depreciatory work of Libri. The dispute over the priority of particular discoveries concerns us even less, since we hold that, at any time and among any civilized people, a man may appear who, starting with very scanty preparation, is irresistibly driven into the path of investigation, and through his native gifts achieves the most astonishing success. Gerbert of Reims [Pope Sylvester II] and Roger Bacon were such men; that in their special subjects they were

133. *The Commentaries of Pius II,* Book I. — That he did not always observe correctly and sometimes filled in the picture from his fancy is clearly shown, for example, by his description of Basel. Yet on the whole, his merit is great.

134. In the sixteenth century Italy continued to be the home of geographical literature, at a time when the discoverers themselves belonged almost exclusively to the countries that bordered on the Atlantic.

masters of the entire knowledge of their times was a natural
consequence of the spirit in which they worked. When once
the veil of illusion was torn apart, when once the dread of
nature and the slavery to books and tradition were overcome,
countless problems lay before them. But it is another matter
when a single nation takes a natural delight in the study
and investigation of nature when other nations are indifferent,
that is, when the discoverer is not threatened or wholly
ignored, but can count on the friendly support of congenial
spirits. That this was the case in Italy is unquestionable.
The Italian students of nature trace with pride in the *Divine
Comedy* the hints and proofs of Dante's scientific interest
in nature. We pass no judgment on his claim to priority in
this or that discovery or reference, but every layman must
be struck by the wealth of his observations on the external
world that are already expressed in his images and comparisons. He, more than any other modern poet, takes them
from reality, be it nature or human life, and uses them
never as mere ornament, but in order to give the reader the
fullest and most adequate sense of his meaning. It is in
astronomy that he appears chiefly as a scientific specialist,
though it must not be forgotten that many astronomical
allusions in his great poem, which now appear learned to us,
must have been intelligible to everyone then. Learning apart,
Dante appeals to a popular knowledge of the heavens which
the Italians of his day, from the mere fact that they were a
nautical people, had in common with the ancients. This
knowledge of the rising and setting of the constellations has
been rendered superfluous to the modern world by calendars
and clocks, and with it has gone whatever interest in astronomy the people may once have had. Nowadays, with our
schools and handbooks, every child knows—what Dante did
not know—that the earth moves round the sun; but the
interest once taken in the subject has given place, except
in the case of astronomical specialists, to the most absolute
indifference.

The pseudo-science that dealt with the stars proves nothing
against the inductive spirit of the Italians of that day. That
spirit was frustrated, and at times overcome, only by the
passionate desire to penetrate the future. We shall return to
the subject of astrology when we speak of the moral and
religious character of the people.

The Church almost always treated this and other pseudo-
sciences with toleration, and became hostile even to genuine
science only when a charge—whether true or false—of heresy
and necromancy was in question, which certainly was often

the case. What would be significant is: to decide whether and in what cases the Dominican (and also the Franciscan) Inquisitors in Italy were conscious of the falsity of the charges and yet condemned the accused, either to oblige some enemy of the prisoner or from deep hatred to natural science, and particularly to experiments. The latter surely occurred, but can hardly be proved. What induced such persecutions in the North, namely, the opposition of the upholders of the received official, scholastic system of nature to the new because it was new, was of little or no weight in Italy. Pietro of Abano (at the beginning of the fourteenth century) fell victim to the professional envy of another physician, who accused him before the Inquisition of heresy and magic; and the same may have been true in the case of his Paduan contemporary, Giovannino Sanguinacci, who was known as an innovator in medical practice; he got off with mere banishment. Nor should it be forgotten that the inquisitorial power of the Dominicans was exercised less methodically in Italy than in the North. In the fourteenth century tyrants as well as free cities treated the clergy with such sovereign contempt at times, that very different matters from natural science went unpunished. But when, in the fifteenth century, antiquity became the leading power, the breach it made in the old system was turned to account by every kind of secular study, except that humanism attracted the best strength of the nation, and was probably detrimental to the inductive investigation of nature. Here and there the Inquisition suddenly started into life, and punished or burned physicians as blasphemers or magicians. In such cases it is hard to discover the true motive underlying the condemnation. Nevertheless, Italy, at the close of the fifteenth century, with Paolo Toscanelli, Luca Pacioli, and Leonardo da Vinci, was without an equal and held the highest place among European nations in mathematics and the natural sciences, and the learned men of every country, even Regiomontanus and Copernicus, confessed themselves its pupils. This glory even survived the Counter Reformation, and even today the Italians would hold first place in this respect had it not been made impossible for the most able minds to devote themselves to tranquil research.

A significant proof of the widespread interest in natural history is found in the zeal that showed itself at an early period for collecting, for the comparative study of plants and animals. Italy claims to be the first creator of botanical gardens, though possibly they may have served a chiefly practical end, and the claim to priority may be disputed.

It is of far greater importance that princes and wealthy men, in laying out their pleasure gardens, instinctively made a point of collecting the greatest possible number of different plants in all their species and varieties. Thus in the fifteenth century the magnificent gardens of the Medicean Villa Careggi are described almost as a botanical garden, with countless specimens of different trees and shrubs. At the beginning of the sixteenth century we find a similar case in a villa of Cardinal Trivulzio, in the Roman Campagna toward Tivoli, with hedges made up of various species of roses, with trees of every description—the fruit trees especially showing an astonishing variety—with twenty different sorts of vines and a large kitchen garden. This is evidently very different from the score or two of familiar medicinal plants that were found in the garden of any castle or monastery in Western Europe. Along with a careful cultivation of fruit for the table, we find an interest in the plant for its own sake, for the pleasure it gives to the eye. We learn from the history of art that it was a long time before this passion for botanical collections was laid aside, and gave place to what was considered a picturesque style of landscape gardening.

Even the collections of foreign animals served the higher purposes of observation. The facility of transport from the southern and eastern harbors of the Mediterranean, and the mildness of the Italian climate, made it practicable to buy the largest animals of the south, or to accept them as presents from the Sultans. The cities and princes were especially anxious to keep live lions, even where a lion was not, as it was in Florence, the emblem of the State. The lions' den was generally in or near the government palace, as in Perugia and Florence; in Rome, it lay on the slope of the Capitol. The beasts sometimes served as executioners of political judgments,[135] and, in addition, probably kept alive a certain terror in the people. Their behavior was also held to be ominous of good or evil. Their fertility, especially, was considered a

135. On great occasions combats of wild animals among themselves and with dogs were part of the entertainment. In 1459, at the reception of Pius II and Galeazzo Maria Sforza in Florence, bulls, horses, boars, dogs, lions, and a giraffe were turned out together in an enclosure on the Piazza della Signoria, but the lions lay down and would not attack the other animals. In later years, a second giraffe was presented to Lorenzo the Magnificent by the Mameluke Sultan Kaitbai. In Lorenzo's menagerie a magnificent lion was especially famous; his destruction by the other lions was taken as an omen of Lorenzo's death.

sign of public prosperity, and no less a man than Giovanni Villani thought it worth recording that he was present at the delivery of a lioness. The cubs were often given to allied States and princes, or to *condottieri* as a reward of valor. In addition to the lions, the Florentines began very early to keep leopards, for which a special keeper was appointed. Borso of Ferrara used to set his lions to fight with bulls, bears, and wild boars.

By the end of the fifteenth century, however, true menageries *(serragli)*, considered part of the suitable appointments of a court, were kept by many princes. "It belongs to the position of the great," says Matarazzo, "to keep horses, dogs, mules, falcons and other birds, court jesters, singers, and foreign animals." The menagerie at Naples, in the time of Ferrante, even contained a giraffe and a zebra, presented, it seems, by the ruler of Baghdad. Filippo Maria Visconti not only owned horses that cost him 500 or 1,000 pieces of gold each, and valuable English dogs, but also many leopards brought from all parts of the East; the care of his hunting birds, which were collected from the countries of Northern Europe, cost 3,000 pieces of gold a month. King Emanuel the Great of Portugal knew what he was about when he presented Leo X with an elephant and a rhinoceros. It was under such circumstances that the foundations of a scientific zoology and botany were laid.

A practical side of these zoological studies was the establishment of studs, of which the Mantuan, under Francesco Gonzaga, was esteemed the best in Europe. The knowledge of the different breeds of horses is probably as old as riding itself, and the crossing of the European with the Asiatic must have been common from the time of the Crusades. In Italy, a special inducement to perfect the breed was offered by the prizes at the horse races that were held in every considerable town. The infallible winners in these contests were bred in the Mantuan stables, as well as the best military chargers, and the horses best suited by their stately appearance for presents to great people. Gonzaga kept stallions and mares from Spain, Ireland, Africa, Thrace, and Cilicia, and for the sake of the last he cultivated the friendship of the Sultans. All possible experiments were tried, in order to produce the most perfect animals.

Even human menageries were not lacking. The famous Cardinal Ippolito de' Medici, bastard of Giuliano, Duke of Nemours, kept at his strange court a troop of barbarians who spoke no less than twenty different languages, and who were all perfect specimens of their races. Among them were incomparable *voltigeurs* of the best blood of the North African Moors, Tartar bowmen, Negro wrestlers, Indian divers, and Turks, who generally accompained the Cardinal on his hunting expeditions. When he was overtaken by an early death (1535), this motley band carried the corpse on their shoulders from Itri to Rome, and mingled with the general mourning for the openhanded Cardinal their medley of tongues and violent gesticulations.[136]

These scattered notices of the relations of the Italians to natural science, and their interest in the wealth and variety of the products of nature, are only fragments of a great subject. No one is more conscious than the author of the defects in his knowledge on this point. Of the multitude of special works in which the subject is adequately treated, even the names are but imperfectly known to him.

But in addition to scientific investigation, there was still another way to draw near to nature, and in a special sense. The Italians were the first among modern peoples by whom the outward world was seen and enjoyed as something beautiful.[137]

This faculty is always the result of a long and complicated development, and its origin is not easily detected, since a dim feeling of this kind may exist long before it betrays itself in poetry and painting and thereby becomes a conscious process. Among the ancients, for example, art and poetry had gone through the whole circle of human interests, before they turned to the representation of nature, and even then nature always had a limited and subordinate place. And yet, from the time of Homer, the powerful impression made by nature upon man is evidenced by countless verses and chance expressions. The Germanic tribes, which founded their States on the ruins of the Roman Empire, were thoroughly and specially fitted to understand the spirit of

136. At this point, a few notes on slavery in Italy at the time of the Renaissance may be in order. In North Italy there were no slaves; elsewhere even Christians, as well as Bulgarians and Circassians, were bought from the Turks and had to serve until they had earned their purchase price. Negroes, on the contrary, remained slaves, but it was not permitted, at least in the kingdom of Naples, to castrate them. — The word *moro* signifies any dark-skinned man; a Negro was called *moro nero*. — Innocent VIII received 100 Moors as a gift from Ferdinand the Catholic and gave them to cardinals and other great men (1488).

137. It is hardly necessary to refer the reader to the famous chapters on this subject in Humboldt's *Cosmos*, vol. 2.

natural scenery; and though Christianity compelled them for a while to see the shapes of evil demons in the springs and mountains, in the lakes and woods that they had revered, this transitional state was certainly soon outgrown. By the year 1200, at the height of the Middle Ages, a genuine, hearty enjoyment of the external world was again in existence, and found lively expression in the minstrelsy of different nations, which gives evidence of the sympathy felt with all the simple phenomena of nature—spring with its flowers, the green fields and the woods. But it is all foreground without perspective, particularly when we realize that the crusaders, who traveled so far and saw so much, are barely recognizable as such in their poems. Even epic poetry, which describes armor and costumes so fully, does not attempt more than a sketch of outward nature; and the great Wolfram von Eschenbach scarcely anywhere gives us an adequate picture of the scene on which his heroes move. From these poems we would never guess that their noble authors in all countries inhabited or visited lofty castles commanding distant prospects. Even in the Latin poems of the wandering clerics, we find no traces of a distant view—of true landscape—but what lies near is sometimes described with a glow and splendor that none of the knightly minstrels can surpass. What picture of the Grove of Love can equal that of the Italian poet—for such we take him to be—of the twelfth century?

> *Immortalis fieret*
> *Ibi manens homo;*
> *Arbor ibi quaelibet*
> *Suo gaudet pomo;*
> *Viae myrrha, cinnamo*
> *Fragrant, et amomo—*
> *Conjectari poterat*
> *Dominus ex domo* etc.[138]

To the Italian mind, at all events, nature had by this time lost its taint of sin and had shaken off all trace of demoniacal powers. St. Francis of Assisi, in his Canticle of the Sun, frankly praises the Lord for creating the heavenly bodies and the four elements.

But the unmistakable proofs of a profound effect of nature

138. *Carmina Burana*, "De Phyllide et Flora," verse 66. [Man would be immortal if/He could there be dwelling;/Every branch on every tree/With ripe fruit swelling;/All the ways with nard and myrrh/And with spice are smelling;/How divine the Master is/All the house is telling. – J.A. Symonds tr.]

on the human spirit begin with Dante. Not only does he
awaken in us by a few vigorous lines the sense of the morning
air and the trembling light on the distant ocean, or of the
storm-beaten forest, but he climbs lofty peaks with the
only possible object of enjoying the view [139]—perhaps one
of the first men since the days of antiquity to do so. Boccaccio suggests rather than depicts how landscape affected
him; yet in his pastoral romances we cannot fail to recognize
that in his imagination, at least, nature had a powerful
presence. But the significance of nature for a receptive spirit
is fully and clearly displayed by Petrarch—one of the first
truly modern men. Alexander von Humboldt, that luminous
spirit who was the first to collect from the literature of all
countries evidence of the origin and progress of the sense
of natural beauty, and who, in his *Aspects of Nature,* achieved
the noblest masterpiece of description, has not done full
justice to Petrarch, so that after the great reaper a few
small gleanings are still left.

Petrarch was not only a distinguished geographer and
cartographer—the first map of Italy is said to have been
drawn under his direction—and a reproducer of the sayings
of the ancients; he was a man who felt the influence of
natural beauty. The enjoyment of nature was, for him, the
favorite accompaniment of intellectual pursuits; it was to
combine the two that he lived in learned retirement at
Vaucluse and elsewhere, that from time to time he fled
from the world and from his age. We should do him wrong
by inferring from his weak and undeveloped power of describing natural scenery that he did not feel it deeply. His picture,
for instance, of the lovely Gulf of Spezia and Portovenere,
which he inserted at the end of the sixth book of the *Africa,*
because neither the ancients nor the moderns had sung of
it, is no more than a simple enumeration. But the same
Petrarch is also conscious of the beauty of rock scenery,
and is perfectly able to distinguish the picturesque quality of
a landscape from the utilitarian. During his stay in the woods
of Reggio, the sudden sight of an impressive landscape so
affected him that he resumed a poem he had laid aside long
before. But the deepest impression of all was made on him
by the ascent of Mont Ventoux, near Avignon. An indefin-
able longing for a distant panorama grew stronger and

139. It would be hard to say what else he could have had to do
at the top of Bismantova. *Purgatorio,* iv, 26. The preciseness
with which he seeks to elucidate all the parts of his supernatural
world shows a remarkable sense of form and space.

stronger in him, till at length the accidental sight of that passage in Livy, where King Philip, the enemy of Rome, ascends the Haemus, decided him. He throught that what was not blameworthy in a gray-headed monarch might well be *excused* in a young man of private station. The ascent of a mountain for its own sake was unheard of, and there could be no thought of the companionship of friends or acquaintances. Petrarch took with him only his younger brother and two country people from the last place he had stopped at. At the foot of the mountain an old herdsman begged them to turn back, saying that he himself had attempted to climb it fifty years before, and had brought home nothing but repentance, broken bones, and torn clothes, and that neither before nor after had anyone else attempted it. Nevertheless, they struggled forward and upward, till the clouds lay beneath their feet, and they finally reached the top. It would be vain to look for a description of the view from the summit, not because the poet was insensible to it, but, on the contrary, because the impression was too overwhelming. His whole past life, with all its follies, rose before his mind; he remembered that ten years ago that day he had quitted Bologna a young man, and he turned a longing gaze toward his native country; he opened a book which was then his constant companion, the *Confessions* of St. Augustine, and his eye fell on the passage in the tenth book, "and men go forth to admire lofty mountains and broad seas, and roaring torrents, and the ocean, and the course of the stars, and yet forget their own selves." His brother, to whom he read these words, could not understand why he closed the book and said no more.

Some decades later, about 1360, Fazio degli Uberti describes, in his rhyming geography, the wide panorama from the mountains of Auvergne, with, it is true, the sympathy of the geographer and antiquarian only, but still showing clearly that he himself had seen it. He must, however, have ascended far higher peaks, since he is familiar with phenomena that only occur at a height of 10,000 feet or more above the sea—mountain sickness and its accompaniments—of which his imaginary comrade Solinus tries to cure him with a sponge dipped in an essence. The ascents of Parnassus and Olympus, of which he speaks, are perhaps only fictions.

In the fifteenth century, the great masters of the Flemish school, Hubert and Jan van Eyck, suddenly lifted the veil from nature. Their landscapes are not merely the fruit of their endeavor to reflect the real world in art, but have, even if expressed conventionally, a certain poetic meaning—in short, a soul. Their influence on the whole art of the West is undeniable, and thus, the landscape painting of the Italians was also affected. But the characteristic interest of the cultivated Italian eye for nature found its own means of expression.

Here, as in scientific geography, Aeneas Sylvius is one of the most important voices of his time. Even if we grant all that has been said against Aeneas the man, we must still admit that in few other men was the picture of the age and its culture so fully reflected, and that few came nearer to the normal type of Early Renaissance man. It may be added parenthetically, that even in respect to his moral character he will not be fairly judged if we listen solely to the complaints of the German Church, which was balked, because of his fickleness, of the Council it so ardently desired.

He interests us here as the first who not only enjoyed the magnificence of the Italian landscape, but described it with enthusiasm down to its minutest details. The ecclesiastical State and the south of Tuscany—his native home—he knew thoroughly, and after he became Pope he spent his leisure during the favorable season chiefly in excursions to the country. Then at last the gouty man was rich enough to have himself carried in a litter across the mountains and valleys; and if we compare his enjoyments with those of the Popes who succeeded him, Pius, whose chief delight was in nature, antiquity, and simple but noble architecture, appears almost a saint. In the elegant and flowing Latin of his *Commentaries* he tells us freely of his happiness.[140]

His eye seems as keen and practiced as that of any modern observer. He enjoys with rapture the panoramic splendor of the view from Monte Cavo, the summit of the Alban Hills, from where he could survey the coast belonging to the Church from Terracina and Monte Cicero as far as Monte Argentario, and the wide expanse of country with the ruined cities of the past and the mountain-chains of Central Italy; and then his eye would turn to the green woods below and the mountain lakes among them. He feels the beauty of the situation of Todi, crowning the vineyards and olive-clad slopes, looking down on distant woods and the valley of the Tiber, where towns and castles rise above the winding river. The lovely

140. The most important passages are: Book IV, spring in his native country; Book V, summer residence in Tivoli; Book VI, the meal at the spring of Vicovaro; Book VIII, the environs of Viterbo, the mountain monastery of San Martino, the lake of Bolsena; Book IX, the splendid description of Monte Amiata; Book X, the situation of Monte Oliveto, the view from Todi; Book XI, Ostia and Porto, description of the Alban Hills; Book XII, Frascati and Grottaferrata.

hills around Siena, with villas and monasteries on all of them, are his own home, and his descriptions of them are touched with a special feeling. But individual picturesque motifs charm him, too, as, for example, the little promontory of Capodimonte that stretches out into the Lake of Bolsena: "Rocky steps, shaded by vines, descend to the water's edge, where the evergreen oaks stand between the cliffs, alive with the singing of thrushes." On the path round the Lake of Nemi, beneath the chestnuts and fruit trees, he feels that here, if anywhere, a poet's soul must awake—here in Diana's hiding place. He often held consistories or received ambassadors under huge old chestnut trees, or beneath the olives on the greensward by some gurgling spring. A view like that of a narrowing gorge, with a bridge arched boldly over it, awakens at once his artistic sense. Even the smallest details delight him by something beautiful, or perfect, or characteristic in them—the blue fields of waving flax, the yellow gorse that covers the hills, even tangled thickets, or single trees, or springs, which seem to him like wonders of nature.

The height of his enthusiasm for natural beauty was reached during his stay on Monte Amiata, in the summer of 1462, when plague and heat made the lowlands uninhabitable. Halfway up the mountain, in the old Lombard monastery of San Salvatore, he and his court made their quarters. There, between the chestnuts that clothe the steep slope, the eye may wander over all southern Tuscany and see in the distance the towers of Siena. The ascent of the highest peak he left to his companions, who were joined by the Venetian envoy; they found at the top two vast blocks of stone one upon the other—perhaps the sacrificial altar of a prehistoric people—and fancied that off in the distance they saw Corsica and Sardinia[141] rising above the sea. In the cool air of the hills, among the old oaks and chestnuts, on the green meadows where there were no thorns to wound the feet, no snakes or insects to hurt or to annoy, the Pope passed days of unclouded happiness. For the Segnatura, which took place on certain days of the week, he selected on each occasion some new shady retreat—*novos in convallibus fontes et novas inveniens umbras, quae dubiam facerent electionem* [finding new springs in the valleys and new patches of shade among which it was hard to choose]. Once the dogs startled a great stag from his lair, and they watched as he defended himself with hoofs and horns and then fled up the mountain. In the evening the Pope would sit before the monastery on the spot from which the whole

141. So must we suppose it to have been, not "Sicily."

valley of the Paglia was visible, holding lively conversations with the cardinals. The curials who ventured down from the heights on their hunting expeditions found the heat below intolerable and the scorched plains like a very hell, while the monastery, with its cool, shady woods, seemed like an abode of the blessed.

All this is genuine modern enjoyment, not a reflection of antiquity. As surely as the ancients felt in the same manner, so surely, nevertheless, were the scanty expressions of the writers whom Pius knew insufficient to awaken in him such enthusiasm.[142]

The second great age of Italian poetry, which now followed at the end of the fifteenth and the beginning of the sixteenth centuries, as well as the Latin poetry of the same period, is rich in proofs of the powerful effect of nature on the human mind. The first glance at the lyric poets of that time will suffice to convince us. Elaborate descriptions of natural scenery are, it is true, very rare, for the reason that, in this energetic age, the novels and the lyric or epic poetry had something else to deal with. Boiardo and Ariosto paint nature vigorously, but as briefly as possible, and with no effort to appeal by their descriptions to the feelings of the reader, which they endeavor to reach solely by their narrative and characters. Letter writers and the authors of philosophical dialogues[143] are, in fact, better evidence than the poets of the growing love of nature. The novelist Bandello, for example, observes rigorously the rules of his department of literature; in his novels he gives us not a word more than is necessary on the natural scenery amid which the action of his tales takes place, but in the dedications that always precede them there are charming descriptions of nature as the setting for his dialogues and social pictures. Among letter writers, Aretino unfortunately must be named as the first who has fully painted in words the splendid effect of light and shadow in an Italian sunset.

Yet even in the poets we occasionally find a remarkable combination of emotion and a tender, realistic description of nature. Tito Strozzi (about 1480) describes in a Latin elegy the dwelling of his mistress: an old ivy-clad house

142. On Leon Battista Alberti's feeling for landscape, cf. Part Two.
143. Agnolo Pandolfini (*Trattato del gov. della famiglia*), another contemporary of Aeneas, is delighted in the country with "the bushy hills, the fair plains, and the rushing water." But perhaps hidden under his name is the great Alberti who, as we have noted, had a completely different feeling for landscape.

covered with weather-stained frescoes of the saints, half-hidden in trees, and near it a chapel much damaged by the violence of the Po, which flows close by; not far off, the priest ploughs his few barren roods with borrowed cattle. This is no reminiscence of the Roman elegists, but true modern sentiment; and the parallel to it—a sincere, unartificial bucolic description of country life—will be found at the end of this section.

It may be objected that the German painters of the beginning of the sixteenth century represented with masterful realism the natural surroundings of human events, as, for example, Albrecht Dürer, in his engraving of the Prodigal Son. But it is one thing if a painter, brought up in a school of realism, introduces such scenery, and quite another if a poet, accustomed to an ideal or mythological framework, descends into realism through inward neccessity. Besides which, priority in point of time is here, as in the descriptions of country life, on the side of the Italian poets.

To the discovery of the outward world the civilization of the Renaissance added a still greater achievement, in that it was the first to discover and bring to light the full, whole nature of man.[144]

First of all, as we have seen, this period gave the highest development to individuality, and then led the individual to the most zealous and thorough study of himself in all forms and under all conditions. Indeed, the development of personality is essentially bound up with the recognition of it in oneself and in others. Between these two great phenomena we have had to place the influence of ancient literature because the mode of conceiving and representing both the individual and human nature in general was defined and colored by that influence. But the power of conception and representation lay in the age and in the people.

The facts we shall quote in evidence of our thesis will be few in number. Here, if anywhere in the course of this discussion, the author is conscious that he is treading on the perilous ground of conjecture, and that what seems to him a clear, if delicate and gradual, transition in the intellectual history of the fourteenth and fifteenth centuries, may not be equally plain to others. The gradual awakening of the soul of a people is a phenomenon that may produce a different impression on each spectator. Time will sift and judge.

144. These striking expressions are taken from the Introduction to the seventh volume of Michelet's *History of France*.

Happily the study of the intellectual side of human nature began not with the search after a theoretical psychology—since for that, Aristotle still sufficed—but with the endeavor to observe and to describe. The indispensable ballast of theory was limited to the popular doctrine of the four temperaments, in its then habitual union with the belief in the influence of the planets. Such conceptions may remain ineradicable in the minds of individuals without hindering the general progress of the age. It is indeed extraordinary to find them used at a time when human nature in its deepest essence and in all its characteristic expressions was not only known by exact observation, but represented by an immortal poetry and art. It sounds almost ludicrous when an otherwise competent observer considers Clement VII to be a melancholy temperament, but defers his judgment to that of the physicians, who recognize the Pope as a sanguine-choleric nature; or when we discover that the same Gaston de Foix, the victor of Ravenna, whom Giorgione painted and Bambaia carved,[145] and whom all the historians describe, had the saturnine temperament. No doubt those who use these expressions mean something by them; but the terms in which they tell us their meaning are strangely out of date.

As examples of the free delineation of the human spirit, we shall speak first of the great poets of the fourteenth century.

If we were to collect the pearls from the courtly and knightly poetry of all the countries of the West during the two preceding centuries, we should have a mass of wonderful divinations and single pictures of the life of the soul, which at first sight would seem to rival the poetry of the Italians. Leaving lyrical poetry out of account, Gottfried von Strassburg already gives us, in *Tristan and Iseult,* a representation of human passion, some features of which are immortal. But these pearls lie scattered in an ocean of artifice and convention, and they are far removed from a complete objective picture of the inner man and his spiritual wealth.

Italy, too, in the thirteenth century had, through the *trovatori* [troubadours], its share in the poetry of the courts and chivalry. To them is mainly due the *canzone,* whose

145. [Although tradition attributes to Giorgione a number of paintings which are supposed to represent Gaston de Foix, modern scholars doubt that Giorgione ever painted him. Burckhardt may be referring here to the portrait in the Louvre, which is now attributed to Savoldo. The effigy by Bambaia is in the Archeological Museum, Milan.]

construction is as difficult and artificial as that of the songs of any Northern minstrel. Their subject and even mode of thought have the conventional tone of the courts, be the poet, burgher or scholar.

But two new paths revealed themselves, along which Italian poetry could advance to another and a characteristic future. They are not less important for being concerned only with the formal side of the art.

To the same Brunetto Latini—the teacher of Dante—who, in his *canzoni*, adopts the customary manner of the *trovatori*, we owe the first-known *versi sciolti*, or blank hendecasyllabic verses, and in this apparent absence of form, a true and genuine passion suddenly showed itself. The same voluntary renunciation of outward effect, through confidence in the power of the inward conception, can be observed some years later in fresco painting, and later still in painting of all kinds, which began to cease to rely on color for its effect and simply used a lighter or darker shade. For an age which laid so much stress on form in poetry, these verses of Brunetto mark the beginning of a new epoch.[146]

About the same time, or even in the first half of the thirteenth century, one of the many strictly balanced forms of verse, in which Europe was then so fruitful, became a normal and recognized form in Italy—the sonnet. The order of rhymes and even the number of lines varied[147] for a whole century, till Petrarch fixed them permanently. In this form all higher lyrical and meditative subjects, and at a later time subjects of every possible description, were treated, and the madrigals, the sestine, and even the *canzoni* were reduced to a subordinate place. Later Italian writers complain, half jestingly, half resentfully, of this inevitable mold, this fourteen-line Procrustean bed, to which they were compelled to make their thoughts and feelings fit. Others were, and still are, quite satisfied with this particular form of verse, which they freely use to express any personal reminiscence or idle singsong without necessity or serious purpose. For which reason there are many more bad or insignificant sonnets than good ones.

Nevertheless, the sonnet seems to us to have been an unspeakable blessing for Italian poetry. The clearness and beauty

146. Blank verse, as is well known, later became the usual form for dramatic compositions. Trissino, in his dedication of the *Sofonisba* to Leo X, expresses the hope that the Pope will recognize this style for what it is—better, nobler, and *less easy* than it looks.

147. Compare, for example, the striking forms adopted by Dante, *La vita nuova* [Book VIII].

of its structure, the invitation to elevate the thought in the second and more rapidly moving half, and the ease with which it could be learned by heart, made it loved and valued even by the greatest masters. Would they have continued to use it down to our own century had they not been convinced of its singular worth? These masters could have given us the same thoughts in other and wholly different forms. But once they had made the sonnet the normal type of lyrical poetry, many other writers of great, if not the highest, gifts, who otherwise would have lost themselves in a sea of diffusiveness, were forced to concentrate their feelings. The sonnet became a condenser of thoughts and emotions such as was possessed by the poetry of no other modern people.

Thus the world of Italian sentiment comes before us in a series of clear, concise, pictures which are most effective in their brevity. Had other nations possessed a similar form of expression, we should perhaps have known more of their inner life; we might have had a number of pictures of inward and outward situations—reflections of the national character and temper—and should not be dependent for such knowledge on the so-called lyrical poets of the fourteenth and fifteenth centuries, who can hardly ever be read with any serious enjoyment. In Italy we can trace a steady progress almost from birth of the sonnet. In the second half of the thirteenth century the *trovatori della transizione*, as they have recently been named, mark the passage from the *trovatori* to the poets—that is, to those poets under the influence of antiquity. The simplicity and strength of their feeling, the vigorous delineation of fact, the precise expression and rounding off of their sonnets and other poems, herald the coming of a Dante. Some political sonnets of the Guelphs and Ghibellines (1260-1270) have about them the ring of his passion, and others remind us of his sweetest lyrical notes.

Of Dante's own theoretical view of the sonnet, we are unfortunately ignorant, since the last books of his work, *De vulgari eloquentia* [*On the Vernacular*], in which he proposed to treat ballads and sonnets, either remained unwritten or have been lost. But, as a matter of fact, he has left us in his sonnets and *canzoni* a treasure of inward experience. And in what a framework they are set! The prose of the *Vita nuova*, in which he gives an account of the origin of each poem, is as wonderful as the verses themselves, and forms with them a uniform whole, inspired with the deepest glow of passion. With unflinching frankness and sincerity he lays bare every shade of his soul's joy and sorrow, and molds it resolutely into the strictest forms of art. Reading attentively these sonnets

and *canzoni* and the marvelous fragments of the diary of his
youth which lie between them, we fancy that throughout the
Middle Ages the poets had purposely been fleeing from themselves, and that he was the first to seek his own soul. Many
an artistic verse had been written before his day, but he is
the first artist in the full sense of the word—the first who
consciously cast immortal matter into an immortal form.
Here subjective feeling has a full objective truth and greatness,
and most of it is so set forth that all ages and peoples can
make it their own. Where he writes in a thoroughly objective
spirit, and betrays the force of his feelings only by some
outward fact, as in the magnificent sonnets *Tanto gentile*,
etc. [My lady looks so gentle and so pure], and *Vede perfet-
tamente*, etc. [For certain he hath seen all perfectness], he
seems to find it neccessary to excuse himself. The most beautiful of these poems really belongs to this class—the *Deh
peregrini che pensosi andate* [Ye pilgrim-folk, advancing
pensively].

Even apart from the *Divine Comedy*, Dante would mark
by these youthful poems the boundary between the Middle
Ages and modern times. Here the human spirit took a
mighty step toward the consciousness of its own secret life.

The revelations in this matter which are contained in the
Divine Comedy itself are simply immeasurable; and it would
be necessary to go through the whole poem, canto by canto,
to do full justice to its value from this point of view.
Happily we do not have to do this, as the *Comedy* has long
been a daily food of all the countries of the West. Its plan,
and the ideas on which it is based, belong to the Middle Ages,
and appeal to our interest only historically; but through the
power and richness of the portrayal of human nature in
every shade and form,[148] it is the beginning of all modern
poetry.

From this time forward poetry may experience unequal
fortunes, and may show, for half a century together, a so-
called relapse—its nobler and more vital principle was saved
forever; and whenever in the fourteenth, fifteenth, and in the
beginning of the sixteenth centuries, an original mind in
Italy devoted himself to it, he represented a more advanced
stage than any poet outside Italy, given—what is certainly
always difficult to settle satisfactorily—an equality of natural
gifts to begin with.

148. For Dante's psychology, the beginning of *Purgatorio*, iv, is
one of the most important passages. See also the respective
passages in the *Convivio*.

Here, as in other things in Italy, culture (to which poetry belongs) preceded the visual arts and, in fact, gave them their chief impulse. More than a century elapsed before the spiritual element in painting and sculpture attained a power of expression in any way analogous to that of Dante. How far the same rule holds good for the artistic development of other nations,[149] and how significant the whole question may be, does not concern us here. For Italian civilization it is of decisive importance.

The position to be assigned to Petrarch in this respect must be settled by the many readers of the poet. Those who come to him in the spirit of a cross-examiner, and busy themselves in detecting the contradictions between the poet and the man, his infidelities in love, and the other weak sides of his character, may perhaps, after sufficient effort, end by losing all taste for his poetry. In place, then, of artistic enjoyment, we may acquire a knowledge of the man in his "totality." What a pity that Petrarch's letters from Avignon contain so little gossip, which might have given us some clue, and that the letters of his acquaintances and of the friends of these acquaintances have either been lost or never existed! Instead of thanking Heaven that we are not forced to inquire how and through what struggles a poet has rescued something immortal from his own poor life and lot, a biography has been stitched together for Petrarch out of such so-called "remains," which reads like an indictment. But the poet may take comfort. If the printing and editing of the correspondence of celebrated people goes on for another half-century as it has begun in England and Germany, he will have illustrious company enough sitting with him on the stool of repentance.

Without shutting our eyes to much that is forced and artificial in his poetry, where the writer is merely imitating himself and singing on in the old strain, we cannot fail to admire the marvelous abundance of pictures of the inmost soul—descriptions of moments of joy and sorrow—which must have been thoroughly his own, since no one before him gives us anything of the kind, and on which his significance rests for his country and for the world. His verse is not everywhere equally transparent; his most beautiful thoughts are not infrequently joined to an allegorical conceit, a sophistical trick of logic altogether foreign to our present taste. But the balance is on the side of excellence.

149. The portraits of the school of Van Eyck would prove the contrary for the North. For a long time they remained far in advance of all verbal descriptions.

BOCCACCIO, too, in his too-little-known sonnets, succeeds sometimes in giving a most powerful and effective picture of his feeling. The return to a spot consecrated by love (son. 22), the melancholy of spring (son. 33), the sadness of the poet who feels himself growing old (son. 65), are admirably celebrated by him. And in the *Ameto* he has described the ennobling and transfiguring power of love in a manner that would hardly be expected from the author of the *Decameron*. In the *Fiammetta* we have another great and minutely painted picture of the human soul, full of the keenest observation, though executed with anything but uniform power and in parts marred by the passion for high-sounding language and by an unlucky mixture of mythological allusion and learned quotation. The *Fiammetta*, if we are not mistaken, is a sort of feminine counterpart to the *Vita nuova* of Dante, or at any rate owes its origin to it.

It goes without saying that the ancient poets, particularly the elegists and the fourth book of the *Aeneid*, were not without influence on the Italians of this and the following generation; but powerful feelings surged in their souls. If we compare them in this respect with their contemporaries in other countries, we shall find in them the earliest complete expression of modern European feeling. The question, be it remembered, is not to know whether eminent men of other nations did not feel so deeply and so nobly, but who were the first to give documentary proof of the widest knowledge of the movements of the human heart.

Why, then, did the Italians of the Renaissance produce nothing but second-rate tragedy? There was the field on which to display human character, intellect, and passion in the thousand forms of their growth, their struggles, and their decline. In other words: why did Italy produce no Shakespeare? For the Italians were equal to the theater of the other Northern countries of the sixteenth and seventeenth centuries; and with the Spaniards they could not enter into competition, since Italy had long lost all traces of religious fanaticism, treated the chivalrous code of honor only as a form, and was both too proud and too intelligent to bow down before its tyrannical and illegitimate nobility. We have, therefore, only to consider the English stage in the brief period of its splendor.

It is an obvious reply that all Europe produced but one Shakespeare, and that such a genius is the rarest of Heaven's gifts. It is further possible that the Italian stage was on the way to something great when the Counter Reformation broke in upon it, and, aided by the Spanish rule (over Naples and

Milan, and indirectly over almost the whole peninsula), blighted and withered the best flowers of the Italian spirit. It would be hard to conceive of Shakespeare himself under a Spanish viceroy, or in the neighborhood of the Holy Inquisition at Rome, or even in his own country a few decades later, at the time of the English Revolution. The stage, which in its perfection is a late product of every civilization, must wait for its own time and fortune.

We must not, however, quit this subject without mentioning certain circumstances that were of a character to hinder or delay a vigorous growth of the drama in Italy, until it was too late.

As the most important of these circumstances we must mention without doubt that the love of spectacle was directed elsewhere, chiefly to the mysteries and other religious processions. Throughout all Europe dramatic representations of sacred history and legend formed the source and beginning of drama and the theater; but Italy, as will be discussed more fully in the next section, had spent on the mysteries such a wealth of decorative splendor that the dramatic element had to suffer. Out of all the countless and costly presentations, there sprang not even a branch of poetry such as the *Autos sacramentales* of Calderón and other Spanish poets, much less any advantage or foundation for the secular drama.

And when the latter did at length appear, it immediately gave itself up as much as it could to the magnificence of scenic effects, to which the mysteries had already accustomed the public taste to far too great an extent. We learn with astonishment how rich and splendid the *décor* was in Italy at a time when in the North the simplest indication of place was thought sufficient. This alone might have had no unfavorable effect on the drama, if the attention of the audience had not been drawn away from the poetic conception of the play partly by the splendor of the costumes, partly, and chiefly, by fantastic intermezzi.

That in many places, particularly in Rome and Ferrara, Plautus and Terence, as well as pieces by the old tragedians, were given in Latin or in Italian, that the academies of which we have already spoken made this one of their chief tasks, and that the poets of the Renaissance followed these models too servilely, were all untoward conditions for the Italian stage at the period in question. Yet I hold them to be of secondary importance. Had not the Counter Reformation and the rule of foreigners intervened, these very disadvantages might have been turned into useful means of transition. At all events, by the year 1520 the victory of the mother tongue

in tragedy and comedy was, to the great disgust of the humanists, as good as won. On this side, then, no obstacle stood in
the way of the most developed people in Europe, to hinder
them from raising the drama, in its noblest forms, to be a
true reflection of human life and destiny. It was the Inquisitors and Spaniards who cowed the Italian spirit and
rendered impossible the dramatic portrayal of the greatest and
most sublime themes, especially when they were associated
with patriotic memories. At the same time, there is no doubt
that the distracting intermezzi did serious harm to the drama.
We must now consider them more closely.

When the marriage of Alfonso of Ferrara and Lucrezia
Borgia was celebrated, Duke Ercole himself showed his illustrious guests the 110 costumes that were to serve at the presentation of five comedies of Plautus, so that all might see
that not one of them was to be used twice. But all this display
of silk and camlet was as nothing compared to the ballets
and pantomimes that served as interludes between the acts
of the Plautine dramas. That, in comparison, Plautus himself
seemed mortally dull to a lively young lady like Isabella
Gonzaga, and that while the play was going on everybody
longed for the interludes, is quite intelligible when we think
of the brilliancy with which they were put on the stage.
There were combats of Roman warriors who brandished their
weapons to the sound of music, torch dances executed by
Moors, a dance of savages with horns of plenty out of which
streamed waves of fire—all as the ballet of a pantomime in
which a maiden was delivered from a dragon. Then came a
dance of fools, got up as Punches, beating one another with
pigs' bladders, and more of the same. At the court of Ferrara
no comedy was ever given without "its" ballet (*moresca*).
In what style the *Amphitruo* of Plautus was presented there
(1491, at the first marriage of Alfonso, to Anna Sforza), is
difficult to know. Possibly it was given more as a pantomime
with music than as a drama. In any case, the accessories
were more considerable than the play itself. There was a
choral dance of ivy-clad youths, moving in intricate figures
to the music of a ringing orchestra; then came Apollo, striking the lyre with the plectrum and singing an ode to the
praise of the House of Este; then followed, as an interlude
within an interlude, a kind of rustic farce, after which the
stage was again occupied by classical mythology—Venus,
Bacchus, and their followers—in a pantomime representing
the judgment of Paris. Not till then was the second half of
the fable of Amphitruo performed, with unmistakable references to the future birth of a Hercules out of the House of

Este. At a former presentation of the same piece in the courtyard of the palace (1487), "a paradise with stars and other wheels" burned constantly, that is, an illumination, probably with fireworks, that undoubtedly absorbed most of the attention of the spectators. It was certainly better when such performances were given separately, as was the case at other courts. We shall speak of the entertainments given by Cardinal Pietro Riaro, by the Bentivogli at Bologna, and by others, when we discuss festivals in general.

This scenic magnificence, which became the normal practice, had a disastrous effect on Italian tragedy. "In Venice formerly," writes Francesco Sansovino, about 1570, "besides comedies, tragedies by ancient and modern writers were put on the stage with great pomp. The fame of the scenic arrangements (*apparati*) brought spectators from far and near. Nowadays, performances are given by private individuals in their own houses, and the custom has long been fixed of passing the carnival in comedies and other cheerful entertainments." In other words, scenic display had helped kill tragedy.

The various starts or attempts of these modern tragedians, among which the *Sofonisba* of Trissino (1515) was the most celebrated, belong to the history of literature. The same may be said of genteel comedy, modeled on Plautus and Terence. Even an Ariosto could do nothing of the first order in this style. On the other hand, popular prose-comedy, as treated by Machiavelli, Bibbiena, and Aretino, might have had a future had its subject matter not condemned it to destruction. This was, on the one hand, licentious to the last degree, and on the other, aimed at certain classes in society, which, after the middle of the sixteenth century, ceased to afford a ground for public attacks. If in the *Sofonisba* the portrayal of character gave place to brilliant declamation, this brilliant declamation combined with its half sister, caricature, became ruthless in these comedies.

The writing of tragedies and comedies continued without interruption, and there was no lack of numerous performances of ancient and modern plays; but they provided only motive and occasion, in order to develop the appropriate magnificence at festivals, and the national genius turned as completely from this as from a living form. When the opera and the pastoral fable appeared, these attempts were wholly abandoned.

Only one form was and remained national—the unwritten *commedia dell' arte*, which was improvised after an established plot. It was of no great benefit in the delineation of character, since the masks were few in number and familiar to everybody. But the talent of the nation had such affinity for this style, that often in the middle of written comedies the actors would throw themselves on their own inspiration, so that in some places a new mixed form of comedy came into existence. The plays given in Venice by Burchiello, and afterward by the company of Armonio, Val. Zuccato, Lod. Dolce, and others, were perhaps of this character. We know that Burchiello used to heighten the comic effect by mixing Greek and Slavonic words with the Venetian dialect. A partial or quite complete *commedia dell' arte* was that of Angelo Beolco, called Il Ruzzante (1502-1542), whose customary masks were Paduan peasants (Menato, Vezzo, Billora, etc.). He would study their dialect while spending the summer at the villa of his patron Luigi Cornaro at Codevico. Gradually all the famous local masks appeared, whose remains still delight the Italian populace: Pantalone, the Doctor, Brighella, Pulcinella, Arlecchino, and the rest. Most of them are certainly much older and are possibly connected with the masks of old Roman farces; but it was not till the sixteenth century that several of them were combined in one piece. At the present time this is less often the case; but every great city still keeps to its local mask—Naples to the Pulcinella, Florence to the Stentorello, Milan to its often so admirable Meneghino.

This is indeed scanty compensation for a people that possessed the power, perhaps to a greater degree than any other, to reflect and contemplate its own highest qualities in the mirror of the drama. But this power was destined to be marred for centuries by hostile forces, for whose introduction the Italians were only in part responsible. The universal talent for dramatic representation could not indeed be uprooted, and in music Italy long made good its claim to supremacy in Europe. Those who can find in this world of sound a compensation for the drama, to which all future was denied, have, at all events, no meager source of consolation.

May we expect to find in epic poetry what the stage failed to produce? Yet the chief reproach made against the heroic poetry of Italy is precisely that it is at its weakest in the portrayal and delineation of character.

Other merits are not to be denied it, among them, that for over three centuries it has actually been read and constantly reprinted, whereas almost all the epic poetry of other nations has become a mere matter of literary or historical curiosity. Or does this perhaps lie in the taste of the readers, who demand something different from what would satisfy a Northern public? Certainly, without the power of entering to some degree into Italian sentiment, it is impossible to appreciate the characteristic excellence of these poems, and many distinguished men declare that they can make nothing of them. And in truth, if we criticize Pulci, Boiardo, Ariosto, and Berni solely with an eye to their thought and subject matter, we shall fail to do them justice. They are artists of a singular kind, who write for a people that is distinctly and eminently artistic.

The medieval legends had lived on after the gradual extinction of the poetry of chivalry, partly in the form of rhyming adaptations and collections, and partly as novels in prose. The latter was the case in Italy during the fourteenth century; but the newly awakened memories of antiquity were growing to gigantic proportions, and soon cast into the shade all the fantastic creations of the Middle Ages. Boccaccio, for example, in his *Amorosa visione*, names among the heroes in his enchanted palace Tristan, Arthur, Galeotto, and others, but briefly, as if he were ashamed; and succeeding writers either do not name them at all, or name them only for purpose of ridicule. But the people remembered them, and in the fifteenth century they passed from the people back to the poets. These were now able to conceive and represent their subjects in a wholly new manner. But they did more. They introduced into their subjects a multitude of fresh elements, and in fact recast them from beginning to end. It must not be demanded of them that they should treat such subjects with the respect once felt for them. All other countries must envy them the advantage of having a popular interest of this kind to appeal to; but they could not without hypocrisy treat these myths with any respect.

Instead of this, they moved with victorious freedom in the new field that poetry had won. Their chief aim seems to have been that their poems, when recited, should produce the most harmonious and exhilarating effect. Indeed, these works gain immensely when they are repeated piecemeal and excellently, with a slight touch of comedy in voice and gesture. A deeper and more detailed portrayal of character would do little to enhance this effect; though the reader may desire it, the hearer, who sees the rhapsodist standing before him, and who hears only one piece at a time, does not think about it at all. With respect to the figures, which the poet found ready made for him, his feeling was of a double kind: his humanistic culture protested against their medieval character, whereas their combats as counterparts of the battles and tournaments of the poet's own age exercised all his knowledge and artistic power, while at the same time they called forth all the highest qualities in the reciter. Even in Pulci,[150] accordingly, we find no parody, strictly speaking, of chivalry, as close as the rough humor of his paladins at times approaches it. By their side stands the ideal of pugnacity —the droll and jovial Morgante—who masters whole armies with his bell clapper, and who is himself thrown into relief by contrast with the grotesque and most interesting monster Margutte. Yet Pulci lays no special stress on these two rough and vigorous characters, and his story, long after they have disappeared from it, maintains its singular course. Even Boiardo [151] treats his characters with the same mastery, using them for serious or comic purposes as he pleases; he has his fun even out of supernatural beings, whom he sometimes intentionally depicts as louts. But there is one artistic aim which he pursues as earnestly as Pulci, namely, the lively and exact description of all that occurs. – Pulci recited his poem, as one book after another was finished, before the society of Lorenzo the Magnificent, and in the same way Boiardo recited his at the court of Ercole of Ferrara. It is easy to imagine what sort of excellence such an audience demanded, and how little thanks a profound exposition of character would have earned for the poet. Under these circumstances the poems naturally formed no complete whole, and might just as well be half or twice as long as they are. Their composition is not that of a great historical picture, but rather that of a frieze, or of some rich festoon entwined among groups of picturesque figures. And just as in the figures or tendrils of a frieze we do not look for minuteness of execution in the individual forms, or for distant perspectives and different planes, so must we as little expect anything of the kind from these poems.

The varied richness of invention which continually aston- ishes us, especially in the case of Boiardo, turns to ridicule all our school definitions as to the essence of epic poetry. For that age, this form of literature was the most agreeable diversion from archeological studies, and, indeed, the only possible means of re-establishing an independent class of narrative poetry. For the versification of ancient history could only lead to the false paths trod by Petrarch in his *Africa,* written in Latin hexameters, and, a hundred and fifty years

150. The *Morgante,* first printed before 1488. – For the tourna- ments, see below.
151. The *Orlando innamorato,* first printed 1496.

later, by Trissino in his *Italia liberata dai Goti* [Italy Delivered from the Goths], composed in *versi sciolti* [free verse] —a never-ending poem of faultless language and versification, which only makes us wonder whether this unlucky alliance has been more disastrous to history or to poetry. And whither did the example of Dante beguile those who imitated him? The visionary *trionfi* [triumphs] of Petrarch were the last works written under this influence which satisfy our taste. The *Amorosa visione* of Boccaccio is at bottom no more than an enumeration of historical or fabulous characters, arranged under allegorical categories. Others preface what they have to tell with a baroque imitation of Dante's first canto, and provide themselves with some allegorical companion to take the place of Vergil. Uberti, for example, chose Solinus for his geographical poem (*Dittamondo*) and Giovanni Santi, Plutarch for his encomium on Federigo of Urbino. The only salvation from these false tendencies lay in the new epic poetry, which was represented by Pulci and Boiardo. The admiration and curiosity with which it was received—the like of which will perhaps never again fall to the lot of epic poetry—is brilliant proof of how greatly it was needed. It is idle to ask whether that epic ideal which our own day has formed from Homer and the Nibelungenlied is or is not realized in these works; an ideal of their own age certainly was. By their endless descriptions of combats, which to us are the most fatiguing part of these poems, they satisfied, as we have already said, a practical interest of which it is hard for us to form a just conception—as hard, indeed, as of the esteem in which a lively and faithful reflection of the passing moment was then held.

Nor can a more inappropriate test be applied to Ariosto than to search in his *Orlando furioso* [152] for the representation of character. Characters there are, and drawn with an affectionate care; but the poem does not depend on them for its effect, and would lose, rather than gain, if more stress were laid on them. But the demand for them is part of a wider and more general desire which Ariosto fails to satisfy as our day would wish it satisfied. From a poet of such fame and such mighty gifts we would gladly receive something better than the adventures of Orlando. From him we might have hoped for a work expressing the deepest conflicts of the human soul, the highest thoughts of his time on things human and divine—in a word, one of those supreme syntheses, as the *Divine Comedy* or *Faust*. Instead of which he

152. First edition, 1516.

goes to work like the visual artists of his own day, not caring for originality in our sense of the word, simply reproducing a familiar circle of figures, and even, when it suits his purpose, using details left him by his predecessors. The excellence which, in spite of all this, can nevertheless be attained, will be the more incomprehensible to people born without artistic sense, learned and intelligent as they may otherwise be. The artistic aim of Ariosto is brilliant, living "action," which he distributes equally throughout the great poem. For this end he must be excused not only from all deeper expression of character, but also from maintaining any strict connection in his narrative. He must be allowed to take up lost and forgotten threads when and where he pleases; his heroes must come and go, not because their character demands it, but because the story requires it. Yet in this apparently irrational and arbitrary style of composition he displays a harmonious beauty, never losing himself in description, but giving only such a sketch of scenes and persons as does not hinder the flowing movement of the narrative. Still less does he lose himself in conversation and monologue, but maintains the lofty privilege of the true epos, by transforming everything into living narrative. His pathos does not lie in the words, not even in the famous twenty-third and following cantos, where Orlando's madness is portrayed. That the love stories in the heroic poem are without all lyrical tenderness, must be reckoned a merit, though from a moral point of view they cannot always be approved. Yet at times they are of such truth and reality, notwithstanding all the magic and romance that surrounds them, we might think them personal affairs of the poet himself. In the full consciousness of his own genius, he does not scruple to weave the events of his own day into the poem, and to celebrate the fame of the House of Este in visions and prophecies. The wonderful stream of his octaves carries it all forward in even and dignified movement.

With Teofilo Folengo, or, as he calls himself here, Limerno Pitocco, the parody of the whole system of chivalry attained the end it had so long deserved.[153] But here comedy, with its realism, demanded a stricter delineation of character. Exposed to all the rough usage of the half-savage street lads in a Roman country town, Sutri, the little Orlando grows up before our eyes into the hero, the priest hater, and the disputant. The conventional fantasy world that had been recognized since the time of Pulci and had served as a framework for

153. *Orlandino,* first edition, 1526.

the epos here falls to pieces. The origin and position of the paladins is openly ridiculed, as in the tournament of donkeys in the second book, where the knights appear with the most ludicrous armament. The poet utters his ironical regrets over the inexplicable faithlessness which seems implanted in the house of Gano of Mainz, over the toilsome acquisition of the sword Durindana, and so forth. Tradition, in fact, serves him only as a substratum for episodes, ludicrous fancies, allusions to events of the time (among which some, e.g., the close of vi, are exceedingly fine), and indecent jokes. Mixed with all this, a certain derision of Ariosto is unmistakable, and it was fortunate for the *Orlando furioso* that the *Orlandino*, with its Lutheran heresies, was soon put out of the way by the Inquisition. The parody is evident when (vi, 28) the House of Gonzaga is deduced from the paladin Guidone, since the Colonna claimed Orlando, the Orsini Rinaldo, and the House of Este—according to Ariosto—Ruggiero as their ancestors. Perhaps Ferrante Gonzaga, the patron of the poet, was party to this sarcasm on the House of Este.

That, finally, in the *Jerusalem Delivered* of Torquato Tasso the delineation of character is one of the chief tasks of the poet, proves only how far his mode of thought differed from that prevalent half a century before. His admirable work is a true monument of the Counter Reformation which had meanwhile been accomplished, and of the spirit and tendency of that movement.

Outside the sphere of poetry, the Italians were the first of all European nations to have a remarkable power and inclination accurately to describe man as shown in history, according to his inward and outward characteristics.

It is true that in the Middle Ages considerable attempts were made in the same direction; and the legends, as a kind of standing biographical task, must, to some extent, have kept alive the interest and the gift for such descriptions. In the annals of the monasteries and cathedrals, many of the churchmen, such as Meinwerk of Paderborn, Godehard of Hildesheim, and others, are brought vividly before our eyes; and descriptions exist of several of the German emperors, modeled after old authors—particularly Suetonius—which contain admirable features. Indeed, these and other profane *vitae* [Lives] came in time to form a continuous counterpart to the sacred legends. Yet neither Einhard nor Wippo nor Radevicus [Rahewin] can be set next to Joinville's picture of St. Louis, which certainly stands almost alone as the first complete spiritual portrait of a modern European nature.

Characters like St. Louis are rare at all times, and his was favored by the rare good fortune that a sincere and naïve observer caught the spirit of all the events and actions of his life, and represented it admirably. From what scanty sources are we left to guess at the inward nature of Frederick II or of Philip the Fair. Much of what, till the close of the Middle Ages, passed for biography, is actually nothing but contemporary narrative, written without any sense of what is individual in the subject of the memoir.

Among the Italians, on the contrary, the search for the characteristic features of remarkable men was a prevailing tendency; and it is this that separates them from the other Western peoples, among whom the same thing happens only accidentally, and in exceptional cases. This keen eye for individuality belongs only to those who have emerged from the race and have become individuals.

Under the influence of the prevailing conception of fame an art of comparative biography arose which no longer found it necessary, like Anastasius, Agnellus, and their successors, or like the biographers of the Venetian doges, to adhere to a dynastic or ecclesiastical succession. It felt itself free to describe a man if and because he was remarkable. In addition to Suetonius, it took as models Nepos, the *viri illustres* [illustrious men], and Plutarch, so far as he was known and translated; for sketches of literary history, the lives of the grammarians, rhetoricians, and poets, which we know as the appendixes to Suetonius,[154] seem to have served as patterns, as well as the widely read life of Vergil by Donatus.

It has already been mentioned that biographical collections —lives of famous men and famous women—began to appear in the fourteenth century. Where they do not describe contemporaries, they are naturally dependent on earlier narratives. The first great original effort is the life of Dante by Boccaccio. Lightly and rhetorically written, and full of arbitrary fancies, this work nevertheless gives us a lively sense of the extraordinary features in Dante's nature. Then follow, at the end of the fourteenth century, the *vite* of illustrious Florentines, by Filippo Villani. They are men of every calling: poets, jurists, physicians, scholars, artists, statesmen, and soldiers, some of them still living. Florence

---

154. How early Philostratus was used in this way, I am unable to say. ‖ Suetonius, of course, had provided a model at a very early date. Most important for the twelfth century in this respect are, apart from Einhard's *Life of Charlemagne,* William of Malmesbury's descriptions of William the Conqueror (Book III), William II (Book IV), and Henry I (Book V). ‖

is here treated like a gifted family, in which all the members are noticed in whom the spirit of the house is vigorously expressed. The descriptions are brief, but they show a remarkable eye for what is characteristic, and are even more remarkable for the combination of the outward physiognomy with the inner. From that time forward, the Tuscans never ceased to consider the description of man as lying within their special competence, and to them we owe the most valuable portraits of the Italians of the fifteenth and sixteenth centuries. Giovanni Cavalcanti (in the appendixes to his Florentine history, written before the year 1450) collects instances of civil virtue and abnegation, of political discernment and military valor, all shown by Florentines. In his *Commentaries,* Pius II gives valuable portraits of famous contemporaries; and not long ago a work of his earlier years, which seems preparatory to these portraits but which has color and features that are very singular, was reprinted [*De viris illustribus*]. To Jacopo da Volterra we owe piquant sketches of members of the Curia after Pius. We have mentioned Vespasiano Fiorentino often; as a historical source a high place must be assigned to him, but his gift as a painter of character is not to be compared with that of Machiavelli, Niccolò Valori, Guicciardini, Varchi, Francesco Vettori, and others, by whom European historical writing has probably been as much influenced in this direction as by the ancients. It must not be forgotten that some of these authors soon found their way into Northern countries by means of Latin translations. And without Giorgio Vasari of Arezzo and his incomparable work, we should perhaps to this day have no history of Northern art, or of the art of modern Europe, at all.

Among the biographers of North Italy in the fifteenth century, Bartolommeo Fazio of Spezia holds a high rank. Platina, born in the territory of Cremona, gives us, in his Life of Paul II, examples of biographical caricature. The description of the last Visconti, written by Piercandido Decembrio—an enlarged imitation of Suetonius—is of special importance. Sismondi regrets that so much trouble has been spent on so unworthy a subject, but the author would hardly have been equal to deal with a greater man, whereas he was thoroughly competent to describe the mixed nature of Filippo Maria, and in and through it to represent with accuracy the conditions, the forms, and the consequences of this particular kind of depotism. The picture of the fifteenth century would be incomplete without this unique biography, which is characteristic down to its minutest details. – Later, Milan possessed, in the historian Corio, an excellent portrait painter; and after him came Paolo Giovio of Como, whose larger biographies and shorter eulogies have achieved a world-wide reputation and became models for subsequent writers in all countries. It is easy to prove, in hundreds of places, how superficial and even dishonest he was; nor can any high and serious purpose be expected from the kind of man he was. But the breath of the age moves through his pages, and his Leo, his Alfonso, his Pompeo Colonna, live and act before us with such perfect truth and reality, that we seem admitted to the deepest recesses of their nature.

Among Neapolitan writers, Tristano Caracciolo, so far as we are able to judge, indisputably holds first place in this respect, although his purpose was not strictly biographical. In the figures that he brings before us, guilt and destiny are wondrously mingled. He is, in fact, a kind of unconscious tragedian. That genuine tragedy which found no place on the stage, stalked the palaces, the streets, and the public squares. – The "Words and Deeds of Alfonso the Great" [*De dictis et factis Alphonsi*], written by Antonio Panormita during the lifetime of the king, is remarkable as one of the first of such collections of anecdotes and of wise and witty sayings.

The rest of Europe followed the example of Italy in this respect only gradually, although great political and religious movements had broken so many bonds, and had awakened so many thousands to new spiritual life. Italians, whether scholars or diplomats, still remain, on the whole, the best source of information for the characters of the most important personalities of all Europe. It is well known how speedily and unanimously in recent times the reports of the Venetian embassies in the sixteenth and seventeenth centuries have been recognized as authorities of the first order for personal description.

Here and there among the Italians even autobiography took a bold and vigorous flight, and sets before us, together with the most varied incidents of external life, striking revelations of the inner man; whereas among other nations, even in Germany at the time of the Reformation, it is confined to remarkable external experiences, and leaves us to guess at the spirit within from the style of the narrative. It is as though Dante's *Vita nuova*, with its inexorable truthfulness, had shown his people the way.

The beginnings of autobiography lie in the family histories of the fourteenth and fifteenth centuries, a goodly number of which are still supposedly preserved in manuscript form, particularly in the Florentine libraries—unaffected narratives written for the sake of the individual or of his family, as, e.g., that of Buonaccorso Pitti.

Nor should we look for a profound self-analysis in the *Commentaries* of Pius II. What we learn of him here as a man seems at first sight to be chiefly confined to the account he gives of the various steps in his career. But further reflection leads us to a different conclusion with regard to this remarkable book. There are men who are by nature mirrors of what surrounds them. It would be irrelevant to ask incessantly after their convictions, their spiritual struggles, their inmost victories and achievements. Aeneas Sylvius lived fully in the world around him, without troubling himself about the problems and contradictions of life. For this his Catholic orthodoxy gave him all the help he needed. And after taking part in every intellectual movement that interested his age, and notably furthering some of them, at the close of his earthly course he still retained character enough to preach a crusade against the Turks, and to die of grief when it came to nothing.

Nor is the autobiography of Benvenuto Cellini, any more than that of Pius II, founded on introspection. And yet it describes the whole man—not always willingly—with marvelous truth and completeness. It is no small matter that Benvenuto, whose most important works remained half finished and consequently perished, and who, as an artist, appears to us perfect only in his decorative aspect, but in other respects, if judged by those works that remain, is surpassed by so many of his greater contemporaries—that Benvenuto as a man will interest mankind to the end of time. It does him no harm when the reader often detects him bragging or lying; the stamp of a mighty, energetic, and thoroughly developed nature remains. By his side the Northern autobiographers, though their tendency and moral character may stand much higher, appear incomplete beings. He is a man who can do all and dares do all, and who carries his measure in himself. Whether we like him or not, he lives, such as he was, as a wholly recognizable prototype of modern man.

Another man deserves a brief mention in connection with this subject—a man who, like Benvenuto, was not always a model of veracity: Girolamo Cardano of Milan (b. 1500). His little book, *De propria vita* [*The Book of My Life*],[155] will outlive and eclipse his fame in philosophy and natural

155. Written in his old age, about 1576.

science, just as Benvenuto's *Life*, though its value is of another kind, has thrown his works into the shade. Cardano is a physician who feels his own pulse, and describes his own physical, moral, and intellectual nature together with all the conditions under which it had developed, and this, to the best of his ability, honestly and sincerely. The work that he avowedly took as his model—the *Meditations* of Marcus Aurelius—he was able, hampered as he was by no stoical maxims, to surpass in this particular. He desires to spare neither himself nor others, and begins the narrative of his career with the statement that his mother tried, and failed, to procure abortion. It is worth remark that he attributes to the stars that presided over his birth only the events of his life and his intellectual gifts, but not his moral qualities; he confesses (ch. 10) that the astrological prediction that he would not live to the age of forty or fifty years did him much harm in his youth. But there is no need to quote from so well-known and accessible a book; whoever opens it will not lay it down till the last page. Cardano admits that he cheated at play, that he was vindictive, incapable of all compunction, purposely cruel in his speech. He confesses it without impudence and without feigned contrition, without even wishing to make himself an object of interest, but with the same simple and sincere love of fact that guided him in his scientific researches. And, what is to us most shocking, the seventy-six-year-old man, after the most terrible experiences [156] and with all his confidence in his fellow men gone, finds himself tolerably happy. He still has a grandson, immense learning, the fame of his works, money, rank and credit, powerful friends, the knowledge of many secrets, and, best of all, belief in God. After this, he counts the teeth in his head: he still has fifteen.

Yet when Cardano wrote, Inquisitors and Spaniards were already busy in Italy either hindering the development of such natures, or, where they existed, by some means or other putting them out of the way. There is a gulf between this book and the memoirs of Alfieri.

Yet it would be unjust to close this list of autobiographers without listening to the words of a man who was both worthy and happy. This is the well-known philosopher of practical life, Luigi Cornaro, whose dwelling at Padua was already classical as an architectural work and at the same time the home of all the Muses. In his famous treatise *On the Sober*

---

156. E.g., the execution of his eldest son, who had taken vengeance for his wife's infidelity by poisoning her.

Life,[157] he describes the strict regimen by which he succeeded, after a sickly youth, in reaching an advanced and healthy age, at that time of eighty-three years. He goes on to answer those who despise life after the age of sixty-five as a living death, showing them that his own life has nothing of death in it. "Let them come and see, and wonder at my good health, how I mount my horse without help, how I run up stairs and hills, how cheerful, good-humored, and contented I am, how free from care and troublous thoughts. Peace and joy never quit me. . . . My friends are wise, learned, and distinguished people of position, and when they are not with me I read and write, and try by this as by all other means, to be useful to others. Each of these things I do at the proper time and at my ease in my dwelling, which is beautiful and lies in the best part of Padua, and is arranged both for summer and winter with all the resources of architecture, and also has gardens by the running streams. In the spring and autumn, I go for awhile to my place in the most beautiful part of the Euganean Hills, where I have fountains and gardens, and a comfortable dwelling; and there I amuse myself with some easy and pleasant hunting, such as is suitable to my age. At other times I go to my villa in the plain; there all the streets converge onto an open square, in the middle of which stands a pretty church; an arm of the Brenta flows through the fertile, well-cultivated fields, now fully peopled, which the marshes and the foul air once made fit rather for snakes than for men. It was I who drained the district; then the air became good, and people settled there and multiplied, and the country became developed as we see it today, so that I can truly say: On this spot I gave to God an altar and a temple and souls to worship Him. This is my consolation and my happiness whenever I come here. In the spring and autumn I also visit the neighboring towns and see and converse with my friends through whom I make the acquaintance of other distinguished men, architects, painters, sculptors, musicians, and cultivators of the soil. I see what new things they have done, I look again at what I know already, and always learn much that is of use to me. I see palaces, gardens, antiquities, public grounds,

157. *Discorsi delle vita sobria* [*Discourses on the Sober Life*], consisting of the *trattato* [treatise] proper, a *compendio* [compendium], an *esortazione* [exhortation], and a *lettera* [letter] to Daniel Barbaro. — The book has often been reprinted [and translated, under a variety of titles, *The Art of Living Long, How to Live to Be 100, Sure Methods of Attaining a Long and Healthful Life*, etc.].

churches, and fortifications. But what delights me most of all when I travel is the beauty of the country and the towns and villages lying now in the plain, now on the slopes of the hills, or on the banks of rivers and streams, surrounded by gardens and villas. And these enjoyments are not diminished through weakness of the eyes or ears; all my senses, thanks be to God, are in the best condition, including the sense of taste, for I enjoy more the simple food which I now take in moderation, than all the delicacies I ate in my intemperate years."

After mentioning the works he had undertaken on behalf of the Republic for draining the marshes, and the projects he had constantly advocated for preserving the lagoons, he concludes: "These are the true recreations of an old age that God has permitted to be healthy, and that is free from those mental and bodily sufferings to which so many young people and so many sickly older people succumb. And if it be allowed to add the little to the great, to add jest to earnest, it is also as a result of my moderate life, that in my eighty-third year I have written a most amusing comedy, full of blameless wit. Such works are generally the business of youth, as tragedy is the business of old age. If it is reckoned to the credit of the famous Greek [Sophocles] that he wrote a tragedy in his seventy-third year, must I not, with my ten years more, be more cheerful and healthy than he was? – And that no consolation may be wanting in the overflowing cup of my old age, I see before my eyes a sort of bodily immortality in the persons of my descendants. When I come home I see before me, not one or two, but eleven grand-children, between the ages of two and eighteen, all from the same father and mother, all healthy and (so far as can already be judged) all gifted with the talent and disposition for learning and a good life. I always have one of the younger ones as my playmate (*buffoncello*), since children from the third to the fifth year are born to tricks; the elder ones I treat as my companions, and, as they have admirable voices, I take delight in hearing them sing and play on different instruments. And I sing myself, and find my voice better, clearer, and louder than ever. These are the pleasures of my last years. My life, therefore, is alive and not dead; nor would I exchange my age for the youth of such as live in the service of their passions."

In the Exhortation which Cornaro added at a much later time, in his ninety-fifth year, he reckons it among the elements of his happiness that this Treatise had made many converts. He died at Padua in 1565, at the age of over a hundred years.

This gift was not, however, confined to the criticism and description of individuals, but could deal with the qualities and characteristics of whole peoples. During the Middle Ages cities, families, and nations of all Europe had carried on a reciprocal barrage of insult and derision, which, with much distortion, generally contained a kernel of truth. But from the first the Italians surpassed all others in their quick apprehension of the mental differences among their cities and provinces. Their local patriotism, stronger probably than that of any other medieval people, soon found expression in literature and allied itself with the conception of fame; topography became the counterpart of biography. While all the more important cities began to celebrate themselves in prose and verse, writers appeared who made the chief towns and districts the subject partly of a serious comparative description, partly of satire, and sometimes of notices in which jest and earnest are not easily distinguished.

Next to some famous passages in the *Divine Comedy*, is the *Dittamondo* of Uberti (about 1360). Here, as a rule, only single remarkable things are mentioned: the Feast of the Crows at Sant' Apollinare in Ravenna, the springs at Treviso, the great cellar near Vicenza, the high duties at Mantua, the forest of towers at Lucca. Yet mixed up with all this, we find laudatory and satirical criticisms of another kind: Arezzo is distinguished for the crafty disposition of its citizens, Genoa for the artificially blackened eyes and teeth (?) of its women, Bologna for its prodigality, Bergamo for its coarse dialect and hardheaded people, etc. In the fifteenth century it was the fashion to belaud one's own city even at the expense of others. Michele Savonarola allows that, in comparison with his native Padua, only Rome and Venice are more splendid, and Florence perhaps more joyous—by which, naturally, our knowledge is not much extended. At the end of the century, Giovano Pontano, in his *Antonius*, wrote an imaginary journey through Italy, simply as a vehicle for malicious observations. But in the sixteenth century there begins a series of exact and profound studies of national characteristics of a kind that no other people of that time possessed. Machiavelli sets forth in some of his valuable essays the character and the political condition of the Germans and French in such a way that the born Northerner, familiar with the history of his own country, is grateful to the Florentine thinker for his flashes of insight. The Florentines begin to take pleasure in describing themselves and bask in the well-earned sunshine of their intellectual glory; perhaps their pride attains its height when, for example, they derive the artistic pre-eminence of Tuscany among Italians not from any special gifts of nature, but from hard, patient work.[158] The homage of famous men from other parts of Italy, as, for example, the magnificent sixteenth *capitolo* of Ariosto, they accepted as a merited tribute to their excellence.

Of one, which seems to be an excellent description of the differences among the Italian people, we can only give the title.[159] Leandro Alberti is not so fruitful as might be expected in his description of the character of the different cities. A small, anonymous Commentary contains, among many absurdities, some valuable information about the unfortunate conditions prevailing at the middle of the century.

To what extent this comparative study of national and local characteristics may, by means of Italian humanism, have influenced the rest of Europe, we are not able to indicate more precisely. Italy, at all events, holds the priority in this respect, as in the description of the world in general.

But the discovery of man was not confined to the spiritual characteristics of individuals and nations; his outward appearance was the object of an entirely different interest in Italy from that of the North.

We do not venture to speak of the position held by the great Italian physicians with respect to the progress of physiology, and the artistic study of the human figure belongs not to a work like the present, but to the history of art. But something must be said here of that universal education of the eye, which rendered perfect and final the judgment of the Italians on physical beauty or ugliness.

On reading the Italian authors of that period attentively, we are astounded at the keenness and accuracy with which outward features are characterized, and at the completeness with which personal appearance in general is described. Even today the Italians, and especially the Romans, can sketch a man's portrait with a few words. This rapid apprehension of the characteristic is an essential condition for detecting and representing the beautiful. In poetry, it is true, circumstantial description may be a fault, since a single feature, suggested by deep passion or insight, will often awaken in the reader a far more powerful impression of the figure in question. Nowhere does Dante give us a more splendid idea of his

158. Vasari, Life of Michelangelo, the beginning.
159. Landi, *Quaestiones Forcianae*, Naples, 1536, used by Ranke, *History of the Popes*, vol. I.

Beatrice than where he only describes her influence on all around her. But here we have not to do with poetry, which pursues its own ends, but rather with the general capacity to paint in words real as well as imaginary forms.

In this, Boccaccio is a master—not in the *Decameron*, where the character of the tales forbids lengthy description, but in the romances, where he is free to take his time. In his *Ameto* he describes a blonde and a brunette much as an artist a hundred years later would have painted them—for here, too, imagination long precedes art. In the account of the brunette—or, strictly speaking, of the less blonde of the two—there are already touches that we would be tempted to call classical. In his words *la spaziosa testa e distesa* [the grand, expanding head] lies the feeling for monumental forms which go beyond graceful prettiness; the eyebrows are no longer two bows, as in the Byzantine ideal, but a sweeping wavy line; the nose was probably seen as aquiline; [160] the wide, full breast, the arms of moderate length, the beautiful hand as it lies on the purple mantle—all foretell the sense of beauty of a future time, and unconsciously approach the ideal of classical antiquity. In other descriptions Boccaccio mentions a flat (not medievally rounded) brow, a long, earnest, brown eye, and a round, not hollowed neck, as well as—in a very modern tone—the "little feet" and the "two roguish eyes" of a black-haired nymph.

Whether the fifteenth century has left any written account of its ideal of beauty, I am not able to say. The works of the painters and sculptors do not render such an account as unnecessary as might appear at first sight, since possibly, as opposed to their realism, a more ideal type may have been favored and preserved by the writers. In the sixteenth century Firenzuola appeared with his remarkable work on female beauty. We must clearly distinguish in it what he had learned from old authors or from artists, such as establishing proportions according to the length of the head, and certain abstract conceptions. What remains is his own genuine observation, illustrated with examples of women and girls of Prato. Since his little work is a kind of lecture, delivered before the women of this city—that is, before very severe critics—he must have kept pretty closely to the truth. His principle is avowedly that of Zeuxis and of Lucian—the creation of an ideal beauty out of a number of beautiful parts. He defines the shades of color which occur in the hair and skin, and gives preference to the *biondo* [blonde] as the most beautiful shade for

160. The reading is evidently corrupt here.

the hair, meaning by it a soft honey shading to brown. He requires the hair to be thick, long, and curly; the forehead serene, and twice as broad as it is high; the skin bright and clear (*candida*), but not dead white (*bianchezza*); the eyebrows dark, silky, most strongly marked in the middle and shading off toward the ears and the nose; the white of the eye faintly touched with blue, the iris not actually black, though all the poets praise the *occhi neri* [black eyes] as a gift of Venus, despite the fact that goddesses had sky-blue eyes, and that soft, joyous, brown eyes were much admired. The eye itself should be large and full and prominent; the lids are most beautiful when they are white and streaked with barely visible tiny red veins; the lashes should be neither too long, nor too thick, nor too dark. The hollow of the eye should have the same color as the cheek. The ear, neither too large nor too small, firmly and neatly fitted on, should have more color in the winding than in the even parts, with the edge of the transparent rosiness of the pomegranate. The temples must be white and even, and for the most perfect beauty ought not to be too narrow.[161] The cheeks should be reddest at their roundest part. The nose, which determines the value of the profile, must recede gently and evenly in the direction of the eyes; where the cartilage ends, there may be a slight elevation, but not so marked as to make the nose aquiline, which is not pleasing in women; the lower part must be less strongly colored than the ears, but not of a chilly whiteness, and the middle partition above the lips should have a slightly reddish tint. Our author would have the mouth rather small, and neither too pointed nor quite flat, with the lips not too thin and fitting neatly together; an accidental opening (that is, when the woman is neither speaking nor laughing) should not display more than six upper teeth. As special delights, he mentions a dimple in the upper lip, a certain fullness of the lower lip, a tempting smile in the left corner of the mouth, and so on. The teeth should not be too small, should be regular, well marked off from one another, and of the color of ivory; and the gums must not be too dark or even like red velvet. The chin must be round, neither pointed nor protuberant, and slightly red as it rises; its special glory is the dimple. The neck should be white and round and rather too

161. Referring to the fact that the appearance of the temples can be completely changed by the arrangement of the hair, Firenzuola makes a comical attack on the overcrowding of the hair with flowers, which causes the head to "look like a pot of pinks or a quarter of a goat on the spit." He is, as a rule, thoroughly at home in caricature.

long than too short, with the hollow and the Adam's apple
only suggested; and the skin must form pleasing contours
with every movement. The shoulders he desires broad, and
in the breadth of the bosom he sees the first condition of its
beauty. No bone may be visible upon it, its fall and swell
must be gentle and gradual, its color *candidissimo* [snow
white]. The leg should be long and slender in the lower parts,
but not without flesh on the shin, and must have white, full
calves. He likes the foot small, but not bony, the instep (it
seems) high, and the color white as alabaster. The arms
should be white, with a rosiness in the upper parts; they
should be fleshy and muscular, but as soft as those of Pallas
when she stood before the shepherd on Mount Ida—in brief:
ripe, fresh, and firm. The hand should be white, especially
toward the wrist, but *large* and plump, as soft as silk to the
touch; the rosy palm should have a few, distinct but not
intricate lines, its elevations should not be too great, the space
between thumb and forefinger brightly colored and without
wrinkles, the fingers long, delicate, and scarcely thinner
toward the tips, with nails clear, even, neither too long nor
too square, and cut so as to show a white margin about
the breadth of a knife's back.

Aesthetic principles of a general character occupy a very
subordinate place to these particulars. The ultimate principles
of beauty, according to which the eye judges *senza appello*
[directly and intuitively], are a secret even for Firenzuola,
he frankly confesses; and his definitions of *leggiadria* [charm],
grazia [grace], *vaghezza* [loveliness], *venustà* [beauty], *aria*
[grand air], *maestà* [majesty], are partly, as has been re-
marked, philological, and partly vain attempts to utter the
unutterable. Laughter he defines—probably following some
old author—as a radiance of the soul.

The literature of all countries shows, at the close of the
Middle Ages, certain attempts to lay down theoretical principles of beauty; but no other work can be compared to that of
Firenzuola. Brantôme, who came a good half-century later,
is a bungling critic by his side, governed as he was by
lasciviousness and not by a sense of beauty.

To the discovery of man we must add, in conclusion,
the interest taken in descriptions of the daily course of human
life.

The comical and satirical literature of the Middle Ages
could not dispense with pictures of everyday events. But it is
something quite different when the Italians of the Renaissance paint this picture for its own sake, because it is

inherently interesting, because it forms part of that great, universal life of the world whose magic breath they feel all around them. Instead of and along with the satirical comedy that wanders through houses, villages, and streets, seeking food for its derision in parson, peasant, and burgher, we find here in literature the beginnings of a true genre, long before it appeared in painting. That genre and satire were then often combined does not prevent them from being wholly different things.

How much earthly business Dante must have watched with active interest, before he was able to make the events of his spiritual world so perceptible.[162] The famous pictures of the busy movement in the arsenal at Venice, of the blind men laid side by side before the church door,[163] and the like, are by no means the only instances of this kind; his art, the expression of the state of the soul by the outward gesture, shows a close and constant study of human life.

The poets who came after him rarely approached him in this respect, and the novelists were forbidden by the laws of their literary style to linger over details. Their prefaces and narratives might be as long as they pleased, but what we understand by genre was outside their province. The taste for this class of description was not fully awakened till the time of the revival of antiquity.

And here we meet again *the* man who was receptive to everything—Aeneas Sylvius. Not only natural beauty, not only matters of antiquarian or geographical interest excite him to description, but any living scene of daily life. Among the numerous passages in his memoirs in which he describes scenes that hardly one of his contemporaries would have thought worth a line of notice, we mention here only the boat race on the Lake of Bolsena.[164] It is impossible to determine which ancient letter writer or storyteller stimulated him to such vigorous descriptions, but then, the whole spiritual communion between antiquity and the Renaissance is full of delicacy and of mystery.

Next we should include those descriptive Latin poems of which we have already spoken—hunting scenes, journeys, ceremonies, and so forth. There are also the same kind of things in Italian, as, for example, the descriptions of the famous Medicean tournament by Politian and Luca Pulci. The true epic poets, Luigi Pulci, Boiardo, and Ariosto, are

162. For the accuracy of his sense of space, see footnote 139.
163. *Inferno*, xxi, 7; *Purgatorio*, xiii, 61.
164. *The Commentaries of Pius II*, Book VIII.

driven onward more rapidly by the stream of their narrative; yet in all of them we must recognize as a chief element of their greatness the lightness and precision of their descriptive touch. Franco Sacchetti on one occasion amuses himself with repeating the short speeches of a troop of pretty women caught in the woods by a shower of rain.

We find other scenes of active life primarily in the military historians. In a lengthy poem, dating from an earlier period, there is a faithful picture of a combat of mercenary soldiers in the fourteenth century, chiefly in the form of shouts, commands, and conversations that take place at such an event.[165]

But the most remarkable productions of this kind are the realistic descriptions of country life, which are found especially in Lorenzo the Magnificent and the poets around him.

Since the time of Petrarch,[166] an unreal and conventional style of bucolic poetry had been in vogue, which, whether written in Latin or Italian, was essentially a copy of Vergil. Parallel to this, we find the pastoral novel of Boccaccio and other works of the same kind down to the *Arcadia* of Sannazaro, and later still, the pastoral comedy of Tasso and Guarini. They are works, whether poetry or prose, that are finished and perfect, but in which pastoral life is only an ideal dress for sentiments that belong to a wholly different sphere of culture.[167]

But alongside all this, a more realistic treatment of rustic life appeared in Italian poetry toward the end of the fifteenth century. This was possible only in Italy, for only here did the peasant (whether laborer or proprietor) possess human dignity, personal freedom, and the right of settlement, hard as his lot might sometimes be in other respects. The difference between town and country was far from being so marked here as it was in the North. Many of the smaller towns were peopled almost exclusively by peasants who, at nightfall, could call themselves townsfolk. The stonecutters of Como

165. Even Machiavelli's description of Florence during the plague of 1527 belongs, to a certain extent, to this class of works. It is a series of living, speaking pictures of a frightful calamity.
166. According to Boccaccio (*Life of Dante*), Dante had already written two eclogues, probably in Latin.
167. In his *Ameto*, Boccaccio renders a kind of mythical *Decameron*, and sometimes fails ludicrously to maintain the character. One of his nymphs is a good Catholic, and in Rome prelates shoot glances of unholy love at her. Another marries. In the *Ninfale Fiesolano*, the pregnant nymph Mensola takes counsel of an "old and wise nymph."

wandered over nearly all Italy; the child Giotto was free to leave his sheep and join a guild in Florence; there was on the whole a steady flow from the country into the cities, and some mountain populations seemed born to supply this current. It is true that pride of culture and local conceit supplied poets and novelists with abundant motives for making fun of the *villano* [peasant], and what they left undone was taken care of by the comic improvisers. But nowhere do we find a trace of that brutal and contemptuous class-hatred against the *vilains* [villeins] which inspired the aristocratic poets of Provence, and often, too, the French chroniclers. On the contrary, Italian authors of every sort gladly recognized and accentuated what was great or remarkable in the life of the peasant. Gioviano Pontano mentions with admiration instances of the fortitude of the savage inhabitants of the Abruzzi; in the biographical collections and in the novelists we meet the figure of the heroic peasant maid who hazards her life to defend her family and her honor.[168]

Such conditions made the poetic treatment of country life possible. The first instance we shall mention is that of Baptista Mantuanus, whose eclogues (written in his youth, about 1480) were once much read and are still worth reading. They are a mixture of real and conventional rusticity, but the former tends to prevail. They represent the mode of thought of a well-meaning village clergyman, not without a certain leaning to liberal ideas. As Carmelite monk, the writer may have had occasion to mix freely with the peasantry.

But it is with a power of a wholly different kind that Lorenzo the Magnificent transports himself into the peasant's world.[169] His *Nencia di Barberino* reads like an abstract of genuine popular songs of the Florentine country, fused into a great stream of octaves. The objectivity of the writer is such that we are in doubt whether the speaker—the young peasant Vallera, who declares his love to Nencia—awakens

168. We are unable to discuss more specifically the condition of the Italian peasantry in general and the details of that condition in several provinces in particular. The proportions between freehold and leasehold property, and the burdens laid on each in comparison with those borne at the present time, must be gathered from special works that we have not had the opportunity to consult. In stormy times the country people were apt to have appalling relapses into savagery.

169. The remarkable poems of the German *Minnesänger* which bear the name of Neidhart von Reuenthal portray the life of the peasant only in so far as the knight chooses to mix with it.

his sympathy or ridicule. The deliberate contrast to the conventional eclogue of Pan and nymphs is unmistakable. Lorenzo surrenders himself purposely to the realism of simple, rough country life, and yet his work makes upon us the impression of true poetry.

The *Beca da Dicomano* of Luigi Pulci is an admitted counterpart to the *Nencia* of Lorenzo. But the deeper purpose is lacking. The *Beca* is written not so much from an inner need to give a picture of popular life, as from the desire to win the approbation of the educated Florentine world. Hence the greater and more deliberate coarseness of the scenes, and the indecent jokes. Nevertheless, the point of view of the rustic lover is admirably maintained.

Third in this company of poets is Angelo Politian and his *Rusticus* in Latin hexameters. Keeping clear of all imitation of Vergil's *Georgics*, he describes the year of the Tuscan peasant, beginning with the late autumn, when the countryman carves his new plough and prepares the seed for the winter. The picture of the meadows in spring is exuberant and beautiful, and the Summer has fine passages; but the vintage feast in autumn is one of the gems of modern Latin poetry. Politian wrote poems in Italian as well as Latin, from which we may infer that in Lorenzo's circle it was possible to render realistically the passionate life of the lower classes. His gypsy's love song is one of the earliest products of that wholly modern tendency to put oneself with poetic consciousness into the position of another class. This had been attempted for ages for comic effect, and the opportunity for it was offered in Florence at every carnival by the songs of the maskers. But the sympathetic understanding of the feeling of another class was new; and with it the *Nencia* and this *Canzone zingaresca* mark a new starting point in the history of poetry.

Here, too, we must note how culture prepared the way for art. Eighty years elapsed between the time of the *Nencia* and the rustic genre painting of Jacopo Bassano and his school.

In the next section we shall show how differences of birth had lost their significance in Italy. Much of this was doubtless due to the fact that it was here that men and mankind were first thoroughly and profoundly understood. This one single result of the Renaissance is enough to fill us with everlasting thankfulness. The logical idea of humanity was old enough—but here the idea became a fact.

The loftiest conceptions on this subject were uttered by Pico della Mirandola in his speech On the Dignity of Man,

which may justly be called one of the noblest bequests of
that great age. God, he tells us, made man at the close of the
creation, to know the laws of the universe, to love its beauty,
to admire its greatness. He bound him to no fixed place, to
no prescribed form of work, and by no iron necessity, but
gave him mobility and free will. "I have set thee," says the
Creator to Adam, "in the center of the world, that thou
mayest the more easily behold and see all that is therein.
I created thee a being neither heavenly nor earthly, neither
mortal nor immortal, that thou mightest be free to shape and
to overcome thyself. Thou canst sink to the level of a beast
and be reborn in the likeness of God. The beasts bring from
their mother's body what they will have; the higher spirits
are from the beginning, or soon after,[170] what they will be
throughout eternity. Thou alone hast a growth and a development according to thine own free will. Thou bearest within
thee the germs of a universal life."

170. An allusion to the fall of Lucifer and his followers.

———◆———

PART FIVE

SOCIETY AND FESTIVALS

EVERY period of civilization that forms a complete and consistent whole not only manifests itself in political life, in religion, art, and science, but sets its characteristic stamp even on social life. Thus, the Middle Ages had their courtly and aristocratic manners and etiquette, which differed very little among the various countries of Europe, and a burgher class with its distinct form of life.

Italian customs at the time of the Renaissance offer a sharp contrast to the Middle Ages in the most important respects. The foundation was wholly different, for social intercourse in its highest and most perfect form no longer depended on caste distinction, but was based on the existence of an educated class in the modern sense, in which birth and origin had influence only when they were combined with inherited wealth and guaranteed leisure. This is not meant in an absolute sense, since medieval class distinctions still asserted themselves occasionally, if only to maintain some kind of rank with the non-Italian European aristocracy. But the main current of the time went steadily toward the fusion of classes in the sense of the modern world.

Of greatest importance for this was the circumstance that from at least the twelfth century onward, noble and burgher dwelt together in the cities. Thus interests and pleasures were shared, and from the first, a view of the world that was centered on the castle was prevented. In Italy the Church never suffered itself to be used as a means of providing for the younger sons of noble families, as in the North. Bishoprics, abbacies, and canonries were often given from the most unworthy motives, but still not according to the pedigrees of the applicants; and if the bishops were more numerous in Italy, poorer, and, as a rule, destitute of all sovereign rights, still they lived in the cities where their cathedrals stood, and formed, together with their chapters, an important element of educated society. As despots and absolute princes prospered, the nobility in most of the cities had occasion and leisure to devote themselves to a private life that, free from political danger and adorned with everything elegant and enjoyable, was in other respects hardly distinguishable from that of the wealthy burgher. And after the time of Dante, when the new poetry and literature were in the hands of everyone,[171] when to this was added the revival of ancient culture and the new interest in man as such, when the successful *condottiere* became a prince, and not only good birth but legitimate birth ceased to be indispensable for a throne, it might well have seemed that the age of equality had dawned and the belief in nobility had vanished forever.

From a theoretical point of view, when the appeal was made to antiquity, the conception of nobility could be both justified and condemned from Aristotle alone. Dante, for example,[172] derives from Aristotle's definition, "Nobility rests on excellence and inherited wealth," his own saying, "Nobility rests on personal excellence or on that of forefathers." But elsewhere he is not satisfied with this conclusion. He blames himself,[173] because even in Paradise, while talking with his ancestor Cacciaguida, he had thought of his noble origin, which is no more than a mantle at which time forever cuts away if nothing of value is added to it daily. And in the *Convivio* [174] he separates almost completely *nobile* [noble] and *nobiltà* [nobility] from every condition of birth, and identifies the idea with the capacity for moral and intellectual eminence, at the same time laying special stress on high culture by calling *nobiltà* the sister of *filosofia*.

The greater the influence of humanism on the Italian mind, the firmer and more widespread the conviction became that birth decides nothing as to the worth of a man. In the fifteenth century this was the prevailing opinion. Poggio, in his dialogue On Nobility, agrees with his interlocutors— Niccolò Niccoli and Lorenzo de' Medici, brother of the great Cosimo—that there is no other nobility than that of personal merit. The keenest shafts of his ridicule are directed

---

171. This was the case long before printing. A large number of manuscripts, and among them the best, belonged to Florentine artisans. Had it not been for Savonarola's great bonfire, many more would be left.

172. *De monarchia,* Book II, ch. 3.

173. *Paradiso,* xvi, at the beginning.

174. *Convivio,* nearly all of Book IV, and elsewhere.

against much of what vulgar prejudice thinks indispensable
to an aristocratic life. "A man is all the further removed
from true nobility, the longer his forefathers plied the trade
of brigands. The taste for hawking and hunting savors no
more of nobility than the nests and lairs of the hunted
creatures of balsam. The cultivation of the soil, as practiced
by the ancients, would be much nobler than this senseless
wandering through the hills and woods, by which men make
themselves liker to the beasts than to the reasonable creatures.
It may serve well enough as a recreation, but not as the
business of a lifetime." The life of the English and French
chivalry in the country or in the woody fastnesses seems to
him thoroughly ignoble, and worst of all, the doings of the
robber-knights of Germany. Lorenzo then begins to take the
part of the nobility, but not—which is characteristic—by
appealing to any natural sentiment, but because Aristotle
in the fifth book of the *Politics* recognizes the nobility as
existent, and defines it as resting on excellence and inherited
wealth. To this Niccoli retorts that Aristotle gives this not as
his own conviction, but as the popular impression; in his
Ethics, where he speaks as he thinks, he calls that man noble
who strives after that which is truly good. Lorenzo urges
upon him vainly that the Greek word for nobility (*eugeneia*)
means good birth; Niccoli thinks the Roman word *nobilis*
(i.e., remarkable) a better one, since it makes nobility
depend on a man's deeds.[175] In addition to these observations,
the conditions of the nobles in various parts of Italy are
outlined as follows: In Naples they will not work, and busy
themselves neither with their own estates nor with trade
and commerce, which they hold to be discreditable; they
either loiter at home or ride about on their horses. The
Roman nobility also despise trade, but they farm their own
property; the cultivation of the land even opens the way
to a title;[176] "it is a respectable even if boorish nobility." In
Lombardy the nobles live on the rent of their inherited
estates; descent and the abstinence from any regular calling
constitute nobility. In Venice, the *nobili,* the ruling caste,
are all merchants; and likewise in Genoa nobles and non-
nobles alike are merchants and sailors, and are separated
only by birth; a few, it is true, still lurk as brigands in
their mountain castles. In Florence a part of the old nobility
devoted themselves to trade; another (and certainly the

175. This contempt of noble birth is common among the humanists.
176. Throughout Italy the owner of large landed property was
equal with the nobles.

smaller part by far) enjoyed the satisfaction of their titles, and spent their time, either in doing nothing at all, or in hunting and hawking.[177]

The decisive fact was, that nearly everywhere in Italy even those who might be disposed to pride themselves on their birth could not maintain any superiority in the face of culture and wealth, and that their privileges in politics and at court were not sufficient to encourage any strong feeling of caste. Venice offers only an apparent exception to this, for there the *nobili* led the same life as their fellow citizens, and were distinguished by few honorary privileges. The case was certainly different at Naples, which was excluded from the spiritual movement of the Renaissance chiefly because of the strict isolation and the ostentatious vanity of its nobility. The Aragonese rule, which had already been established before the middle of the fifteenth century, was added to strong survivals of Lombardic and Norman medievalism and Late Gothic aristocracy, and thus there first occurred here what was to prevail throughout all Italy only a hundred years later: the partial Spaniardization of life, characterized primarily by a contempt for work and a passion for titles. The effect of this was evident before the year 1500 even in the smaller towns. There are complaints from La Cava: the place had been proverbially rich, so long as it was filled with masons and weavers; now, since instead of looms and trowels only spurs, stirrups, and gilded belts were to be seen, since everybody was trying to become Doctor of Laws or of Medicine, Notary, Officer, or Knight, the most intolerable poverty prevailed. In Florence an analogous change appears to have taken place by the time of Cosimo, the first Grand Duke; he is thanked for adopting the young people, who now despise trade and commerce, as knights of his order of St. Stephen. This is an exact opposite of the good old Florentine custom, by which fathers left property to their children on the condition that they have some occupation.

But a curious kind of social ambition, especially among the Florentines, thwarted the leveling influence of art and culture in a way that was often comical. This was the

177. The severe judgment of Machiavelli (*Discourses*, Book I, ch. 55) refers only to those of the nobility who still retained feudal rights and who were thoroughly idle and politically mischievous. – Agrippa of Nettesheim, who owes his most notable ideas to his life in Italy, has a chapter on the nobility and princes, the extreme bitterness of which is due to the social ferment then prevailing in the North.

passion for knighthood, which became a craze just when
it had lost every shadow of significance.

"A few years ago," writes Franco Sacchetti toward the
end of the fourteenth century, "everybody saw how all the
workmen down to the bakers, down to wool carders, usurers,
money-changers, and blackguards became knights. Why does
an official need knighthood when he goes to preside over
some provincial town? Certainly this title has nothing to do
with any ordinary breadwinning pursuit? How art thou
sunken, unhappy dignity! Of all the long list of knightly
duties, what single one do these knights of ours discharge? I
wished to speak of these things that the reader might see
that knighthood is dead. And as we have gone so far as to
confer knighthood upon dead men, why not upon figures of
wood and stone, and why not upon an ox?" – The stories
that Sacchetti tells by way of illustration speak plainly
enough. We read how Bernabò Visconti knighted the victor
of a drunken brawl, and then derisively did the same to the
vanquished; how German knights with their decorated hel-
mets and devices were ridiculed, etc. At a later period Poggio
mocks the many knights who have neither horse nor military
training. Whoever wished to assert the privilege of the order,
e.g., ride out with lance and colors, in Florence had to face
the government as well as the jokers.

On considering the matter more closely, we shall find that
this belated chivalry, independent of all nobility of birth
though partly the fruit of an insane passion for titles, had
another side. Tournaments still existed, and no one could
take part in them who was not a knight. But combat in the
lists, and especially the difficult and perilous tilting with the
lance, offered an opportunity for the display of strength,
skill, and courage, which no one, whatever his origin, would
willingly neglect in an age that laid such stress on personal
merit.

It was in vain that even Petrarch had already denounced
the tournament as a dangerous folly. No one was converted
by his pathetic appeal: "In what book do we read that Scipio
and Caesar were skilled at the joust?" The practice became
more and more popular, especially in Florence. Every citizen
came to consider his tournament—now, no doubt, less dangerous than formerly—as a fashionable sport, and Franco
Sacchetti has left us a very funny picture of one of these
Sunday cavaliers. He rides out on horseback to Peretola,
where the tournament was cheap, on a jade hired from a
dyer. A thistle is stuck by some wag under the tail of the
steed who takes fright, runs away, and carries the helmeted

rider, bruised and shaken, back into the city. The inevitable conclusion of the story is a severe lecture from the wife, who is enraged at these breakneck follies of her husband.[178]

Finally, the early Medici developed a passionate interest in this sport, as if they—private citizens without noble blood —wished to show that the society that surrounded them was equal to any court. Even under Cosimo (1459), and afterward under the elder Pietro, brilliant tournaments were held at Florence. The younger Pietro neglected the duties of government for these amusements and would only be painted clad in armor. Even at the court of Alexander VI tournaments took place, and when Cardinal Ascanio Sforza asked the Turkish Prince Djem how he liked the spectacle, the latter replied with much discretion that in his country such combats took place only among slaves, since then, if any were killed, no one was the worse for it. The Oriental was unconsciously in accord with the old Romans as against the manners of the Middle Ages.

Apart from this particular prop of knighthood, there were already, for example at Ferrara, orders of courtiers whose members had a right to the title of *cavaliere*.

But great as the individual ambitions and vanities of nobles and knights might be, the Italian noble took his place in the center of life and not at the periphery. He mixed with other classes on an equal footing, and culture and intelligence were members of his household. It is true that for the genuine courtier a certain rank of nobility was required,[179] but this is expressly declared to be caused by a prejudice rooted in the public mind *(per l'oppenion universale)* and was never held to imply the belief that the personal worth of one who was not of noble blood was in any degree lessened thereby. Nor did it follow that the prince was limited to the nobility for his society. It meant simply that the perfect man— the true courtier—should not be wanting in any conceivable advantage. If in all the relations of life he was specially bound to maintain a dignified and reserved demeanor, the reason was not found in the blood that flowed in his veins, but in the perfection of his manner. We have here a modern distinction, in which culture and wealth are the standard of measurement,

---

178. This is one of the oldest parodies of the tournament. Sixty years passed before Jacques Coeur, the burgher Minister of Finance under Charles VII, placed a relief of a tournament of donkeys in the courtyard of his palace at Bourges (about 1450). The most brilliant of all these parodies, the second canto of the *Orlandino*, was not published till 1526.
179. Castiglione, *The Courtier*, Book I.

and the latter only because it enables men to devote their lives to the former, and effectually to promote its interests and advancement.

The less distinctions of birth conferred any special privilege, the more the individual as such was compelled to make the most of his personal qualities, and society to find its worth and charm in itself. The demeanor of individuals and the higher forms of social intercourse became a free, conscious work of art.

Even the outward appearance of men and women and the habits of daily life were more accomplished, more beautiful, and more refined than among the other people of Europe. The dwellings of the upper classes fall within the province of the history of art; here we only note how far these surpassed in comfort, order, and harmony the castles and city mansions or city palaces of the Northern nobles. The style of dress varied so continually that it is impossible to make any thorough comparison with the fashions of other countries, especially because from the end of the fifteenth century imitations of the latter were frequent. The costumes that the Italian painters render are the most beautiful and most becoming that were to be found in Europe at that time; but we cannot be sure whether they represented the prevalent fashion, or if they reproduced it faithfully. But we can be certain that nowhere was so much importance attached to dress as in Italy. The nation was, and is, vain; and even serious men looked on a handsome and becoming costume as an element in the perfection of the individual. At Florence, indeed, there was a brief period when dress was a purely personal matter, and every man set the fashion for himself, and far into the sixteenth century there were exceptional people who still had the courage to do so; and the rest at least knew how to set an individual mark on the prevailing fashion. It is a symptom of decline when Giovanni della Casa warns his readers not to be singular or to depart from prevailing fashion. Our own age, which, in men's dress at any rate, treats uniformity as the supreme law, gives up by this far more than it is aware of. But it saves itself much time, and this (according to our notions of business) outweighs all other disadvantages.

In Venice [180] and Florence at the time of the Renaissance

---

180. See, on this point, the Venetian books of fashion. The fashion prescribed for the betrothal—a white dress, hair falling freely over the shoulders—can be seen in Titian's *Flora* [Uffizi Gallery, Florence].

there were rules and regulations that prescribed the dress of the men and restrained the luxury of the women. Where the fashions were free, as in Naples, the moralists confess with regret that no difference can be observed between noble and burgher. They further deplore the rapid changes of fashion and (if we interpret the words correctly) the senseless idolatry of whatever comes from France, though often the fashions that were received back from the French had originally been Italian. It is not necessary to examine how far these frequent changes and the adoption of French and Spanish ways contributed to the national passion for display; but they are additional evidence of the rapid movement of life in Italy in the decades around 1500.

We should note in particular the efforts of the women to alter their appearance by every means the toilette could provide. In no country of Europe since the fall of the Roman Empire had so much trouble been taken to modify the face, the color of the skin, the growth of the hair as was the case in Italy at this time. All was directed toward the formation of a conventional type, at the cost of the most striking and transparent deceptions. Leaving out of account costume in general, which in the fourteenth century,[181] was extremely colorful and loaded with ornament, and at a later period assumed a more harmonious richness, we limit ourselves here to the toilette in the narrower sense.

Most prevalent was the use of false hair, often made of white or yellow silk. The law denounced and forbade it in vain, till some preacher of repentance touched the worldly minds of the wearers; then, in the middle of the public square, a lofty pyre (*talamo*) would arise, on which, beside lutes, dice boxes, masks, magical charms, song books, and other vanities, lay masses of false hair, which the purging fires soon turned into nothing. The ideal color, desired for both natural and artificial hair, was blonde. And since the sun was supposed to be able to make hair blonde, many ladies would not go out of the sun on good days. Dyes and other mixtures were also used freely. Besides all these, there was a whole arsenal of beautifying waters, plasters, and paints for every single part of the face—even for the teeth and eyelids—of which our time has no conception. The ridicule of the poets, the invectives of the preachers, and the warning

181. In the celebrated edict on fashion of 1330, embroidered figures only were allowed on the dresses of women, to the exclusion of those that were painted (*dipinto*). The nature of these decorations is uncertain.

of the baneful effects of these cosmetics on the skin were powerless to hinder women from giving their faces new forms and colors. It is possible that the frequent and splendid representations of Mysteries, at which hundreds of people appeared painted and masked,[182] helped to further this practice in daily life. In any case, it was widespread, and the countrywomen held their own with their sisters in the towns. It was vain to preach that such decorations were the mark of the courtesan; the most respectable matrons, who all the year round never touched paint, used it on holidays, just when they appeared in public. – But whether we look on this bad habit as a remnant of barbarism, to which the painting of savages is a parallel, or as a consequence of the desire for perfect youthful beauty in feature and in color, as the art and complexity of the toilette would lead us to think—in either case there was no lack of good advice on the part of the men.

The use of perfumes, too, went beyond all reasonable limits. They were applied to everything with which human beings came into contact. At festivals even the mules were treated with scents and ointments, and Pietro Aretino thanks Cosimo I for a perfumed roll of money.[183]

The Italians of that day were convinced that they lived more cleanly than the Northerners. There are in fact general historical reasons that make us grant rather than reject this conviction. Cleanliness is indispensable to our modern notion of social perfection, and this was developed in Italy earlier than elsewhere. That the Italians were one of the richest nations of that time is another point in their favor. Proof, either for or against, can never, of course, be established, and if it is a question of priority in establishing rules of cleanliness, the chivalrous poetry of the Middle Ages may be able to produce earlier evidence. So much, however, is certain: the singular neatness and cleanliness of some distinguished representatives of the Renaissance, especially their table manners, was noticed expressly, and "German" was the synonym in Italy for all that was filthy. The dirty habits that Massimiliano Sforza picked up in the course of his German education, and the notice they attracted on his

182. Cennino Cennini, *Trattato della pittura* [*The Craftsman's Handbook*], gives, in ch. 161, a recipe for painting the face, evidently only for the purpose of Mysteries or masquerades, since, in ch. 162, he solemnly warns his readers against the general use of cosmetics and the like.

183. Some objects which date from that period have not yet lost their scent.

return to Italy, are mentioned by Giovio. It is at the same time very curious that, at least in the fifteenth century, the inns and hotels were left chiefly in the hands of Germans, who probably, however, made their profit mostly out of the pilgrims journeying to Rome. Yet the statements on this point may refer primarily to the country districts, since it is well-known that in the larger cities Italian hotels held first place. The lack of decent inns in the country may also be explained by the general insecurity of life and property.

From the first half of the sixteenth century we have the manual of polite conduct which Giovanni della Casa, a Florentine by birth, published under the title *Il Galateo*. Not only cleanliness in the strict sense of the word, but the correction of all the habits that we consider "improper," is prescribed with the same unfailing tact with which the moralist discerns the highest ethical truths. In the literature of other countries the same lessons are taught, though less systematically, by the indirect influence of repulsive descriptions.

In other respects also, the *Galateo* is a graceful and intelligent guide to good manners—a school of tact and delicacy. Even now it may be read with much profit by people of all classes, and the politeness of European nations is not likely to outgrow its precepts. So far as tact is an affair of the heart, it has been inborn in some men from the dawn of civilization, and acquired through force of will by others; but the Italians were the first to recognize it was a universal social duty and a mark of culture and education. And Italy itself had changed very much in the course of two centuries. We feel distinctly that the time of practical jokes between friends and acquaintances, of *burle* and *beffe,* was over in good society, that the people had emerged from behind the walls of their cities and had learned a cosmopolitan politeness and consideration. We shall speak later on of the intercourse of society in the narrower sense.

In the fifteenth and the early part of the sixteenth centuries outward life was polished and ennobled as among no other people in the world. We know that a countless number of those little things and big things which combine to make up what we mean by comfort appeared first in Italy. In the well-paved streets of the Italian cities, driving became common, whereas elsewhere in Europe walking or riding was the custom, and at all events no one drove for amusement. The novelists tell of soft, springy beds, of costly carpets and bedroom furniture, of which we hear nothing in other countries. The abundance and beauty of the linen is often given

special mention. Many of these things belong equally to the
realm of art. We note with admiration the thousand ways
in which art ennobled luxury, adorning the massive sideboard or the delicate whatnot with magnificent vases, cover-
ing the walls with splendid tapestries, decorating the bedside
table with numberless graceful trifles, and, above all, making
woodcarving a full-fledged art. All Western Europe, as soon
as its wealth enabled it to do so, behaved this way at the
close of the Middle Ages. But it produced either picturesque
trifles or works that were confined within the narrow bounds
of a Gothic decorative style, whereas the Renaissance moved
freely, guided by the meaning of the given task and working
for a broader range of patrons and admirers. The rapid
victory of Italian decorative art over Northern in the course
of the sixteenth century is due partly to this, although there
are greater and more general reasons.

The higher forms of social intercourse, which emerged
here as a work of art, as a conscious product and one of
the highest products of national life, have their most important preliminary conditions and basis in language.

At the height of the Middle Ages, the nobility of Western
Europe had tried to establish a "courtly" speech for social
intercourse as well as for poetry. In Italy, too, where the
dialects differed so greatly, we find in the thirteenth century
a so-called *curiale*, which was common to the courts and to
the poets. It is of decisive importance that a serious and
deliberate attempt was made to turn this into the language
of literature and society. The introduction to the *Hundred
Old Tales*, which were put into their present shape before
1300, avows this object openly. Language is considered apart
from its uses in poetry; its highest function is clear, simple
intelligent utterance in short speeches, epigrams, and answers.
This faculty was admired as it had been admired only among
the Greeks and Arabs: "How many in the course of a long
life have produced even one *bel parlare* [beautiful dis-
course]."

But the matter was rendered more difficult by the diversity
of aspects under which it was considered. Dante's writings
take us into the center of the struggle. His work *On the
Vernacular* is not only of the utmost importance for the
subject itself, but is also the first complete treatise on any
modern language.[184] His method and results belong to the

---

184. *De vulgari eloquentia.* According to Boccaccio, *Life of
Dante*, it was written shorly before Dante's death. In the begin-

history of linguistic science, in which they will always hold a high place. We must content ourselves here with the remark that long before the appearance of this book the subject must have been of daily and pressing importance, that the various dialects of Italy had long been the objects of eager study and dispute, and that the birth of the one national language was not accomplished without the greatest pain.

Dante himself contributed most by his great poem. The Tuscan dialect became the basis of the new national speech.[185] If this assertion seems to go too far, may a foreigner be excused, in a matter on which much difference of opinion prevails, for following the general belief.

Literature and poetry probably lost more than they gained by the dispute over the purism of this language, which probably marred the freshness and vigor of many an able writer. And others, who were masters of this language, relied on its harmony and flow, as on an excellence that was independent of content. A very insignificant melody played upon such an instrument can produce a very great effect. But however this may be, this language had great social value. It was the crown of a noble and dignified appearance, and compelled the gentleman, both in his daily behavior and in exceptional moments, to observe external propriety. This classical garment undoubtedly covered much that was foul and malicious, as had been the case with the purest Atticism; but it was also the valid expression of all that was noblest and most refined. It was from a national point of view, however, that it was of supreme importance, serving as an ideal home for the educated classes in all the States of the peninsula that had so early been divided. Nor was it the special property of the nobles or of any one class; the poorest and humblest had time and means enough to learn it if he wished. Even now (and perhaps more than ever)

---

ning of the *Convivio* Dante mentions the rapid and striking changes that took place in the Italian language during his lifetime.

185. The gradual progress that this dialect made in literature and social intercourse could be tabulated without difficulty by a native scholar. It could be shown to what extent in the fourteenth and fifteenth centuries the various dialects retained their hold, wholly or in part, in correspondence, in official documents, in historical works, and in literature generally. The continued use of the Italian dialects along with a more or less impure Latin which at that time served as the official language, would also be discussed.

in those parts of Italy where, as a rule, the most unintelligible dialect prevails, the stranger is often astonished at hearing pure and well-spoken Italian from the mouths of peasants or artisans, and he looks in vain for anything analogous in France or in Germany where even the educated classes retain traces of a provincial speech. There is certainly a larger number of people able to read in Italy than we should be led to expect from the condition of many parts of the country, e.g., the States of the Church, in other respects; but it would have been of little value without the general and undisputed respect for pure language and pronunciation as something precious and sacred. One part of the country after another officially adopted this purity; Venice, Milan, and Naples did so at the noontime of Italian literature, and partly through its influences. It was not till the present century that Piedmont, of its own free will, became a genuine Italian province by sharing in this chief treasure of the people—pure speech.[186] From the beginning of the sixteenth century dialect was intentionally reserved for a certain class of subjects, serious as well as comic,[187] and the style that was thus developed proved equal to all its tasks. A conscious separation of this kind did not occur among other nations till much later.

The opinion of educated people on the social value of language is set forth fully in the *Courtier*.[188] Already then, at the beginning of the sixteenth century, there were people who purposely kept to the antiquated expressions of Dante and the other Tuscan writers of his time simply because they were old. Our author flatly forbids their use in speech, and is unwilling to permit them even in writing, which he considers merely a form of speech. Upon which follows the admission: the best style of speech is that which most resembles good writing. We can clearly recognize the author's feeling that people who have anything of importance to say must shape their own speech, and that language is flexible and changing because it is a living thing. Any expression may be used, however ornate, as long as it is used by the

186. Tuscan, it is true, was read and written in Piedmont long before this—but very little reading and writing was done at all.
187. When and when not to use dialect in daily life was also clearly understood. Gioviano Pontano expressly warned the Prince of Naples against the use of it. The last Bourbons, as is well known, were less scrupulous in this respect.
188. Baldassare Castiglione, *The Courtier,* Book I. Although the book is written in the form of a dialogue, the personal opinion of the writer comes through constantly.

people; nor are non-Tuscan words, or even French and Spanish words forbidden, if custom has accepted them for definite purposes.[189] Thus care and intelligence will produce a language, which, if not the pure old Tuscan, is still Italian, rich as a well-kept garden, full of fruit and flowers. It is part of the completeness of the courtier that his wit, his polished manners, and his poetry, must be clothed only in this perfect dress.

When style and language had once become the property of a living society, all the efforts of purists and archaists failed to attain their goal. Tuscany itself was too rich in excellent writers and talkers who ignored and ridiculed these endeavors, and ridiculed especially the foreigner who came and explained to them, the Tuscans, how little they understood their own language. The life and influence of a writer such as Machiavelli was enough to sweep away all these cobwebs in so far as his vigorous thoughts, his clear and simple mode of expression appeared in a language that had any merit but that of a pure *trecentismo*. On the other hand there were too many North Italians, Romans, and Neapolitans who must have been thankful if the demand for purity of style in literature and conversation was not pressed too far. Indeed, they repudiated the forms and idioms of their dialect; and a foreigner might suspect false modesty, when Bandello, for example, solemnly protests: "I have no style; I do not write like a Florentine, but like a barbarian; I do not yearn to give new graces to my language; I am a Lombard, and from the Ligurian border to the bargain." But the rigorous purists were most easily defeated in fact by the express renunciation of the higher claims and the adoption instead of the vigorous, popular language. Few could hope to equal Pietro Bembo who, though born in Venice, wrote the purest Tuscan all his life although it was almost a foreign language, or the Neapolitan Sannazaro, who did the same. But the essential point was that language, whether spoken or written,

---

189. There was, however, a limit to this. The satirists drop in bits of Spanish, and Folengo (under the pseudonym Limerno Pitocco, in his *Orlandino*) inserts fragments of French, but only for the purpose of ridicule. It is an exceptional fact that a street in Milan, which at the time of the French (1500–12, 1515–22) was called Rue Belle, now bears the name Rugabella. Almost no trace of the long Spanish rule is left in the language—at most, the name of some governor in streets and public buildings. It was not until the eighteenth century that, together with French modes of thought, many French words and phrases found their way into Italian. The purism of our century is still busy removing them.

was held to be an object of respect. As long as this feeling
prevailed, the fanaticism of the purists—their linguistic con-
gresses and the rest of it[190]—did little harm. They became
harmful only later, when the original power of Italian
literature relaxed and yielded to other and far worse influences. At last it became possible for the Accademia della
Crusca to treat Italian like a dead language. But this association was so powerless, that it could not even hinder the
invasion of Gallicism in the eighteenth century.

This language—loved, tended, and trained to every use—
now served as the basis of social intercourse. In the North,
the nobles and princes passed their leisure either in solitude,
or in hunting, fighting, drinking, and the like, the burghers
in their games and exercises, with a mixture of literary or
festive amusements. But in Italy there existed in addition a
neutral ground, where people of every origin, provided they
had the necessary talent and culture, spent their time in
conversation and the polished interchange of jest and earnest.
As eating and drinking were only a secondary part of such
entertainments, it was not difficult to keep at a distance the
obtuse and the greedy. If we take the writers of dialogues
literally, the loftiest problems of human existence were not
excluded from the conversation of thinking men, and the
production of noble thoughts was not, as was commonly
the case in the North, the work of solitude, but of society.
But we prefer to limit ourselves here to the less serious side
of social intercourse—to the side that existed only for the
sake of amusement.

This society, at least at the beginning of the sixteenth
century, had an ordered beauty, and rested on tacit, and
often avowed, rules of good sense and propriety, which are
the exact opposite of all mere etiquette. In less polished
circles, where society took the form of a permanent corporation, there were statutes and a prescribed mode of entrance,
as for example, those wild sets of Florentine artists of whom
Vasari tells, who were capable of giving representations of
the best comedies of the day.[191] In the easier intercourse of
society it was not unusual to select some distinguished lady

190. Such a congress appears to have been held at Bologna at
the end of 1531 under the presidency of Bembo.
191. Vasari, *Lifa of Giovan Francesco Rustici*. – For the School
for Scandal of needy artists, see the Life of Bastiano da Sangallo,
called Aristotile. – Machiavelli's *capitoli* for a circle of pleasure
seekers are a ludicrous caricature of these social statutes. – The
well-known description of the evening meetings of artists in Rome
in Benvenuto Cellini, Book I, ch. 30, is incomparable.

as president, whose word was law for the evening. Everyone knows the introduction to Boccaccio's *Decameron*, and looks on the presidency of Pampinea as a graceful fiction. That it was so in this particular case is a matter of course, but the fiction was based on a practice that often occurred in reality. Firenzuola, who nearly two centuries later prefaces his collection of tales in a similar manner, certainly comes nearer to the truth when he puts into the mouth of the queen of the society a formal speech on the mode of spending the hours during the stay in the country which the company proposed to make: first, a philosophical morning hour during a stroll among the hills; then, breakfast,[192] with music and singing; next, in some cool spot, the recitation of a new poem, the subject of which had been given the night before; in the evening, a walk to a spring where all sit down and each one tells a tale; finally, supper and lively conversation "of such a kind that we women may listen to it without shame and you men may not seem to be speaking under the influence of wine." Bandello, in the introductions and dedications to single novels, does not, it is true, give us such inaugural discourses, since the groups before which the stories are told are represented as already formed; but he gives us to understand in other ways how rich, how manifold, and how charming the conditions of society were. Some readers may hold that no good was to be got from a world that was willing to be amused by such immoral literature. It would be juster to wonder at the secure foundations of a society that notwithstanding these tales, still observed the rules of order and decency, and knew how to vary such pastimes with serious and solid discussion. The need of noble forms of social intercourse was felt to be stronger than all others. To convince ourselves, we are not obliged to take as our standard the idealized society that Castiglione depicts at the court of Guidobaldo of Urbino, and Pietro Bembo at the castle of Asolo, as discussing the loftiest sentiments and aims of human life. It is the society of a Bandello, with all its frivolities, that gives us the best notion of the easy and polished dignity, of the urbane kindliness, of the intellectual freedom, of the wit and graceful dilettantism that distinguished these circles. A significant proof of the value of such society lies in the fact that the leading women could become famous and illustrious without in any way compromising their reputation. Among the patronesses of Bandello, for example, Isabella Gonzaga (born an Este) was talked

192. Which must have been taken about ten or eleven o'clock.

of unfavorably not through any fault of her own, but because of the dissolute young ladies who filled her court. Giulia Gonzaga Collona, Ippolita Sforza married to a Bentivoglio, Bianca Rangona, Cecilia Gallerana, Camilla Scarampa, and others were either completely irreproachable, or their social fame threw into the shade whatever they may have done amiss. The most famous woman of Italy, Vittoria Colonna, enjoyed the reputation of a saint. It is difficult to describe the unconstrained intercourse of these circles in the city, in the country, at the spas in a way that would furnish literal proof of the superiority over the rest of Europe. But let us read Bandello, and then ask ourselves if anything of the same kind would have been possible, say, in France, before this kind of society was introduced there by people like himself. – Certainly the supreme achievements of the human mind were produced without the help of such salons; but it would be unjust to rate their influence on art and poetry too low, if only because that society helped shape that which existed in no other country—a widespread interest in artistic production and an intelligent and critical public opinion. And apart from this, this kind of society was in itself a natural flower of that life and culture which was then purely Italian, and which since then has extended to the rest of Europe.

In Florence, society was strongly affected by literature and politics. Lorenzo the Magnificent was master of his circle, not, as we might believe, because of his princely position but because of the wonderful tact with which he gave perfect freedom of action to the many and varied natures that surrounded him. We see, for example, how gently he dealt with his great tutor Politian, and how the sovereignty of the poet and scholar was reconciled with the inevitable reserve prescribed by the approaching change in the position of the House of Medici and by consideration for the sensitiveness of the wife. And in return Politian became the herald and the living symbol of Medicean glory. Lorenzo, after the fashion of a true Medici, delighted in giving outward and artistic expression to his social amusements. In his brilliant improvisation, the Hawking Party, he gives us a humorous description of his comrades, and in the *Simposio* a burlesque of them, but in both cases in a way that lets us see clearly his capacity for more serious intercourse.[193] His correspond-

193. The title *Simposio* is inaccurate; it should be called "The Return from the Vintage." Lorenzo, in a parody of Dante's *Inferno,* gives an amusing account of meeting in the Via Faenza

ence and the reports of his literary and ph…
versation give ample proof of this intercourse. So…
social unions that were formed in Florence later we…
part political clubs, though not without a certain poetical
and philosophical character, as, for example, the so-called
Platonic Academy which met after Lorenzo's death in the
Rucellai gardens.

At the courts of the princes, society naturally depended
on the character of the ruler. After the beginning of the
sixteenth century, it is true, there were less and less of these
courts, and these few soon lost their importance. In the
unique court of Leo X, Rome had a society to which the
history of the world offers no parallel.

It was for these courts, but even more for his own sake,
that the courtier described by Castiglione educated himself.
He was the ideal man of society, and was regarded by the
civilization of that age as its choicest flower; and the court
existed for him rather than he for the court. Indeed, such
a man would have been unnecessary at a court, since he
himself possessed the gifts and the bearing of an accomplished
ruler, and his calm supremacy in all things, both outward
and spiritual, implied too independent a nature. The impulse
that inspired him was directed, though our author does not
acknowledge the fact, not to the service of the prince, but to
his own perfection. One example will make this clear. In
time of war the courtier refuses [194] even useful and perilous
tasks if they are not beautiful and dignified in themselves,
such as, for instance, the capture of a herd of cattle; what
urges him to take part in war is not duty but *l'onore*
[honor]. The moral relation to the prince, as prescribed in
the fourth book, is singularly free and independent. The
theory of well-bred love-making (set forth in the third book)
is full of delicate psychological observation, which perhaps
would be more in place in a treatise on human nature
generally; and the magnificent lyrical praise of ideal love
(at the end of the fourth book) has no connection whatever with the special object of the work. Yet here, as in the

---

all his good friends coming back from the country more or less
tipsy. In the eighth chapter there is a very funny picture of
Piovano Arlotto who sets out in search of his lost thirst armed
with dry meat, a herring, a piece of cheese, a sausage, and four
sardines, *e tutte si cocevan nel sudore* [and all of them cooking
in his perspiration].
194. *The Courtier*, Book II.

...re of the time reveals itself in
.... this sentiment is represented and
........uld not take these writers literally;
.....ses they give us were actually frequent
.... cannot be doubted, and that it was no
.... genuine passion that appeared in this guise,
.... further on.

.....ion, especially in the so-called knightly arts, was
exp....d from the courtier in all outward accomplishments,
and besides these much that could exist only at cultured,
highly organized courts based on personal emulation, such
as were not to be found outside Italy. Obviously, there was
much that rested on an abstract notion of individual perfection. The courtier must be at home in all noble sports,
among them running, leaping, swimming, and wrestling; above
all, he must be a good dancer and (as a matter of course) an
accomplished rider. In addition, however, he must be master
of several languages, at least of Latin and Italian; he must
be familiar with literature and have some knowledge of the
fine arts. In music he should have a certain practical skill,
which he must, nevertheless, keep as secret as possible. All
this is not to be taken too seriously, except what relates to
the use of weapons; the mutual interaction of these gifts and
accomplishments results in the perfect man, in whom no one
quality usurps the place of the rest.

So much is certain, that in the sixteenth century the
Italians had all Europe for their pupils both theoretically
and practically in every noble physical exercise and in the
habits and manners of good society. Their instructions and
their illustrated books on riding, fencing, and dancing set
the fashion; gymnastics as an art, apart from both military
training and mere amusement, was probably taught first by
Vittorino da Feltre and after his time became essential to a
complete education. The important fact is that they were
taught systematically, though what the exercises were, and
whether they resembled those now in use, we are unable to
say. But we can be sure, not only from the general character
of the people, but from positive evidence that has been left
us, that grace of movement, as well as strength and skill, was
one of the main objects of physical training. It is enough to
recall the great Federigo of Urbino directing the evening
games of the young peoples committed to his care.

The games and contests of the popular classes did not
differ essentially from those which prevailed elsewhere in
Europe. In the maritime cities there was also boat racing,

and the Venetian regattas were famous at an early period.[195]
The classical game of Italy was and is ball; and even at the
time of the Renaissance this game was probably played with
more zeal and brilliancy than anywhere else in Europe. But
it is not at all easy to present positive evidence in support of
this view.

A few words on music are in order at this point.[196] Even
around 1500, musical composition was chiefly in the hands
of the Flemish school, whose originality and artistic dexterity
were greatly admired. But there was also an Italian school,
which was probably closer to our present taste. Half a century later came Palestrina, whose genius still affects us
powerfully. We discover that he was a great innovator; but
whether he or others took the decisive part in shaping the
musical language of the modern world lies beyond the judgment of the layman. Since we are ignoring completely the
history of musical composition, we shall try to undertand
the position music held in the social life of the day.

A fact most significant for the Renaissance and for Italy
is the specialization of the orchestra, the search for new instruments and modes of sound, and—closely connected with
this—the formation of a class of virtuosos who devoted their
whole attention to particular instruments or particular branches
of music.

195. They are said to have arisen through the rowing out to
the Lido, where the practice with the crossbow took place. The
great regatta on the Feast of St. Paul was prescribed by law from
1315. – In early times there was much riding in Venice, before
the streets were paved and the level wooden bridges were turned
into arched stone ones. Petrarch describes a brilliant tournament
held in 1364 on the Piazza di San Marco, and Doge Steno, about
the year 1400, had as fine a stable as any prince in Italy. But
riding in the neighborhood of the Piazza was prohibited as a rule
after the year 1291. – At a later time the Venetians were,
naturally, considered bad riders.

196. Outside Italy it was still hardly permissible for persons
of consequence to be musicians; at the Flemish court of the young
Charles V a serious dispute took place on the subject.

There is a remarkable and comprehensive passage on music
where we would not expect it, in the *Macaroneide, Phant.* xx. It
is a comic description of a quartette, from which we see that
Spanish and French songs were often sung, that music already
had its enemies (1520), and that the orchestra of Leo X and
the still earlier composer, Josquin des Prés, whose principal works
are mentioned, were the chief subjects of enthusiasm in the
musical world of that time. The same author (Folengo), writing
under the name Limerno Pitocco, displays in his *Orlandino* a
musical fanaticism of a thoroughly modern sort.

Of the more complex instruments, which were perfected and widely diffused at a very early period, we find not only the organ, but a corresponding string instrument, the gravicembalo or clavicembalo. Fragments of these, dating from the beginning of the fourteenth century, have come down to us because they were decorated by the greatest painters. Among other instruments, first place was held by the violin, which even then conferred great celebrity on the successful player. At the court of Leo X, who already as a cardinal had filled his house with singers and musicians and who enjoyed the reputation of a critic and performer, the Jew Giovanni Maria and Jacopo Sansecondo were among the most famous. The former received from Leo the title of count and a small town; the latter has been taken to be the Apollo in Raphael's *Parnassus*. [197] In the course of the sixteenth century, celebrities in every branch of music appeared, and Lomazzo (about 1584) names the three most distinguished masters of the art of singing, of the organ, the lute, the lyre, the viola da gamba, the harp, the cittern, the horn, and the trumpet, and wishes that their portraits might be painted on the instruments themselves.[198] Such comprehensive criticism would have been impossible at that time anywhere but in Italy, even though almost the same instruments may have been in use.

The variety of these instruments is betrayed by the fact that it was worth forming collections of them for the sake of curiosity. In Venice, which was one of the most musical cities of Italy, there were several such collections, and when a sufficient number of virtuosos happened to be on the spot, a concert was immediately improvised. (In one of these collections there were many instruments made after ancient pictures and descriptions, but we are not told if anybody could play them or what they sounded like. It must not be forgotten that such instruments were ofen magnificently decorated, and could be arranged beautifully. Thus they were frequent in collections of other rarities and works of art.

Apart from the genuine virtuosos, the players were either

---

197. [In the Stanza della Segnatura, The Vatican.]
198. Lomazzo, *Treatise on the Art of Painting*. – When he discusses the lyre, he mentions Leonardo da Vinci and Alfonso (Duke?) of Ferrara. The author includes in his work all the celebrities of his age, among them several Jews. – The most complete list of the famous musicians of the sixteenth century, divided into an earlier and a later generation, is to be found in Rabelais, Book IV, The Author's Prologue. – A virtuoso, the blind Francesco of Florence (d. 1390), was crowned at Venice with a wreath of laurel by the King of Cyprus.

individual amateurs, or whole orchestras of them, organized into a corporate "Academy."[199] Many artists were skilled in music, too, and were often masters. – People of position were averse to wind instruments, for the same reason that made them distasteful to Alcibiades and Pallas Athene. In good society singing, either alone or accompanied with the violin, was usual, also string quartettes and, because of its versatility, the piano. In singing, only the solo was permitted, "for a single voice is heard, enjoyed, and judged far better." In other words, since singing, notwithstanding all conventional modesty, is an exhibition of the individual man of society, it is better that each be heard (and seen) separately. Since it is taken for granted that tender feelings are produced in the fair listeners, elderly people are therefore recommended to abstain from such forms of art, even though they still sing and play beautifully. It was considered important that the effect should be a harmonious mixture of sound and sight. We hear nothing, however, of the recognition in these circles of musical composition as an independent branch of art. On the other hand, sometimes the subject of the song was some terrible event that had befallen the singer himself.

This dilettantism, which pervaded the middle as well as the upper classes, was more widespread and at the same time more genuinely artistic in Italy than in any other country. Wherever social intercourse is described, music and singing are always and expressly mentioned. Hundreds of portraits portray people, often in groups, playing or holding the lute, etc., and even the angel concerts in ecclesiastical pictures prove how familiar the painters were with the living effects of music. And we learn of the lute player Antonio Rota at Padua (d. 1549), who became rich by his lessons, and even published a handbook on the lute.

At a time when opera had not yet begun to concentrate and monopolize musical talent, this impulse must have been wonderfully varied, intelligent, and original. It is something else if we ask how much we should find to satisfy us in these forms of music, could they be reproduced for us now.

To understand the higher forms of social intercourse

199. The Accademia de' Filarmonici at Verona is mentioned by Vasari, Life of Sanmicheli. – In 1480, Lorenzo the Magnificent was already the center of a "school of harmony," which consisted of 15 members, among them the famous organist Squarcialupi. Lorenzo's son, Leo X, seems to have inherited his love of music from his father. Lorenzo's eldest son, Pietro, was also very musical.

during the Renaissance, it is, finally, essential to know that women were regarded as equal to men. We must not allow ourselves to be misled by the sophistical and often malicious talk about the supposed inferiority of the female sex, which occurs now and then in the dialogues, nor by such satires as the third of Ariosto,[200] where woman is considered a dangerous grown-up child whom a man must learn how to manage, in spite of the great gulf between them. There is, indeed, a certain amount of truth in what he says. Precisely *because* the educated woman was equal to man, that form of marriage in which man and wife form a deep spiritual union, or in which man and wife complement each other in a higher sense could not develop as it did later in the moral world of the North.

The education of the women in the upper classes was essentially the same as that of the men. The Italian of the Renaissance did not have the slightest misgiving about putting sons and daughters alike under the same course of literary and even philological instruction. Indeed, since he viewed this ancient culture as the chief treasure of life, he was glad that his girls should have a share in it. We have seen what perfection was attained by the daughters of princely houses in writing and speaking Latin. Many others must have been able at least to read it, in order to follow the conversation of the day, which turned largely on classical subjects. Many actively engaged in Italian poetry through *canzoni,* sonnets, and improvisations, whereby a large number of Italian women, from the time of the Venetian Cassandra Fedele (about the close of the fifteenth century), made themselves famous;[201] in fact, Vittoria Colonna can even be called immortal. If any proof were needed of the assertion made above, it would be found in the manly tone of this female poetry. The love sonnets like the religious poems are so precise and definite, and so far removed from the tender twilight of sentiment and all the dilettantism we commonly find in the poetry of women, that we should not hesitate to attribute them to male authors, if names, reports, and definite external evidence did not prove the contrary.

For with education, the individuality of women in the upper classes was developed in the same way as that of men, whereas outside Italy, till the time of the Reformation, the

200. To Annibale Maleguccio, sometimes also called the fifth or sixth.
201. Whereas the part played by women in the visual arts is absolutely insignificant.

personality of women, even of royal rank, does not stand out very much. Exceptions such as Isabella of Bavaria, Margaret of Anjou, and Isabella of Castille, are the result of very unusual, actually forced, circumstances. In Italy, throughout the entire fifteenth century, almost all the wives of the rulers, and still more those of the *condottieri*, have a distinct, recognizable personality, and take their share of notoriety and glory. Gradually there was a crowd of famous women of the most varied kind, even if their sole distinction lay in the fact that their beauty, disposition, education, virtue, and piety combined to render them harmonious human beings. There was no question of "woman's rights" or "emancipation," simply because the thing itself was a matter of course. The educated woman of that time strove, exactly like the man, after a characteristic and complete individuality. The same intellectual and emotional development that perfected the man was demanded for the perfection of the woman. Active literary work was not demanded of her, and if she were a poet, some powerful utterance of feeling, rather than the confidences of the novel or the diary, was expected. These women had no thought of the public; their function was to influence distinguished men, and to moderate male impulse and caprice.

The highest praise that could be given at that time to the great Italian women was that they had the mind and courage of men. We have only to observe the thoroughly manly bearing of most of the women in the heroic poems, especially those of Boiardo and Ariosto, to realize that we are looking at a definite ideal. The title *virago*, which is an equivocal compliment in the present day, at that time implied nothing but praise. It was borne in all its glory by Caterina Sforza, wife and later widow of Girolamo Riario, whose hereditary possession, Forlì, she gallantly defended first against his murderers and then against Cesare Borgia. Though finally vanquished, she retained the admiration of her countrymen and the title *prima donna d'Italia*. This heroic vein can be detected in many of the women of the Renaissance, though none found the same opportunity of showing their heroism to the world. In Isabella Gonzaga this type is clearly recognizable.

Women of this stamp could listen to novels like those of Bandello without social intercourse suffering by it. The ruling genius of society was not, as now, womanhood, that is, the respect for certain presuppositions, mysteries, and susceptibilities, but the consciousness of energy, of beauty, and of a social state full of danger and opportunity. And for this reason we find, side by side with the most measured and polished social forms, something our age would call immodesty because we can no longer imagine the counterbalance—the powerful characters of the women who were exposed to it.

That in all the dialogues and treatises put together we can find no absolute evidence on these points is only natural, however freely the nature of love and the position and capacities of women were discussed.

What seems to have been lacking in this society were the young girls who, even when not brought up in the convents, were still carefully kept away from it. It is difficult to know whether their absence was the cause of the greater freedom of conversation, or whether they were removed because of it.

Even the intercourse with courtesans seems to have assumed a more elevated character, as if the relation of the ancient Athenians to their hetaerae were being revived. The famous Roman courtesan Imperia was a woman of intelligence and culture, had learned from a certain Domenico Campana the art of composing sonnets, and was not without musical accomplishments.[202] The beautiful Isabella de Luna, of Spanish extraction, who was reckoned amusing company, seems to have been an odd compound of a kind heart and a shockingly foul tongue. At Milan, Bandello knew the majestic Caterina di San Celso, who played and sang and recited superbly. And so on. All this makes it clear that the distinguished people who visited these women, and occasionally lived with them, demanded from them a considerable degree of intelligence, and that the more famous courtesans were treated with the greatest respect. Even when relations were broken off, their good opinion was still desired, because departed passion had left behind a permanent significant impression. But on the whole this intellectual intercourse is not worth mentioning alongside that sanctioned by the recognized forms of social life, and the traces it has left in poetry and literature are for the most part of a scandalous nature. We may well be astonished that among the 6,800 persons of this class, who were to be found in Rome in 1490[203]—that is, before the appearance of syphilis—scarcely

202. Ariosto says of a courtesan: she knows by heart all Petrarch and Boccaccio, and many beautiful verses of Vergil, Horace, Ovid, and a thousand other authors.
203. The public women only—not the kept women—are meant. The number, compared with the population of Rome, is certainly enormous, perhaps because of a clerical error.

a single woman seems to have been remarkable for any higher gifts. Those whom we have mentioned all belong to the subsequent period. The mode of life, the morals and philosophy of the public women who, with all their sensuality and greed, were not always incapable of deeper passions, as well as the hypocrisy and devilish malice shown by some in their later years, are best set forth by Giraldi, in the novels that form the introduction to the *Hecatommithi.* Pietro Aretino, on the other hand, gives us, in his *Ragionamenti,* a picture of his own depraved character rather than of this unhappy class of women as they really were.

The mistresses of the princes, as has already been pointed out, formed the subject matter of poets and artists, and have thus become personally familiar to their contemporaries and to posterity. But we hardly know more than the names of an Alice Perries, a Clara Dettin (mistress of Frederick the Victorious), and of Agnes Sorel we have only a half-legendary story. The situation is different later with the concubines of the Renaissance monarchs Francis I and Henry II.

After the intercourse of society, the domestic life of the Renaissance deserves our notice. We are commonly disposed to look on the family life of the Italians at this time as hopelessly ruined by the national immorality, and this side of the question will be discussed more fully in the next part. For the moment we must content ourselves with pointing out that conjugal infidelity had by no means so disastrous an influence on family life in Italy as in the North, so long as certain limits were not overstepped.

The domestic life of the Middle Ages was a product of popular morals, or if we prefer, a result of the inborn tendencies of national life modified by position and property. Chivalry at its height left domestic economy untouched. The knight wandered from court to court, and from one battlefield to another. His homage was given systematically to some woman other than his wife, and things went how they might at home in the castle. It was the Renaissance that made the first conscious attempt to systematize domestic life, indeed, to make it a work of art. A highly developed economy and a rational style of domestic architecture served to promote this end. But the main point was the thoughtful study of all questions relating to social intercourse, to education, to domestic service and organization.

The most precious document on this subject is the treatise

on the management of the home by Agnolo Pandolfini.[204]
A father speaks to his grown-up sons, and initiates them
into his method of administration. We are introduced into
a large and wealthy household, which, if governed with
moderation and reasonable economy, promises happiness and
prosperity for generations to come. A considerable landed
estate, whose produce furnishes the table of the house and
serves as the basis of the family fortune, is combined with
some industrial pursuit, such as the weaving of wool or silk.
The dwelling is solid and the food good. Everything that has
to do with the plan and arrangement of the house is great,
durable, and costly, but the daily life within it is as simple
as possible. All other expenses, from those involving the
family honor down to the pocket money of the younger
sons, are in a rational, not a conventional relation. Nothing is
considered of so much importance as education, which the
head of the house gives not only to the children, but to the
whole household. He first develops his wife from a shy girl,
brought up in careful seclusion, to the true woman of the
house, capable of commanding and guiding the servants. The
sons are brought up without any undue severity,[205] carefully
watched and counseled, and controlled "by authority rather
than by force." And finally the servants are chosen and
treated on such principles that they gladly and faithfully
hold by the family.

We must mention one other feature of this book which is by
no means peculiar to it but which it treats with special warmth
—the love of the educated Italian for country life. In the
North at that time the nobles lived in the country in their
castles and the monks of the higher orders lived in their well-
guarded monasteries, while the wealthiest burghers dwelt
year in and year out in the cities. But in Italy, at least so
far as the neighborhood of certain towns was concerned, the

204. *Trattato del governo della famiglia*. Cf. notes 63 and 68.
Pandolfini died in 1446; L.B. Alberti, to whom the work has
also been attributed, died in 1472. Cf. also note 143.
205. A fundamental, psychologically oriented history of "flogging"
among the Germanic and Latin people would be worth volumes
of dispatches and negotiations. When and through what influence
did flogging become a daily practice in the German household?
Not till after Walther sang: *Nieman kan mit gerten kindes zuht
beherten* [corresponding, roughly, to our "Spare the rod and
spoil the child"]. In Italy, a child past the age of seven was
no longer beaten. The small Roland (*Orlandino*, vii, 42) lays down
the principle: *Sol gli asini si ponno bastonare,/Se una tal bestia
fussi patirei* [Only donkeys will respond to the stick,/Were I such
a beast, I would suffer].

security of life and property was so great, and the passion for a country residence was so strong, that men were willing to risk a loss in time of war. Thus arose the villa, the country house of the well-to-do citizen. A precious inheritance of the old Roman world was thus revived, as soon as the wealth and culture of the people were sufficiently advanced.

At his villa our author finds a peace and happiness that only his own words can describe. The economic side of the matter is that one single property must, if possible, contain everything—corn, wine, oil, pasture land, and woods, and that the high price of such property should be paid willingly since nothing need then be bought on the market. But the higher enjoyment derived from the villa is betrayed by some words of the introduction to this subject: "Round about Florence lie many villas in a transparent atmosphere, amid cheerful scenery, and with a splendid view; there is little fog and no injurious winds; all is good, and the water is pure and healthy. Of the numerous buildings many are like palaces, many like castles, costly and beautiful to behold." He is speaking of those unrivaled villas, of which the greater number were sacrificed—vainly—by the Florentines themselves in the defense of their city in 1529.

In these villas, as in those on the Brenta, on the Lombard hills, at Posilippo, and on the Vomero, social life assumed a freer and more rural character than in the palaces within the city. Here and there we find charming descriptions of the intercourse of the guests, the hunting parties, and all the open-air pursuits and amusements. But even the noblest achievements of poetry and thought are sometimes dated from these scenes of rural peace.

It is no mere arbitrariness when we include the processions and performances that formed part of the festivals in our discussion of social life. The artistic power the Italians of the Renaissance displayed on such occasions [206] was attained only by means of that free intercourse of all classes which formed the basis of Italian society. In Northern Europe the monasteries, the courts, and the burghers had their special feasts and shows as in Italy; but in the North they were separated according to form and substance, whereas in Italy an art and culture common to the whole nation brought them to a universal brilliance. The decorative architecture that served these festivals deserves a chapter to itself in the

---

206. Cf. above, Part Four, where the magnificence of the festival is shown to have hindered the higher development of the drama.

history of art, although our imagination can only form a picture of it from the descriptions that have been left. Here we are concerned with the festival itself as a heightened moment in the life of the people, in which its religious, moral, and poetic ideals took visible shape. The Italian festivals in their best form mark the true transition from life to art.

The two chief forms of the festival entertainment were derived, as was the case throughout the West, from the Mystery, that is, the dramatization of sacred history and legend, and the Procession, that is, the magnificent pagaentry of any ecclesiastical occasion.

The performances of the Mysteries were more frequent and splendid in Italy than elsewhere, and were most favorably affected by the parallel development of the visual arts and poetry. In the course of time not only did the farce and the secular drama branch off from the Mystery, as in other countries of Europe, but also the pantomime, with singing and dancing, whose effect depended on the richness and beauty of the spectacle.

The Procession, in the broad,[207] level, and well-paved streets of the Italian cities, soon developed into the *trionfo* [triumph], that is, the train of masked figures on foot and in chariots, whose ecclesiastical character gradually gave way to the secular. The processions at the Carnival and at the feast of Corpus Christi were alike in the pomp and brilliancy with which they were conducted, and set the pattern followed later by the royal or princely progresses. Other nations were willing to spend vast sums of money on these occasions, but only in Italy do we find an artistic method of treatment which arranged the procession as a significant whole.

What is left of these festivals is but a poor remnant of what once existed. Religious as well as royal processions have abandoned the dramatic element—the costumes—partly from fear of ridicule and partly because the cultivated classes, which formerly gave their whole energies to these things, have for several reasons lost their interest in them. Even at the Carnival, the great processions of masks are out of fashion. What still remains, such as the costumes adopted in imitation of certain religious confraternities, or even the brilliant festival of St. Rosalia at Palermo, shows clearly how far the higher culture of the country has withdrawn from such interests.

The festivals did not reach their full development till after the decisive victory of the modern spirit, in the fifteenth

207. In comparison with the cities of the North.

century,[208] unless perhaps Florence was here, as in other things, in advance of the rest of Italy. In any case, here the quarters of the city had already in early times been organized for public performances, which demanded a great expenditure of artistic effort. Thus there was the representation of Hell, with a scaffold and boats in the Arno, on May 1, 1304, when the Ponte alla Carraia broke down under the weight of the spectators. That at a later time Florentines traveled through Italy as directors of festivals (*festaiuoli*), shows that the art was perfected early at home.

If we try to establish the essential areas of superiority of the Italian festivals over those of other countries, we must place first the sense of the developed individual for representing the individual, that is, the capacity to invent a given mask, and to act the part with dramatic propriety. Painters and sculptors not only participated in the decoration of the place where the festival was held, but helped in getting up the characters themselves, and prescribed the dress, the paints, and other ornaments. The second fact to be pointed out is the universal familiarity of the people with the poetic basis of the show. The Mysteries, indeed, were equally well understood all over Europe, since the biblical story and the legends of the saints were the common property of Christendom; but in all other respects the advantage was on the side of Italy. For the recitations, whether of religious or secular-ideal heroes, she possessed a lyric poetry so rich and harmonious that neither great nor small could resist its charm.[209] And the majority of the spectators—at least in the cities—understood the meaning of mythological figures, and could guess, at least easier then anywhere else, the allegorical and historical ones, which were drawn from sources familiar to the mass of Italians.

This point should be discussed more fully. The Middle Ages was essentially the time of allegory. Theology and philosophy treated their categories as independent beings, and it was quite simple for poetry and art to add whatever still lacked personality. In this, all the countries of the West were on the same level. Their world of ideas was rich enough in types and figures, but when these were put into concrete shape, costume and attributes were likely to be unintelligible

---

208. Despite their splendor, the festivities that took place in 1395 when Visconti was made Duke of Milan still had a medieval coarseness about them, and the dramatic element was totally absent.

209. In the Mysteries, dialogue was generally in octaves, monologues in tercets.

and unsuited to the popular taste. Even in Italy this was often the case, and not only during the whole period of the Renaissance, but down to a still later time. To produce the confusion, it was enough if a predicate of the allegorical figure referred to was wrongly translated by an attribute. Even Dante is not completely free from such errors,[210] and, actually, he is on the whole proud of his allegories.[211] Petrarch, in his *trionfi* tries to give clear if short descriptions of at least the figures of Love, of Chastity, of Death, of Fame, etc. But others load their allegories with inappropriate attributes. In the satires of Vinciguerra, for example, Envy is depicted with "rough, iron teeth," Gluttony as biting its own lips and with a shock of tangled hair, the latter probably to show its indifference to all that is not edible. We cannot discuss in detail here the unfortunate effects of these misunderstandings in the visual arts. They, like poetry, might think themselves fortunate if allegory could be expressed by a mythological figure—by a figure which antiquity saved from absurdity—if Mars might stand for war, and Diana for the love of the chase, etc.

Nevertheless art and poetry had better allegories than these to offer, and we may assume with regard to those figures of this kind which appeared in the Italian festivals, that the public required them to be clearly and vividly characterized, since its previous training had fitted it to be a competent critic. Elsewhere, particularly at the Burgundian court, the most inexpressive figures, and even mere symbols, were allowed, since to understand, or to seem to understand them, was a part of aristocratic breeding. At the famous Oath of the Pheasant in the year 1453,[212] the beautiful young horsewoman, who rode as Queen of Pleasure, was the only pleasing allegory. The huge epergnes with automatons or even living figures are either mere curiosities or are loaded with some clumsy moral lesson. A naked female statue on a sideboard guarding a live lion was supposed to represent Constantinople and its future savior, the Duke of Burgundy. The rest, with the exception of a pantomime—Jason in Colchis—

---

210. To this must be attributed, e.g., his creating images from metaphors, as when at the door of Purgatory the middle, cracked step is supposed to symbolize contrition (*Purgatorio*, ix, 97), whereas the slab, by being broken, loses its value as a step; or when (*Purgatorio*, xviii, 94) those who were lazy in this world must do penance by running in the next, whereas running could also symbolize flight, etc.

211. *Inferno*, ix, 61; *Purgatorio*, viii, 19.

212. Actually 1454. Cf. Olivier de la Marche, *Mémoires*, ch. 29.

seems either too recondite or to have no sense at all. Olivier himself, to whom we owe the description of the scene, appeared as the "Church" in a tower on the back of an elephant, and sang a long elegy on the victory of the unbelievers.

But although the allegorical element in Italian poetry, art, and festivals is superior both in good taste and in unity of conception, it is not in these qualities that it is most characteristic and unique. The decisive advantage[213] lay much more in the fact that, besides the personifications of abstract qualities, even historical representatives of these abstract qualities were introduced in great number—that both poetry and the visual arts were accustomed to represent famous men and women. The *Divine Comedy*, the *trionfi* of Petrarch, the *Amorosa visione* of Boccaccio—all of them works based on this principle—and the great diffusion of culture that took place under the influence of antiquity had made the nation familiar with this historical element. These figures now appeared at festivals, either individualized, as definite masks, or in groups, as characteristic attendants on some leading allegorical figure. The art of grouping and composition was thus learned in Italy at a time when the most splendid exhibitions in the North were made up of unintelligible symbolism or meaningless puerilities.

We begin with the kind that is perhaps the oldest—the Mysteries. In their main features they resembled those performed in the rest of Europe. In the public squares, in the churches, and in the cloisters, extensive scaffolding was constructed, with the top serving as a Paradise that could be locked and the bottom sometimes serving as a Hell, while between the two lay the stage proper, representing the scene of all the earthly events of the drama. In Italy, as elsewhere, the biblical or legendary play often began with an introductory dialogue between Apostles, Prophets, Sibyls, Virtues, and Fathers of the Church, and sometimes ended with a dance. It goes without saying that there was no lack of the half-comic intermezzi of secondary characters in Italy, yet this feature was hardly so broadly marked as in the Northern countries.[214] The artificial means by which figures were made to rise and float in the air—one of the chief delights of these representations—were probably much better understood in

213. That is, an advantage for very great poets and artists who knew how to use it.
214. True, a Mystery in a church at Siena on the Massacre of the Innocents ended with a scene of the disconsolate mothers tearing each other's hair.

Italy than elsewhere; and already in the fourteenth century the hitches in these performances were a stock subject of ridicule in Florence. Soon afterward Brunelleschi invented for the Feast of the Annunciation in the Piazza San Felice a marvelous apparatus consisting of a heavenly globe surrounded by two circles of angels, out of which Gabriel flew down in a machine shaped like a *mandorla*. Cecca, too, devised mechanisms for such displays.[215] The spiritual corporations or the quarters of the city which undertook the management and in part the performance of these plays, at all events in the larger towns, spared no trouble and expense to render them as perfect and artistic as possible. The same was no doubt the case at the great court festivals, when Mysteries were performed in addition to the pantomimes and secular dramas. The court of Pietro Riario, that of Ferrara, etc. certainly lacked nothing that human invention could produce. When we imagine the theatrical talent and the splendid costumes of the actors, the scenes constructed in the style of the architecture of the period, hung with garlands and tapestry, and in the background the noble buildings of an Italian piazza or the slender columns of some great courtyard or cloister, the effect is one of great brilliance. But just as the secular drama suffered from this passion for display, the higher poetic development of the Mystery was arrested by the same cause. In the texts that are left we find for the most part the poorest dramatic texture relieved now and then by a fine lyrical or rhetorical passage, but no trace of the grand symbolic enthusiasm that distinguishes the *Autos sacramentales* of Calderón.

In the smaller towns, where there was less scenic display, the effect of these spiritual plays on the character of the spectators may have been greater. One of the great preachers of repentance, Roberto da Lecce, whom we shall discuss in the last section, closed his Lenten sermons at Perugia during the plague of 1448 with a representation of the Passion. The cast was small, but the entire assembly wept aloud. It is true that on such occasions emotional stimulants were resorted to which depended on the crudest realism. We are reminded of the pictures of Matteo da Siena, or of the groups of clay figures by Guido Mazzoni, when we read that the actor who took the part of Christ appeared covered with weals and apparently sweating blood, and even bled from a wound in the side.[216]

215. Vasari, Life of Brunelleschi, Life of Girolamo della Cecca. Compare the Life of Don Bartolommeo della Gatta.
216. For the last, see, e.g., *The Commentaries of Pius II*, Book

The special occasions on which these Mysteries were performed, apart from the great festivals of the Church, princely weddings, etc., were of various kinds. When, for example, St. Bernardino of Siena was canonized by the Pope (1450), a sort of dramatic imitation of the ceremony *(rappresentazione)* took place, probably on the great square of his native city, with meat and drink for all comers. We are told that a learned monk celebrated his promotion to the degree of Doctor of Theology by giving a representation of the legend about the patron saint of the city. Charles VIII had scarcely entered Italy before he was welcomed at Turin by the widowed Duchess Bianca of Savoy with a sort of half-religious pantomime, in which there was first a pastoral scene symbolizing the Law of Nature, then a procession of patriarchs symbolizing the Law of Grace, then the stories of Lancelot of the Lake, and "of Athens." And no sooner had the King reached Chieri than he was received with another pantomime, in which a woman in childbed was shown surrounded by distinguished visitors.

If any church festival by universal consent called for exceptional efforts, it was the feast of Corpus Christi, which in Spain gave rise to a special class of poetry. For Italy we have at least the splendid description of the feast that was celebrated at Viterbo by Pius II in 1462.[217] The procession itself, which advanced from a vast and gorgeous tent in front of San Francesco along the main street to the cathedral, was the least part of the ceremony. The cardinals and wealthy prelates had divided the route into portions which they not only decorated with curtains, tapestry, garlands, etc., but in which they had also erected stages on which short historical and allegorical scenes were performed during the procession. It is not clear from the account whether all the characters were living beings or whether some were merely draped figures; in any case, the expense was very great. There was a suffering Christ amid singing angels, the Last Supper with a figure of St. Thomas Aquinas, the combat between the Archangel Michael and the devils, fountains of wine and orchestras of angels, the grave of Christ with the whole scene of the Resurrection, and finally, on the square before

---

VIII. – Even the poetry of the fifteenth century sometimes shows the same coarseness. A *canzone* by Andrea da Basso traces in detail the corruption of the corpse of a hardhearted mistress. And in a monastery drama of the twelfth century, King Herod was depicted on stage as being eaten by worms.

217. *The Commentaries of Pius II*, Book VIII. [Burckhardt has 1482, which would seem to be a printer's error.]

the cathedral, the tomb of the Virgin. It opened after High
Mass and Benediction, and the Mother of God accompanied
by angels ascended singing to Paradise, where she was
crowned by her Son and led into the presence of the Eternal
Father.

Among the series of representations in the public streets,
the one given by the Cardinal Vice-Chancellor Roderigo
Borgia—later Pope Alexander VI—was remarkable for its
splendor and obscure symbolism.[218] It also offers an early
instance of the fondness for salvos of artillery,[219] which was
characteristic of the House of Borgia.

Pius II is less detailed in his account of the procession held
the same year in Rome on the arrival of the skull of St.
Andrew from Greece. Here, too, Roderigo Borgia distinguished himself by his magnificence; but this festival had a
more secular character than the other, since, besides the
inevitable choirs of angels, other masks were exhibited, as
well as "strong men," who seem to have performed various
feats of muscular prowess.

The representations that were wholly or chiefly secular
were arranged, especially at the more important princely
courts, mainly with a view to splendid and striking scenic
effects. The subjects were mythological or allegorical, and
the interpretation commonly lay on the surface. There was
no lack of extravagances: huge figures of animals from which
a crowd of masked figures suddenly emerged, as at Siena
in the year 1465 when at a public reception a ballet of twelve
persons came out of a golden wolf; living table ornaments,
not always, however, showing the tasteless exaggeration of
the Burgundian court. Most of them showed some artistic
or poetic feeling. The mixture of pantomime and drama at
the court of Ferrara has already been referred to in the
discussion of poetry. The entertainments given in 1473 by
Cardinal Pietro Riario at Rome when Leonora of Aragon,
the intended bride of Prince Ercole of Ferrara, passed
through the city, were famous far beyond the limits of Italy.
The plays were Mysteries on some ecclesiastical subject, but
the pantomimes were mythological. There were Orpheus with

218. Five kings with an armed retinue, a savage who fought with
a (timid?) lion, the latter perhaps an allusion to the name of the
Pope—Sylvius.
219. At the accession of Alexander VI there were great salvos of
artillery. – Fireworks, a beautiful invention of the Italian festivals,
belong, as do the festival decorations, more properly to the history
of art than to our present work. – So, too, the brilliant illumina-
tions we read of in connection with many festivals, as well as
the table ornaments and the hunting trophies.

the beasts, Perseus and Andromeda, Ceres drawn by dragons, Bacchus and Ariadne drawn by panthers, and the education of Achilles; then a ballet of the famous lovers of ancient times, with a troop of nymphs; this was interrupted by an attack of predatory centaurs, who in their turn were vanquished and put to flight by Hercules. A fact, which is in itself a trifle, may be mentioned as characteristic of the taste of the time: at all festivals, the human beings who appeared as statues in niches or on pillars and triumphal arches and then showed themselves to be alive by singing or speaking, retained their natural complexion and natural costume, and thus the sense of incongruity was removed; but in the house of Riario a living child was exhibited, gilt from head to foot, who showered water round him from a fountain.[220]

Brilliant pantomimes of the same kind were given at Bologna, at the marriage of Annibale Bentivoglio to Lucrezia d'Este. Instead of the orchestra, choral songs were sung, while the fairest of Diana's nymphs flew over to the Juno Pronuba, and Venus walked with a lion—which in this case was a disguised man—among a troop of savages. The decorations were a faithful representation of a forest. At Venice, in 1491, the princesses of the House of Este were met and welcomed by the Bucentaur, and entertained by boat races and a splendid pantomime, "Meleager," in the court of the ducal palace. At Milan, Leonardo da Vinci directed the festivals of the Duke and of some leading citizens. One of his machines, which must have rivaled that of Brunelleschi, represented the heavenly bodies with all their movements on a colossal scale. Whenever a planet approached Isabella, the bride of the young Duke, the divinity whose name it bore stepped forth from the globe and sang some verses written by the court poet Bellincioni (1490). At another festival (1493) the model of the equestrian statue of Francesco Sforza appeared with other objects under a triumphal arch on the square before the castle. From Vasari we know of the ingenious automata that Leonardo invented to welcome the French kings as masters of Milan. Even in the smaller cities great efforts were sometimes made on these occasions. In 1453, when Duke Borso came to Reggio to receive the homage of the city, he was met at the gate by a great machine on which St. Prospero, the patron saint of the town, appeared to float shaded by a baldachin held by angels,

220. Vasari, *Life of Jacopo da Pontormo*, tells how after such a festival at Florence in 1513, a child died from the effects of the exertion—or perhaps of the gilding. The poor boy had to represent the "golden age."

while below him was a revolving disk with eight singing angels, two of whom received from the saint the scepter and keys of the city, which they then delivered to the Duke. Then a chariot drawn by concealed horses advanced, bearing an empty throne behind which stood a figure of Justice attended by a genius. At the corners of the chariot sat four gray-headed lawgivers surrounded by angels with banners; on each side rode standard-bearers in complete armor. It need hardly be added that the goddess and the genius did not suffer the Duke to pass by without an address. A second car, drawn it seems by a unicorn, bore a Charity with a burning torch; but amid all this they could not deny themselves the ancient spectacle of a car in the form of a ship, moved by men concealed inside it. The whole procession now advanced toward the Duke. In front of the church of San Pietro, a halt was again made. A St. Peter attended by two angels floated down in an aureole from the façade, placed a wreath of laurel on the head of the Duke, and then floated back to his former position. The clergy provided another allegory of a purely religious kind: Idolatry and Faith stood on two lofty pillars, and after Faith, represented by a beautiful girl, had uttered her welcome, the other column and the figure upon it fell to pieces. Then came a Caesar with seven beautiful women, who were presented to Borso as the Virtues, which he was exhorted to pursue. At last the cathedral was reached, but after the service the Duke was again seated outside on a lofty golden throne, and a second time received the homage of some of the masks already mentioned. To conclude all, three angels flew down from an adjacent building, and, amid songs of joy, delivered to him palm branches, as symbols of peace.

Let us now glance at those festivals whose chief feature was the procession itself.

There is no doubt that from an early period of the Middle Ages the religious processions gave rise to the use of masks, whether it was angels accompanying the sacrament or the sacred pictures and relics, or characters in the Passion, such as Christ with the cross, the thieves and the soldiers, or the faithful women. But the great feasts of the Church were from an early time accompanied by a civic procession, and the naïveté of the Middle Ages found nothing unfitting in the many secular elements it contained. We may mention especially the naval car (*carrus navalis*), which had been inherited from pagan times, and which, as an instance already quoted shows, was admissible at festivals of very various kinds, and has left its name on one of them in particular—the Carnival.

Such ships, decorated with all possible splendor, delighted the eyes of spectators long after their original meaning was forgotten. When Isabella of England met her bridegroom, Emperor Frederick II, at Cologne, she was met by a number of such chariots filled with music-making priests, drawn by invisible horses.

But the ecclesiastical processions were not only enriched with all kinds of accessories, they were often replaced by processions of religious masks. Their origin lies perhaps in the parties of actors who wound their way through the streets of the city to the place where they were about to act the Mystery; but it is possible that there may have been a kind of religious procession completely independent of this. Dante describes [221] the triumph of Beatrice, with the twenty-four Elders of the Apocalypse, the four mystical Beasts, the three Christian and four Cardinal Virtues, and St. Luke, St. Paul, and other Apostles in a way that almost forces us to conclude that such processions actually occurred before his time. We are led to this conclusion chiefly by the chariot in which Beatrice rides, which in the miraculous forest of the vision would have been unnecessary, in fact, out of place. Or did Dante look on the chariot only as a symbol of triumph? and was it his poem that first gave rise to these processions, the form of which was borrowed from the triumph of the Roman Emperors? However this may be, poetry and theology continued to make free use of the symbol. Savonarola in his Triumph of the Cross imagines [222] Christ on a triumphal chariot, above his head the shining sphere of the Trinity, in his left hand the Cross, in his right the Old and New Testaments; below, the Virgin Mary; in front of the chariot, Patriarchs, Prophets, Apostles, and preachers; on either side, the Martyrs and Doctors with open books; behind him, all the converts; further back, the countless crowd of enemies, emperors, powerful rulers, philosophers, heretics, all vanquished, their idols destroyed and their books burned. (A large picture by Titian, which is known only as a woodcut, has a good deal in common with this description.) The ninth and tenth of Sabellico's thirteen Elegies on the Mother of God contain a minute account of her triumph, richly adorned with allegories, and are especially interesting from that matter-of-fact air with

221. *Purgatorio*, xxix, 43 to the end, and xxx, at the beginning. – According to [xxix] 115, the chariot is more splendid than the triumphal chariot of Scipio, of Augustus, and even of the Sun God.
222. Ranke, *History of the Latin and Teutonic Nations*, p. 125.

which the realistic painting of the fifteenth century represents such scenes.

Nevertheless, the secular *trionfi* were far more frequent than the religious. They were modeled on the procession of the Roman Imperator, as it was known from the old reliefs and the writings of ancient authors. The historical conceptions then prevalent in Italy, with which these processions were closely connected, have already been discussed.

Now and then we read of the actual triumphal entrance of a victorious general, which was organized as far as possible on the ancient pattern, even against the will of the hero himself. Francesco Sforza had the courage (1450) to refuse the triumphal chariot that had been prepared for his return to Milan, on the ground that such things were monarchial superstitions. Alfonso the Great, on his entrance into Naples (1443), had the grace to decline the wreath of laurel, which, as is well-known, Napoleon did not disdain to wear at his coronation in Notre-Dame. For the rest, Alfonso's procession (which passed through a breach in the wall and then through the city to the cathedral) was a strange mixture of antique, allegorical, and purely comic elements. The car, drawn by four white horses, on which he sat enthroned was lofty and covered with gilding; twenty patricians carried the poles of the golden baldachin that shaded his head. The part of the procession which the Florentines who were present in Naples had undertaken was composed of elegant young cavaliers, skillfully brandishing their lances, of a chariot with the figure of Fortune, and of seven Virtues on horseback. The goddess herself, in accordance with the inexorable logic of allegory to which even the painters at that time conformed, had hair only on the front part of her head, while the back part was bald, and the genius who sat on the lower steps of the car and who symbolized the fugitive character of Fortune, had his feet immersed (?) in a basin of water. Then followed, equipped by the same Florentines, a troop of horsemen in the costumes of various nations, dressed as foreign princes and nobles, and then, on a high car, crowned with laurel and standing above a revolving globe, a Julius Caesar who explained to the king in Italian verse the meaning of all the allegories, and then took his place in the procession. Sixty Florentines, all in purple and scarlet, closed this splendid display of what their home could achieve. But then a band of Catalans advanced on foot, with lay figures of horses fastened on to them before and behind, and engaged in a mock combat with a band of Turks, as though in derision of the Florentine sentimentalism. Last of all came a gigantic tower, the door guarded by an angel with a drawn sword; on it stood, in their turn, four Virtues, who each addressed the king with a song. The rest of the show had nothing specially characteristic about it.

At the entrance of Louis XII into Milan in 1507 we find, besides the inevitable chariot with Virtues, a living group representing Jupiter, Mars, and a figure of Italy caught in a net. After which came a car laden with trophies, etc.

And when there were no actual triumphs to celebrate, the poets found a compensation for themselves and their patrons. Petrarch and Boccaccio had described the representation of every sort of fame as attendants of an allegorical figure; the celebrities of past ages were now made attendants of the prince. The poetess Cleofe Gabrielli of Gubbio paid this honor to Borso of Ferrara. She gave him seven queens—the seven liberal arts—as his handmaids, with whom he mounted a chariot; further, a crowd of heroes, made distinguishable by names written on their foreheads; then followed all the famous poets; and after them the gods driving in their chariots. At this time there is, in fact, simply no end to the mythological and allegorical charioteering, and the most important work of art of Borso's time—the frescoes in the Palazzo Schifanoia—shows us a whole frieze filled with this subject.[223] When Raphael had to paint the Stanza della Segnatura, he found this mode of artistic thought completely vulgarized and worn out. The new and final consecration which he gave to it will remain a wonder to all ages.

The actual triumphal processions of victorious generals were only exceptions. But all the festive processions, whether they celebrated any special event or were held only for their own sakes, assumed more or less the character and nearly always the name of a *trionfo*. It is a wonder that funerals were not also treated in the same way.

It was the practice, both at the Carnival and on other occasions, to represent the triumphs of ancient Roman commanders, such as those in Florence of Paulus Aemilius (under Lorenzo the Magnificent) and of Camillus (on the visit of Leo X), both under the direction of the painter Francesco

223. Even panel paintings of similar scenes are by no means rare, and no doubt often represent masquerades which had actually been performed. The wealthy classes soon became accustomed to chariots at every ceremony. Annibale Bentivoglio, eldest son of the ruler of Bologna, returned to the palace after presiding as umpire at the regular military exercises *cum triumpho more romano* [with a triumph in the Roman manner].

Granacci.[224] In Rome, the first complete festival of this kind
was the triumph of Augustus after the victory over Cleopatra,
given under Paul II, where, besides the comic and mythological masks (which, as a matter of fact, were not lacking in
the ancient triumphs), all the other requisites were present—
kings in chains, silk tablets with decrees of the senate and
the people, a senate clothed in the ancient costume, praetors,
aediles, and quaestors, four chariots filled with singing masks,
and, doubtless, cars laden with trophies. Other processions
aimed rather at setting forth, in a general way, the universal
empire of ancient Rome; and in answer to the very real
danger of the Turks there was a parade of a cavalcade of
camels bearing masks representing Ottoman prisoners. Later,
at the Carnival of 1500, Cesare Borgia, with a bold allusion
to himself, celebrated the triumph of Julius Caesar, with a
procession of eleven magnificent chariots, doubtless to the
scandal of the pilgrims who had come for the Jubilee. – Two
trionfi, famous for their taste and beauty, were given by rival
companies in Florence, on the election of Leo X to the
Papacy. [225] One represented the three Ages of Man, the other
the Ages of the World, ingeniously set forth in five scenes
of Roman history and two allegories of the golden age of
Saturn and its final return. The imagination displayed in the
decoration of the chariots, when great Florentine artists undertook the work, made the scene so impressive that a permanent, periodic repetition of such spectacles was found
desirable. Hitherto the subject cities had been satisfied merely
to present their symbolical gifts—costly stuffs and wax
candles—on the day when they annually did homage. The
guild of merchants now built ten chariots (to which more
were to have been added) not so much to carry the tribute
as to symbolize it, and Andrea del Sarto, who painted some
of them, no doubt did his work to perfection.[226] These cars,
whether for tribute or trophies, now formed part of all such
celebrations, even when there was not much money. In 1477,
the Sienese announced the alliance between Ferrante and
Sixtus IV, with which they themselves were associated, by
driving a chariot round the city, with "one clad as the
goddess of peace standing on a hauberk and other arms."

At the Venetian festivals instead of the chariots, the processions on water became marvelous in their fantastic splendor.

224. Vasari, Life of Granacci.
225. Vasari, Life of Jacopo da Pontormo. A most important
passage of its kind.
226. Vasari, Life of Andrea del Sarto.

The sailing of the Bucentaur to meet the princesses of Ferrara in 1491 seems to have been something out of fairyland. Countless vessels with garlands and hangings, filled with the richly dressed youth of the city, moved in front; genii with attributes symbolizing the various gods floated on machines hung in the air; below were others grouped as tritons and nymphs; the air was filled with music, sweet odors, and the fluttering of embroidered banners. The Bucentaur was followed by such a crowd of boats of every sort that for a mile around, the water could not be seen. With regard to the rest of the festivities, besides the pantomime mentioned above, we may notice as something new a boat race of fifty powerful girls. In the sixteenth century the nobility were divided into corporations for the production of these festivals, whose most noteworthy feature was some extraordinary machine placed on a ship. Thus, for example, in the year 1541, at the festival of the Sempiterni, a round "universe" moved along the Grand Canal, and a splendid ball was given inside it. The Carnival, too, in this city was famous for its dances, processions, and exhibitions of every kind. The Piazza di San Marco was found to give space enough not only for tournaments but for *trionfi* similar to those common on the mainland. At a festival held on the conclusion of peace, the pious brotherhoods (*scuole*) each took its part in the procession. There one saw, among golden candelabra with red candles, among crowds of musicians and winged boys with golden bowls and horns of plenty, a car on which Noah and David sat together enthroned; then came Abigail, leading a camel laden with treasures, and a second car with a group of political significance: Italy sitting between Venice and Liguria, and on a raised step three female symbolical figures with the arms of the allied princes. This was followed by a great globe with, it seems, the constellations round it. The bodily representatives of the princes appeared on other chariots with their servants and their coats of arms, if we have interpreted the report correctly.

The Carnival proper, apart from these great triumphal marches, had perhaps nowhere in the fifteenth century so varied a character as in Rome. There were races of every kind—of horses, asses, buffaloes, old men, young men, Jews, and so on. Paul II fed crowds of people before the Palazzo di Venezia, in which he lived. The games in the Piazza Navona, which had probably never completely ceased since classical times, were remarkable for their warlike splendor; there was a sham fight of cavalry, and a review of all the citizens in arms. The greatest freedom existed with regard to the use of masks, which were sometimes allowed for several months at a time. Sixtus IV was not afraid to make his way through crowds of masks in the most populous part of the city—at the Campofiore and near the Banchi—but he refused to receive them as visitors in the Vatican. Under Innocent VIII a discreditable usage, which had already appeared among the cardinals, attained its height. In the Carnival of 1491, they sent one another chariots full of splendid masks, singers, and buffoons chanting scandalous verses, all accompanied by men on horseback. – Apart from the Carnival, the Romans seem to have been the first to discover the effect of a great procession by torchlight. When Pius II came back from the Congress of Mantua in 1459,[227] the people waited on him with a squadron of horsemen bearing torches, who rode in shining circles before his palace. Sixtus IV, however, thought it better to decline a nocturnal visit of the people, who wanted to come with torches and olive branches.[228]

But the Florentine Carnival surpassed the Roman in a certain class of processions, which have left their mark even in literature.[229] Among a crowd of masks on foot and on horseback appeared a huge, fantastic chariot, and upon it an allegorical figure or group of figures with the proper accompaniments, such as Jealousy with four spectacled faces on one head; the four temperaments with the planets belonging to them; the three Fates; Prudence enthroned above Hope and Fear, who lay bound before her; the four Elements, Ages, Winds, Seasons, etc.; as well as the famous chariot of Death with the coffins which presently opened. Or there was a splendid scene from classical mythology—Bacchus and Ariadne, Paris and Helen, etc. Or, finally a chorus of figures forming some single class or category, such as beggars, hunters and nymphs, lost souls who in their lifetime were hardhearted women, hermits, astrologers, vagabonds, devils, sellers of various kinds of wares, and even on one occasion *il popolo*, the people, who then reviled one another in their songs. The songs that have been collected and still remain explain the masquerade sometimes in a pathetic, sometimes in a humorous, and sometimes in an excessively indecent tone. Some of the worst in this respect are attributed to

227. *The Commentaries of Pius II,* Book IV.
228. They wanted to thank him for a peace he had concluded, but they found the gates to the palace locked and troops posted on all the squares.
229. Vasari, Life of Piero di Cosimo, to whom a leading role in the development of these processions is assigned.

Lorenzo the Magnificent, probably because the real author did not dare to declare himself. However this may be, we must certainly ascribe to him the beautiful song that accompanied the scene of Bacchus and Ariadne, whose refrain still echoes to us from the fifteenth century like a regretful presentiment of the brief splendor of the Renaissance itself:

> *Quanto è bella giovinezza,*
> *Che si fugge tuttavia!*
> *Chi vuol esser lieto, sia:*
> *Di doman non c'è certezza.*[230]

230. [Fair is youth and void of sorrow;/But it hourly flies away./Youth and maids enjoy today;/Naught ye know about tomorrow. – J.A. Symonds tr.]

PART SIX

MORALITY AND RELIGION

THE relation of individual nations to the highest things of life, to God, virtue, and immortality, may be investigated up to a certain point, but a strict parallel can never be drawn. In fact, the more distinctly our evidence in these matters seems to speak, the more must we be on our guard against unqualified assumptions and rash generalizations.

This is especially true with regard to our judgment on questions of morality. It may be possible to indicate many contrasts and nuances among different nations, but to formulate absolutes is not given to human understanding. The ultimate truth with respect to the character, the conscience, and the guilt of a people remains a secret forever, if only because its defects have another side, where they appear as national peculiarities or even as virtues. We must leave those authors who find pleasure in passing sweeping censures on whole nations to do so as they like. The nations of the West can maltreat each other but, fortunately, cannot judge one another. A great nation, interwoven by its civilization, its achievements, and its fortunes with the whole life of the modern world can afford to ignore both its advocates and its accusers. It lives on with or without the approval of theorists.

Accordingly, what follows here is no judgment, but a series of marginal notes suggested by a study of the Italian Renaissance extending over some years. Their value is all the more limited, since they refer mainly to the life of the upper classes, about which we have far more information, good as well as evil, in Italy than in any other country of Europe. But though both fame and infamy ring louder here than anywhere else, it does not bring us any closer to forming an adequate moral estimate of the people.

What eye can pierce the depths in which the character and fate of nations are formed? in which the innate and the experienced combine to form a new whole and a second, a third nature? in which even those intellectual capacities which at first sight we would take to be primary are in fact evolved late and slowly? Did, for example, the Italian before the thirteenth century possess that flexible activity and certainty in his whole being, that power to shape whatever subject he dealt with in word or in form, which has been characteristic of him ever since? – And if we do not know, how can we possibly form an opinion of the infinitely rich and intricate channels through which character and intellect incessantly pour their influence on each other? Fortunately, there is a personal tribunal, whose voice is conscience; but let us have done with generalities about nations. For the people who seem to be most sick, the cure may be at hand; and those who appear healthy may carry within them the ripening germs of death, which only danger will bring to light.

At the beginning of the sixteenth century, when the civilization of the Renaissance had reached its highest pitch and, at the same time, the political ruin of the nation seemed inevitable, there was no lack of serious thinkers who saw a connection between this disaster and the prevalent immorality. It was not one of those preachers of repentance who in every age and among every people think themselves called to declaim against the wickedness of the time, but it was Machiavelli, who, in one of his best-considered works, declared: we Italians are irreligious and bad.[231] – Another would perhaps have said, "We are individually highly developed; we have outgrown the limits of morality and religion that were natural to us in our undeveloped state, and we despise outward law, because our rulers are illegitimate, and their judges and officers wicked men." – Machiavelli himself adds: because the Church and her representatives set the worst example.

And shall we add: "because the influence of antiquity was unfavorable?" Such a statement requires careful qualification. It may possibly be true of the humanists, especially as regards the profligacy of their lives. With the others it may have been that after they became familiar with antiquity, they substituted for holiness—the Christian ideal of life—the cult of historical greatness. It is easy to understand how easily they could view as negligible the very faults despite which the great had become great. They were probably scarcely conscious of this, for if theoretical evidence is re-

---

231. *The Discourses*, Book I, ch. 12. Also. ch. 55: Italy is more corrupt than all other countries; then come the French and the Spanish.

quired, we must look for it in the humanists, such as, for example, Paolo Giovio, who excuses the perjury of Gian Galeazzo Visconti, through which he was enabled to found an empire, by the example of Julius Caesar. The great Florentine historians and statesmen are completely free from such servile quotations, and what seems antique in their deeds and their judgments is so because the nature of their political life necessarily fostered in them a mode of thought that had some analogy to that of antiquity.

Be this as it may, at the beginning of the sixteenth century Italy found itself in the midst of a grave moral crisis, out of which the best men saw hardly any escape.

Let us begin by saying a few words about that moral force which was then the strongest bulwark against evil. Those highly gifted men thought they would find it in the form of a sense of honor. This is that enigmatic mixture of conscience and egotism which often survives in the modern man after he has lost, whether by his own fault or not, faith, love, and hope. This sense of honor is compatible with much selfishness and great vices, and is capable of astonishing illusions; yet, all the noble elements that are left in a character may gather around it, and from this source may draw new strength. It has become, in a far wider sense than is commonly believed, a decisive rule of conduct for the cultivated Europeans of our own day, and many who still hold faithfully by religion and morality are unconsciously guided by this feeling in the gravest decisions.

It is not our task to show that the men of antiquity also experienced a peculiar form of this feeling, and that later, in the Middle Ages, a special sense of honor became the mark of a particular class. Nor shall we argue with those who hold that conscience, rather than honor, is the motive force. It would be better and nobler if it were; but since it must be granted that even our worthier resolutions result from "a conscience more or less dimmed by selfishness," it is better to call the mixture by name. True, it is sometimes difficult, when discussing the Italian of the Renaissance, to distinguish this sense of honor from the passion for fame, into which it easily passes. Yet they remain two essentially different things.

There is no lack of statements on this subject. One of particular clarity may be quoted here instead of many others; it comes from the recently published aphorisms of Guicciardini.[232] "He who esteems honor highly succeeds in all that

232. Franc. Giucciardini, *Ricordi*, no. 118.

he undertakes, since he fears neither trouble, danger, nor expense; I have found it so in my own case, and may say it and write it; empty and dead are the deeds of those men who do not have this as their fiery spur." We should add that, from what is known of the life of the writer, he can be speaking here only of honor and not of fame. Rabelais has put the matter more clearly than perhaps any Italian. Indeed, we quote him unwillingly in these pages. What the great, always baroque Frenchman gives us is a picture of what the Renaissance would look like without form and without beauty. But his description of an ideal state in the Thelemite monastery is decisive as historical evidence, and without this excellent fantasy the picture of the sixteenth century would not be complete. In speaking of his gentlemen and ladies of the Order of Free Will, he tells, among other things, the following: [233]

> *En leur reigle n'estoit que ceste clause: Fay ce que vouldras. Parce que gens liberes, bien nayz,* [234] *bien instruictz, conversans en compaignies honnestes, ont par nature ung instinct et aguillon qui tousjours les poulse à faictz vertueux, et retire de vice: lequel ilz nommoyent honneur.*

This is the same faith in the goodness of human nature that inspired the men of the second half of the eighteenth century, and helped prepare the way for the French Revolution. Among the Italians, too, each man appealed to his own noble instinct, and though society as a whole—chiefly in consequence of the national disasters—began to have judgments and views of a more pessimistic sort, the importance of this sense of honor must still be rated highly. If the boundless development of individuality was the work of a historical providence, if it was stronger than the will of the individual, no less so was the opposing force which then

233. *Gargantua and Pantagruel*, Book I, ch. 57. [In all their rule . . . there was but this one clause to be observed, DO WHAT THOU WILT. Because men that are free, well-born, well-bred, and conversant in honest companies, have naturally an instinct and spur that prompteth them unto virtuous actions, and withdraws them from vice, which is called honour. – T. Urquhart tr.]
234. That is, well-born in the higher sense of the word, since Rabelais, son of the innkeeper of Chinon, has no reason to assign any privilege to the nobleman. – The preaching of the Gospel, which is mentioned in the inscription on the gate of the abbey, would hardly fit with the rest of the life of the Thelemites; it must be understood in a negative sense, as defiance of the Roman Church.

manifested itself in Italy. How often, and against what passionate attacks of selfishness it won the day, we do not quite know, and therefore no human judgment can estimate with certainty the absolute moral value of the nation.

A force that we must constantly take into account in considering the morality of the more highly developed Italian of this period is that of the imagination. It, more than anything else, gives to his virtues and vices a peculiar color, and under its influence his unbridled egotism shows itself in its most terrible form.

The force of his imagination explains, for example, the fact that he was the first gambler on a large scale in modern times. Images of future wealth and enjoyment rose in such lifelike colors before his eyes, that he was ready to hazard everything to reach them. The Mohammedan nations would doubtless have preceded him in this respect, had not the Koran from the beginning set up the prohibition against gambling as a chief safeguard of Islamic morals, and directed the imagination of its followers to the search after buried treasures. In Italy the passion for play reached an intensity that often threatened or shattered the existence of the gambler. At the end of the fourteenth century Florence had already had its Casanova, a certain Buonaccorso Pitti who, in the course of his incessant journeys as merchant, political agent, diplomat, and professional gambler, won and lost sums so enormous that only princes like the Dukes of Brabant, Bavaria, and Savoy could play with him. Even that great lottery bank, as the Roman Curia was called, accustomed people to a need of excitement, which found its release in dice games during the intervals between one intrigue and another. Once, for example, Franceschetto Cibo, in two games with Cardinal Raffaello Riario, lost 14,000 ducats, and then complained to the Pope that his opponent had cheated him. As we know, Italy subsequently became the home of the lottery.

It was also imagination that gave vengeance its special character. The sense of justice was exactly the same throughout Europe, and any violation of it, as much as it remained unpunished, must have been felt in the same manner. But other nations, though they found it no easier to forgive, nevertheless forgot more easily, while the Italian imagination kept the picture of the wrong alive with frightful vividness.[235] The fact that, according to the popular morality, the avenging

235. This opinion of the gifted Stendhal (*The Charterhouse of Parma*) seems to me to rest on profound psychological observation.

of blood was a duty, and a duty often performed in the most monstrous way, gave this passion a peculiar and still firmer basis. The government and the tribunals recognized its existence and justification, and sought only to keep it within certain limits. Even among the peasantry there were Thyestean banquets and mutual assassination on the widest scale. Let us look at only one example.

In the district of Acquapendente three young shepherds were watching the cattle, and one of them said: "Let us find out how people are hanged." While one was sitting on the shoulders of the other, and the third, after fastening the rope round the neck of the first, was tying it to an oak, a wolf came, and the two who were free ran away and left the other hanging. Afterward they found him dead, and buried him. On the Sunday his father came to bring him bread, and one of the two confessed what had happened, and showed him the grave. The old man then killed him with a knife, cut him up, brought away the liver, and entertained the boy's father with it at home. After dinner, he told him whose liver he had eaten. Hereupon began a series of reciprocal murders between the two families, and within a month thirty-six persons were killed, women as well as men.

And such vendettas, handed down from father to son and extending to friends and distant relations, extended to the upper classes also. Chronicles as well as novels of the period are full of such examples, especially of vengeance taken for the violation of women. The classic land for these feuds was Romagna, where the vendetta was interwoven with intrigues and party divisions of every conceivable sort. The popular legends present an awful picture of the savagery that seized this brave and energetic people. As, for example, the story of a nobleman at Ravenna, who had got all his enemies together in a tower, and could have burned them; instead of which he let them out, embraced them, and entertained them sumptuously; whereupon shame drove them mad, and they conspired against him. Pious and saintly monks exhorted unceasingly to reconciliation, but they can scarcely have done more than restrain to a certain extent the feuds already established; their influence hardly prevented the growth of new ones. The novelists often describe this effect of religion, the sentiments of generosity and forgiveness that were suddenly awakened, and then paralyzed by the force of what had once been done and could never be undone. The Pope himself was not always lucky as a peacemaker: "Pope Paul II desired that the quarrel between Antonio Caffarello and the family of Alberino should cease, and ordered Giovanni Alberino and

Antonio Caffarello to come before him, bade them kiss one another, and threatened them with a fine of 2,000 ducats if they harmed each other again, and two days later Antonio was stabbed by the same Giacomo Alberino, son of Giovanni, who had wounded him once before; and Pope Paul was full of anger, and confiscated the goods of Alberino, and destroyed his houses, and banished father and son from Rome." The oaths and ceremonies by which reconciled enemies attempted to guard themselves against a relapse are sometimes utterly horrible. When the parties of the Nove and the Popolari met and kissed one another by twos in the cathedral at Siena on New Year's Eve, 1494, an oath was read by which all salvation in time and eternity was denied to the future violator of the treaty, "an oath more astonishing and dreadful than had ever been heard." Even the last consolations of religion in the hour of death were to turn to the damnation of the man who would break the oath. It is clear, however, that such a ceremony represents the despairing mood of the mediators and does not offer any real guarantee of peace, since the truest reconciliation has the least need of such oaths.

This need of personal vengeance felt by the cultivated and highly placed Italian, resting on the solid basis of an analogous popular custom, was played out in thousands of ways and received, as we can tell from the novelists, the unqualified approval of public opinion. It was unanimously agreed that in those cases of injuries and insults for which Italian justice offered no redress, and, even more, in those cases against which no human law can ever adequately provide, each man was free to take the law into his own hands. Only there must be art in the vengeance, and the satisfaction must be compounded of material injury and moral humiliation of the offender. A mere brutal, clumsy triumph of force was held by public opinion to be no satisfaction. The whole man, with his sense of fame and scorn, must triumph, not only his fist.

The Italian of that time shrank, it is true, from no dissimulation in order to attain his ends, but he was wholly free from hypocrisy in matters of principle. In these he attempted to deceive neither himself nor others. Accordingly, even this revenge was declared with perfect frankness to be a necessity of human nature. Coolheaded people declared that it was most worthy of praise when it was disengaged from passion and performed simply from motives of expedience, "in order that others may learn to leave us unharmed." Yet such instances must have formed only a small minority in comparison with those in which passion sought an outlet. This sort of revenge clearly differs from the avenging of blood; whereas the latter keeps more or less within the limits of retaliation—the *ius talionis*—the former necessarily goes much further, not only requiring the sanction of the sense of justice, but craving admiration, and even striving to get the laugh on its own side.

This is why men were willing to wait so long for their revenge. A *bella vendetta* generally demanded a combination of circumstances for which it was necessary to wait patiently. The gradual ripening of such opportunities is described by the novelists with heartfelt delight.

There is no need to discuss the morality of actions in which plaintiff and judge are the same person. If this Italian thirst for vengeance is to be vindicated at all, it must be by proving the existence of a corresponding national virtue, namely gratitude. The same force of imagination that retains and magnifies wrong once suffered, might also be expected to keep alive the memory of kindness received. It will never be possible to prove this with regard to the nation as a whole, though traces of it may be seen in the Italian character of today. The gratitude shown by the inferior classes for kind treatment and the good memory of the upper for politeness in social life are instances of this.

This relation between the imagination and the moral qualities of the Italian repeats itself continually. If we find more cold calculation in cases where the Northerner would follow his impulses, this is because individual development in Italy was not only more marked and earlier in point of time, but also far more frequent. Where this is the case in other countries, the results also are analogous; for example, the early emancipation of the young from domestic and paternal authority is common to North America and Italy. Later, in the more generous natures, a tie of freer affection grows up between parents and children.

It is, in fact, extremely difficult to judge other nations in the sphere of character and feeling. In these respects a people may be highly developed, and yet in a manner so strange that a foreigner is utterly unable to understand it. Perhaps all the nations of the West are equally favored in this respect.

But where the imagination exercised the most powerful and despotic influence on morals was in the illicit intercourse of the two sexes. It is well known that the Middle Ages had no aversion to common prostitution, before the appearance of syphilis, and a comparative study of prostitution does not belong here. What seems characteristic of Renaissance Italy, however, is that here marriage and its rights were more often and more deliberately trampled underfoot than anywhere else. The girls of the higher classes, carefully secluded, are of no moment; all passion was directed to the married women.

Under these circumstances it is remarkable that, so far as we know, there was no decrease in the marriage rate, and that family life by no means underwent that disorganization which a similar state of things would have produced in the North. Men wished to live as they pleased, but by no means to renounce the family, even when they were not sure that it was all their own. Nor did the race decline, either physically or mentally, because of this—for that apparent intellectual deterioration which showed itself toward the middle of the sixteenth century may be accounted for by political and ecclesiastical causes, even if we are not to assume that the circle of achievements possible to the Renaissance had been completed. Notwithstanding their profligacy, the Italians continued to be, physically and mentally, one of the healthiest populations in Europe,[236] and have retained this position, with improved morals, down to our own time.

When we look more closely at the ethics of love at the time of the Renaissance, we are struck by a remarkable contrast. The novelists and comic poets give the impression that love consists only of sensual enjoyment, and that to win this, all means, tragic or comic, are not only permitted but are interesting in proportion to their audacity and unscrupulousness. But if we turn to the better lyric poets and writers of dialogues, we find a deep and spiritual passion of the noblest kind, whose ultimate and highest expression is a revival of the ancient belief in an original unity of souls in the Divine Being. And both modes of feeling were genuine then, and could coexist in the same individual. It is not exactly laudable but it is a fact that, in the cultivated man of modern times, this coexistence of feelings on various levels can be present not merely unconsciously, but may also manifest itself openly, and even artistically. Modern man, like the man of antiquity, is in this respect, too, a microcosm, which medieval man was not and could not be.

To begin, the morality of the novelists. They are chiefly

---

236. It is true that when the Spanish rule was fully established there was a certain decline in population. Had this been due to the demoralization of the people, it would have appeared much earlier.

concerned, as we have said, with married women and, consequently, adultery.

Of greatest importance to this subject is the opinion we expressed above on the equality of the sexes. The highly developed and cultivated woman conducted herself with a freedom unknown in Northern countries; and her unfaithfulness did not disastrously upset her life, so long as she protected herself from outward consequences. The husband's claim on her fidelity did not have that firm foundation which it acquired in the North through the poetry and passion of courtship and betrothal. After the briefest acquaintance with her future husband, the young wife quit the convent or the paternal roof and only then did she enter the world, in which her character began to develop rapidly. This is the chief reason the rights of the husband were only conditional, and even the man who regarded them as a *ius quaesitum* [unnatural law] thought only of the outward conditions of the contract, not of the affections. The beautiful young wife of an old man sends back the presents and letters of a youthful lover, firmly resolved to keep her honor *(honestà)*. "But she rejoiced in the love of the youth for his great excellence; and she perceived that a noble woman may love a man of merit without loss to her honor." But how short is the road from such a distinction to a complete surrender.

Indeed, the latter seemed as good as justified when there was unfaithfulness on the part of the husband. The woman, conscious of her own dignity, experienced this not only as a pain, but also as humiliation and deceit, and set to work, often with the calmest consciousness of what she was about, to devise the vengeance the husband deserved. Her tact had to decide the measure of punishment suited to the particular case. The deepest wound might, for example, prepare the way for a reconciliation and a peaceful life in the future, if only it remained secret. The novelists, who experienced such things themselves or invented them according to the spirit of their time, are full of admiration when the vengeance is skillfully adapted to the particular case— when it is a work of art. Of course, the husband never really recognized this right of retaliation, and submitted to it only from fear or prudence. Where these motives were absent, where his wife's unfaithfulness exposed him or might expose him to the derision of outsiders, the affair became tragic. Violent vengeance and murder were not rare. It is characteristic of the real motive for these deeds, that not only the husband, but the brothers [237] and the father of the woman not only felt justified in taking vengeance, but bound to take it. Jealousy, therefore, had nothing to do with the matter, moral reprobation little; the chief reason was the wish to spoil the triumph of others. "Nowadays," says Bandello, "we see a woman poison her husband to gratify her lusts, thinking that then, as a widow, she will be able to do whatever she likes. Another, fearing the discovery of an illicit amour, has her husband murdered by her lover. Then fathers, brothers, and husbands rise to extirpate the shame with poison, with the sword, and by every other means, and women still follow their passions, careless of their lives and their honor." Another time, in milder strain, he exclaims: "If only we were not forced every day to hear: this one has murdered his wife because he suspected her of infidility; that one has killed his daughter because of a secret marriage; that one has had his sister murdered because she would not marry as he wished! It is great cruelty that we claim the right to do whatever we please and will not allow the poor women to do the same. If they do anything which does not please us, there we are at once with cords and daggers and poison. What folly it is of men to suppose that their own and their house's honor depend on the appetite of a woman!" The tragedy in which such affairs commonly ended was so well known that the novelist looked on the threatened gallant as a dead man, even while he went about alive and merry. The physician and lute player Antonio Bologna had secretly married the widowed Duchess of Amalfi, of the house of Aragon. Soon afterward her brothers seized both her and her children, and murdered them in a castle. Antonio, ignorant of their fate and still cherishing the hope of seeing them again, was staying at Milan, closely watched by hired assassins, and one day at a party of Ippolita Sforza sang to the accompaniment of his lute the story of his misfortunes. A friend of the house, Delio, "told the story up to this point to Scipione Atellano, and added that he would make it the subject of a novel, since he knew for a fact that Antonio would be murdered." The manner in which this took place, almost under the eyes of both Delio and Atellano, is movingly described by Bandello.

Meanwhile, however, the novelists always sympathize with all the ingenious, comic, and cunning features that attend

237. There is a particularly gruesome example of the vengeance taken by a brother at Perugia in the year 1455. The brother forces the gallant to tear out the sister's eyes, and then beats him from the place. True, the family was a branch of the Oddi and the lover was merely a ropemaker.

adultery. They describe with delight how the lover manages to hide himself in the house, all the means and devices by which he communicates with his mistress, the boxes with cushions and sweetmeats in which he can be hidden and transported, etc. The deceived husband is described sometimes as a fool to be laughed at, sometimes as a bloodthirsty avenger of his honor; there is no third situation except when the woman is portrayed as wicked and cruel, and the husband or lover is the innocent victim. It should be noted, however, that narratives of the latter kind are not actually novels, but warning examples taken from real life.

With the Spaniardization of Italian life during the course of the sixteenth century, the means with which jealousy was satisfied perhaps became more violent. But this new phase must be distinguished from the punishment of infidelity which had existed before, and which had been founded in the spirit of the Italian Renaissance itself. As the influence of Spain declined, these excesses of jealousy declined also, till toward the end of the seventeenth century they were replaced by their exact opposite, by that indifference which regarded the *cicisbeo* [gallant] as an indispensable figure in every household, and took no offense at one or two concurrent lovers (*patiti* [sufferers]).

But who can undertake to compare the vast sum of wickedness that all these facts imply, with what happened in other countries? Was the marriage tie, for instance, really more sacred in France during the fifteenth century than in Italy? The fabliaux and farces make us doubt it, and lead us to believe that unfaithfulness was equally common, but its tragic consequences were less frequent, because the individual was less developed and his claims were less. In fact, there might be evidence in favor of the Germanic peoples, namely, the social freedom enjoyed by girls and women, which impressed Italian travelers so pleasantly in England and in the Netherlands. And yet we must not attach too much importance to this. Unfaithfulness was certainly just as frequent, and here, too, the cultivated man drove it to tragedy. We have only to remember how the Northern princes of that time dealt with their wives on the first suspicion of infidelity.

But it was not merely the sensual desire, not merely the vulgar appetite of the ordinary man that trespassed upon forbidden ground among the Italians of that day, but also the best and noblest passions; and this, not only because the unmarried girl did not appear in society, but also because it was precisely the complete man who was most strongly attracted by the woman whom marriage had developed. These are the men who struck the loftiest notes of lyrical poetry, and who have attempted in their treatises and dialogues to give us an idealized image of the devouring passion: *l'amor divino* [divine love]. When they complain of the cruelty of the winged god, they are not only thinking of the coyness or hardheartedness of the loved one, but also of the unlawfulness of the passion itself. They seek to rise above this misfortune by that spiritualization of love which found a support in the Platonic doctrine of the soul and which found its most famous representative in Pietro Bembo. His thoughts on this subject are set forth directly in the third book of his *Asolani*, and indirectly by Castiglione, who puts in his mouth the splendid speech with which the fourth book of the *Courtier* concludes. Neither of these writers was a stoic in his conduct, but at that time it meant something to be a famous and yet a good man, and this praise can be denied to neither of them; their contemporaries accepted what these men said as a true expression of their feeling, and thus we should not despise it as affectation. Those who take the trouble to study the speech in the *Courtier* will see how poor an idea of it can be given by an extract. There were at that time several distinguished women in Italy, who owed their celebrity chiefly to relations of this kind, such as Giulia Gonzaga, Veronica da Correggio, and, above all, Vittoria Colonna. The land of profligates and scoffers respected these women and this sort of love—what more can be said in their favor? Who can tell how much vanity had to do with the matter, how far Vittoria was flattered to hear around her the sublimated utterances of hopeless love from the most famous men in Italy. If the thing occasionally became a fashion, it was still no trifling praise for Vittoria that she, as least, never went out of fashion, and in her last years still produced the most profound impressions. – It was long before other countries had anything similar to show.

The imagination then, which governed this people more than any other, is one general reason why the course of every passion was violent, and why the means used for the gratification of passion were often criminal. There is a violence that cannot control itself because it is born of weakness; but what we find in Italy is the corruption of powerful natures. Sometimes this corruption assumes a colossal shape, and crime seems to acquire almost a personal existence of its own.

Restraints were few. Everyone, even the common people, felt themselves inwardly emancipated from the control of the illegitimate State that was founded on violence, and its police, and no one believed any longer in the justice of the law. When a murder was committed, the sympathies of the people were instinctively on the side of the murderer even before the circumstances of the case were known. A proud, manly bearing before and at the execution excited such admiration that the narrator often forgets to tell us why the victim was condemned. But when to this inward contempt of law and to the countless grudges and enmities that called for satisfaction we add the impunity that crime enjoyed during times of political disturbance, we can only wonder that the State and society were not dissolved. Crises of this kind occurred at Naples, during the transition from the Aragonese to the French and Spanish rule, and at Milan, on the repeated expulsions and returns of the Sforza; at such times those men who had never in their hearts recognized the bonds of law and society came forward and gave free play to their instincts of murder and rape. Let us take, by way of example, a picture drawn from a humbler sphere.

About the year 1480, when the Duchy of Milan was suffering from the disorders that followed the death of Galeazzo Maria Sforza, all safety ceased in the provincial cities. This was the case in Parma, where the Milanese Governor, terrified by threats of murder, opened the jails and let loose the most abandoned criminals, where burglary, the demolition of houses, public assassination and murders became everyday occurrences, where at first masked criminals prowled about singly, then large gangs of armed men went boldly to work every night. Threatening letters, satires, and scandalous jests circulated freely; and a sonnet in ridicule of the Government seems to have roused its indignation far more than the frightful condition of the city The fact that in many churches the sacred vessels with the host were stolen betrays still another quality and direction of these outrages. It is impossible to say what would happen now in any country of the world if the government and police ceased to act and yet, by their presence, hindered the establishment of a provisional authority; but what occurred in Italy at that time has its special character because of the great share revenge had in it.

In general, it would seem that in Renaissance Italy great crimes were commoner than in other countries even in quiet times. We may, it is true, be misled by the fact that we have far fuller details on such matters here than elsewhere,

and that the same force of imagination that gave a special
character to crimes actually committed invented much that
never really happened. The amount of violence was perhaps
as great elsewhere. It is hard to say for certain, whether
men were any safer, whether human life was any better
protected in the powerful, wealthy Germany of 1500, with
its robber knights, extortionate beggars, and daring highwaymen. But one thing is certain, that premeditated crimes,
committed professionally and for hire by third parties, occurred in Italy with great and appalling frequency.

So far as regards brigandage, Italy, especially in the more
fortunate provinces, such as Tuscany, was certainly not
more, and probably less, troubled than the countries of the
North. But there are characteristically Italian figures. It
would be hard, for instance, to find anywhere else the case
of priests gradually driven by passion from one excess to
another, till at last they became leaders of bands of robbers.
That age offers us the following example, among others.
On August 12, 1495, the priest Don Niccolò de' Pelegati of
Figarolo was imprisoned in an iron cage outside the tower
of San Giuliano at Ferrara. He had twice celebrated his first
mass; the first time he had committed a murder on the same
day, but afterward received absolution at Rome; then he
killed four people and married two wives, with whom he
traveled about. Subsequently he took part in many assassina-
tions, violated women, carried others away by force, plundered
far and wide, murdered many more, and infested the territory
of Ferrara with a band of followers in uniform, extorting
food and shelter by every sort of violence. – When we think
of what all this implies, the guilt of the priests assumes
massive proportions. There were plenty of murderers and
other malefactors among the priests and monks who had
many privileges and little supervision—but hardly a second
Pelegati. It is another matter, though by no means creditable,
when ruined characters sheltered themselves in the cowl in
order to escape the arm of the law, as, for example, the
corsair Massuccio knew in a convent at Naples. What the
real truth was with regard to Pope John XXII in this
respect, is not known with certainty.[238]

The age of the famous brigand chief did not begin till

238. If in his youth he was a corsair in the war between the two
lines of Anjou for the possession of Naples, he may have become
one as a political partisan, which, according to the ideas of the
time, implied no dishonor. Archbishop Paolo Fregoso of Genoa,
in the second half of the fifteenth century, probably allowed
himself much more.

later, in the seventeenth century, when the political strife of Guelph and Ghibelline, of Frenchman and Spaniard no longer agitated the country. The robber then took the place of the partisan.

In certain districts of Italy, where civilization had made little progress, the country people were disposed to murder any stranger who fell into their hands. This was especially the case in the more remote parts of the Kingdom of Naples, where the barbarism probably dated from the days of the Roman latifundia, and when the stranger and the enemy, *hospes* and *hostis,* were in all good faith held to be the same. These people were not at all irreligious. A herdsman once appeared in great trouble at the confessional, avowing that, while making cheese during Lent, a few drops of milk had found their way into his mouth. The confessor, familiar with the customs of the country, discovered in the course of his examination that the penitent and his friends often robbed and murdered travelers, but that this, through force of habit, did not give rise to twinges of conscience. We have already mentioned to what degree of barbarism the peasants of other regions could sink in times of political confusion.

A worse sympton than brigandage of the morality of that time was the frequency of paid assassination. In this respect Naples, it was admitted, stood at the head of all the other cities. "Nothing," says Pontano, "is cheaper here than human life." But other districts could show a terrible list of these crimes. It is hard, of course, to classify them according to motive, since political expediency, personal hatred, party hostility, fear, and revenge were intermingled. It is to the great honor of the Florentines, the most highly developed people of Italy, that offenses of this kind occurred more rarely among them than anywhere else,[239] perhaps because there was a justice at hand for legitimate grievances that was recognized by all, or because the higher culture of the individual gave him different views as to the right of men to interfere with the decrees of fate. In Florence, if anywhere, men were able to feel the incalculable consequences of a deed of blood, and to understand how uncertain the author of a so-called profitable crime is of any true and lasting gain. After the fall of Florentine liberty, assassination, especially by hired agents, seems to have increased rapidly, and continued till the government of Cosimo I had attained

239. Absolute proof of this cannot be given, but few murders are mentioned, and the imagination of the Florentine writers of the best period is not filled with this kind of suspicion.

such strength that the police were at last able to repress it.

Elsewhere in Italy the rate of paid crimes probably depended on the number of powerful and solvent buyers. No one would dream of making a statistical account, yet if only a fraction of the deaths that rumor attributed to violence were actually murders, we arrive at a huge sum. The worst example was set by princes and governments, who without the faintest scruple reckoned murder as one of the instruments of their power. It did not require a Cesare Borgia; the Sforza, the Aragonese monarchs, and, later, even the agents of Charles V resorted to it whenever it suited their purpose.

The imagination of the people gradually became so accustomed to facts of this kind that the death of any powerful man was seldom attributed to natural causes. There were certainly absurd notions current with regard to the effect of various poisons. There may be some truth in the story of that terrible white powder used by the Borgias, which did its work at the end of a definite period, and it is possible that it really was a *venenum atterminatum* [measured poison] that the Prince of Salerno handed to the Cardinal of Aragon, with the words: "In a few days you will die, because your father, King Ferrante, wanted to trample on us all." But the poisoned letter that Caterina Riario sent to Pope Alexander VI would hardly have caused his death even if he had read it; and when Alfonso the Great was warned by his physicians not to read the Livy that Cosimo de' Medici had presented to him, he told them rightly not to talk like fools. Nor can that poison with which the secretary of Piccinino wished to anoint the sedan chair of Pius II have affected any other organ than the imagination. The proportion which mineral and vegetable poisons bore to one another cannot be ascertained precisely. The liquid with which the painter Rosso Fiorentino destroyed himself (1541) was evidently a powerful acid, which would have been impossible to administer to another person without his knowledge.[240] – The use of weapons, especially of the dagger for secret violence, was habitual among the powerful men of Milan, Naples, and other cities, since among the crowds of armed retainers who were necessary for the personal safety of the great, sheer idleness had to lead, now and again, to a lust for blood. Many a deed of horror would never have been committed, had not the master known that he had only to give a sign to one or another of his followers.

240. Vasari, Life of Il Rosso.

Among the secret means of destruction—so as intention—we find magic, though practiced Where *malefici* [witchcraft], *malie* [bewitchments], e mentioned, they appear mainly as a means of heaping tional horror on some hated or loathsome individual. At th courts of France and England in the fourteenth and fifteenth centuries, magic practiced with a view to death and destruction played a far more important part than among the upper classes in Italy.

Finally, we find in this country, where individuality of every sort attained its highest development, instances of that ideal and absolute wickedness which delights in crimes for their own sake and not as means to an end, or at any rate as means to ends that are beyond the realm of normal psychology.

At first glance it would seen that some of the *condottieri* [241] belong among these appalling figures, a Braccio da Montone, a Tiberto Brandolino, and even a Werner von Urslingen whose silver hauberk bore the inscription: Enemy of God, of pity, and of mercy. In this class of men we have the earliest instances of criminals deliberately repudiating every moral restraint. Yet we shall be more reserved in our judgment when we remember that the worst part of their guilt—in the estimate of those who record it—lay in their defiance of spiritual threats and penalties, and that it is this that gives them that sinister air which seems to surround them. In the case of Braccio, the hatred of the Church went so far that he was infuriated at the sight of monks at their psalms, and had them thrown down from the top of a tower, "but he was loyal to his soldiers and a great general." As a rule, the crimes of the *condottieri* were committed to gain some advantage, and must be attributed to their highly demoralizing position. Even their apparently gratuitous cruelty generally had its purpose, if only to strike terror. The barbarities of the House of Aragon, as we have seen, were due mainly to fear and to the desire for vengeance. A thirst for blood for its own sake, a devilish delight in destruction, is exemplified best in the case of the Spaniard Cesare Borgia, whose cruelties were certainly out of all proportion to the end he had in view. A similar disinterested love of evil may be detected in Sigismondo Malatesta, tyrant of Rimini. It

241. Ezzelino da Romano might be put first, were it not that he acted under the influence of ambitious motives and astrological delusions.

ɔman Curia,[242] but the verdict of history
ɔf repeated murder, rape, adultery, incest,
and treason. But the most shocking crime
ɪral attempt on his own son Roberto, who
his drawn dagger—may well have been
erely of moral corruption, but perhaps of
astrological superstition. The same conjecture
has ᴜₑₑ___ to account for the rape of the Bishop of
Fano by Pierluigi Farnese of Parma, son of Paul III.

If we now attempt to sum up the principal features of the
Italian character of that time, as we know it from a study
of the life of the upper classes, we shall obtain something
like the following. The fundamental defect of this character
was at the same time a condition of its greatness, namely,
excessive individualism. The individual first inwardly cast
off the authority of a State that was in most cases tyrannical
and illegitimate, and what he then thought and did was,
rightly or wrongly, called treason. The sight of victorious
egotism in others drove him to defend his own right in his
own way. And, while he thought he was restoring his inner
peace, he fell, through the vengeance that he executed, into
the hands of the powers of darkness. His love was directed
mainly to an equally cultivated individual, namely, to his
neighbor's wife. In face of all objective facts, of all kinds of
laws and restraints, he retained the feeling of his own sovereignty, and in each single instance formed his decision
independently, depending only on whether his sense of honor
and advantage dictated passion or calculation, revenge or
renunciation.

If, therefore, egotism is, in its wider as well as its narrower
sense, the root and fountain of all evil, this is the reason the
more highly developed Italian of that time was more inclined
to wickedness than the members of other nations.

But this individual development did not come to him
through any fault of his own, but rather through a historical
necessity. It did not come only to him, but also, and chiefly
by means of Italian culture, to the other nations of Europe,
and has since then constituted the higher atmosphere that
they breathe. In itself it is neither good nor bad, but
necessary; within it there has grown up a modern standard
of good and evil—a sense of moral responsibility—which is
essentially different from that of the Middle Ages.

But the Italian of the Renaissance had to bear the first
mighty surging of a new age. Through his gifts and his

242. *The Commentaries of Pius II*, Book VII.

passions he became the most characteristic representative of
all the heights and all the depths of his time. By the side
of profound corruption there developed human personalities
of the noblest harmony and an artistic splendor that shed
on the life of man a luster that neither antiquity nor medievalism could or would bestow.

The morality of a people stands in the closest connection
with its consciousness of God, that is, with its firmer or
weaker faith in a divine government of the world, whether
this faith views the world as destined to happiness or to
misery and speedy destruction.[243] The nonbelief prevalent
in Italy at that time is notorious, and whoever takes the
trouble to look for proofs, will find them by the hundred. Our
present task, here as elsewhere, is to separate and discrim-
inate; refraining here, too, from an absolute and final verdict.

The belief in God at earlier times had its source and chief
support in Christianity and the outward symbol of its power,
the Church. When the Church became corrupt, men ought to
have drawn a distinction and kept their religion in spite of it.
But this is more easily said than done. It is not every people
who is calm enough, or dull enough, to tolerate a lasting
contradiction between a principle and its outward expression.
But history does not record a heavier responsibility than that
which rests upon the decaying Church. By the most violent
means she had set up as absolute truth a doctrine that she
had distorted in the interest of her omnipotence, and secure
in the sense of her inviolability, she abandoned herself to the
most scandalous profligacy. In order to maintain herself in
this state, she leveled mortal blows against the conscience
and the intellect of nations, and drove multitudes of the
noblest spirits, whom she had inwardly estranged, into the
arms of nonbelief and despair.

Here we are faced with the question: Why did not Italy,
intellectually so great, react more energetically against the
hierarchy; why did she not accomplish a reformation similar
to that which occurred in Germany, and accomplish it at an
earlier date?

The answer seems to be: The Italian mind never went
further than the denial of the hierarchy, whereas the origin

---

243. On which point feeling differs according to the place and
the people. The Renaissance prevailed in times and in cities where
the tendency was to enjoy life heartily. The general darkening
of the spirits of thoughtful men did not begin to show itself till
the time of the foreign supremacy in the sixteenth century.

and the vigor of the German Reformation was due to its positive religious doctrines, most of all to the doctrines of justification by faith and of the inefficacy of good works.

It is certain that these doctrines affected Italy only through the influence of Germany, and much too late, since the power of Spain was sufficiently great to root them out without difficulty, partly by itself and partly by means of the Papacy and its instruments.[244] Nevertheless, in the earlier religious movements of Italy, from the Mystics of the thirteenth century down to Savonarola, there was a large amount of positive religious doctrine which, like the very definite Christianity of the Huguenots, failed to achieve success only because circumstances were against it. The details of the outbreak and development of such colossal events like the Reformation of the sixteenth century elude the deductions of the philosophers, however clearly their general necessity may be demonstrated. The life of the spirit, its sudden flashes, its expansions, its pauses, must forever remain a mystery, since we can only know this or that force at work in it, never all of them.

The feeling of the upper and middle classes in Italy with regard to the Church at the culmination of the Renaissance was compounded of deep and contemptuous aversion, of acquiescence in the outward ecclesiastical customs that entered into daily life, and of a sense of dependence on sacraments and ceremonies. The great personal influence of religious preachers may be added as a fact characteristic of Italy.

How the hostility of the Italians to the hierarchy is revealed in literature and history, especially from the time of Dante, has been fully treated by several writers. We have already had something to say on the attitude of public opinion with regard to the Papacy. Those who want the strongest evidence from the best authorities, can find it in the famous passages of Machiavelli's *Discourses* and in (the unabridged edition of) Guicciardini. Outside the Roman Curia, there seems to have been some respect chiefly for the better bishops,[245] and for many of the parochial clergy. On the other hand, the mere holders of benefices, the canons, and

244. What is termed the spirit of the Counter Reformation was developed in Spain some time before the Reformation itself, and chiefly through the sharp suveillance and partial reorganization of the Church under Ferdinand and Isabella.
245. It should be noted that the novelists and other satirists almost never mention the bishops, although they could have altered the place names and included them with all the rest.

the monks were held in almost universal suspicion, and were often the objects of the most scandalous slander, which extended to their whole order.

It has been said that the monks were made the scapegoats for the whole clergy because only they could be ridiculed without danger. But this is absolutely incorrect. They are so frequent in the novels and comedies, because these forms of literature need fixed and well-known types where the imagination of the reader can easily fill in an outline. Besides which, the novelists do not as a fact spare the secular clergy.[246] In the third place, we have ample proof in the rest of Italian literature of how boldly men spoke about the Papacy and the Roman Curia; in works of imagination we cannot expect to find criticism of this kind. Fourthly, even the monks were occasionally capable of taking a terrible vengeance.

So much, however, is true; the monks were the most unpopular class of all, and they were reckoned as living proof of the worthlessness of conventual life, of the whole ecclesiastical organization, of the system of dogma, indeed, of religion altogether, whichever way men pleased, rightly or wrongly, to draw their conclusions. We may also assume that Italy retained a clearer recollection of the origin of the two great mendicant orders than other countries, and had not forgotten that they were the chief agents in the reaction against what is called the heresy of the thirteenth century, that is, against an early and vigorous movement of the modern Italian spirit. And that spiritual policing which was permanently entrusted to the Dominicans certainly never excited any other feeling than secret hatred and contempt.

After reading the *Decameron* and the novels of Franco Sacchetti, we might imagine that the vocabulary of abuse directed at the monks and nuns was exhausted. But toward the time of the Reformation this abuse became still fiercer. We prefer to omit Aretino who, in the *Ragionamenti*, uses conventual life merely as a pretext for giving free play to his own poisonous nature. But there is one author we must

246. Bandello, e.g., prefaces [a novel] with the statement that the vice of avarice is more discreditable to priests than to any other class of men, since they have no families to provide for. On this ground he justifies the disgraceful attack made on a parsonage by two soldiers or brigands at the order of a young gentleman, on which occasion a sheep was stolen from the stingy and gouty old priest. A single story of this kind illustrates the ideas by which men lived and acted better than all the dissertations in the world.

name, as typical of the rest—Massuccio, in the first ten of his fifty novels. They are written in a tone of deepest indignation, and with the purpose of making this indignation general, and are dedicated to men in the highest position, such as King Ferrante and Prince Alfonso of Naples. Many of the stories are old, and some are familiar to readers of Boccaccio. But others reflect, with frightful realism, the actual state of things at Naples. The way in which the priests deceive and plunder the people by means of spurious miracles, in addition to their own scandalous lives, is enough to drive any thoughtful observer to despair. Of the Minorite friars who traveled around collecting alms, he says: "They cheat, steal, and fornicate, and when they are at the end of their resources they set up as saints and work miracles, one displaying the cloak of St. Vincent, another the handwriting of St. Bernardino, a third the bridle of Capistrano's donkey. . . ." Others "provide themselves with confederates who pretend to be blind or afflicted with some mortal disease, and after touching the hem of the monk's cowl, or the relics which he carries, are suddenly healed before the eyes of the multitude. All then shout 'Misericordia,' the bells are rung, and the miracle is recorded in a solemn protocol." Or else a monk in the pulpit is denounced as a liar by another who stands below among the audience; the accuser is immediately possessed by the devil, and then healed by the preacher. The whole thing was a prearranged comedy, in which the principal with his assistant made so much money that he was able to buy a bishopric from a cardinal, on which the two confederates lived comfortably to the end of their days. Massuccio makes no great distinction between Franciscans and Dominicans, finding the one worth as little as the other. "And yet the foolish public lets itself be drawn into their hatreds and divisions, and quarrels about them in public places,[247] and calls itself *franceschino* or *domenichino*." The nuns are the exclusive property of the monks. Those nuns who have anything to do with the laity are prosecuted and put in prison, while others are formally wedded to monks, with the accompaniments of mass, a marriage contract, and a liberal indulgence in food and wine. "I myself," says the author, "have been there not once, but several times, and have seen it all with my own eyes. The nuns afterward bring forth pretty little monks or else use means to hinder

247. He adds: and in the *seggi,* i.e., the clubs into which the Neopolitan nobility was divided. – The rivalry of the two orders is often ridiculed.

that result. And if anyone charges me with falsehood, let him search the sewers of the nunneries well, and he will find there as many little bones as in Bethlehem at Herod's time." Such things, and more, are among the secrets of monastic life. The monks are by no means too strict with one another in the confessional, and impose a Paternoster for things for which they would refuse all absolution to a layman as if he were a heretic. "Therefore may the earth open and swallow up the wretches alive, together with those who protect them!" In another place Massuccio, remarking that the influence of the monks depends chiefly on the dread of another world, utters the following extraordinary wish: "The best punishment for them would be for God to abolish Purgatory; they would then receive no more alms, and would be forced to go back to their spades."

If men were free to write this way in the time of Ferrante, and to him, it is perhaps because the King himself had been incensed by a false miracle which had been palmed off on him. An attempt had been made to urge him to a persecution of the Jews, like the one in Spain, by producing a tablet with an inscription said to have been buried at Taranto and afterward dug up again. When he discovered the fraud, the monks defied him. He had also managed to detect and expose a pretended instance of fasting, as his father, Alfonso, had done before him. At least the court was no accomplice in maintaining these blind superstitions.

We have been quoting from an author who wrote in earnest, and he is by no means the only one of his kind. All Italian literature is full of ridicule and invective against the begging friars. It can hardly be doubted that the Renaissance would soon have destroyed these two orders, had it not been for the German Reformation and the Counter Reformation. Their saints and popular preachers could hardly have saved them. It would only have been necessary to come to an understanding at a favorable moment with a Pope such as Leo X, who despised the mendicant orders. If the spirit of the age found them ridiculous or repulsive, they could no longer be anything but an embarrassment to the Church. And who can say what fate awaited the Papacy itself, had the Reformation not saved it?

The influence that the Father Inquisitor of a Dominican monastery constantly exercised in the city where it was situated, was, in the latter part of the fifteenth century, just considerable enough to hamper and irritate cultivated people, but not strong enough to extort any lasting fear or obedience.[248] It was no longer possible, as it had been, to punish men for their thoughts, and those whose tongues wagged most impudently against the clergy could easily keep clear of heretical doctrine. Except when some powerful party had an end to serve (as in the case of Savonarola) or when there was a question of the use of magic (as was often the case in the cities of North Italy), we seldom read of men being burned at the stake at the end of the fifteenth and beginning of the sixteenth centuries. The Inquisitors were frequently satisfied, it seems, with the most superficial retraction, and at times the victim was taken out of their hands on the way to the place of execution. In Bologna (1452) the priest Niccolò da Verona had been publicly degraded on a wooden scaffold in front of San Domenico as a wizard and profaner of the sacraments, and was about to be led to the stake, when he was set free by a gang of armed men sent by Achille Malvezzi, a noted friend of heretics and violator of nuns. The legate, Cardinal Bessarion, was able to catch and hang only one of the party; Malvezzi lived on in peace.

It deserves to be noticed that the higher monastic orders— e.g., the Benedictines and their many branches—were, notwithstanding their great wealth and easy lives, far less disliked than the mendicant friars. For ten novels which treat of *frati* [friars], hardly one can be found in which a *monaco* [monk] is the subject and the victim. It was no small advantage to these orders that they were founded earlier, and not as an instrument of police, and that they did not interfere with private life. They contained men of learning, wit, and piety, but the average has been described by a member of it, Firenzuola, who says: "These well-fed gentlemen in their capacious cowls do not pass their time in barefooted journeys and sermons, but sit in elegant slippers with their hands crossed over their paunches, in charming cells wainscoted with cyprus wood. And when they are obliged to go somewhere, they ride comfortably, as if for their amusement, on mules and sleek, quiet horses. They do not overstrain their minds with the study of many books, for fear that knowledge might produce the pride of Lucifer in place of monkish simplicity."

Those who are familiar with the literature of that time will see that we have mentioned only what is absolutely

248. The story in Vasari, Life of Sandro Botticelli, shows that the Inquisition was sometimes treated jocularly. True, the *vicario* [vicar] mentioned here may have been the Archbishop's deputy rather than that of the Dominican Inquisitor.

necessary for the understanding of the subject.[249] That the reputation attaching to the monks and the secular clergy must have shattered the faith of multitudes in all that is sacred is, of course, obvious.

And some of the judgments that we read are terrible; in conclusion we will quote one of them, which has been published only lately and is still little known. The historian Guicciardini, who was for many years in the service of the Medicean Popes, says (1529) in his aphorisms:[250] "No man is more disgusted than I am with the ambition, the avarice, and the profligacy of the priests, not only because each of these vices is hateful in itself, but because each of them alone and all of them together are so little suited to those who profess a life that depends on God, and also because they are vices so opposed to one another, that they can coexist only in very singular natures. Nevertheless, my position under several Popes forced me to desire their greatness for the sake of my own interest. But for this, I should have loved Martin Luther as myself, not in order to free myself from the laws prescribed by the Christian religion, as generally interpreted and understood, but to see this swarm of scoundrels (*questa caterva di scelerati*) put in their proper place, so that they might live either without vices or without power."

The same Guicciardini believes, moreover, that we are in the dark as to all that is supernatural, that philisophers and theologians have nothing but nonsense to tell us about it, that miracles occur in every religion and prove the truth of none in particular, and that all of them may be explained as unfamiliar phenomena of nature. The faith that moves mountains, then common among the followers of Savonarola, is mentioned by Guicciardini as a curious phenomenon but without any bitter remark.

Against this hostile public opinion, the clergy and the monks had the great advantage that the people were used to them, and that their existence touched and was interwoven with the everyday existence of all. This is the advantage that every old and powerful institution possesses. Everybody had some cowled or frocked relative, some prospect of assistance or future gain from the treasure of the Church; and in the

---

249. Pius II was on principle in favor of abolishing the celibacy of the clergy. One of his favorite sentences was: *Sacerdotibus magna ratione sublatas nuptias maiori restituendas videri* [There was great reason for prohibiting priests from marrying, but there seems to be greater reason for permitting it again]. Platina, *The Lives of the Popes*.

250. *Ricordi*, no. 28.

center of Italy stood the Roman Curia, where men sometimes became rich in a moment. Yet it must never be forgotten that all this did not hinder people from writing and speaking freely. Indeed, the authors of the most scandalous satires were themselves monks, beneficed priests, etc. Poggio, who wrote the *facetiae*, was a clergyman; Francesco Berni held a canonry; Teofilo Folengo was a Benedictine;[251] Matteo Bandello, who ridiculed his own order, was a Dominican, and nephew of a general of this order. Were they encouraged by the sense that they ran no risk? Or did they feel an inward need to clear themselves personally from the infamy attached to their order? Or were they moved by that selfish pessimism which takes for its maxim, "it will last our time?" Perhaps there was a little of each. In the case of Folengo, the unmistakable influence of Lutheranism must be added.

The sense of dependence on rites and sacraments, which we have already mentioned in speaking of the Papacy, is not surprising among that part of the people which still believed in the Church. Among those who were more emancipated, it testifies to the strength of youthful impressions and to the magical force of traditional symbols. The universal desire of dying men—whoever they might be—for priestly absolution shows that the last remnants of the dread of hell had not, even in the case of that Vitellozzo, been entirely extinguished. It would hardly be possible to find a more instructive instance than this. The doctrine taught by the Church of the *character indelebilis* of the priesthood, independent of the personality of the priest, had so far borne fruit that it was possible to loathe the individual and still desire his spiritual gifts. It is true that there were defiant natures like Galeotto of Mirandola, who died unabsolved in 1499, after living for sixteen years under the ban of the Church. During this time the city, too, lay under an interdict, so that no mass was celebrated and no Christian burial took place.

A splendid contrast to all this is offered by the power exercised over the nation by its great preachers of repentance. Other countries of Europe were from time to time moved by the words of saintly monks, but only superficially in comparison with the periodic upheaval of the Italian conscience. The only man, in fact, who produced a similar effect in Germany during the fifteenth century, was an Italian born in the Abruzzi, Giovanni Capistrano.[252] In the North at that

---

251. By no means a faithful one.
252. He had with him a German and a Slavonian interpreter. St. Bernard had to use the same means when he preached in the Rhineland.

time, those natures which bear within them this religious vocation and this commanding earnestness had an intuitive and mystical aspect. In the South they were practical and expansive, and shared in the national gift of oratorical skill. The North produced an *Imitation of Christ,* which influenced quietly, at first only within the walls of the monastery, but influenced the ages; the South produced men who made on their fellows an immediate and mighty but passing impression.

This impression consisted chiefly in the awakening of the conscience. The sermons were moral exhortations, free from abstract notions and full of practical application, rendered more impressive by the saintly and ascetic character of the preacher and by the miracles which, even against his will, the inflamed imagination of the people attributed to him.[253] The most powerful argument was not the threat of Hell and Purgatory, but rather the living results of the *maledizione,* the temporal ruin wrought on the individual by the curse that clings to wrongdoing. The grieving of Christ and the saints has its consequences in this life. And only thus could men, sunk in passion and guilt, be brought to repentance and atonement, which was the chief object of these sermons.

Among these preachers of the fifteenth century were Bernardino da Siena, Alberto da Sarzana, Jacopo della Marca, Giovanni Capistrano, Roberto da Lecce, and others; and finally, Girolamo Savonarola. No prejudice was stronger than that against the mendicant friar; they overcame it. They were criticized and ridiculed by a scornful humanism;[254] but when they raised their voices, no one heard the humanists. The thing was no novelty, and the scoffing Florentines had already in the fourteenth century learned to caricature it whenever it appeared in the pulpit. But when Savonarola appeared, he carried the people so triumphantly with him, that soon all their beloved art and culture melted away in the furnace he lighted. Even the grossest profanation by hypocritical monks, who produced an effect in the audience by means of confederates, could not bring the thing itself into discredit. Men

253. Capistrano, for example, contented himself with making the sign of the cross over the thousands of sick persons brought to him, and with blessing them in the name of the Trinity and of his master St. Bernardino, after which some of them, not unnaturally, got well. The Brescian chronicle puts it this way: "He worked fine miracles, yet not so many as were told of him."
254. E.g., Poggio. He finds that they have an easy time of it, since they say the same thing in every city and send the people away more stupid than they came.

kept on laughing at the ordinary monkish sermons with their spurious miracles and manufactured relics, but did not cease to honor the great and genuine preachers. These are a true Italian speciality of the fifteenth century.

The order—generally that of St. Francis, and more particularly the so-called Observantines—sent them out as they were wanted. This was commonly the case when there was some important public or private feud in a city, or some alarming outbreak of violence, immorality, or disease. Once the reputation of a preacher was made, the cities were all anxious to hear him even without any special occasion. He went wherever his superiors sent him. A special form of this work was the preaching of a Crusade against the Turks; but here we are concerned primarily with the exhortations to repentance.

The order of the sermons, if a methodical order was observed, seems to have followed the customary list of the deadly sins. The more pressing, however, the occasion was, the more directly did the preacher make for his main point. He began perhaps in one of the great churches of the order, or in the cathedral. Soon the largest piazza was too small for the crowds that thronged to hear him, and he himself could hardly move without risking his life. The sermon was usually followed by a great procession; but even the principle officers of the city, who surrounded him, could barely save him from the multitude who kissed his hands and feet, and cut off fragments from his cowl.

The most immediate consequences, which were the easiest to accomplish, of the preacher's denunciations of usury, luxury, and scandalous fashions were the opening of the jails—which meant no more than the discharge of poor debtors—and the burning of various instruments of luxury and amusement, whether innocent or not. Among these were dice, cards, games of all kinds, written incantations, masks, musical instruments, song books, false hair, and so forth. All these were then, without doubt gracefully, arranged on a scaffold (talamo), a figure of the devil fastened to the top, and the whole set on fire.

Then came the turn of the more hardened consciences. Men who had not been near the confessional for years, now confessed. Ill-gotten gains were restored, and insults which might have drawn blood retracted. Orators like Bernardino da Siena entered diligently into all the details of the daily life of man, and the moral laws involved. Few theologians nowadays would feel tempted to give a morning sermon "on contracts, restitutions, the public debt (monte), and the por-

tioning of daughters," as he once did in the cathedral at
Florence. Imprudent preachers easily fell into the mistake
of attacking particular classes, professions, or offices with
such energy that the enraged hearers proceeded to violence
against those whom the preacher had denounced. A sermon
that Bernardino once preached in Rome (1424) had another
consequence besides a bonfire of vanities on the Capitol:
"After this," we read, "the witch Finicella was burned, because by her diabolical arts she had killed many children and
bewitched many other persons, and all Rome went to see
the sight."

But the most important aim of the preacher was, as has already been said, to reconcile enemies and persuade them to
give up thoughts of vengeance. Probably this end was seldom
attained till toward the close of a course of sermons, when the
tide of penitence flooded the city and the air resounded
with the cry of the whole people: "Misericordia!" – Then
followed those solemn embracings and treaties of peace,
which even previous bloodshed on both sides could not hinder.
Banished men were recalled to the city to take part in these
sacred transactions. It appears that these *paci* were on the
whole faithfully observed, even after the mood that prompted
them was over, and the memory of the monk was blessed
from generation to generation. But there were sometimes
terrible crises like those in the families Della Valle and Croce
in Rome (1482), where even the great Roberto da Lecce
raised his voice in vain. Shortly before Holy Week he had
preached to immense crowds in the square before the Minerva. But on the night before Maundy Thursday a terrible
combat took place in front of the Palazzo della Valle, near
the Ghetto. In the morning Pope Sixtus gave orders for its
destruction, and then performed the customary ceremonies
of the day. On Good Friday, Roberto preached again with
a crucifix in his hand; but he and his hearers could do nothing
but weep.

Violent, disintegrated natures often resolved to enter a
convent, under the impression made by these preachers.
Among such were not only brigands and criminals of every
sort, but soldiers without employment. This resolve was
stimulated by their admiration of the holy man, and by the
desire to copy at least his outward position.

The concluding sermon was a general benediction, summed up in the words: *la pace sia con voi* [peace be with you]!
Throngs of hearers accompanied the preacher to the next
city, and there listened for a second time to the whole course
of sermons.

The enormous influence exercised by these preachers made it important, both for the clergy and the government, not to have them as opponents; one means to this end was to permit only monks or priests who had received at least the lesser consecration to enter the pulpit, so that the order or corporation to which they belonged was, to some extent, responsible for them. But it was not easy to observe the rule strictly, since the Church and pulpit had long been used as a means of publicity in many ways—judicial, educational, and others—and since sermons were sometimes delivered by humanists and other laymen. There was, in addition, a dubious class of persons who were neither monks nor priests, but who had renounced the world—that is, the hermits who were so numerous in Italy and who appeared from time to time in the pulpit on their own authority, and often carried the people with them.[255] A case of this kind occurred at Milan in 1516, after the second French conquest, at a time, to be sure, when public order was much disturbed. A Tuscan hermit, possibly an adherent of Savonarola, maintained his place in the pulpit of the cathedral for many months, denounced the hierarchy with great violence, caused a new candelabrum and a new altar to be set up in the church, worked miracles, and only abandoned the field after a long and desperate struggle. During the decades in which the fate of Italy was decided, the spirit of prophecy was unusually active, and it was never confined, no matter where it appeared, to any one particular class. We know, for example, with what a tone of true prophetic defiance the hermits came forward before the sack of Rome. To make up for their own lack of eloquence, these men made use of messengers with symbols of one kind or another, as, for example, the ascetic near Siena (1496) ||1429|| who sent a "little hermit," that is, a pupil, into the terrified city with a skull on a pole, to which was attached a paper with a threatening text from the Bible.

Nor did the monks themselves scruple to attack princes, governments, the clergy, or even their own order. A direct

255. Even then, their reputation oscillated between two extremes. They must be distinguished from the hermit monks. – The line was not always clearly drawn in this respect. The Spoletans, who traveled about working miracles, took St. Anthony and, because of the snakes they carried with them, St. Paul as their patrons. Even in the thirteenth century they got money from the peasantry by a sort of clerical conjuring, and their horses were trained to kneel at the name of St. Anthony. They pretended to collect for hospitals.

exhortation to overthrow a despotic house, as that uttered by Fra Jacopo Bussolaro at Pavia in the fourteenth century,[256] no longer occurs in the following period; but there is no want of courageous reproof, addressed even to the Pope in his own chapel, and of naïve political advice given in the presence of rulers who did not feel themselves in need of it. In the Piazza del Castello at Milan, a blind preacher from the Incoronata—consequently an Augustinian—ventured in 1494 to exhort Il Moro from the pulpit: "My lord, beware of showing the French the way, else you will repent it."[257] There were prophetic monks who, without exactly preaching political sermons, drew such appalling pictures of the future that the hearers almost lost their senses. Soon after the election of Leo X (1513) a whole association of these men, twelve Franciscan Conventuals, journeyed through the various districts of Italy, to which each one had been assigned. The one who appeared in Florence, Fra Francesco di Montepulciano, struck terror into the people. The alarm was not diminished by the exaggerated reports of his prophecies that reached those who were too far off to hear him. After one of his sermons he suddenly died "of pain in the chest." The people thronged in such numbers to kiss the feet of the corpse that it had to be buried secretly at night. But the newly inflamed spirit of prophecy, which seized even women and peasants, could not be dampened without great difficulty. "In order to restore to the people their cheerful humor, the Medici—Giuliano (Leo's brother) and Lorenzo—gave on St. John's Day, 1514, those splendid festivals, tournaments, processions, and hunting parties, which were attended by many distinguished persons from Rome, and among them, though disguised, no less than six cardinals."

But the greatest prophet and apostle had already been burned in Florence in the year 1498—Fra Girolamo Savonarola of Ferrara. We must be satisfied with a few words about him.

The instrument by means of which he transformed and ruled the city of Florence (1494-1498) was his eloquence, of which the meager reports that are left to us, which were taken down mostly on the spot, obviously give us a very limited

256. He first preached against tyranny in general, and then, when the ruling house of the Beccaria tried to have him murdered, he began to preach a change of government and constitution, and forced the Beccaria to flee (1357).
257. Sometimes, at critical moments, the ruling house itself would employ the services of monks to exhort the people to loyalty.

idea. It was not that he possessed any striking outward advantages, for voice, accent, and rhetorical skill constituted precisely his weakest side; and those who required the preacher to be a stylist went to his rival Fra Mariano da Gennazzano. But the eloquence of Savonarola was the expression of a lofty and commanding personality, the like of which was not seen again till the time of Luther. He himself held his own influence to be the result of a divine illumination, and could therefore, without presumption, assign a very high place to the office of the preacher: in the great hierarchy of spirits, the preacher occupies the place directly below the angels.

This man, whose nature seemed made of fire and flame, accomplished another and greater miracle than any of his oratorical triumphs. His own Dominican monastery of San Marco, and then all the Dominican monasteries of Tuscany, adopted his views and undertook voluntarily the work of inward reform. When we reflect what the monasteries were then, and what endless difficulty attends the least change where monks are concerned, we are doubly astonished at so complete a revolution. While the reform was still in progress large numbers of Savonarola's followers entered the order, and thereby greatly facilitated his plans. Sons of the first houses in Florence entered San Marco as novices.

This reform of the order in a particular province was the first step to a national Church, in which, had the reformer himself lived longer, it must infallibly have ended. To be sure, Savonarola himself desired the regeneration of the whole Church, and near the end of his career sent pressing exhortations to the great potentates urging them to call a Council. But his order and party became the only possible organ of his spirit, the salt of the earth, in Tuscany, while the neighboring provinces continued in their old condition. Fantasy and asceticism tended more and more to produce in him a state of mind to which Florence appeared as the scene of the kingdom of God upon earth.

The prophecies, whose partial fulfillment conferred on Savonarola a supernatural credit, were the means by which the powerful Italian imagination seized control of the soundest and most cautious natures. At first the Franciscans of the Observantines, trusting in the reputation that had been bequeathed to them by St. Bernardino of Siena, fancied that they could compete with the great Dominican. They put one of their own men into the cathedral pulpit, and outbid the jeremiads of Savonarola by still more terrible warnings, till Pietro de' Medici, who still ruled over Florence, forced them both to be silent. Soon after, when Charles VIII came to Italy and the Medici were expelled, as Savonarola had clearly foretold, he alone was believed in.

It must be frankly confessed that he never judged his own premonitions and visions critically, as he did those of others. In the funeral oration on Pico della Mirandola he deals somewhat harshly with his dead friend. Since Pico, notwithstanding an inner voice which came from God, would not enter the order, he had himself prayed to God to chasten him for his disobedience. He certainly had not desired his death, and alms and prayers had obtained the favor that Pico's soul was safe in Purgatory. With regard to a comforting vision that Pico had on his sickbed, in which the Virgin had appeared and promised him that he should not die, Savonarola confessed that he had long regarded it as a deceit of the Devil, till it was revealed to him that the Madonna meant the second, that is, the eternal death. — If these and similar things are proof of presumption, it must be admitted that this great soul paid a bitter penalty for his fault. In his last days Savonarola seems to have recognized the vanity of his visions and prophecies. And yet enough inward peace was left to him to enable him to meet death like a Christian. His adherents held to his doctrine and predictions for thirty years.

He undertook the reorganization of the State only because otherwise his enemies would have got the government into their own hands. It is unfair to judge him by the semi-democratic constitution of the beginning of the year 1495. It was neither better nor worse than other Florentine constitutions.[258]

He was at bottom the most unsuitable man who could be found for such a work. His ideal was a theocracy, in which all men were to bow in blessed humility before the Unseen, and all conflicts of passion were as a matter of course never to arise. His whole mind is contained in that inscription on the Palazzo della Signoria, the substance of which was his maxim as early as 1495, and which was solemnly renewed by his partisans in 1527: *Jesus Christi Rex populi florentini S.P.Q. decreto creatus* [Jesus Christ decreed King of Florence by the Senate and the people]. He had as little relation to mundane affairs and their actual conditions as any other inhabitant of a monastery. Man, according to him, has only

---

258. Savonarola was perhaps the only man who could have made the subject cities free and yet kept Tuscany together. But he seems never to have thought of it.

to attend to those things which make directly for his salvation.

This temper comes out clearly in his opinions on ancient literature: "The only good thing that we owe to Plato and Aristotle is that they brought forward many arguments which we can use against the heretics. Yet they and other philosophers are now in Hell. An old woman knows more about Faith than Plato. It would be good for religion if many books that seem useful were destroyed. When there were not so many books and not so many arguments (*ragioni naturali*) and disputes, religion grew more quickly than it has since." He wanted to limit the classical instruction of the schools to Homer, Vergil, and Cicero, and to supply the rest from SS. Jerome and Augustine. Not only Ovid and Catullus, but Terence and Tibullus were to be banished. This may be no more than the expression of a nervous morality, but elsewhere, in a separate work, he admits that science as a whole is harmful. He holds that only a few people should learn it, so that the tradition of human knowledge may not perish, and particularly that there may be no want of intellectual athletes to confute the sophisms of the heretics. For all others, grammar, morals, and religious teaching (*sacrac literae*) suffice. Culture and education would thus return wholly into the charge of the monks, and since, in his opinion, the "most learned and the most pious" are to rule over the States and empires, these rulers would also be monks. Whether he really foresaw this conclusion we need not inquire.

A more childish method of reasoning cannot be imagined. The simple reflection that the resurrected antiquity and the boundless enlargement of human thought and knowledge might give splendid confirmation to a religion able to adapt itself to it seems never to have occurred to the good man. He wanted to forbid what could not be removed by any other means. In fact, he was anything but liberal, and was ready, for example, to send the astrologers to the same stake at which he himself later died.

How mighty must have been the soul that dwelt with this narrow intellect! And what a fire must have burned within him before he could constrain the Florentines, possessed as they were by the passion for knowledge and culture, to surrender themselves to a man who could thus reason!

How much of their art and their worldliness they were ready to sacrifice for his sake is shown by those famous bonfires next to which all the *talami* of Bernardino da Siena and others were certainly of small account.

All this could not, however, be effected without the agency

of a tyrannical police. He did not shrink from the most vexatious interferences with the much-prized freedom of Italian
private life, using, for example, the espionage of servants on
their masters as a means of carrying out his moral reforms.
That transformation of public and private life which the
iron Calvin was only able to effect at Geneva with the aid
of a permanent state of siege, proved impossible at Florence,
and the attempt only served to drive the enemies of Savonarola to a more implacable hostility. Among his most unpopular measures may be mentioned those organized parties of
boys, who forced their way into the houses and laid violent
hands on any objects that seemed suitable for the bonfire.
Since they were sometimes sent away with a beating, they
were afterward attended, in order to keep up the figment of
a pious "rising generation," by a bodyguard of adults.

And so on the last day of the Carnival in the year 1497,
and on the same day the year after, the great autos-da-fé
could take place on the Piazza della Signoria. In the center of
the piazza rose a high stepped pyramid, like the *rogus* on
which the Roman Emperors were commonly burned. On the
lowest tier were arranged false beards, masks, and Carnival
disguises; above came volumes of the Latin and Italian poets,
among others Boccaccio, the *Morgante* of Pulci, and
Petrarch, some of which were valuable printed parchments
and illuminated manuscripts; then women's ornaments and
toilet articles, scents, mirrors, veils, and false hair; higher
up, lutes, harps, chessboards, playing cards; and finally, on
the two uppermost tiers, nothing but paintings, especially of
female beauties, partly fancy pictures bearing the classical
names of Lucretia, Cleopatra, or Faustina, partly portraits
of the beautiful Bencina, Lena Morella, Bina, and Maria
de' Lenzi. On the first occasion a Venetian merchant who
happened to be present offered the Signoria 22,000 gold
florins for the objects on the pyramid; the only answer he
received was that his portrait, too, was painted, and burned
along with the rest. When the pile was lighted, the Signoria
appeared on the balcony, and the air echoed with song, the
sound of trumpets, and the pealing of bells. The people then
adjourned to the Piazza di San Marco, where they danced
round in three concentric circles. The innermost was composed of monks of the monastery, alternating with boys
dressed as angels; then came young laymen and ecclesiastics;
and on the outside, old men, citizens, and priests, the latter
crowned with wreaths of olive.

All the ridicule of his victorious enemies, who in truth had
no lack of justification or of talent for ridicule, was unable

...iscredit the memory of Savonarola. The more tragic t... fortunes of Italy became, the brighter grew the halo that surrounded the figure of the great monk and prophet in the recollection of the survivors. Though his predictions may not have been confirmed in detail, the great and general calamity that he foretold was fulfilled with appalling truth.

Great, however, as the influence of all these preachers may have been, and brilliantly as Savonarola justified the claim of the monks to this office, this class as a whole could not escape the contempt and condemnation of the people. Italy showed that she could give her enthusiasm only to individuals.

If, apart from priests and monks, we try to evaluate the strength of the old faith, it will appear great or small depending on the point of view from which it is considered. We have already spoken of the need felt for the rites and sacraments. Let us now glance for a moment at the position of faith and worship in daily life. Both were determined by the habits of the people and by the policy and example of the rulers.

Everything concerned with repentance and the attainment of salvation by means of good works was in much the same stage of development or corruption as in the North, among both the peasantry and the poorer inhabitants of the cities. And even the educated classes were occasionally influenced. Those aspects of popular Catholicism which had their origin in the old pagan ways of invoking, rewarding, and propitiating the gods had fixed themselves ineradicably in the consciousness of the people. Baptista Mantuanus' eighth eclogue, which has already been quoted, contains the prayer of a peasant to the Madonna, in which she is called upon as the patroness of specific agricultural interests. And what conceptions the people formed of their protectress! What was in the mind of the Florentine woman who gave an ex-voto of a keg of wax to the Annunziata, because her lover, a monk, had gradually emptied a barrel of wine without her absent husband finding out! At that time, as still in our own day, each area of human life had its special patron. Many attempts have been made to trace a number of the commonest rites of the Catholic Church back to pagan ceremonies, and no one doubts that many local and popular customs associated with religious festivals are unconscious remnants of ancient European paganisms. But in Italy there are instances in which we cannot fail to recognize a conscious remnant of pagan belief. As, for example, the custom of setting out food for the dead four days before the Feast of the Chair of St. Peter,

that is, on February 18th, the date of the ancient Feralia.[259]
Many other practices of this kind may have prevailed then
and have only been extirpated since then. Perhaps it only
seems paradoxical when we say that in Italy the strength of
popular faith depended on the degree to which it was pagan.

The extent to which this form of belief prevailed in the
upper classes can to a certain point be shown in detail. It had,
as we have said in speaking of the influence of the clergy, the
power of custom and early impressions on its side. The love
of ecclesiastical pomp and display helped to confirm it, and
now and then there came one of those epidemics of revivalism,
which even the scoffers and skeptics could not withstand.

But in questions of this kind it is dangerous to grasp too
hastily at absolute results. We might believe for example,
that the feeling of educated men toward relics of saints
would be a key by which some chambers of their religious
consciousness might be opened. And in fact, some difference
of degree may be distinguished, though by no means as
clearly as we might wish. The government of Venice in the
fifteenth century seems to have shared fully in the reverence
felt thoughout the rest of Europe for the remains of the
bodies of saints. Even strangers who lived in Venice found
it well to adapt themselves to this superstition. If we can
form a judgment of scholarly Padua from the testimony of
its topographer, Michele Savonarola, things were no different
there than they were in Venice. With a mixture of pride and
pious awe, Michele tells how in times of great danger the
saints were heard to sigh at night along the streets of the city,
how the hair and nails on the corpse of a holy nun in Santa
Chiara kept growing, and how the same corpse, when any
disaster impended, would make noise and raise its arms.
When he describes the chapel of St. Anthony in the Santo,
the author loses himself in ejaculations and fantastic dreams.
In Milan the people at least showed a fanatical devotion to
relics; and when once (1517) the monks of San Simpliciano
carelessy exposed six holy corpses during certain alterations
of the high altar, after which there were heavy rains, the
people attributed the visitation to this sacrilege and gave the
monks a sound beating whenever they met them in the street.

259. When the army of John XXII entered the Marches to attack
the Ghibellines, the pretext was avowedly *eresia* [heresy] and
idolatria [idolatry]. Recanati, which surrendered voluntarily, was
nevertheless burned, "because idols had been worshiped there."
— Most astonishing is what happened in the Forum at Rome under
Leo X: to stay the plague, a bull was solemnly offered up with
pagan rites.

In other parts of Italy, and even among the Popes, the sincerity of this feeling is much more dubious, though here, too, it is difficult to come to a definite conclusion. It is well known amid what general enthusiasm Pius II acquired the head of the Apostle Andrew, which had been taken from Greece to Santa Maura, and solemnly deposited it in St. Peter's (1462); but we gather from his own account that he only did it from a kind of shame, since so many princes were competing for the relic. It was not till then that the idea struck him of making Rome the common refuge for the remains of the saints that had been driven from their own churches.[260] Under Sixtus IV, the people were more zealous than the Pope himself, and the magistracy (1483) complained bitterly that Sixtus had sent to Louis XI, the dying King of France, some of the Lateran relics.[261] A courageous voice was raised about this time at Bologna, advising the sale of the skull of St. Dominic to the King of Spain and the application of the money to some useful public object. But it was the Florentines who had the least reverence for relics. Between the decision to honor St. Zenobius, their patron saint, with a new sarcophagus and the actual commission to Ghiberti, nineteen years elapsed (1409-1428), and even then the commission was granted only because the master had skillfully executed a smaller work of a similar kind.[262] Perhaps through being tricked by a cunning Neapolitan abbess (1352), who sent them a spurious arm of the patroness of the cathedral, St. Reparata, made of wood and plaster, they began to tire of relics. Or perhaps it would be truer to say that their aesthetic sense turned them away in disgust from dismembered corpses and moldy clothes. Or perhaps their feeling was rather due to that sense of glory which held Dante and Petrarch worthier of a splendid grave than all the twelve apostles put together. But it is possible that in Italy (apart from Venice and Rome, which was an exceptional case) the worship of relics had long been giving way[263] to the adoration

260. *The Commentaries of Pius II,* Book VIII.
261. Louis was able to pay his devotion to the gift, but he died anyway.
262. [Ghiberti's Shrine of St. Zenobius (1432-42) is still in the cathedral at Florence. The "smaller order of a similar kind" is Ghiberti's Shrine of SS. Protus, Hyacinth, and Nemesius, which was completed in 1428 and is now in the Museo Nazionale (Bargello) at Florence.]
263. We must further distinguish between the growing cult in Italy of the bodies of saints of historically recent date and the Northern practice of collecting bones and relics dating from early

of the Madonna to a greater extent than anywhere else in Europe, and this despite its disguised form, may well be an early triumph of aesthetic sensibility.[264]

It may be questioned whether in the North, where the greatest cathedrals are nearly all dedicated to Our Lady, and where an extensive branch of Latin and indigenous poetry sang the praises of the Mother of God, a greater devotion to her was possible. In Italy, however, the number of miraculous pictures of the Virgin was far greater, and the part they played in the daily life of the people was much more important. Every town of any size contained a whole series of them, from the ancient, or ostensibly ancient, "paintings by St. Luke" down to the works of contemporaries who not seldom lived to see the miracles wrought by their own pictures. The work of art was by no means as harmless as Baptista Mantuanus thinks; sometimes it suddenly acquired a magical virtue. The popular craving for the miraculous, especially strong in women, may have been fully satisfied by these pictures, and for this reason the relics may have been less esteemed. It cannot be said with certainty how far the respect for genuine relics suffered from the ridicule the novelists aimed at the spurious.

The attitude of the educated classes in Italy toward Mariolatry is more clearly recognizable than toward the worship of images. One cannot but be struck with the fact that in Italian literature Dante's *Paradiso* [265] is the last poem in honor of the Virgin, while among the people hymns in her praise have

---

Christianity. These last, particularly important to pilgrims, were preserved in great abundance in the Lateran. But on the sarcophagi of St. Dominic and St. Anthony of Padua, and on the mysterious tomb of St. Francis, there glowed not only the halo of sanctity, but the splendor of historical fame.

264. ‖It would not be without interest to determine precisely how much in the religious decrees of the Popes and theologians of that time proceeded from a specifically Italian impulse. The advocacy of Sixtus IV of the Immaculate Conception should probably be ascribed to this. On the other hand, there is more of a Northern influence in the growing cult of Joseph and the parents of Mary, which was already popular in northern France at the beginning of the fifteenth century and officially sanctioned in 1414 by a legate of John XXIII. It was not until a half century later that Sixtus IV established for the whole Church the Feast of the Presentation of Mary in the Temple, the Feasts of St. Anne and of St. Joseph.‖

265. ‖Especially *Paradiso*, xxxiii, 1, the famous prayer of St. Bernard: *Vergine madre, figlia del tuo figlio* [Virgin mother, daughter of thy son].‖

been produced down to our own day. The names of Sannazaro, Sabellico, and other writers of Latin poems prove
little, since their object was chiefly literary. The poems
written in Italian in the fifteenth and at the beginning of the
sixteenth centuries, in which we meet with genuine religious
feeling, such as the hymns of Lorenzo the Magnificent, the
sonnets of Vittoria Colonna, of Michelangelo, ||of Gaspara
Stampa||, etc., might just as well have been composed by
Protestants. Besides the lyrical expression of faith in God, we
notice chiefly in them the sense of sin, the consciousness of
deliverance through the death of Christ, the longing for a
better world. The intercession of the Mother of God is only
mentioned by the way. The same phenomenon is repeated in
French classical literature at the time of Louis XIV. Not till
the time of the Counter Reformation did Mariolatry reappear
in the literary poetry of Italy. Indeed, the visual arts had
meanwhile done their utmost to glorify the Madonna. It may
be added that the worship of the saints among the educated
classes often took an essentially pagan form.

We might thus critically examine various aspects of Italian
Catholicism at this period, and establish with a certain degree
of probability the attitude of the educated classes toward
popular faith. Yet an absolute and positive result cannot be
reached. We meet contrasts that are hard to explain. Whereas
architects, painters, and sculptors were working with restless
activity in and for the churches, we hear at the beginning
of the sixteenth century the bitterest complaints of the
slackening of public worship and the neglect of these very
churches: *Templa ruunt, passim sordent altaria, cultus Paula-
tim divinus abit* [The temples are ruined, the altars are defiled,
the divine cult of Paul is dying]! . . . It is well known how
Luther was scandalized by the irreverence with which the
priests in Rome said Mass. And at the same time the feasts
of the Church were celebrated with a taste and magnificence
of which Northern countries had no conception. It would appear that this most imaginative of nations was easily tempted
to neglect everyday things, and was as easily captivated by anything extraordinary.

It is to this imagination that we must attribute the epidemic
of religious revivals, on which we must again say a few
words. They should be clearly distinguished from the excitement generated by the great preachers; they were called forth
by general public calamities, or by the dread of such.

In the Middle Ages all Europe was periodically flooded by
these great tides, which carried away whole peoples, as, for
example, the Crusades and the Flagellant movement. Italy

took part in both waves. The first great companies of Flagellants appeared, immediately after the fall of Ezzelino and his house, in the neighborhood of the same Perugia that has already been mentioned as a major visiting point of the revivalist preachers. Then followed the Flagellants of 1310 and 1334, and then the great pilgrimage without scourging, which Corio describes in 1399. It is not impossible that the Jubilees were founded partly in order to regulate and render harmless this sinister passion for pilgrimage which seized whole populations at times of religious excitement. In the meantime certain sanctuaries of Italy, such as Loreto, had become famous, and diverted a certain part of this enthusiasm.

But years later terrible crises could still reawaken the flame of medieval penitence, and the conscience-stricken people, especially when there were signs and wonders, sought the mercy of Heaven by wailings and scourgings. So it was at Bologna during the plague of 1457, and so in 1496 at a time of internal discord at Siena, to mention only two out of countless instances. But truly staggering is what happened at Milan in 1529, when the dread sisters—famine, plague, and war—and Spanish extortion reduced the city to the depths of despair. The monk who had the ear of the people, Fra Tommaso Nieto, happened to be a Spaniard. He had the Host borne along in a novel fashion, amid barefooted crowds of old and young. It was placed on a decorated bier, which rested on the shoulders of four priests in linen garments—an imitation of the Ark of the Covenant [266] which the children of Israel once carried round the walls of Jericho. Thus did the afflicted people of Milan remind their ancient God of His ancient covenant with man; and as the procession re-entered the cathedral, and it seemed as if the vast building must fall in with the agonized cry of *Misericordia!*, many who stood there may have believed that the Almighty would indeed subvert the laws of nature and of history, and send a miraculous deliverance.

There was, however, one government in Italy, that of Duke Ercole I of Ferrara, which assumed the direction of public feeling and compelled the popular revivals to move in regular channels. When Savonarola was powerful in Florence, and the movement that he began spread far and wide among the population of Central Italy, the people of Ferrara voluntarily

266. It was also called *l'arca del testimonio* [ark of witness] and people told how it was *conzado* (constructed) *con gran misterio* [with great mystery].

entered on a general fast (at the beginning of 1496). A
Lazarist announced from the pulpit the approach of a season
of war and famine such as the world had never seen, but
the Madonna had assured a pious couple that these evils
might be avoided by fasting. The court itself had no choice
but to fast, but it took the conduct of the public devotions
into its own hands. On the 3rd of April (Easter Day) a
proclamation on morals and religion was issued, forbidding
blasphemy, prohibiting games, sodomy, concubinage, the
letting of houses to prostitutes or panders, and the opening
of all shops on feast days, excepting those of the bakers and
greengrocers. The Jews and marranoes, who had taken refuge
from the Spaniards at Ferrara, were now again compelled
to wear the yellow O upon their breasts. Contraveners were
threatened not only with the punishments already provided by
law, but also "with such severer penalties as the Duke might
think fit to inflict." After this, the Duke and the court went
several days in succession to hear sermons in church, and
on the 10th of April all the Jews in Ferrara were compelled
to do the same. On the 3rd of May, the director of police—
that Zampante to whom we have already referred—announced that whoever had given money to the police officers
in order not to be denounced as a blasphemer, might, if he
came forward, have it back with a further indemnification.
These wicked officers, he said, had extorted as much as two
or three ducats from innocent persons by threatening to lodge
a denunciation against them. They had then mutually informed against one another, and so all had found their way
into prison. But since the money had been paid precisely in
order not to have to do with Zampante, it is probable that
his proclamation induced few people to come forward. – In
the year 1500, after the fall of Il Moro, when a similar
outbreak of popular feeling took place, Ercole ordered [267] a
series of nine processions, in which there was no lack of
children dressed in white bearing the standard of Jesus. He
himself rode on horseback, as he could not walk without
difficulty. Then followed an edict of the same kind as that
of 1496. It is well known how many churches and monasteries
were built by this ruler. He even sent for a live saint, Suor
Colomba, shortly before he married his son Alfonso to
Lucrezia Borgia (1502). A special messenger fetched the saint
and fifteen other nuns from Viterbo, and the Duke himself

267. *Per buono rispetto a lui noto e perchè sempre è buono a
star bene con Iddeo* [as an act of self-respect and because it is
a good thing to stand well with God], says the chronicler.

conducted her on her arrival at Ferrara into a convent prepared for her reception. Do we do him an injustice if we attribute all these measures to the strictest political calculation? For the conception of government formed by the House of Este, as we have described it above, this employment of religion for the ends of statecraft is almost a logical necessity.

———————

But in order to reach a definite conclusion with regard to the religious sense of the men of this period, we must adopt a different method. Their intellectual attitude in general can make clear their relation both to the Divine idea and to the existing religion of their age.

These modern men, the representatives of the culture of Italy, were born with the same religious instincts as the men of the Middle Ages. But their powerful individuality made them in religion, as in other matters, completely *subjective*, and the intense charm that the discovery of the inner and outer universe exercised upon them rendered them markedly *worldly*. In the rest of Europe religion remained for a long time something objectively given, and in practical life egotism and sensuality alternated with devotion and repentance. The latter had no spiritual competitors, as in Italy, or only to a far lesser degree.

Further, the close and frequent relations of Italy with Byzantium and the Mohammedan peoples had produced a dispassionate *tolerance* which weakened the ethnographical conception of a privileged Christendom. And when, finally, classical antiquity with its men and institutions became an ideal of life, because it was the greatest Italian memory, ancient speculation and *skepticism* sometimes obtained a complete mastery over the minds of the Italians.

Since, in addition, the Italians were the first modern people of Europe who gave themselves boldly to speculations on freedom and necessity, and since they did so under violent and lawless political circumstances in which evil seemed often to win a splendid and lasting victory, their belief in God began to waver, and their view of the world became *fatalistic*. And when their passionate natures refused to remain in the sense of uncertainty, many sought a solution in ancient, Oriental, or medieval *superstition*. They became astrologers and magicians.

Finally, these intellectual giants, these representatives of the Renaissance, show, in respect to religion, a quality that is common in youthful natures: they distinguish keenly between good and evil, yet they are conscious of no sin. They believe that every disturbance to their inward harmony will be resolved by virtue of their own plastic resources, and therefore they feel no repentance. Thus the need for salvation became weaker, while the ambitions and the intellectual activity of the present either shut out altogether every thought of a world to come, or caused it to assume a poetic instead of a dogmatic form.

If we see all this as pervaded and often perverted by the all-powerful Italian *imagination,* we obtain a picture of that time which is certainly closer to the truth than are vague declamations against modern paganism. And closer investigation will reveal that underneath this outward shell much genuine religion still survived.

The fuller discussion of these points must be limited to the more essential explanations.

That religion should again become an affair of the individual and of his own personal feeling was inevitable when the Church became corrupt in doctrine and tyrannous in practice, and is proof that the European mind was still alive. It is true that this showed itself in many different ways. While the mystical and ascetical sects of the North lost no time in creating new outward forms for their new modes of thought and feeling, in Italy each individual went his own way, and thousands wandered on the sea of life without any religious guidance whatever. All the more must we admire those who attained and held fast to a personal religion. They were not to blame for being unable to have any part of the old Church, as she then was; nor would it be reasonable to expect that individuals should go through that mighty spiritual labor which was appointed to the German reformers. We shall try to show at the close of our work what the better minds generally aimed for with this personal religion.

The worldliness, through which the Renaissance seems to offer so striking a contrast to the Middle Ages, owed its first origin to the flood of new thoughts, purposes, and views which transformed the medieval conception of nature and man. In itself this spirit is no more hostile to religion than that "culture" which now holds its place, but this culture, as we pursue it, can give us only a feeble notion of the universal ferment that the discovery of a new world of greatness then called forth. Thus this worldliness was earnest, and, in addition, was ennobled by art and poetry. It is a lofty necessity of the modern spirit that this attitude, once gained, can never be lost, that an irresistible impulse forces it to the investigation of men and things, and that this inquiry becomes its proper end and work.[268] How soon and by what paths this search leads back to God, and in what ways the religious temper of the individual will be affected by it, are questions that cannot be resolved by any general answer. The Middle Ages, which spared itself the trouble of induction and free inquiry, cannot impose its dogmatic verdict in a matter of such vast importance.

The study of man, but also the study of many other things, was responsible for the tolerance and indifference with which the Mohammedan religion was regarded. The knowledge and admiration of the remarkable civilization that Islam had attained, particularly before the Mongol inundation, was peculiar to Italy from the time of the Crusades. This sympathy was fostered by the half-Mohammedan government of some Italian princes, by the dislike, even contempt, for the existing Church, and by constant commercial intercourse with the harbors of the eastern and southern Mediterranean.[269] It can be shown that in the thirteenth century the Italians recognized a Mohammedan ideal of nobleness, dignity, and pride, which they loved to connect with the person of a Sultan. A Mameluke Sultan is commonly meant; if any name is mentioned, it is the name of Saladin. Even the Osmanli Turks, whose destructive tendencies were no secret, gave the Italians only half a fright, and whole populations were accustomed to the thought of a possible agreement with them.

The truest and most characteristic expression of this religious indifference is the famous story of the Three Rings, which Lessing, among others, put into the mouth of his Nathan, after it had already been told centuries earlier, with some reserve in the *Hundred Old Tales* (nov. 72 or 73), and more boldly in Boccaccio.[270] In what language and in what corner of the Mediterranean it was first told can never be known; most likely the original was much more plain-spoken than the two Italian adaptations. The religious postulate on which it rests, namely Deism, will be discussed later in its wider significance for this period. The same idea is repeated, though in a clumsy caricature, in the famous proverb of "the three who have deceived the world," that is, Moses, Christ, and Mohammed. If Emperor Frederick II, who is supposed

268. Cf. the portion of Pico's Speech on the Dignity of Man quoted above [Part Four].
269. Let alone the fact that a similar tolerance or indifference was not uncommon among the Arabs themselves.
270. *Decameron*, Book I, nov. 3. Boccaccio is the first to name the Christian religion, whereas the *Hundred Old Tales* does not.

to have originated this saying, really thought so, he would probably have expressed himself with more wit. Similar sayings were also current in Islam at that time.

At the height of the Renaissance, toward the close of the fifteenth century, Luigi Pulci offers us an example of the same mode of thought in the *Morgante maggiore*. The imaginary world in which his story takes place is divided, as in all heroic poems of romance, into a Christian and a Mohammedan camp. In accordance with the medieval temper, the victory of the Christian and the final reconciliation among the combatants was attended by the baptism of the defeated Islamites, and the *improvisatori*, who preceded Pulci in the treatment of these subjects, must have made free use of this stock incident. It was Pulci's object to parody his predecessors, particularly the worst among them, and this he does by the invocations of God, Christ, and the Madonna, with which each canto begins; and still more clearly by the sudden conversions and baptisms, the utter senselessness of which must have struck every reader or hearer. This ridicule leads him further, to the confession of his faith in the relative goodness of all religions, a faith which, notwithstanding his profession of orthodoxy, rests on an essentially theistic basis. In another point, too, he departs widely from medieval conceptions. The alternatives in past centuries had been: orthodox believer or heretic; Christ, or pagan and Mohammedan. Pulci draws a picture of the Giant Margutte who, in opposition to every single religion, jovially confesses to every form of vice and sensuality, and reserves to himself only one merit: he has never committed treason. Perhaps the poet intended to make something of this—in his way—honest monster, possibly to have led him into virtuous paths by Morgante, but he soon tired of his own creation and in the next canto brought him to a comic end.[271] Margutte has been brought forward as proof of Pulci's frivolity; but he is needed to complete the picture of the poetry of the fifteenth century. Somewhere it had to present in grotesque proportions the figure of an untamed egotism insensible to all established rule, in which only a remnant of honorable feeling remained. In other poems, too, sentiments which no Christian knight should utter are put into the mouths of giants, fiends, infidels, and Mohammedans.

Antiquity exercised a completely different kind of influence from that of Islam, and this not through its religion, which

271. Pulci touches, although hastily, on a similar conception in his characterization of Prince Chiaristante, who believes in nothing and causes himself and his wife to be worshiped. One is reminded of Sigismondo Malatesta.

was too much like the Catholicism of this period, but through its philosophy. Ancient literature, now honored as something incomparable, is full of the victory of philosophy over religious tradition. An endless number of systems and fragments of systems were suddenly presented to the Italian mind, not as curiosities or even as heresies, but almost with the authority of dogmas which had now to be reconciled rather than discriminated. In nearly all these various opinions and doctrines a certain kind of belief in God was implied; but taken all together they formed a marked contrast to the Christian faith in a Divine government of the world. And there was one central question, which medieval theology had striven in vain to solve and which now urgently demanded an answer from the wisdom of the ancients, namely, the relation of Providence to human freedom and necessity. Even a superficial consideration of the history of this question from the fourteenth century onward would lead to an entire book. Here a few hints must suffice.

If we take Dante and his contemporaries as evidence, we find that ancient philosophy first came into contact with Italian life in the form which offered the most marked contrast to Christianity, that is to say, Epicureanism. The writings of Epicurus were no longer preserved, and even at the close of antiquity a more or less one-sided conception had been formed of his philosophy. Nevertheless, that phase of Epicureanism which could be studied in Lucretius, and especially in Cicero, was sufficient enough to make men familiar with a godless universe. To what extent his teaching was actually understood, and whether the name of the problematic Greek sage was not rather a catchword for the multitude, is hard to say. It is probable that the Dominican Inquisition used the word against men who could not be reached by a more definite accusation. In the case of premature skeptics, whom it was difficult to accuse of specific heretical teachings and expressions, a moderate degree of luxurious living may have sufficed to provoke the charge. The word is used in this conventional sense by Giovanni Villani, for example, when he explains the Florentine fires of 1115 and 1117 as Divine judgment on heresies, "among others, on the luxurious and gluttonous sect of Epicureans." Of Manfred he says, "His life was Epicurean, since he believed neither in God, nor in the Saints, but only in bodily pleasure."

Dante speaks more clearly in the ninth and tenth cantos of the *Inferno*. That terrible fiery field covered with half-opened tombs, from which cries of hopeless agony issue, is peopled by the two large groups that the Church had vanquished or expelled in the thirteenth century. One was the heretics who opposed the Church by deliberately spreading false doctrine; the other was the Epicureans, and their sin against the Church lay in their general disposition, which was summed up in the belief that the soul dies with the body. The Church was well aware that this one doctrine, if it gained ground, must be more ruinous to her authority than all the teachings of the Manichaeans and Patarines, since it removed all reason for her interference in the destiny of man after death. That she herself, by the means she used in her struggles, had driven precisely the most gifted natures to nonbelief and despair, she would, naturally, not admit.

Dante's loathing of Epicurus, or of what he took to be his doctrine, was certainly sincere. The poet of the other world had to detest the denier of immortality; and a world neither made nor ruled by God, as well as the lowly aim of existence which the system seemed to advocate, were intensely antipathetic to a man like Dante. But if we look closer, we find that even he was so impressed by certain doctrines of the ancients that the biblical doctrine of Divine government retreated. Or was it his own speculation, the influence of prevailing opinion, loathing for the injustice that ruled the world, which made him give up the belief in a special Providence.[272] His God leaves all the details of the world's government to a deputy, Fortune, whose sole work is to change and thoroughly shake all earthly things, and who can disregard the wailings of men with indifferent bliss. Therefore Dante insists on the moral responsibility of man: he believes in free will.

The popular belief in freedom of the will had prevailed in the West before; at all times men have as a matter of course been held responsible for their actions. The case is otherwise with religious and philosophical doctrine, which must harmonize the nature of the will with the laws of the universe. We have here a question of more or less, which every moral estimate must take into account. Dante is not wholly free from those astrological superstitions which illumined the horizon of his time with deceptive light, but they do not hinder him from rising to a worthy conception of human nature. "The heavens," he has his Marco Lombardo say, "set your impulses in motion, but a light is given you to know good and evil, and free will, which, if it endure the strain

272. *Inferno*, vii, 67-96.

in its first battlings with the heavens, at length gains the whole victory, if it be well nurtured." [273]

Others might seek the necessity that annulled human freedom in a power other than the stars, but the question was henceforth an open and inevitable one. To the extent that it remained a question for the schools or the pursuit of isolated thinkers, it belongs to the history of philosophy. But the extent to which it passed over into the consciousness of a wider public, demands some discussion.

The fourteenth century was stimulated primarily by the writings of Cicero who was considered an eclectic that exercised the influence of a skeptic since he set forth the opinions of different schools without coming to any satisfactory conclusions. Next in line came Seneca, and the few works of Aristotle which had been translated into Latin. The immediate fruit of these studies was the capacity to reflect on great subjects, if not in direct opposition to the authority of the Church, at least independently of her.

In the course of the fifteenth century the writings of antiquity were, as we have seen, discovered and diffused with extraordinary rapidity; eventually all the extant Greek philosophers became available, at least in Latin translation. It is a curious fact that some of the most zealous apostles of this new culture were men of the strictest piety, or even ascetics. We do not include among these Fra Ambrogio Camaldolese who devoted himself exclusively to the translation of the Greek Fathers of the Church and only reluctantly, at the urging of the elder Cosimo de' Medici, translated Diogenes Laërtius into Latin. But his contemporaries, Niccolò Niccoli, Giannozzo Manetti, Donato Acciaiuoli, and Pope Nicholas V, combined a many-sided humanism with profound biblical scholarship and deep piety. We have already noted a similar temper in Vittorino da Feltre. The same Maffeo Vegio who added a thirteenth book to the *Aeneid* had an enthusiasm for the memory of St. Augustine and his mother, Monica, that cannot have been without a deeper influence on him. The result of all these tendencies was that the Platonic Academy at Florence deliberately chose for its object the reconciliation of the spirit of antiquity with that of Christianity. It was a remarkable oasis in the humanism of the period.

This humanism was in fact profane, and became more and

273. *Purgatorio*, xvi, 73. To which the theory of the influence of the planets in the *Convivio* should be compared. — Even Pulci's demon Astaroth (*Morgante*) attests the freedom of the human will and the justice of God.

more so as its sphere widened in the fifteenth century. Its representatives, whom we have already described as the advance guard of an unbridled individualism, display as a rule such a character that even their religion, which is sometimes professed very definitely, becomes a matter of indifference to us. They easily got the name of atheists if they were indifferent to religion and spoke freely against the Church; but not one of them ever professed, or dared to profess, a formal, philosophical atheism. If they sought for any leading principle, it must have been a kind of superficial rationalism—a careless inference from the many and contradictory opinions of antiquity with which they busied themselves, and from the discredit into which the Church and her doctrines had fallen. This was the sort of reasoning that almost brought Galeotto Marzio to the stake, had not his former pupil, Pope Sixtus IV, speedily saved him from the hands of the Inquisition. Galeotto had ventured to write that the man who lived uprightly and acted according to the natural law born within him would go to heaven, whatever people he belonged to.

Let us, by way of example, take the religious attitude of one of the lesser men in the great army, Codrus Urceus, who was first the tutor of the last Ordelaffo, Prince of Forlì, and afterward for many years professor at Bologna. Against the Church and the monks his language is as abusive as that of the rest. His tone in general is reckless to the last degree, and he constantly introduces himself into all his local history and gossip. But he knows how to speak with devotion of the true God-Man, Jesus Christ, and to commend himself by letter to the prayers of a saintly priest. On one occasion, after enumerating the follies of the pagan religions, he carries on: "Our theologians, too, often waver and quarrel *de lana caprina* [split hairs] about the Immaculate Conception, the Antichrist, the Sacraments, Predestination, and other things, which were better let alone than talked of publicly." Once, when he was not at home, his room and manuscripts were burned. When he heard the news he stood opposite a figure of the Madonna in the street, and cried to it: "Listen to what I tell you; I am not mad, I am saying what I mean. If I ever call upon you in the hour of my death, you need not hear me or take me among your own, for I will go and spend eternity with the devil." After which speech he found it desirable to spend six months in retirement at the home of a woodcutter. With all this, he was so superstitious that prodigies and omens gave him incessant frights, leaving him no belief to spare for the immortality of the soul. When his hearers questioned him on the matter, he answered that no one knew what became of a man, of his soul *or* his spirit, after death, and all talk about another life was only fit to frighten old women. But as he lay dying, he commended his soul *or* his spirit to Almighty God, exhorted his weeping pupils to fear the Lord, and especially to believe in immortality and future retribution, and received the Sacrament with much fervor. – We have no guarantee that more famous men in the same calling, however significant their opinions may be, were any more consistent in practical life. It is probable that inwardly most of them wavered between incredulity and a remnant of the faith in which they were brought up, and outwardly, for prudential reasons, held to the Church.

Through the combination of rationalism and the newly born science of historical investigation, some timid attempts at biblical criticism may here and there have been made. A remark of Pius II has been recorded,[274] which seems intended to prepare the way for such criticism: "Even if Christianity were not confirmed by miracles, it ought still to be accepted on account of its morality." The legends of the Church, in so far as they contained arbitrary versions of the biblical miracles, were freely ridiculed, and this in turn affected the religious attitude of the people. Where Judaizing heretics are mentioned, we must understand chiefly those who denied the Divinity of Christ, which was probably the offense for which Giorgio da Novara was burned at Bologna about the year 1500. But at about the same time (1497) in the same Bologna the Dominican Inquisitor was forced to let the physician Gabriele da Salò, who had powerful patrons, escape with a simple expression of penitence, although he was in the habit of maintaining that Jesus was not God, but son of Joseph and Mary, and conceived in the usual way; that by his cunning he had deceived the world to its ruin; that he may have died on the cross for crimes he had committed; that his religion would soon come to an end; that his body was not really contained in the sacrament; and that he performed his miracles not through any divine power but through the influence of the heavenly bodies. This latter statement is most characteristic of the time: Faith is gone, but magic still holds its ground.

With respect to the moral government of the world, the humanists seldom get beyond a cold and resigned consideration of the prevailing violence and misrule. This is the temper that gave rise to the numerous books "On Fate," or whatever name they may bear. They are mostly concerned with the

274. Platina, *The Lives of the Popes.*

turning of the wheel of Fortune, the instability of earthly, especially political, things. Providence is brought in only because the writers would still be ashamed of undisguised fatalism, of the avowal of their ignorance, or of useless complaints. Gioviano Pontano ingeniously illustrates the nature of that mysterious something which men call Fortune by a hundred incidents, most of which belonged to his own experience. The subject is treated more humorously by Aeneas Sylvius, in the form of a vision seen in a dream. The aim of Poggio, on the other hand, in a work written in his old age, is to represent the world as a vale of tears, and to fix the happiness of various classes as low as possible. This tone became the prevalent one. Distinguished men drew up a debit and credit of the happiness and unhappiness of their lives, and generally found that the latter outweighed the former. The fate of Italy and the Italians, so far as it could be told in the year 1510, has been described with dignity and almost elegiac pathos by Tristano Caracciolo. Applying this general tone of feeling to the humanists themselves, Pierio Valeriano afterward composed his famous treatise. Some of these themes, as, for example, the fortunes of Leo X, were most suggestive. The good that could be said of him politically was briefly and admirably summed up by Francesco Vettori; the picture of Leo's pleasures is given by Paolo Giovio and in the anonymous biography; and the shadows that attended this prosperity are drawn with inexorable truth by the same Pierio Valeriano.

On the other hand, a kind of terror is aroused by the way men sometimes boasted of their fortune in public inscriptions. Giovanni II Bentivoglio, ruler of Bologna, ventured to carve in stone on the newly built tower near his palace that his merit and his fortune had given him richly all that could be desired—and this a few years before his expulsion.[275] When the ancients spoke in this tone, they at least had a sense of the envy of the gods. In Italy it was probably the *condottieri* who first ventured to boast so loudly of their fortune.

Resuscitated antiquity affected religion most powerfully, however, not through any doctrines or philosophical system, but through a general tendency which it fostered. The men, and in some respects the institutions, of antiquity were

275. The chronicler does not make clear, however, whether this inscription was outside and visible or, like another mentioned by him, hidden on one of the foundation stones. In the latter case, a fresh idea is involved: by this secret inscription, known perhaps only to the chronicler, Fortune is to be magically bound to the building.

preferred to those of the Middle Ages, and in the eager attempt to imitate and reproduce them religious differences became a matter of indifference. The admiration for historical greatness absorbed everything.

The philologians added many special follies of their own and thereby attracted universal attention. How far Paul II was justified in calling his Abbreviators and their associates to account for their paganism is certainly a matter of great doubt, as his chief victim and biographer, Platina, has shown masterly skill in explaining his vindictiveness on other grounds and, especially, in making him appear a ludicrous figure. The charges of irreligion, paganism, denial of immortality, etc., were brought against the accused only when the charge of high treason had broken down. And Paul, if we are correctly informed about him, was by no means the man to judge intellectual matters, considering that it was he who exhorted the Romans to teach their children nothing beyond reading and writing. In his priestly narrowness of view he resembles Savonarola, except that to Pope Paul one could have retorted that it was he and his kind who were most to blame if culture made men hostile to religion. Nevertheless, it cannot be doubted that he felt a real anxiety about the pagan tendencies that surrounded him. And what, in truth, may not the humanists have allowed themselves at the court of the profligate pagan, Sigismondo Malatesta? How far these men, destitute for the most part of fixed principle, dared to go, certainly depended on their surroundings. Nor could they touch Christianity without paganizing it. It is curious, for instance, to notice how far a Gioviano Pontano carried this confusion; a saint is not only *divus,* but *deus;* to him the angels are identical with the genii of antiquity;[276] and his notion of immortality reminds us of the abode of the shades. This attitude occasionally results in the most fantastic extravagances. In 1526, when Siena was attacked by the exiled party, the worthy Canon Tizio, who tells the story himself, rose from his bed on July 22nd, remembered what is written in the third book of Macrobius, celebrated Mass, and then pronounced against the enemy the curse with which his author had provided him, only altering *Tellus mater teque Jupiter obtestor* [I call as witness you Mother Earth and you Jupiter] into *Tellus teque Christe Deus obtestor* [I call as witness you Earth and Christ our Lord]. After he had repeated this

276. Whereas the visual arts at least distinguished between angels and *putti,* and used the former for all serious purposes.

on the following two days, the enemy retreated. On one
side, these things strike us as a matter of mere style and
fashion; on the other, as a symptom of religious apostasy.

But antiquity exercised another, completely different perilous influence, and of a dogmatic kind: it imparted to the
Renaissance its own kind of superstition. Some fragments
of this had survived in Italy all through the Middle Ages,
and its reawakening was that much easier. That imagination
played a powerful part, goes without saying. Only imagination could have so thoroughly silenced the critical intellect
of the Italians.

The belief in a Divine government of the world was, as
we have said, shaken for some by the spectacle of so much
injustice and misery. Others as, for example, Dante, surrendered earthly life to the caprices of chance, and if they
nevertheless retained a sturdy faith, it was because they
held that the higher destiny of man would be accomplished
in the life to come. But when the belief in immortality
began to waver, Fatalism got the upper hand—or sometimes
the latter came first and had the former as its consequence.

The gap thus opened was filled chiefly by the astrology
of antiquity, or even of the Arabs. According to the relation
of the planets among themselves to the signs of the zodiac,
future events and the course of whole lives were divined
and the most weighty decisions arrived at. In many cases
the course of action adopted at the suggestion of the stars
may not have been any more immoral than that which
would have been followed without their influence. But too
often the decision must have been made at the cost of
honor and conscience. It is profoundly instructive to observe
how powerless culture and enlightenment were against this
delusion, since the latter was supported by the passionate
imagination of the people, by the burning desire to penetrate
and determine the future, and because antiquity sanctioned
it.

In the thirteenth century astrology suddenly became a
predominant feature in Italian life. Emperor Frederick II
always traveled with his astrologer Theodorus; and Ezzelino
da Romano had a large, well-paid court of such people,
among them the famous Guido Bonatto and the long-bearded
Saracen, Paul of Baghdad. They had to fix the day and hour
for all his important undertakings, and the gigantic atrocities
of which he was guilty may have been in part practical
inferences from their prophecies. Soon all scruples about
consulting the stars ceased. Not only princes, but even

cities[277] had their regular astrologers, and from the four-teenth to the sixteenth century, professors of this pseudo-science were appointed at the universities,[278] side by side with genuine astronomers. The Popes [279] made no secret of their stargazing, though Pius II, who also despised magic, omens, and the interpretation of dreams, is an honorable exception. Even Leo X seems to have thought the flourishing of astrology a credit to his Pontificate, and Paul III never held a Consistory unless the stargazers fixed the hour.

It may fairly be assumed that the better natures did not allow their actions to be determined by the stars beyond a certain point, and that there was a limit where conscience and religion made them pause. In point of fact, not only did pious and excellent people share the delusion, but they actually came forward to profess it publicly. One of these was Maestro Pagolo of Florence, in whom we can detect the same desire to turn astrology to moral account that we find in the late Roman Firmicus Maternus. His life was that of a saintly ascetic. He ate almost nothing, despised all temporal goods, and collected only books. A skilled physician, he practiced only among his friends, and made it a condition of his treatment that they confess their sins. He frequented the small but famous circle that assembled in the Monastery of the Angeli around Fra Ambrogio Camaldolese—and also the company of Cosimo the Elder, especially in his last years; for Cosimo accepted and used astrology, though probably only for situations of lesser importance. As a rule, however, Pagolo interpreted the stars only to his most confidential friends. But even without this severity of morals, the astrol-oger might be highly respected and show himself every-where; also, there were far more of them in Italy than in other European countries, where they appeared only at the great courts, and there not always. All the great householders in Italy, once the fashion was established, kept an astrologer, who, it must be added, was not always sure of his supper. The literature of this science, which was widely diffused even before the invention of printing, created a dilettantism which, as far as possible, followed in the steps of the masters. The worst species of astrologers were those who used the stars either as an aid or a cloak to magical arts.

277. Florence, for example, where Bonatto filled the office for some time.
278. At Bologna this professorship is said to have existed in 1125.
279. About 1260, Pope Alexander IV compelled a cardinal and shamefaced astrologer, Bianco, to bring out a number of political prophecies.

Yet even without this additional adornment, astrology is a miserable feature in Italian life of that time. What a figure all these highly gifted, many-sided, original characters cut when the blind passion for knowing and determining the future forces them to abdicate their powerful will and resolution! Now and then, when the stars send them too cruel a message, they manage to brace themselves, act for themselves, and say boldly: *Vir sapiens dominabitur astris*—the wise man is master of the stars [280]—and then relapse again into the old delusion.

In all the better families the horoscope of the children was drawn as a matter of course, and sometimes men were haunted for half their lives by the idle expectation of events that never occurred.[281] The stars were consulted whenever a great man had to make an important decision, even as to the hour at which the undertaking was to be begun. The journeys of princes, the reception of foreign ambassadors, the laying of the foundation stones of public buildings depended on the answer. A striking example of the latter occurs in the life of the aforenamed Guido Bonatto who, by his personal activity as well as his great systematic work on the subject, deserves to be called the restorer of astrology in the thirteenth century. In order to put an end to the struggle of the Guelphs and Ghibellines at Forlì, he persuaded the inhabitants to rebuild the city walls and to begin the works under a constellation he would indicate. If then, two men, one from each party, put a stone into the foundation at the same moment, henceforth and forever there would be no more party divisions in Forlì. A Guelph and a Ghibelline were selected for this office; the solemn moment arrived, each held the stone in his hands, the workmen stood ready with their tools. Bonatto gave the signal, and the Ghibelline threw his stone on to the foundation. But the Guelph hesitated, and then refused to do anything at all, on the ground that Bonatto was thought to be a Ghibelline

280. It was in such a moment of resolution that Il Moro had the cross with this inscription made, which is now in the Minster at Chur. Sixtus IV, too, once said that he would try to see if the proverb were true.

281. The father of Piero Capponi, himself an astrologer, put his son into trade lest he should get the dangerous wound in the head which threatened him. – The physician and astrologer Pierleoni of Spoleto believed that he would be drowned, therefore avoided all watery places and refused brilliant positions offered him at Venice and Padua.

and might be devising some mysterious mischief against the Guelphs. Upon which the astrologer addressed him: "God damn thee and thy Guelph party, with your distrustful malice! This constellation will not appear above our city for another 500 years." In fact God soon afterward did destroy the Guelphs of Forlì, but now (writes the chronicler about 1480) the two parties are thoroughly reconciled, and their very names are no longer heard.

Next important among those things which depended on the stars were the decisions in time of war. The same Bonatto procured a whole series of victories for the great Ghibelline leader Guido da Montefeltro by telling him the propitious hour for marching. When Bonatto no longer accompanied Montefeltro,[282] he lost the courage to maintain his despotism, and entered a Minorite monastery, where he lived as a monk for many years till his death. In the war with Pisa in 1362, the Florentines commissioned their astrologer to fix the hour for the march, and almost came too late because of a sudden order to take a circuitous route through the city. On former occasions they had marched out by the Via di Borgo Santi Apostoli, and had been unsuccessful; it was clear that there was some bad omen connected with this street when going out against Pisa, and thus the army was now led out by the Porta Rossa. But as the tents stretched out there to dry had not been taken away, the flags—a new bad omen— had to be lowered. The influence of astrology in war was confirmed by the fact that nearly all the *condottieri* believed in it. Jacopo Caldora was cheerful in the most serious illness, knowing that he was fated to fall in battle, which in fact happened. Bartolommeo Alviano was convinced that his head wounds were as much a gift of the stars as his military command. Niccolò Orsini-Pitigliano asked the physicist and astrologer Alessandro Benedetto to fix a favorable hour for the conclusion of his bargain with Venice (1495). When, on June 1, 1498, the Florentines solemnly invested their new *condottieri* Paolo Vitelli with his office, the Marshal's staff

282. When constellations auguring victory appeared, Bonatto ascended with his book and astrolobe to the tower of San Mercuriale above the Piazza and, when the right moment came, gave the signal for the great bell to be rung. Yet it was admitted that he was often wide of the mark and foresaw neither his own death nor the fate of Montefeltro. Not far from Cesena he was killed by robbers while on his way back to Forlì from Paris and from Italian universities where he had been lecturing.

they presented to him was, at his own wish, decorated with pictures of the constellations.[283]

Sometimes it is not completely clear whether in important political events the stars were questioned beforehand, or whether the astrologers were simply impelled afterward by curiosity to determine which constellation had decided the result. When Gian Galeazzo Visconti by a master stroke of policy imprisoned his uncle Bernabò and the latter's family (1385), we are told by a contemporary that Jupiter, Saturn, and Mars stood in the house of the Twins, but we do not learn whether the circumstance determined the deed. It is also probable that the astrologers were often influenced more by political calculation than by the course of the planets.

During the latter part of the Middle Ages all Europe had been terrified by predictions, spread from Paris and Toledo, of plagues, wars, floods, and earthquakes, and in this respect Italy was no exception. The unlucky year 1494, which opened forever the gates of Italy to the stranger, was undeniably ushered in by many prophecies of misfortune—only we cannot say whether such prophecies were not ready for every year.

This mode of thought was extended with thorough consistency into regions where we should hardly expect to meet it. If the whole outward and spiritual life of the individual is determined by the facts of his birth, the same law also governs groups of individuals, that is, nations and religions; and as the constellation of these things changes, so do the things themselves. The idea that each religion has its day first came into Italian culture in connection with these astrological beliefs. The conjunction of Jupiter with Saturn brought forth, we are told, the faith of Israel; that of Jupiter with Mars, the Chaldean; with the Sun, the Egyptian; with Venus, the Mohammedan; with Mercury, the Christian; and the conjunction of Jupiter with the Moon will one day bring forth the religion of Antichrist. Cecco d'Ascoli had already blasphemously calculated the nativity of Christ, and deduced from it his death on the cross. For this he was burned at the stake in 1327 at Florence.[284] Doctrines of this sort led

283. The same decoration was not uncommon on clothing and utensils. At the reception of Lucrezia Borgia in Ferrara, the mule of the Duchess of Urbino wore trappings of black velvet with astrological signs in gold.
284. There were also other reasons, among them, the jealousy of his colleagues. — Bonatto had taught similar things, e.g., the miracle of Divine Love in St. Francis as the effect of the planet Mars.

finally to the darkening of men's perception of spiritual things.

All the more worthy of recognition, then, is the warfare which the clear Italian spirit waged against this army of delusion. Side by side with the great monumental glorifications of astrology, such as the frescoes in the Salone at Padua and those in Borso's summer palace (Schifanoia) at Ferrara, side by side with the shameless praises of even such a man as the elder Beroaldus, there was always the sound of thoughtful and independent minds. Here, too, the way had been prepared by antiquity, but they did not merely parrot the ancients; they spoke from their own common sense and observation. Petrarch's attitude toward the astrologers, whom he knew personally, is one of bitter contempt,[285] and he saw through their system of lies. The novels, from the time they first began to appear—from the time of the *Hundred Old Tales* —were almost always hostile to the astrologers. The Florentine chroniclers guarded themselves valiantly against the delusions which, being part of historical tradition, they were compelled to record. Giovanni Villani says more than once, "No constellation can subjugate either the free will of man or the counsels of God." Matteo Villani declares astrology to be a vice which the Florentines had inherited, along with other superstitions, from their pagan ancestors, the Romans. It did not, however, remain a matter of mere literary discussion; the parties for and against disputed publicly. After the terrible floods of 1333, and again in 1345, astrologers and theologians discussed with great minuteness the influence of the stars, the will of God, and the justice of his punishments. These struggles never ceased throughout the whole course of the Renaissance, and we may conclude that the protestors were in earnest, since it was easier for them to recommend themselves to the great by defending rather than opposing astrology.

Among the most distinguished Platonists in the circle of Lorenzo the Magnificent opinions on the subject were divided. Marsilio Ficino defended astrology and drew the horoscopes of the children of the House, and is supposed to have predicted that the little Giovanni—afterward Leo X— would be Pope. On the other hand, Pico della Mirandola's famous refutation of the subject is of real epochal significance. He points out that belief in the stars is a root of all impiety and immorality; if the astrologer is to believe in anything,

285. His letter is addressed to Boccaccio, who must have been of a similar frame of mind.

he must worship the planets as gods, since it is from them that all good and evil proceed. Also, all other superstitions find a ready instrument here, since geomancy, chiromancy, and magic of every kind for the selection of the appropriate hour turn chiefly to astrology. With regard to morality, he maintains that nothing can more foster evil than the opinion that heaven itself is the cause of it, in which case faith in eternal happiness and punishment must also disappear. Pico even took the trouble to check the astrologers, and found that in the course of a month three fourths of their weather prophecies turned out false. But his main achievement was to set forth (in the Fourth Book) a positive Christian doctrine of the freedom of the will and the government of the universe, which seems to have made a greater impression on the educated classes throughout Italy than all the revivalist preachers put together. The latter, in fact, often failed to reach these classes any longer.

The first result of his book was that the astrologers ceased to publish their doctrines, and those who had already printed them were more or less ashamed. Gioviano Pontano, for example, in his book On Fate, had recognized the whole deluded science, and in a large work of his own had expounded the theory in the style of the old Firmicus. Now in his dialogue *Aegidius* he abandoned the astrologers, though not astrology, sounded the praises of free will, and limited the influence of the stars to mundane matters. Astrology remained more or less in fashion, but seems not to have dominated human life as it had formerly done. Painting, which in the fifteenth century had done its best to foster the delusion, now expressed the altered tone: in the cupola of the Chigi Chapel,[286] Raphael represents the symbols of the planets and the firmament, but watched and guided by beautiful angels and receiving from above the blessing of the Eternal Father. There seems to have been still another enemy of astrology in Italy: the Spaniards were not interested in it, not even the generals, and those who wished to gain their favor declared open war against the half-heretical, because it was half-Mohammedan, science. True, in 1529 Guicciardini still remarks: "How happy are the astrologers, who are believed if they tell one truth to a hundred lies, whereas other people lose all credit if they tell one lie to a hundred truths." But the contempt for astrology did not necessarily

286. In Santa Maria del Popolo, Rome. — The angels remind us of Dante's theory at the beginning of the *Convivio*.

lead to a return to the belief in Providence; it could also retreat to a general, indefinite Fatalism.

In this respect, as in others, Italy was unable to make its own way healthily through the ferment of the Renaissance, because the foreign invasion and the Counter Reformation intervened. Without such interference its own strength would have enabled it to rid itself thoroughly of these fantastic illusions. Those who hold that invasion and Catholic reaction were necessities for which the Italian people were themselves solely responsible will look on the spiritual bankruptcy they produced as a just retribution. But it is a pity that the rest of Europe had to pay so large a part of the penalty.

The belief in omens seems a much more innocent matter than astrology. The Middle Ages had inherited a large number of them from the various pagan religions, and Italy did not differ in this respect from other countries. What is characteristic of Italy is the support lent by humanism to the popular superstition. The inherited pagan fragment was backed up by a developed pagan literature.

The popular superstition of the Italians rested largely on premonitions and inferences drawn from ominous occurrences, with which a good deal of magic, mostly of an innocent sort, was connected. There was, however, no lack of learned humanists who boldly ridiculed these delusions, and have thereby reported them. Gioviano Pontano, the author of the great astrological work mentioned above, enumerates with pity in his *Charon* a long string of Neapolitan superstitions—the grief of the women when a fowl or goose caught the pip; the deep anxiety of the nobility if a hunting falcon did not come home, or if a horse sprained its foot; the magical formulas of the Apulian peasants, recited on three Saturday evenings, when mad dogs were at large. As in antiquity, the animal kingdom was regarded as specially significant in this respect, and the behavior of those lions, leopards, and other beasts kept by the State gave the people all the more food for reflection, because they had come to be considered as living symbols of the State. When, during the siege of Florence in 1529, an eagle that had been shot at flew into the city, the Signoria gave the bearer four ducats because the omen was good. Certain times and places were favorable or unfavorable, or even decisive, for certain actions. The Florentines, so Varchi tells us, held Saturday to be the fateful day on which all important events, good as well as bad, commonly happened. Their prejudice against marching out to war through a particular street has already been mentioned. At Perugia one of the gates, the Porta Eburnea was considered lucky, and the Baglioni always marched out through that gate on their way to war. Meteors and the appearance of the heavens were as significant as in the Middle Ages, and in an unusual formation of clouds the popular imagination saw warring armies and heard the clash of their collision high in the air. Superstition became a more serious matter when it attached itself to sacred things, when figures of the Virgin wept or moved their eyes, or when public calamities were associated with some alleged act of impiety, for which the people demanded expiation. In 1478, when Piacenza was visited with a violent and prolonged rainfall, it was said that there would be no dry weather till a certain usurer, who had lately been buried in San Francesco, had ceased to rest in consecrated earth. As the bishop was not obliging enough to have the corpse dug up, the young fellows of the town took it by force, dragged it round the streets amid frightful confusion, and at last threw it into the Po. Even an Angelo Politian accepted this point of view with regard to Giacomo Pazzi, one of the leaders of the Florentine conspiracy of 1478 that is called after his family. When he was put to death, he committed his soul to Satan with fearful words. Here, too, rain followed and threatened to ruin the harvest; here, too, a party of men (mostly peasants) dug up the body in the church, and immediately the clouds departed and the sun shone—"so gracious was fortune to the opinion of the people," adds the great scholar. The corpse was first cast into unhallowed ground, the next day dug up again, and after a horrible procession through the city, thrown into the Arno.

These and similar things bear a popular character, and might have occurred in the tenth century just as well as in the sixteenth. But now comes the literary influence of antiquity. We know positively that the humanists were peculiarly accessible to prodigies and auguries, and instances of this have already been mentioned. If further evidence were needed, it would be found in Poggio. The same radical thinker who denied the rights of noble birth and the inequality of men, not only believed in all the medieval stories of ghosts and devils, but also in prodigies of the ancient sort, like those said to have occurred on the last visit of Pope Eugenius IV to Florence. "Near Como there were seen one evening four thousand dogs, who took the road to Germany; these were followed by a great herd of cattle, and these by an army on foot and horseback, some with no heads and some with almost invisible heads, and then a gigantic horseman with another herd of cattle behind him." Poggio also believes in a battle of magpies and jackdaws. He even relates, perhaps without being aware of it, a well-preserved piece of ancient mythology. On the Dalmatian coast a bearded and horned Triton had appeared, a genuine sea satyr, ending in fins and a tail; he carried away women and children from the shore, till five stouthearted washerwomen killed him with sticks and stones. A wooden model of the monster, which was exhibited at Ferrara, makes the whole story credible to Poggio. Though there were no more oracles, and it was no longer possible to take counsel of the gods, it again became the fashion to open Vergil at hazard, and take as an omen the passage hit upon *(sortes virgilianae)*.[287] Nor can the belief in demons current in the later period of antiquity have been without influence on the Renaissance. The work of Iamblichus or Abammon on the Mysteries of the Egyptians, which could have contributed to this, was already printed in a Latin translation at the end of the fifteenth century. The Platonic Academy at Florence was not wholly free from these and other neoplatonic delusions of the Roman decadence. A few words must be given here to the belief in demons and to the magic that was connected with this belief.

The popular faith in what is called the spirit world was nearly the same in Italy as elsewhere in Europe. In Italy, too, there were ghosts, that is, reappearances of deceased persons; and if the view differed in any respect from that which prevailed in the North, the difference betrayed itself only in the ancient name *ombra*. Even nowadays if such a shade presents itself, a couple of Masses are said for its repose. That the spirits of evil men appear in a dreadful shape, is a matter of course, but along with this we find the notion that the ghosts of the departed are generally malicious. The dead, says the priest in a novel by Bandello, kill the little children. It seems as though this means that a certain shade was thought of as separate from the soul, since the latter suffers in Purgatory, and when *it* appears, does nothing but wail and pray. At other times what appears is not the ghost of a man, but of an event—of a past condition of things. Thus did the neighbors explain the diabolical appearances in the old palace of the Visconti near San Giovanni in Conca at Milan, since it was here that Bernabò Visconti had caused countless victims of his tyranny to be tortured and strangled, and small wonder if strange things were to be seen. One evening a swarm of poor people with candles in

287. In 1529 two suspected persons decided to flee because they opened the *Aeneid* at Book III, 44. Cf. Rabelais, *Pantagruel*, Book III, ch. 10.

their hands appeared to a dishonest guardian of the poor at
Perugia, and danced around him; a great figure spoke in
threatening tones on their behalf—it was St. Alò, the patron
saint of the poorhouse. – These beliefs were so much a
matter of course that the poets could use them as universally
valid motifs. The appearance of the slain Lodovico Pico under
the walls of besieged Mirandola is finely represented by Castiglione. It is true that poetry made the freest use of these
conceptions when the poet himself had outgrown them.

Italy shared the belief in demons that was common to the
other nations of the Middle Ages. Men were convinced that
God sometimes allowed bad spirits of every degree to exercise a destructive influence on parts of the world and of human
life. The only reservation made was that the man to whom
the Evil One came as tempter, could use his free will to
resist. In Italy the demonic influence, especially as shown
in natural events, easily assumed a character of poetic greatness. The night before the great inundation of the Val d'Arno
in 1333, a pious hermit above Vallombrosa heard a diabolical
tumult in his cell, crossed himself, stepped to the door, and
saw a crowd of black and terrible knights in armor gallop
by. When conjured to stand, one of them said: "We go to
drown the city of Florence because of its sins, if God will
let us." We may compare with this the nearly contemporary
vision at Venice (1340) out of which a great master of the
Venetian school, probably Giorgione, made a marvelous picture of a galley full of demons which speeds with the swift-
ness of a bird over the stormy lagoon to destroy the sinful
island-city, till the three saints, who have stepped unobserved
into a poor boatman's skiff, exorcize the fiends and send
them and their vessel to the bottom of the waters.[288]

To this belief was now added the illusion that by means of
magical arts it was possible to enter into relations with the
evil ones, and to use their help to further the purposes of
greed, ambition, and sensuality. Many persons were probably
accused of doing so before the time when many were guilty;
only when the so-called magicians and witches began to be
burned, did the deliberate practice of the black art become
more frequent. With the smoke of the fires in which the suspected victims were sacrificed were spread the narcotic fumes
by which numbers of ruined characters were drugged into
magic. They were joined by many calculating impostors.

288. [Burckhardt probably refers here to the *Miracle of St. Mark*
in the Biblioteca dell' Ospedale Civile, Venice, which is now
catalogued as by Palma Vecchio.]

The primitive and popular form in which the superstition had probably lived on uninterruptedly from the time of the Romans was the art of the witch *(strega)*. So long as she limited herself to mere divination,[289] she might be completely innocent, were it not that the transition from prophecy to active help could easily, though often imperceptibly, be a fatal downward step. Once it became a matter of causative magic, she was endowed primarily with the power of exciting love or hatred between man and woman, but also with purely destructive and malignant arts, especially with the sickness of little children, even when the malady obviously came from the neglect and stupidity of the parents. It is still questionable how far she was supposed to act by mere magical ceremonies and formulas, or by a conscious alliance with the fiends, apart from the poisons and drugs which she administered with a full knowledge of their effect.

The more innocent form of the superstition, in which the mendicant friar could venture to appear as the competitor of the witch, is shown, for example, in the case of the witch of Gaeta, of whom we read in Pontano. His traveler Suppatius reaches her dwelling while she is giving audience to a girl and a servant maid, who come to her with a black hen, nine eggs laid on a Friday, a duck, and some white thread—for it is the third day since the new moon. They are sent away, and told to return at twilight. It is to be hoped that nothing worse than divination is intended. The mistress of the servant maid is pregnant by a monk; the girl's lover has proved untrue and has entered a monastery. The witch complains: "Since my husband's death I support myself in this way, and I would make a good thing of it, since the Gaetan women have plenty of faith, were it not that the monks balk me of my gains by explaining dreams, appeasing the anger of the saints for money, promising husbands to the girls, men children to the pregnant women, offspring to the barren, and, besides all this, visiting the women at night when their husbands are away fishing, having made the assignations in daytime at church." Suppatius warns her against the envy of the monastery, but she has no fear, since the guardian is an old acquaintance of hers.

But the superstition gave rise to a worse sort of witch, those who deprived men of their health and life. In these

---

289. This was probably the case with the possessed woman who in 1513 at Ferrara and elsewhere was consulted by distinguished Lombards as to future events; her name was Rodogine. See also Rabelais, *Pantagruel,* Book IV, ch. 58.

cases the mischief, when not sufficiently accounted for by the evil eye and the like, was naturally attributed to the aid of powerful spirits. The punishment, as we have seen in the case of Finicella, was the stake; and yet a compromise with fanaticism was still possible. According to the laws of Perugia, for example, a witch could settle the affair by paying 400 pounds. At that time the matter was not yet treated with the seriousness and consistency of later times. In the territories of the Church, in the upper Apennines, indeed at Norcia, the home of St. Benedict, there was a perfect nest of witches and sorcerers. No secret was made of it. One of the most remarkable letters of Aeneas Sylvius, dating from his youth, tells us about it. He writes to his brother: "The bearer of this came to me to ask if I knew of a Mount of Venus in Italy, for in such a place magical arts were taught, and his master, a Saxon and a great astronomer, was anxious to learn them. I told him that I knew of a Porto Venere not far from Carrara, on the rocky coast of Liguria, where I spent three nights on the way to Basel; I also found that there was a mountain called Eryx, in Sicily, which was dedicated to Venus, but I did not know whether magic was taught there. But it came into my mind during the conversation, that in Umbria, in the old Duchy (Spoleto), not far from the town of Norcia, there is a cave beneath a steep rock, in which water flows. There, as I remember to have heard, are witches *(striges)*, demons, and nightly shades, and he that has the courage can see and speak to ghosts *(spiritus)*, and learn magical arts.[290] I have not seen it, nor taken any trouble to see it, for that which is learned with sin is better not learned at all." He nevertheless names his informant, and begs his brother to take the bearer of the letter to him, should he still be alive. Aeneas goes far here in his politeness to a man of position, but personally he was not only freer from superstition than his contemporaries, but he also stood a test on the subject which not every educated man of our own day could endure. At the time of the Council of Basel, when he lay sick of the fever for seventy-five days at Milan, he could never be persuaded to listen to the magic doctors, though a man was brought to his bedside who a short time before had marvelously cured 2,000 soldiers of fever in the camp of

290. In the fourteenth century there existed a kind of hell gate near Anselonia in Tuscany. It was a cave with footprints of men and animals in the sand, which, whenever they were effaced, reappeared the next day.

Piccinino. While still an invalid, Aeneas rode over the mountains to Basel, and recovered during the journey.[291]

We learn something more about the neighborhood of Norcia through the necromancer who tried to get the eminent Benvenuto Cellini into his power. A new book of magic was to be consecrated,[292] and the best place for the ceremony was among the mountains in that district. True, the master of the magician had once done the same thing near the Abbey of Farfa, but had found difficulties there which did not present themselves at Norcia; further, the peasants in the latter neighborhood were trustworthy people who had had practice in the matter and could afford considerable help in case of need. The expedition did not take place, else Benvenuto would probably have been able to tell us something of the impostor's assistants. At that time the whole neighborhood was proverbial. Aretino says somewhere of an enchanted well, "there dwell the sisters of the sibyl of Norcia and the aunt of the Fata Morgana." And about the same time Trissino could still, in his great epic, celebrate the place with all the resources of poetry and allegory as the home of authentic prophecy.

After the notorious bull of Innocent VIII (1484), witchcraft and the persecution of witches grew into a great and revolting system. The chief representatives of this system of persecution were German Dominicans; and Germany and, curiously enough, those parts of Italy nearest Germany were the regions most afflicted by this plague. The bulls and injunctions of the Popes themselves refer, for example, to the Dominican Province of Lombardy, to Cremona, to the dioceses of Brescia and Bergamo. We learn from Sprenger's famous theoretico-practical guide, the *Malleus maleficarum,* that forty-one witches were burned at Como in the first year after the publication of the bull; crowds of Italian women took refuge in the territory of Archduke Sigismund, where they believed they would still be safe. Witchcraft finally took firm root in a few unlucky Alpine valleys, especially in the Val Camonica; the system of persecution had succeeded in permanently infecting with the delusion those populations which were in any way predisposed to it. This essentially German form of witchcraft is what we should think of when reading the stories and novels of Milan, Bologna, etc. That it did not make further progress in Italy is probably due to the fact that here a highly developed *stregheria* was already in existence, resting on a different set

291. *The Commentaries of Pius II,* Book I.
292. Benv. Cellini, Book I, ch. 65.

of ideas. The Italian witch practiced a trade, and needed money and, above all, sense. She has nothing of the hysterical dreams of the Northern witch, of marvelous journeys through the air, of Incubus and Succubus; the business of the *strega* was to provide for other people's pleasures. If she was credited with the power of assuming different shapes, or of transporting herself suddenly to distant places, she was content to accept this reputation just so far as her influence was thereby increased; on the other hand, it was perilous for her when the fear of her malice and vengeance, and especially of her power for enchanting children, cattle, and crops, gained ground. Inquisitors and magistrates could become most popular if they burned her.

By far the most important field for the activity of the *strega* lay, as has been said, in love affairs, and included the stirring up of love and hatred, the producing of abortion, the pretended murder of the unfaithful man or woman by magical arts, and even the manufacture of poisons. Owing to the unwillingness of many persons to have to do with these women there arose a class of occasional practitioners who secretly learned this and that from them, and then used this knowledge on their own. The Roman prostitutes, for example, tried to enhance their personal attractions by another kind of magic in the style of the Horatian Canidia. Aretino may not only have known but also have, in this particular, told the truth about them. He gives a list of the loathsome messes that could be found in their boxes—hair, skulls, ribs, teeth, dead men's eyes, human skin, the navels of little children, the soles of shoes, and pieces of clothing from graves. They themselves went to the graveyard and fetched bits of rotten flesh which they slyly fed to their lovers—with more that is still worse. Pieces of the hair and nails of the lover were boiled in oil stolen from the ever-burning lamps in the church. The most innocuous of their charms was to make a heart of glowing ashes, and then to piece it while singing:

> *Prima che'l fuoco spenghi,*
> *Fa ch'a mia porta venghi;*
> *Tal ti punga mio amore*
> *Quale io fo questo cuore.* [293]

There were other charms practiced by moonlight, with drawings on the ground and figures of wax or bronze, which

293. [Before the fire goes out,/Make him come to my door;/ Let my love pierce you/As I pierce this heart.]

doubtless represented the lover and were treated according to circumstances.

These things were so customary that a woman without youth and beauty, who nevertheless exercised a powerful charm on men, naturally became suspected of witchcraft. The mother of Sanga (secretary to Clement VII) poisoned her son's mistress, who was a woman of this kind. Unfortunately the son died too, as well as a party of friends who had eaten of the poisoned salad.

Next came, not as helper but as competitor to the witch, the magician or enchanter—*incantatore*—who was still more familiar with the perilous business of the craft. Sometimes he was as much or more of an astrologer than a magician; he probably often presented himself as an astrologer to avoid being prosecuted as a magician, and some astrology was essential in order to determine the favorable hour for a magical process. But since many spirits are good or indifferent, the magician could sometimes maintain a very tolerable reputation, and in 1474 Sixtus IV had to proceed expressly against some Bolognese Carmelites, who asserted in the pulpit that there was no harm in seeking information from the demons. Very many people believed in the possibility of the thing itself; an indirect proof of this lies in the fact that the most pious men believed that by prayer they could obtain visions of good spirits. Savonarola's mind was filled with these things; the Florentine Platonists speak of a mystic union with God; and Marcellus Palingenius gives us to understand clearly that he consorted with consecrated spirits.[294] The same writer is convinced of the existence of a whole hierarchy of bad demons, who range from the moon downward, and are ever on the watch to do some mischief to nature and human life. He even tells of his own personal acquaintance with some of them, and as the scope of our book does not allow a systematic exposition of the then prevalent belief in spirits, the narrative of Palingenius may be given as one instance out of many.[295]

At San Silvestro, on Soracte, he had been receiving instruction from a pious hermit on the nothingness of earthly things and the worthlessness of human life, and when night drew near he set out on his way to Rome. On the road, in the full light of the moon, he was joined by three men, one of whom called him by name and asked him whence he came. Palingenius answered: "From the wise man on the mountain."

294. *The Zodiac of Life,* XII, 363-539; cf. X, 393ff.
295. *Ibid.,* X, 770ff.

"O fool," replied the stranger, "do you in truth believe that anyone on earth is wise? Only higher beings *(divi)* have wisdom, and such are we three, although we wear the shapes of men. I am named Saracil, and these two Sathiel and Jana. Our kingdom lies near the moon, where dwell that multitude of intermediate beings who have sway over earth and sea." Palingenius then asked, not without an inward tremor, what they were going to do at Rome. The answer was: "One of our comrades, Ammon, is kept in servitude by the magic arts of a youth from Narni, one of the attendants of Cardinal Orsini; for mark it, O men, there is proof of your own immortality therein, that you can control one of us: I myself, shut up in crystal, was once forced to serve a German, till a bearded monk set me free. This is the service that we wish to render at Rome to our friend, and shall also take the opportunity of sending one or two distinguished Romans to the nether world." At these words a light breeze arose, and Sathiel said: "Listen, our messenger is coming back from Rome, this wind announces him." And in fact another being appeared, whom they greeted joyfully and asked about Rome. His utterances are strongly anti-Papal: Clement VII was again allied with the Spaniards and hoped to root out Luther's doctrines, not with arguments but by the Spanish sword. This is pure profit for the demons, since the impending bloodshed would enable them to carry into hell the souls of thousands. After this conversation, in which Rome and its immorality is represented as completely given over to the Evil One, the apparitions vanish, and leave the poet sadly to pursue his way alone.

Those who want to form a conception of the extent of those relations to demons which could be openly avowed in spite of the penalties attaching to witchcraft, should turn to the much-read work of Agrippa von Nettesheim, On Occult Philosophy. He seems originally to have written it before he was in Italy, but in the dedication to Trithemius he mentions, among others, many important Italian authorities, if only by way of disparagement. In the case of equivocal persons like Agrippa, or of the knaves and fools that made up the majority, there is little that is interesting in the system they profess with its formulas, fumigations, ointments, bones of the dead,[296] and the rest. But this system was filled

296. Yet murder is hardly ever the end, and perhaps never the means. A monster such as Gilles de Retz (about 1440), who sacrificed more than 100 children to the demons, has not even a distant counterpart in Italy.

with quotations from the superstitions of antiquity, the influence of which on the life and passions of the Italians is at times most remarkable and fruitful. We might think that a great mind must be thoroughly ruined before it surrenders itself to such influences; but the violence of hope and desire led even vigorous and original men of all classes to have recourse to the magician, and the belief that the thing was feasible at all weakened to some extent the faith in a moral order of even those who kept at a distance. At the cost of a little money and danger it seemed possible to defy with impunity the universal reason and morality of mankind, and to spare oneself the intermediate steps which otherwise lie between a man and his lawful or unlawful ends.

Let us glance here for a moment at an older and now decaying form of superstition. From the darkest period of the Middle Ages, or even from the days of antiquity, many cities of Italy had kept the remembrance of the connection of their fate with certain buildings, statues, etc. The ancients had left records of consecrating priests or *telestae*, who were present at the solemn foundation of cities and magically guaranteed their prosperity by erecting certain monuments or by burying certain objects (*telesmata*). Traditions of this sort were more likely than anything else to live on in the form of popular, unwritten legend; but in the course of centuries the priest naturally became transformed into the magician, since the religious side of his function in antiquity was no longer understood. In some of the Vergilian miracles at Naples[297] there is clearly preserved the ancient remembrance of one of these *telestae* whose name was, in the course of time, supplanted by that of Vergil. The enclosing of the mysterious picture of the city in a vessel is nothing more than a genuine ancient *telesma;* and Vergil, the founder of the walls of Naples, is only a transformation of the officiating priest who took part in the ceremony. The popular imagination went on working at these themes, till Vergil became responsible for the bronze horse, for the heads at the Nolan gate, for the bronze fly over another gate, and even for the Grotto of Posilippo—all of them things which in one respect or other served to put a magical constraint on fate, while the first two seemed to determine the whole fortune of the city. Medieval Rome also preserved confused recollections of the same kind.

297. That Vergil began to take the place of the older *telestae* may be explained partly by the fact that the frequent visits to his grave even in the time of the Empire struck the popular imagination.

At the church of Sant' Ambrogio in Milan, there was an ancient marble Hercules; so long, it was said, as this stood in its place, so long would the Empire last. The Empire of the Germans is probably meant, as the coronation of their emperors at Milan took place in this church. The Florentines were convinced that the temple of Mars (later transformed into the Baptistery) would stand to the end of time, according to the constellation under which it had been built in the time of Augustus; they had, as Christians, removed from it the marble equestrian statue; but since the destruction of the latter would have brought some great calamity on the city—also according to a constellation—they set it up on a tower by the Arno. When Totila [Attila] conquered Florence, the statue fell into the river, and was not fished out again till Charlemagne refounded the city. It was then placed on a pillar at the entrance to the Ponte Vecchio, and on this spot Buondelmonte was slain in 1215. The origin of the great feud between Guelph and Ghibelline was thus associated with the dreaded idol. During the inundation of 1333 the statue vanished forever.

But the same *telesma* reappears elsewhere. Guido Bonatto, already mentioned, was not satisfied, at the refounding of the walls of Forlì, with requiring certain symbolic acts of reconciliation from the two parties. By burying a bronze or stone equestrian statue, which he had produced by astrological or magical arts, he believed that he had defended the city from ruin, and even from capture and plunder. When Cardinal Albornoz was governor of Romagna some sixty years later, the statue was accidentally dug up and shown to the people, probably by the order of the Cardinal, that it might be known by what means the cruel Montefeltro had defended himself against the Roman Church. And again, half a century later (1450), when an attempt to surprise Forlì had failed, men appealed to the power of the statue, which had perhaps been saved and reburied. It was the last time they could indulge themselves; a year later Forlì was really taken. – The foundation of buildings all through the fifteenth century was associated not only with astrology but also with magic. The large number of gold and silver medals which Paul II buried in the foundation of his buildings was noticed,[298] and Platina was by no means displeased to recognize in this an old pagan

---

298. Platina, *The Lives of the Popes: veteres potius hac in re quam Petrum, Anacletum et Linum imitatus* [preferring to imitate in this respect the ancient customs rather than Peter, Anacletus, and Linus].

telesma. Neither Paul nor his biographer were in any way conscious of the medieval religious significance of such an offering.

But this official magic, which in many cases rests only on hearsay, never attained the importance of the secret magic practiced for personal ends.

The part this most often played in daily life is shown by Ariosto in his comedy of the necromancers. His hero is one of the many Jewish exiles from Spain, although he also presents himself as a Greek, an Egyptian, and an African, and is constantly changing his name and costume. He pretends that his incantations can darken the day and lighten the night, that he can move the earth, make himself invisible, and change men into beasts; but these boasts are only an advertisement. His true object is to make profit out of unhappy and troubled marriages, and the trail he leaves behind him is like the slime of a snail, and often like the ruin wrought by a hailstorm. To attain his ends he can persuade people that the box in which a lover is hidden is full of ghosts, or that he can make a corpse talk. It is at least a good sign that poets and novelists could count on popular applause in holding up this class of men to ridicule. Bandello not only treats the sorcery of a Lombard monk as a miserable, and in its consequences terrible, piece of knavery, but he also describes[299] with unaffected indignation the disasters which never cease to pursue the credulous fool. "Such a man hopes that with Solomon's seal and many other magical books he will find the treasures hidden in the bosom of the earth, force his lady to do his will, learn the secret of princes, and transport himself in the twinkling of an eye from Milan to Rome. The more often he is deceived, the more steadfastly he believes. . . . Do you remember the time, Signor Carlo, when a freind of ours, in order to win the favor of his beloved, filled his room with skulls and bones, like a churchyard?" The most loathsome tasks were prescribed—to draw three teeth from a corpse or a nail from its finger, and the like; and while the hocus-pocus of the incantation went on, the unhappy participants sometimes died of terror.

Benvenuto Cellini did not die during the well-known incantation (1532) in the Colosseum at Rome,[300] although both he and his companions witnessed no ordinary horrors; the

299. The magician exacts a promise of secrecy strengthened by solemn oaths, in this case by an oath at the high altar of San Petronio at Bologna, when no one else was in the church.
300. Benv. Cellini, Book I, ch. 64.

Sicilian priest, who probably expected to find him a useful coadjutor in the future, paid him the compliment, as they went home, of saying that he had never met a man of such courage. Every reader will have his own thoughts on the proceedings themselves. The narcotic fumes and the fact that the imagination of the spectators was predisposed for all possible terrors are the chief points to be noticed, and explain why the young boy who had been brought along, and on whom they made the most impression, saw much more than the others. But it may be inferred that it was Benvenuto himself they were supposed to impress, since the dangerous beginning of the incantation can have had no other aim than to arouse curiosity. For Benvenuto had to think before the fair Angelica occurred to him; and the magician told him afterward that love-making was folly compared with the finding of treasures. Further, it must not be forgotten that it flattered his vanity to be able to say: "The demons have kept their word, and exactly a month later Angelica came into my hands, as they promised" (ch. 68). Even if Benvenuto gradually deluded himself into believing the whole story, it would still be permanently valuable as evidence of the mode of thought prevalent at that time.

As a rule, however, the Italian artists, even "the odd, capricious, and eccentric" among them, had little to do with magic. One of them, in his anatomical studies, may have cut himself a jacket out of the skin of a corpse, but at the advice of his confessor he put it back into the grave.[301] Indeed the frequent study of corpses probably did more than anything else to destroy the belief in the magical influence of various parts of the body, while at the same time the incessant observation and representation of the human form opened to the artist a completely different kind of magic.

In general, notwithstanding the instances that have been cited, magic seems to have been markedly on the decline at the beginning of the sixteenth century—that is, at a time when it first began to flourish vigorously outside Italy; thus, the tours of Italian sorcerers and astrologers in the North seem not to have begun till they were no longer trusted at home. In the fourteenth century it was thought necessary to watch carefully the lake on Mount Pilatus, near Scariotto, to hinder the magicians from consecrating their books there. In the fifteenth century we find, for example, that the offer was made to produce a storm of rain, in order to frighten

301. Vasari, Life of Andrea da Fiesole. It was Silvio Cosini, who also believed in "incantations and similar follies."

away a besieged army; and even then the commander of the besieged town—Niccolò Vitelli in Città di Castello—had the good sense to dismiss the sorcerers as godless persons. In the sixteenth century instances of this official kind no longer appear, although the magicians were still active in private affairs. The classic figure of German sorcery, Dr. Johann Faust, belongs to this time; whereas the Italian ideal, Guido Bonatto, dates back to the thirteenth century.

It must nevertheless be added that the decrease of belief in magic was not necessarily accompanied by an increase of belief in a moral order, but that in many cases, like the decaying faith in astrology, the delusion left behind it nothing but a hollow fatalism.

One or two minor forms of superstition—pyromancy, chiromancy, etc.—which gained ground as the belief in sorcery and astrology declined, may be passed over here, and even the emerging physiognomy has none of the interest that the name might lead us to expect. For it did not appear as the sister and ally of art and psychology, but as a new form of fatalistic superstition and, what it may have been among the Arabs, as the rival of astrology. The author of a manual on physiognomy, Bartolommeo Cocle, who styled himself a "metoposcopist" and whose science, according to Giovio, seemed like one of the most respectable of the liberal arts, was not content with the prophecies he made to the clever people who consulted him daily; he compiled a very serious "catalogue of those who were destined to meet great dangers in life." Giovio, although grown old in the free thought of Rome—*in hac luce romana*—nevertheless finds that the predictions contained therein had only too much truth in them.[302] But on this same occasion we also learn how the people aimed at in these and similar prophecies took vengeance on the seers. Giovanni Bentivoglio had Lucas Gauricus suspended from a rope hanging from a lofty, winding staircase and swung five times against a wall, because Lucas had predicted to him the loss of his authority.[303] Ermes Bentivoglio sent an assassin after Cocle, because the unlucky metoposcopist had—unwillingly—prophesied to him that he would die an exile in battle. The murderer, it seems, mocked the dying man: Cocle himself had foretold that he would

302. It is Giovio the enthusiastic collector of portraits who speaks here.
303. From the stars, since Gauricus did not know physiognomy. For his own fate, however, he had to refer to the prophecies of Cocle, for his father had neglected to draw his horoscope.

shortly commit an infamous murder. – The reviver of chiromancy, Antioco Tiberto of Cesena, came to an equally miserable end at the hands of Pandolfo Malatesta of Rimini, to whom he had prophesied the worst that a tyrant can imagine: death in exile and the most grievous poverty. Tiberto was a man of intelligence, who seems to have given his answers not so much according to any methodical chiromancy as by means of his shrewd knowledge of mankind; and his high culture won him the respect of those scholars who thought little of his divination.

Alchemy, in conclusion, which is not mentioned in antiquity till quite late, under Diocletian, played only a very subordinate part at the height of the Renaissance. Italy had gone through this disease earlier, in the fourteenth century when, Petrarch admitted in his polemic against it, gold making was a general practice. Since that time, the particular kind of faith, devotion, and isolation that the practice of alchemy required became more and more rare in Italy, while in the North, Italian and other adepts began to make full profit out of the great lords. Under Leo X the few Italians who busied themselves with it were called "brooders" (ingenia curiosa) and Aurelio Augurelli, who dedicated to Leo X, the great despiser of gold, his didactic poem on the making of the metal, is said to have received in return a beautiful but empty purse. The mystic science which, besides gold, sought for the omnipotent philosopher's stone is a late Northern growth, which rose from the theories of Paracelsus and others.

The decline of the belief in immortality is closely connected to these superstitions and to ancient modes of thought in general. But, in addition, this question has even broader and deeper bearings on the whole development of the modern spirit.

One great source of doubt in immortality was the inward wish to be under no obligation to the hated Church. We have seen that the Church named those who felt this way Epicureans. In the hour of death many may have turned again to the sacraments, but multitudes during their whole lives, and especially during their most vigorous years, lived and acted according to the other view. That non-belief on this particular point must often have led to a general skepticism, is evident of itself, and is attested by abundant historical proof. These are the men of whom Ariosto says: their faith goes no higher than the roof.[304] In Italy, and especially in

304. The poet says it angrily of an official who had decided against him in a matter of property.

Florence, it was possible to live as an open and notorious non-believer, so long as one refrained from direct acts of hostility against the Church. The confessor, for instance, who was sent to prepare a political offender for death, began by inquiring whether the prisoner was a believer, "for there was a false report that he had no belief at all."[305]

The unhappy transgressor about whom this is told—the same Pierpaolo Boscoli whom we have already mentioned—who in 1513 took part in an attempt against the newly restored Medici, is a faithful reflection of the religious confusion that prevailed at that time. He was first a partisan of Savonarola, but then became possessed with an enthusiasm for the ancient ideals of liberty, and for paganism in general; when he was in prison, however, his early friends regained the control of his mind, and secured for him what they considered a pious ending. The tender witness and narrator of his last hours was a member of the artistic family of the Della Robbia, the learned philologist Luca. "Ah," sighs Boscoli, "drive Brutus out of my head, that I may go my way as a Christian." "If you want to," answers Luca, "it is not difficult; for you know that these deeds of the Romans are not handed down to us straightforwardly, but idealized *(con arte accresciute)."* The penitent forces himself to believe, and bewails his inability to believe voluntarily. If only he could live for a month with pious monks he would become truly spiritual. It turns out that these partisans of Savonarola did not know their Bible very well; Boscoli can only say the Paternoster and the Ave Maria, and earnestly begs Luca to exhort his friends to study the sacred writings, for only what a man has learned in life does he possess in death. Luca then reads and explains to him the story of the Passion according to the Gospel of St. John; the poor listener, strange to say, can perceive clearly the divine nature of Christ, but is perplexed at His manhood; he wishes to get as firm a hold of it "as if Christ came to meet him out of a wood," whereupon his friend exhorts him to be humble, since these are only doubts sent to him by the Devil. Later the penitent remembers that he has not fulfilled a vow made in his youth, to make a pilgrimage to the Impruneta; his friend promises to do it for him. Meanwhile the confessor—a monk from Savonarola's monastery, as he had requested—arrives and after giving him the explanation quoted above of the opinion of St. Thomas Aquinas on tyrannicide, exhorts him to bear

305. The standard expression was *non aver fede* [to have no faith], cf. Vasari, Life of Piero di Cosimo.

death manfully. Boscoli answers: "Father, waste no time on this, for the philosophers are satisfactory enough for that; help me to bear death out of love to Christ." What follows— the communion, the leave-taking and the execution—is very touchingly described. But one point deserves special mention. When Boscoli laid his head on the block, he begged the executioner to delay the stroke for a moment: "During the whole time (since the pronouncement of the sentence) he had been striving after a close union with God, without attaining it, and now in this supreme moment he thought that by a strong effort he could give himself wholly to God." Clearly an expression of Savonarola—half-understood—was troubling him.

If we had more confessions of this kind, the spiritual picture of that age would be richer by many important features, which no poem or treatise gives us. We should see more clearly how strong the inborn religious instinct was, how subjective and how variable was the relation of the individual to religion, and what powerful enemies and competitors religion had. That men whose inward condition is of such a nature are not the men to found a new church is evident; but the history of the Western spirit would be imperfect without considering that agitated period among the Italians, whereas other nations, who have had no share in the evolution of thought, may be passed over without loss. But we must return to the question of immortality.

If non-belief in this respect attained such a significant position among the more highly developed people, this was because the great earthly task of discovering the world and representing it in word and form absorbed most of the higher spiritual faculties. We have already spoken of the inevitable worldliness of the Renaissance. But this investigation and this art were necessarily accompanied by a general spirit of doubt and inquiry. If this spirit manifests itself little in literature, if, for example, it reveals itself only in isolated instances of the beginnings of biblical criticism, we are not to assume that it did not exist. It was only over-powered by what we have just mentioned—the need of representation and creation in all areas, that is, by the artistic instinct; and it was further checked, whenever it tried to express itself theoretically, by the existing despotism of the Church. This spirit of doubt must, for reasons too obvious to need discussion, have inevitably and chiefly concerned itself with the question of the state of man after death.

And here antiquity entered, and affected the whole matter in two ways. In the first place, men set out to master the psychology of the ancients, and tortured the letter of Aristotle for a definitive answer. In one of the Lucianic dialogues of the time, Charon tells Mercury how he questioned Aristotle on his belief in immortality when the philosopher crossed in the Stygian boat; the prudent sage, physically dead yet still alive, declined even then to compromise himself by a straightforward answer; so how could his writings be interpreted now, after so many centuries! — All the more eagerly did men dispute about his opinion and that of other ancient writers on the true nature of the soul, its origin, its pre-existence, its unity in all men, its absolute eternity, even its transformations; and there were men who discussed these things in the pulpit. The debate became especially heated in the fifteenth century; some proved that Aristotle taught the doctrine of an immortal soul; others complained of the hard-heartedness of men who would believe that there was a soul only if they saw it sitting on a chair in front of them; in his funeral oration on Francesco Sforza, Filelfo quotes a long list of opinions of ancient and even Arab philosophers in favor of immortality, and closes the mixture, which covers a folio page and a half of print, with the words, "Besides all this we have the Old and New Testaments, which are above all truth." In the middle of all this came the Florentine Platonists with Plato's doctrine of the soul, supplemented, as in the case of Pico, by Christian teaching. But the opposite opinion prevailed in the instructed world. At the beginning of the sixteenth century the anxiety it caused to the Church was so serious that Leo X set forth a Constitution at the Lateran Council (1513) in defense of the immortality and individuality of the soul, the latter against those who proclaimed the universality of the soul. But a few years later the work of Pomponazzo appeared, in which the impossibility of a philosophical proof of immortality is maintained; and the contest was now waged incessantly with replies and apologies, till it was silenced by the Catholic reaction. The pre-existence of the soul in God, conceived more or less in accordance with Plato's ideas, long remained a common belief, and proved of service to the poets. The consequences that followed from it, as to the mode of the soul's existence after death, were not more closely considered.

The second way in which antiquity made itself felt was chiefly by means of that remarkable fragment of the sixth book of Cicero's *Republic,* which is known as the Dream of Scipio. Without the commentary of Macrobius it would probably have perished, as has the rest of the second part of the work; now it was again diffused in countless manuscript

copies, and, after the discovery of typography, in printed
form, with numerous new commentaries. It is the description
of a transfigured hereafter for great men, pervaded by the
harmony of the spheres. This pagan heaven, for which much
more evidence was gradually assembled from the ancients,
gradually supplanted the Christian heaven to the same degree
that the ideal of fame and historical greatness overshadowed
the ideal of the Christian life; and public feeling was not as
offended by this as it was by the doctrine of total annihilation
after death. Even Petrarch based his hope chiefly on this
Dream of Scipio, on the declarations found in other Ciceronian works, and on Plato's *Phaedo,* without mentioning the
Bible. "Why," he asks elsewhere, "should not I as a Catholic
share a hope that was demonstrably cherished by the
heathen?"   Some time later Coluccio Salutati wrote his
"Labors of Hercules" (still in manuscript), in which he
proved, in conclusion, that the valorous man, who has
endured the great labors of earthly life, is justly entitled to
a seat among the stars. If Dante still firmly believed that the
great pagans, whom he would have gladly welcomed in Paradise, do not come beyond that Limbo at the entrance to
Hell,[306] the poetry of this time accepted joyfully the new
liberal ideas of a future life. Cosimo the Elder, according
to Bernardo Pulci's poem on his death, was received in heaven
by Cicero, who had also been called the "Father of His
Country," by the Fabii, by Curius, Fabricius, and many
others; with them he would adorn the choir where only
blameless spirits sing.

But in the old writers there was another and less pleasing
picture of the world to come—the shadowy realms of Homer
and of those poets who had not sweetened and humanized the
conception. This made an impression on certain temperaments. Gioviano Pontano somewhere attributes to Sannazaro
the story of a vision he beheld one early morning while half
awake. He seemed to see a departed friend, Ferrandus
Januarius, with whom he had often discoursed on the immortality of the soul; he asks him now whether it is true that
the pains of Hell are really dreadful and eternal. After some
moments the shadow gives an answer similar to that of
Achilles when Odysseus questioned him: "So much I tell and
aver to thee, that we who are parted from earthly life have
the strongest desire to return to it again." He then saluted
his friend and disappeared.

We cannot fail to recognize that such views of the state of

306. *Inferno,* iv, 24f. — Cf. *Purgatorio,* vii, 28, xxii, 100.

man after death partly presuppose and partly promote the dissolution of the most essential dogmas of Christianity. The notion of sin and salvation must have almost entirely evaporated. We must not be misled by the effects of the great preachers of repentance or by the epidemic revivals which have been described above. For even granting that the individually developed classes had shared in them like the rest, the main reason for their participation was the need of emotional excitement, the rebound of passionate natures, the horror felt at great national calamities, the cry to heaven for help. The awakening of the conscience was by no means necessarily followed by the sense of sin and the need for salvation, and even a very severe outward penance did not perforce involve any repentance in the Christian sense. When highly developed people of the Renaissance tell us that their principle is: repent nothing, they may have in mind, it is true, matters that have no moral significance, merely faults of unreason or imprudence; but this contempt for repentance must automatically extend to the sphere of morals, because its origin, namely the consciousness of individual force, is universal. The passive and contemplative form of Christianity, with its constant reference to a higher world beyond the grave, no longer controlled these men. Machiavelli ventured still further: it could no longer serve the State and the defense of its freedom.[307]

What form, then, had to be embraced by the strong religious instinct which, notwithstanding all, survived in many natures? It was Theism or Deism, call it what we will. The latter name may be applied to that mode of thought which simply wiped the Christian element out of religion, without either seeking or finding any other substitute for the feelings. In Theism, however, we recognize the elevated, positive devotion to the Supreme Being which was not known in the Middle Ages. This mode of faith does not exclude Christianity, and can either ally itself with the Christian doctrines of sin, redemption, and immortality, or exist and flourish without them.

Sometimes this belief has a childish naïveté and even a half-pagan air; God appears here as the almighty fulfiller of human wishes. Agnolo Pandolfini tells how, after his wedding, he shut himself in with his wife and knelt down before the family altar with the picture of the Madonna, and prayed, not to her, but to God, that He would vouchsafe to them the right use of their property, a long, happy, and harmonious life together, and many male descendants: "For myself I

307. *The Discourses,* Book II, ch. 2.

prayed for wealth, honor, and friends; for her, blamelessness, honesty, and that she might be a good housekeeper." When, in addition, the language has a strong antique flavor, it is not always easy to separate the pagan style and the theistic belief.

Even in times of misfortune this temper is sometimes expressed with striking sincerity. There have come down to us some addresses to God from Firenzuola's old age, when he had lain ill of a fever for years, in which, though he expressly declares himself a believing Christian, he shows that his religious consciousness is essentially theistic. His sufferings seem to him neither as punishment of sin nor as preparation for another world; it is a matter between him and God, who has put the strong love of life between man and his despair. "I curse, but only curse Nature, since Thy greatness forbids me to utter Thy name . . . give me death, Lord, I beseech Thee, give it to me now!"

It would be vain to look for a conscious and consistent Theism in these and similar utterances; the speakers partly believed themselves to be Christians still, and for various other reasons respected the existing doctrines of the Church. But at the time of the Reformation, when men were forced to come to a distinct conclusion on such points, this mode of thought was accepted with a fuller consciousness; a number of the Italian Protestants turned out to be Anti-Trinitarians, and the Socinians, even as exiles in distant countries, made the memorable attempt to found a church on these principles. From what we have said up till now, so much at least should have become clear: that apart from humanistic rationalism, there were other winds that stirred these sails.

One chief center of theistic thought lay in the Platonic Academy at Florence, and especially in Lorenzo the Magnificent himself. The theoretical works and even the letters of these men show us only half their nature. It is true that Lorenzo, from his youth till he died, expressed himself dogmatically as a Christian, and that Pico was drawn by Savonarola's influence to accept the point of view of a monkish ascetic. But in the hymns of Lorenzo, which we are tempted to regard as the highest product of the spirit of this school, an unreserved Theism is set forth—a Theism which strives to treat the world as a great moral and physical Cosmos. Whereas the men of the Middle Ages looked on the world as a vale of tears, which Pope and Emperor must guard against the coming of Antichrist; whereas the fatalists of the Renaissance oscillated between seasons of overflowing energy and seasons of superstition or dull resignation, here, in this circle of chosen spirits, the doctrine was upheld that the visible world was created by God with love, that it is the reproduction of a model pre-existing in Him, and that He will ever remain its eternal mover and restorer. By recognizing God, the soul of the individual can draw *Him* into its narrow boundaries, but also by love of Him it can expand *itself* into the Infinite—and this is blessedness on earth.

Here the stream of medieval mysticism flows in the same current with Platonic doctrine, and with a characteristically modern spirit. Perhaps one of the most precious fruits of the discovery of the world and of man comes to maturity here, on whose account alone the Italian Renaissance must be called the mother of our modern age.

5 Marks

Medival Mysticism: church now has mysteries (rather than truths) which are sure for questioning.

modern Spirit: Renaissance

Conclusion — Renaissance is the leader of modern times

INDEX OF NAMES